Cases on Human Performance Improvement Technologies

Jill E. Stefaniak
Old Dominion University, USA

**International Society for
Performance Improvement** ®

WHERE KNOWLEDGE BECOMES KNOW-HOW

A volume in the Advances in
Human Resources Management and
Organizational Development (AHRMOD)
Book Series

An Imprint of IGI Global

Managing Director:	Lindsay Johnston
Managing Editor:	Austin DeMarco
Director of Intellectual Property & Contracts:	Jan Travers
Acquisitions Editor:	Kayla Wolfe
Production Editor:	Christina Henning
Development Editor:	Erin O'Dea
Typesetter:	Kaitlyn Kulp
Cover Design:	Jason Mull

Published in the United States of America by
Business Science Reference (an imprint of IGI Global)
701 E. Chocolate Avenue
Hershey PA 17033
Tel: 717-533-8845
Fax: 717-533-8661
E-mail: cust@igi-global.com
Web site: http://www.igi-global.com

Library of Congress Cataloging-in-Publication Data

Cases on human performance improvement technologies / Jill E. Stefaniak, editor.
     pages cm
 Includes bibliographical references and index.
 Summary: "This book presents a collection of teaching cases that demonstrate the real-world application of digital tools for human performance enhancement across a variety of settings, utilizing a problem-based instructional technique"-- Provided by publisher.
 ISBN 978-1-4666-8330-3 (hardcover : alk. paper) -- ISBN 978-1-4666-8331-0 (ebook : alk. paper) 1. Performance technology--Case studies. 2. Performance--Case studies. 3. Organizational effectiveness--Case studies. I. Stefaniak, Jill E., 1984-

 HF5549.5.P37C37 2015
 658.3'14--dc23

                    2015006723

This book is published in the IGI Global book series Advances in Human Resources Management and Organizational Development (AHRMOD) (ISSN: 2327-3372; eISSN: 2327-3380)

British Cataloguing in Publication Data
A Cataloguing in Publication record for this book is available from the British Library.

Advances in Human Resources Management and Organizational Development (AHRMOD) Book Series

ISSN: 2327-3372
EISSN: 2327-3380

MISSION

A solid foundation is essential to the development and success of any organization and can be accomplished through the effective and careful management of an organization's human capital. Research in human resources management and organizational development is necessary in providing business leaders with the tools and methodologies which will assist in the development and maintenance of their organizational structure.

The **Advances in Human Resources Management and Organizational Development (AHRMOD) Book Series** aims to publish the latest research on all aspects of human resources as well as the latest methodologies, tools, and theories regarding organizational development and sustainability. The **AHRMOD Book Series** intends to provide business professionals, managers, researchers, and students with the necessary resources to effectively develop and implement organizational strategies.

- Worker Behavior and Engagement
- Corporate governance
- Job Enrichment
- Recruitment Process
- Upward Feedback
- Human Relations Movement
- Process Improvement
- Workplace Discrimination
- Organizational development
- Entrepreneurialism

IGI Global is currently accepting manuscripts for publication within this series. To submit a proposal for a volume in this series, please contact our Acquisition Editors at Acquisitions@igi-global.com or visit: http://www.igi-global.com/publish/.

Titles in this Series

For a list of additional titles in this series, please visit: www.igi-global.com

Handbook of Research on Internationalization of Entrepreneurial Innovation in the Global Economy
Luisa Cagica Carvalho (Universidade Aberta, Portugal & CEFAGE, Universidade de Évora, Portugal)
Business Science Reference • copyright 2015 • 547pp • H/C (ISBN: 9781466682160) • US $335.00 (our price)

Cases on Sustainable Human Resources Management in the Middle East and Asia
Stephanie Jones (Maastricht School of Management, The Netherlands) and Sheena Graham (Graham Reid Associates, Hong Kong)
Business Science Reference • copyright 2015 • 374pp • H/C (ISBN: 9781466681675) • US $195.00 (our price)

Business Ethics and Diversity in the Modern Workplace
Philippe W. Zgheib (Lebanese American University, Lebanon)
Business Science Reference • copyright 2015 • 326pp • H/C (ISBN: 9781466672543) • US $235.00 (our price)

Impact of Diversity on Organization and Career Development
Claretha Hughes (University of Arkansas, USA)
Business Science Reference • copyright 2015 • 342pp • H/C (ISBN: 9781466673243) • US $215.00 (our price)

Organizational Innovation and IT Governance in Emerging Economies
Jingyuan Zhao (University of Toronto, Canada) Patricia Ordóñez de Pablos (Universidad de Oviedo, Spain) and Robert D. Tennyson (University of Minnesota, USA)
Business Science Reference • copyright 2015 • 304pp • H/C (ISBN: 9781466673328) • US $205.00 (our price)

Utilizing Evidence-Based Lessons Learned for Enhanced Organizational Innovation and Change
Susan McIntyre (Defence Research and Development, Canada) Kimiz Dalkir (McGill University, Canada) Perry Paul (Lessons Learned Consultant, Canadian Armed Forces (Retired), Canada) and Irene C. Kitimbo (McGill University, Canada)
Business Science Reference • copyright 2015 • 323pp • H/C (ISBN: 9781466664531) • US $195.00 (our price)

www.igi-global.com

701 E. Chocolate Ave., Hershey, PA 17033
Order online at www.igi-global.com or call 717-533-8845 x100
To place a standing order for titles released in this series,
contact: cust@igi-global.com
Mon-Fri 8:00 am - 5:00 pm (est) or fax 24 hours a day 717-533-8661

Editorial Advisory Board

Table of Contents

Detailed Table of Contents

Chapter 1

 Bonnie Beresford, AMCI Global, USA
 Paige Barrie, Volkswagon Credit, USA

When the learning and development manager of a financial services firm wanted to improve organizational performance, she stated, "I want to understand what the best performers do, and make the rest more like the best." By studying high performing salespeople, the organization discovered what such performers did that made them more successful than their colleagues. Using a structured performance mapping process, the project team elicited and documented the unconscious competence of these in-role experts. A gap analysis of all performers objectively identified, quantified, and prioritized the curriculum and performance support needs. This case study examines an organization that went from simply asking managers what courses their salespeople needed to an evidence-based assessment of real performance gaps. The approach resulted in a highly regarded curriculum, the elimination of development costs for unneeded courseware, and a reduction in training time and time away from the field.

Chapter 2

 Simone G. Symonette, Indiana University, USA

This case study examines the analysis, design, development, implementation, and continuous improvement of a training feedback system. In this case, the system captured sales training participant feedback and distributed that data to stakeholders to analyze and to resolve problems within the learning experience. The intervention set presented in the case is intended for practitioners who have limited time and resources but are interested in creating a feedback system that meets ever changing business demands in a sales training environment.

Chapter 3

Melanie E. Ross, Old Dominion University, USA
Jill E. Stefaniak, Old Dominion University, USA

After consistently missing the contract's monthly-required staffing personnel requests, the senior director and senior manager of recruiting decided the day-to-day operations, procedures, and recruiting processes should be standardized within the recruiting section. The staffing department at Variant Data Systems, Inc. decided to move forward with instructional and noninstructional interventions to address incomplete biography submissions between the recruiters and the technical writer. This case study demonstrates how a layered organizational performance analysis was conducted to dissect recurring performance problems. The case also examines how an internal performance improvement consultant was utilized on the project to identify the performance issue and develop the expectations of the position, a communication plan, the formal instructional unit and knowledge management database, and accountability metrics to ensure it met the needs of the recruiting section in the staffing department.

Chapter 4

Joe Monaco, National LIFTOR Licensing Systems, USA
Edward W. Schneider, Peacham Pedagogics, USA

This case study explores how a performance management system was developed to address recurring health and safety issues in an organization. Performance improvement technologists were recruited to address the problem and ensure that it stayed solved. The authors describe the process that was used to develop a training program that eventually evolved to a full scale Performance Management (PM) System. Today, nearly three decades later, the PM System has endured with its original mission intact; it has influenced the international dialog on forklift operator safety; and it provides, through ongoing field research, insights into how a Performance Management system might endure past the first change in the management that championed it.

Chapter 5

Robert Anthony Jordan, Independent Researcher, USA
Alison Carr-Chellman, Penn State University, USA

This case describes how a federal government agency engaged in a user design process to design, develop, and implement a workplace learning curriculum to be implemented throughout several agency offices. While several offices had developed their own training program, there were inconsistencies and a lack of standardization. The authors describe how a user design process was utilized in the development of a standardized curriculum. User design shifts the responsibility of design from expert designers to frontline users and stakeholders. Several user-driven tools are available to organizations that adopt user design processes. Potential advantages of a curriculum developed through user design include better adoption and diffusion of the curriculum and improved engagement of the users in the workplace.

Chapter 6

This case study describes the processes and outcomes of intentional efforts to formalize and enable learning, communication, and collaboration in a network of nonprofit practitioners to enhance the capacity and effectiveness of member organizations. After identifying a need for nonprofits in Central Illinois to have increased awareness of others' efforts and work together to a greater extent, a technology-enabled Community of Practice (CoP) was formed to facilitate positive change. After a short period of implementation, an evaluation found that the virtual CoP was valued by members as an important source of learning, networking, and finding resources. Further, intentional efforts to facilitate nonprofit network activities and productivity led to meaningful outcomes in this community and members' performance. This case study serves as a non-instructional Human Performance Technology (HPT) example for consideration by organizations seeking to support informal learning among nonprofit employees and stakeholders in order to improve and sustain members' performance.

This case study describes the efforts of performance consultants to improve the extent to which staff and volunteers at a nonprofit agency performed according to their customer service standards. After providing background information about the organization and its service standards, the case study describes the existing performance gap regarding the standards and the consultants' response to the client's initial request for training. The case study describes the performance analysis the consultants conducted, including the gap analysis, organizational analysis, environmental analysis, and cause analysis. The case study also describes the task analysis that the consultants conducted using the critical incident technique. The case study concludes with a description of how the consultants created the resulting training, and the effect of the training on the sponsoring organization.

Chapter 8

This case study explains how a complete overhaul to the national high school equivalency test posed a significant organizational challenge to Grace Centers of Hope, a nonprofit based in Pontiac, Michigan in the United States. All adult clients participating in Grace Centers of Hope's one-year drug and alcohol recovery program who are without a high school diploma or equivalent are required to take in-house adult basic education classes to prepare for taking the high school equivalency test. Faced with the need to completely redesign their existing adult basic education program, Grace Centers of Hope reached out to Designers for Learning, an instructional design and performance improvement consultancy that matches nonprofits with instructional design students in service-learning projects. The resulting 100% virtual e-service-learning collaboration among volunteer college students, their faculty sponsors, and other advisors provided Grace Centers of Hope with educational resources to support the organization.

Chapter 9

The College Advisory Program offered by Total Vision Soccer Club aims at providing young players with the opportunity to learn how to navigate the collegiate recruiting process, market themselves to college coaches, and increase their exposure to potential colleges and universities. A team of external evaluators (authors of this chapter) conducted a formative evaluation to determine what the program needs to do to reach its goal. By following a systemic evaluation process, the evaluation team investigated five dimensions of the program and collected data by reviewing various program materials and conducting surveys and interviews with players and their parents, upstream stakeholders, and downstream impactees. By triangulating the multiple sources of data, the team drew a conclusion that most program dimensions were rated as mediocre although the program had several strengths. The team provided evidence-based recommendations for improving the quality of the program.

This case demonstrates how problem-based learning (PBL) was used as a teaching method to help medical students integrate their knowledge of basic sciences with a clinical application at a medical school. PBL promotes self-directed, problem-solving, and lifelong learning. In the PBL context, students sought out a variety of resources to tackle their learning issues and help them arrive at a solution to a patient problem. The existing strategy for curating resources was not aligned with the type of thinking and activities in the PBL process. Therefore, a knowledge management system was developed to provide an online knowledge base of medical information resources and tools easily accessible at the point of students' needs.

The current case study is situated within a large, land grant hospital located in the Midwestern region of the United States. Although the physicians had seen an increase in medical related human performance technology (HPTs) within the organization (e.g. computer physician ordered entry) some challenges remained as the hospital sought to improve the productivity of the electronic health record (EHRs). Specifically, physicians had difficulty finding information embedded within the chart due to usability problems and information overload. To overcome the challenges, a semantic search within the chart was implemented as a solution for physicians to retrieve relevant results given the conceptual semantic pattern. The case study will discuss many elements of the implementation based on our experience and feedback from clinicians. The case will specifically highlight the importance of training and change agents within an organization.

DiversiCorp Communications grew extremely fast to support Red Oak Health System's enterprise IT needs. Often promoting strong performers from within, DiversiCorp leadership recognized that their directors and managers needed enhanced support to maintain their expected level of service to their health care client. Two performance consultants were engaged who facilitated DiversiCorp leadership through a systematic organizational development process that culminated in the creation of an organizational "competency operating system." This competency/behavioral-based system took as key inputs existing relevant company competencies and was developed with stakeholder involvement using a critical incident approach. Additionally, it was the core mechanism that then drove performance improvement through improved hiring practices, behavioral interview training, job tools and performance support, enhanced job descriptions, and aligned performance expectations and appraisals.

This case study presents FITC's evidence based application of ISPI's 10 Standards of Performance Improvement and theoretical insights from the author's doctoral dissertation to preposition a special purpose not for profit professional services organization in Africa. It describes the FITC mandate, FITC's trajectory and impact on identified stakeholders; reviews the various initiatives taken by FITC from May 2009 to May 2014, with a highlight of results attained. Thus, enabling the reader draw personal connections with interventions articulated in the organization. Consultants, Practitioners and Academics in the field of Performance Improvement, as well as those aspiring to these roles, would find this case study interesting.

Performance problems come in all forms. The method presented in this chapter blends the models of three respected Performance improvement icons – Joe Harless, Thomas Gilbert, and Roger Chevalier. Their theoretical and practical approaches are applied to a case study. The three models – 13 Smart Questions (Front-end analysis), Behavior Engineering Model (BEM), and Updated BEM – when combined show ways practitioners can assess and improve performance. The practitioner will develop effective partnerships with clients, gain valuable perspectives on the issues, and their underlying causes. Finally the practitioner will be able to lead a department or an organization in fully analyzing problems and determining how best to solve them.

Preface

Human performance technology (HPT) is a systematic approach for improving performance that takes into account organizational, environmental, and causal analyses in order to make data-driven decisions regarding intervention design, implementation, and evaluation. (ISPI, 2013). Principles of HPT are used in a variety of different industries to solve problems, assist with qualitative improvement initiatives, and identify future business opportunities. Performance improvement technologists take the entire organizational environment into account when developing strategies and interventions to address an organizational need.

This casebook is a collection of 14 teaching case studies that are intended to provide educators, students, and practitioners with an opportunity to see how principles of human performance technology have been implemented in various contexts and industries. Like most fields, students are taught best practices, but are not always privy to understanding the challenges that can occur when attempting to implement these best practices in the real world. Lack of resources, organizational buy-in and timing can all hinder performance, requiring practitioners to work creatively to implement solutions within a limited timeframe. Often times, performance improvement technologists are tasked with implementing multiple interventions (instructional and non-instructional) at the same time. The success of any intervention is dependent on whether or not it meets the needs identified during initial assessment of the perceived performance problem.

It is in the intent of this casebook to provide those with an interest in human performance technology and performance improvement a repertoire of cases where human performance improvement initiatives were employed. Each case provides insight as to how analyses were carried out, the design of interventions, and how organizational culture contributed to the performance problem being addressed. The goal of this case book is to provide educators, students, and practitioners with in-depth case studies, showcasing real-life applications of HPT in a variety of different industries and contexts, that can be used for instructional purposes in human performance technology and performance improvement courses. The cases featured in this book address how projects were implemented within the following industries: higher education, manufacturing, government, healthcare, and non-profit sectors.

Topics addressed within the case studies include the following:

- Conducting performance analyses
- Solving business problems
- Identifying and selecting performance improvement interventions
- Implementing instructional and/or noninstructional interventions
- Implementing change management strategies within organizations
- Employee development
- Instructional design
- Changes in workflow procedures
- Performance support systems

BOOK OBJECTIVE

The overall mission of this casebook is to provide educators in the field of human performance technology, organizational development, educational technology, and business management with a compilation of case studies based on real-life experiences that can be integrated within their classes utilizing a problem-based instructional technique. The goals for this case book are to 1) provide relevant cases that demonstrate how principles of HPT have been employed within organizations, 2) provide examples of how HPT has been utilized in a variety of different industries, and 3) provide a combination of examples that address business problems, quality improvement initiatives and business opportunities. This case book includes 14 cases from educators and professionals in the performance improvement field who have applied human performance technology standards and principles in a variety of different contexts to solve performance problems. Each case highlights the challenges encountered with conducting analyses, designing interventions, and identifying strategies to implement performance improvement plans.

AUDIENCE

The target audience for this book consists primarily of educators and students in the field of human performance technology. The cases included in this book could be of benefit to courses within business management, performance improvement, organizational development, and instructional design and technology programs. Each case consists of a real-life unique problem or opportunity that was addressed, as well as a detailed account of the steps taken to arrive at a solution. It is the intent of this casebook that educators will be able to utilize this book as a supplemental text to build upon the theoretical textbooks addressing the topics of HPT and provide students with examples of how principles of HPT have been applied to solve real problems in a variety of different organizations and contexts. The cases included in this book can be used as both individual and group assignments in face-to-face and distant learning environments.

ORGANIZATION

This book contains 14 cases that span across a wide variety of contexts, including higher education, manufacturing, government, healthcare, and non-profit sectors. Topics range from strategies employed during performance analyses, instructional and noninstructional solutions, and performance support systems. Each case presents a unique performance problem along with a detailed account of the steps taken to arrive at a solution.

Chapter 1 provides a detailed account of how a learning and development manager of a financial services firm conducted a performance analysis to better understand the organization's high performing salespeople. The project team engaged in gap analysis and performance mapping to conduct an evidence-based assessment to improve training for the firm's salespeople. A gap analysis of all performers objectively identified, quantified, and prioritized the curriculum and performance support needs. This case study examines an organization that went from simply asking managers what courses their salespeople needed to an evidence-based assessment of real performance gaps. The authors demonstrates how performance assessment was used to reduce overall training costs by focusing on key skills expected of employees.

Chapter 2 explores how a performance technologist encountered several issues while attempting to integrate a feedback system into an organization for sales training participants. The purpose of the feedback system was to identify and resolve problems from current sales training practices. The performance technologist utilized rapid prototyping to educate the sales training workforce regarding the feedback initiatives that were being developed and to see necessary input. This case also emphasizes the challenges and time constraints associated with the adoption of new interventions in the workplace. Each case provides a detailed account of how rapid prototyping was used as a human performance technology intervention.

Chapter 3 provides a rich account of how instructional interventions were not successful with addressing recurrent organizational issues for recruitment and selection firms. A performance technologist was consulted to conduct an organizational analysis to identify the root cause of performance problems and develop noninstructional interventions to solve the problem. This case provides examples of how noninstructional interventions can often be more viable than training solutions. The performance technologist incorporated the development of a communication plan, formal instruction, a knowledge management database, and accountability metrics to ensure organizational and client needs were being addressed. This case provides a detailed overview of how multiple interventions (both instructional and noninstructional) were implemented simultaneously to adequately address the performance problem described.

Chapter 4 moves us into the health and safety industry exploring how human performance technology principles were utilized to address frequent forklift injuries for an organization. The case provides a detailed account of how interventions were implemented over the course of 30 years as well as the challenges associated with the adoption of new policies and forklift safety measures over time. The authors emphasize strategies used to embark on changing an organization's longstanding culture and the development of training program that is still being used today. Furthermore, a detailed account is provided regarding the development of a training program and how it evolved into a performance management support system to prevent the recurrence of similar performance problems and safety issues in the workplace.

Chapter 5 describes how a federal government agency utilized a user design process rooted in general systems theory to develop a workplace curriculum. The case emphasizes how a participatory approach was used to engage key stakeholders in the process. The authors discuss how the utilization of a user design approach to developing instructional interventions aided in the adoption and diffusion of the curriculum. Several user-driven tools are available to organizations that adopt user design processes. Potential advantages of a curriculum developed through user design include better adoption and diffusion of the curriculum and improved engagement of the users in the workplace.

Chapter 6 shifts the focus to the nonprofit sector and the implementation of a Community of Practice to engage member organizations. The case serves as a non-instructional intervention that was developed to improve and formalize communication and collaborative efforts among nonprofits in Central Illinois. The case describes in detail how the development of the Community of Practice promoted positive change and led to a smooth adoption process among member organizations. Intentional efforts to facilitate nonprofit network activities and productivity led to meaningful outcomes in this community and members' performance. This case study serves as a non-instructional Human Performance Technology (HPT) example for consideration by organizations seeking to support informal learning among nonprofit employees and stakeholders in order to improve and sustain members' performance.

Chapter 7 provides another example of how human performance improvement technologies were applied in the nonprofit sector. The authors provide a rich account of how they conducted a tiered analysis to identify performance gaps through gap, organizational, environmental, and causal analyses. The case outlines how the findings from the analyses were used to develop an instructional intervention as well as the effects the training had on the organization. After providing background information about the organization and its service standards, the case study describes the existing performance gap regarding the standards and the consultants' response to the client's initial request for training. The authors describe the performance analysis the consultants conducted as well as a detailed account of the training that was develop and the effect of the training on the sponsoring organization.

Chapter 8 shifts the focus to e-service learning and how a performance technologist conducted organizational and performance analyses as part of a needs assessment to identify opportunities to develop basic adult education classes. Faced with the need to completely redesign their existing adult basic education program, a non-profit agency reached out to an instructional design and performance improvement consultancy that matches nonprofits with instructional design students in service-learning projects. The resulting 100% virtual e-service-learning collaboration among volunteer college students, their faculty sponsors, and other advisors provided the non-profit with educational resources to support the organization. The author provides a detailed account of the process that was followed to identify content to be addressed through the development of instructional materials. This case study provides a unique look at how a service-learning project was transformed into an e-service-learning collaboration among instructional designers of varying backgrounds.

Chapter 9 explores how a group of performance technologists conducted a systematic evaluation to identify program needs for a college advisory program. The case provides a detailed account of how data was collected from multiple sources and triangulated to identify the programs strengths and areas for growth. By following a systemic evaluation process, the evaluation team investigated five dimensions of the program and collected data by reviewing various program materials and conducting surveys and interviews with multiple constituents. The use of a tiered evaluative approach allowed for the performance technologists to provide evidence-based recommendations to their client.

Chapter 10 shifts our focus to medical education and how the development of a knowledge management system was developed to assist medical students conduct information searches. The knowledge management system was designed and developed to provide a repository of medical information resources and tools that medical students could access while engaging in problem-based learning activities. This case provides a detailed account for how the need for a performance support system was identified and customized to meet the students' needs.

Chapter 11 provides another account of how human performance technologies can be applied in the healthcare industry. To overcome the challenges, a semantic search within the chart was implemented as a solution for physicians to retrieve relevant results given the conceptual semantic pattern. This case provides a detailed account of how an electronic performance support system was developed to assist healthcare practitioners to improve their use of electronic health records within a hospital. The authors discuss the importance of training and change agents within an organization and explain the need for alignment between instructional and non-instructional interventions.

Chapter 12 shifts the focus to leadership development through the design of an organizational competency operating system. Performance consultants embarked on a systematic organizational development process to identify client needs for leadership development support. The case provides a detailed account of how the performance consultants improved performance through hiring practices, behavioral interview training, job tools and performance support, enhanced job descriptions, and aligned performance expectations and appraisals.

Chapter 13 provides a detailed account of how a performance technologist applied human performance technology standards to FITC's organization performance. This case study demonstrates how HPT practices were applied in an international setting at multiple levels of an organization. The author provides a detailed account of how the development and use of instructional and noninstructional interventions were implemented throughout several years. In addition, the author discusses how the organizational culture was instrumental in rebranding the interventions to create as preserve the organization's cultural identity.

Chapter 14 explores the application of the behavioral engineering model and front-end analysis techniques were applied to a Fortune 500 company. While many models and processes have been published on behavioral engineering, this case highlights how multiple techniques can be used in tandem to solve a performance problem. The author provides a detailed account as to how these performance improvement tools were modified and adapted to address the existing performance problems and develop customized interventions.

CLOSING REMARKS

Organizations, regardless of industry, are in a never-ending search to improve performance and identify opportunities to expand their operations. Depending on the industry, project, and organizational constraints, there are many ways performance improvement technologists may approach any given project. This casebook, focusing on human performance technology business decisions, provides students with opportunities to see how principles of human performance technology are applied in a variety of real situations. The cases featured in this book provide examples of various types of projects that utilized principles of human performance technology and how interventions were implemented in a variety of industries such as higher education, governmental, manufacturing, non-profits, and healthcare.

Jill E. Stefaniak
Old Dominion University, USA

REFERENCE

International Society for Performance Improvement. (2013). *What is HPT?* Retrieved August 5, 2013, from http://www.ispi.org/content.aspx?id=54

Chapter 1
Using Performance Mapping and Gap Analysis to Improve Performance:
An Evidence-Based Assessment of Performance Gaps

Bonnie Beresford
AMCI Global, USA

Paige Barrie
Volkswagon Credit, USA

EXECUTIVE SUMMARY

When the learning and development manager of a financial services firm wanted to improve organizational performance, she stated, "I want to understand what the best performers do, and make the rest more like the best." By studying high performing salespeople, the organization discovered what such performers did that made them more successful than their colleagues. Using a structured performance mapping process, the project team elicited and documented the unconscious competence of these in-role experts. A gap analysis of all performers objectively identified, quantified, and prioritized the curriculum and performance support needs. This case study examines an organization that went from simply asking managers what courses their salespeople needed to an evidence-based assessment of real performance gaps. The approach resulted in a highly regarded curriculum, the elimination of development costs for unneeded courseware, and a reduction in training time and time away from the field.

DOI: 10.4018/978-1-4666-8330-3.ch001

ORGANIZATION BACKGROUND

When most consumers think of the automobile business, they likely think of manufacturing facilities and dealerships. There is another group of vibrant players in this industry: the financing arms of the automobile manufacturers. By law, "captive" finance companies like Ford Credit, Toyota Financial Services, and VW Credit, Inc. are registered as independent companies, yet they maintain a symbiotic relationship with the manufacturer. The finance companies service the manufacturer's two important customer bases: the consumers of the manufacturer's products (buyers and lessees) and its dealerships who sell and service those products.

For dealers, financing plays an important role in providing capital for facility expansion, purchase of vehicles for their lot and equipment for the service department, and funding for consumers. A well-funded dealer is good for the captive as well as for the manufacturer. For consumers, financing enables them to purchase the vehicle of their dreams at a payment they can afford.

Automotive financing is big business. While these captive finance companies may have an edge due to their connection with the manufacturer, they compete every day with banks and other lenders for the lucrative dealer and consumer financing business. The captives strive daily to get a bigger share of each dealer's financing wallet. A good relationship with a dealer can lead to the dealer sending more new and used consumer deals to the captive. Thus, the quality of the finance company's workforce plays an important role in achieving the business goals of both the manufacturer (to profitably sell more vehicles) and the finance company itself (to profitably finance more dealers and consumers).

Volkswagen Group (Volkswagen AG), headquartered in Wolfsburg, Germany, and manufacturer of VW, Audi, Bentley, Lamborghini, Porsche and a number of other automotive products, has set its target to become the global economic and environmental leader among automobile manufacturers by 2018. In particular, they aspire to:

- Be the world leader in customer satisfaction and quality,
- Increase unit sales to more than 10 million vehicles per year,
- Increase return on sales before tax to at least 8 percent,
- Become the top employer across all brands, companies, and regions.

According to an August 2014 study by the Center of Automotive Management, Volkswagen Group is positioned to sell 10.1 million vehicles in 2014 and become the world's largest car manufacturer ahead of their 2018 stated goal, surpassing Toyota and General Motors. Volkswagen Group's strategy includes an intentional focus on environmentally friendly and profitable vehicle projects. They believe the design and environmentally friendly attributes of their vehicles, coupled with a strong brand position in markets around the world, will be key factors that to contribute to their global growth.

VW Credit, Inc. (VCI), the financing arm of Volkswagen Group of America (VWGoA) which is headquartered in Herndon, Virginia, plays a key role in supporting the charge. VCI knows that the capability and commitment of its workforce are crucial to achieving the company's growth and customer satisfaction goals.

VCI Academy is the company's internal training organization, providing learning and professional development to employees across the company, from credit analysts and collection agents to the business development staff that calls on dealerships to ensure that dealers give their financing business to VCI. They also provide training to their dealers' finance and insurance managers, a key role within each dealership. The Academy knows that time in training is time away from the job. As such, they want to be sure the time invested in training truly helps improve performance.

SETTING THE STAGE

One of VCI's most important audiences is the Business Development Manager (BDM). These individuals are the face of the company to the dealers. BDMs are field salespeople who compete with banks and other financial institutions to earn the dealers' financing business. Each BDM has an assigned geographic territory with an average of 24 dealers per territory. The time BDMs spend with the dealers building relationships and building business is critical to their success, so time spent in training needs to be fiercely justified as being able to close a known performance gap.

The Academy had an existing curriculum and certification program in place for BDMs. It was assumed that new courses and new certification requirements would be required every year. Historically, curriculum decisions were made based on opinions and a quick survey of managers, asking them, "What sort of training do your BDMs need?" Being new to the role, Academy Senior Manager Paige Barrie was not convinced that the training content was necessarily addressing the things BDMs really needed. Before embarking on the next year's curriculum plan, she wanted a more objective approach to quantitatively define those performance gaps and to determine what BDMs really needed to best do their jobs.

Barrie knew the Academy needed to do some real investigation into the BDM job and into what high performers were doing that made them so good. This research would require both budget and pulling BDMs out of the field for interviews. Barrie garnered the support of her manager David Bruce, Director of Human Resources, by explaining how findings could go beyond just improvements to training; insights into the BDM role could also help HR with recruitment and onboarding.

The needs and gap assessment approach the Academy selected was based on a model of performance mapping and gap analysis (Stolovitch & Keeps, 2004), and they brought in human performance improvement consultants to guide the work. The mission was to:

- Identify what behaviors make high performing BDMs so effective,
- Identify – and quantify – the skill gaps between high performing BDMs and their colleagues,
- Take action to close the gaps.

CASE DESCRIPTION

VCI Academy wanted to learn from their high performing BDMs. After all, these are the people who are consistently meeting or exceeding their quantifiable business objectives, or key performance indicators (KPIs). As Barrie said, "We want to learn from the best, determine the gaps between the best and the rest, and then bring the rest up to higher levels of performance."

The first step required the identification of high performers. The BDM job role has six very specific KPIs that served as the foundation for selecting candidates for performance mapping interviews The KPIs represent various penetration rates of VCI products across the dealers in the BDM's territory. For example, "New Vehicle Service Contract Penetration" is the percent of new vehicles sold that also include a VCI service contract. Other KPIs include the percent of dealers using VCI to finance their new and used vehicle inventory, the percent of dealers utilizing VCI's lease maturity program, and the percentage of new and used vehicles financed through VCI. BDMs were initially ranked on each KPI. These individual rankings were then turned into a composite score, resulting in each BDM being scored as high, medium, or low.

Barrie quickly realized that the numbers didn't tell the whole story. For VCI, some KPIs were more important than others; hence a weighting scale was applied. Some exceptional BDMs had been transferred to underperforming geographic territories, so their current numbers made them look like under-performers. Looking at historical performance plus engaging regional management in the selection process resolved the problem. The final selection of high performers needed to also provide representation from each of VCI's five regions. Using a combination of past and current KPIs and regional input, Barrie's team identified 10 high performing BDMs who consistently ranked among the top 15 performers. The terminology of "high" vs. "top" performers is very intentional. A "top performer" designation would suggest excellence in all regards when in fact most high performers, while excelling in many areas, may have room for improvement in others. Further, by the very nature of KPIs, a person could be on top one month and third the next. She is still a high performer.

Learning what high performers do that makes them so good requires a guided interview process. Simply asking them what they do is usually futile because they are so proficient that their behaviors and actions may be second nature. They may feel they were born knowing and can't imagine that others don't know what they know. Even though they are aware they perform better, they likely are unable to articulate why. This is called "unconscious competence," the fourth of the four stages of learning, often attributed to psychologist Abraham Maslow and formalized by Noel Burch of Gordon Training International (Adams, 2014). The job of the interviewer then is to tap into the unconscious competence to draw out what these experts do. The task at hand was to codify this high level of competence in the form of a performance map.

The Performance Mapping Methodology

The performance mapping approach engages sets of high performers in an iterative process to build a map of what they do to achieve success. The initial mapping shares similarities with hierarchical task analysis, or job analysis, where tasks are defined, grouped, and further supported by subtasks. Importantly, the tasks are the things the high performers actually do, and as VCI was to find out, they might be different and more robust than what is in the job description.

The mapping process led performance consultants to four of VCI's regional offices to conduct half-day mapping sessions with two to three BDMs at each location. The first session began with the consultants presenting a "performance statement" – a basic definition of success for a BDM. Participants bantered about the accuracy of the statement, quickly noting the naivety of the corporately generated one. They refined it and crafted a statement of success that they felt defined success as a BDM: "Collaborate with all our business partners to leverage VCI products and services for our mutual success." Once the statement was refined, the consultants then asked the BDMs, "If this is what success looks like, what do you do to achieve it?"

Starting at a high level, participants began identifying what it really takes to get the job done. The map was beginning to take shape, but it was nowhere near complete. High level tasks came to light, taking shape as each was explored for further detail. For example, BDMs identified "Building trust relationships with dealer principals" as critical to success. Interviewers then probed deeper, asking "What do you do to do that?" The BDMs played off each other's contribution, refining, challenging, enhancing, clarifying and synthesizing until they agreed that the map was "right."

5

They remarked that they were also learning from each other. After half a day of interviewing and mapping, it was time to move on to the next location to let the next group of high performers critique the initial work, and build on it.

To ensure that the map was truly a "performance" map, the consultants pushed participants to express their tasks in action-oriented, observable terms. Bloom's Taxonomy provides a useful framework for nailing down the verb of what the performer actually *does* in observable, measurable terms (Bloom, 1956; Krathwohl, 2002). This approach pushed the high performing BDMs to really think about what they do and what drives success. As the map was taking shape, many BDMs remarked that it would be an excellent tool for onboarding new BDMs, simply to show them what the job really entails. They also commented that they would like their bosses to see the map so they would understand everything that good BDMs do every day to consciously (and unconsciously) drive the business.

A validation step followed the building of the map. Two managers of BDMs participated in reviewing the map to provide a management perspective. Their charge was to ensure that VCI's goals and values were properly represented, to confirm terminology, and to catch any omissions. Their modest changes were largely in making the map politically correct.

The performance map goes beyond the job analysis. During the course of the mapping and through subsequent follow-up phone calls, the consultants built the "interior" of the map. This additional detail captures information about the conditions needed to perform these activities, the inputs and outputs, and the tools that are needed. It further defines the frequency of each task, how hard it is to learn, how important it is to the job, and the risk of not doing it (Figure 1). Ultimately, the map becomes a roadmap for curriculum design and other performance supports. In fact, because the map uses action-oriented verbs for every task, instructional designers can easily convert performance statements into performance-based learning objectives and the foundation of a course.

The Gap Analysis Methodology

With a robust map, the Academy knew they couldn't and probably shouldn't develop training for every item. In fact, their existing curriculum already addressed many of the tasks. The next step, the gap analysis, would help them to identify where they were not currently meeting BDM needs, and where additional, revised, or new training was necessary. The consultants developed the survey using the tasks from the performance map. The same two managers who validated the map also reviewed and validated the survey which would go to all BDMs and their managers. The manager version asked managers to respond with their perceptions of each of their BDMs. The survey asked respondents to rate each task in two ways:

Figure 1. Excerpt from final Performance Map

Business Development Manager

PERFORMANCE
1.0 Build trust relationships with business partners
ACTIVITIES
1.1 Earn "trusted-advisor" status with Dealer Principal
  1.1.1 Build an understanding of each dealership
    1.1.1.1 Identify dealership business plan and motivators
    1.1.1.2 Identify dealer goals
    1.1.1.3 Identify decision-makers for departments and dealership
  1.1.2 Dialogue with Dealer Principal on strategies to meet goals
    1.1.2.1 Meet regularly with Dealer Principal to discuss dealership issues
    1.1.2.2 Review progress on goals with Dealer Principal
    1.1.2.3 Offer business insights and perspectives
    1.1.2.4 Coach Dealer Principal on how to work effectively with VCI
    1.1.2.5 Build strategies to advance dealer's goals
    1.1.2.6 Have crucial conversations with dealer principal about dealership challenges
    1.1.2.7 Acknowledge dealership success
    1.1.2.8 Notify dealer principal of discretionary incentives to staff
  1.1.3 Support Dealer Principal's initiatives
    1.1.3.1 Support dealer's special events
    1.1.3.2 Support dealer's community service interests
	FREQUENCY
	1=Annual; 2=Quarterly;
	3=Monthly; 4=Weekly;
	5=Continuously
		LEARN
		1=Easy; 3=Moderate;
		5=Very Hard
			IMPORTANCE
			1=Low; 3= Moderate;
			5=High
				RISK
				1=Low; 3= Moderate;
				5=High

	5	3	5	5
	INPUTS • Dealership contact information • List of dealership senior management • Dealer principal hot buttons • Dealership business plan	**OUTPUTS** • Greater influence with Dealer Principal on topics of mutual interest • Input into dealership business plan • Stronger position to protect and promote VCI financial interests	**STANDARDS**	
	TOOLS • *Salesforce* • Dealer file from Region office	**CIRCUMSTANCES/COMMENTS** Analyze dealership marketing to see if marketing message aligns with dealer's business goals. The "learn" rating for this activity is contingent on the BDM being of the right temperament – a "people person" rather than a pure analyst		

- How important is this to your job? (For managers, "…to the BDM job").
- How proficient are you at doing this? (For managers, "how proficient is John…").

Barrie knew that communication around the survey was key, as the Academy needed to get honest responses. If BDMs thought this was a performance appraisal, the results may be gamed. To help with the messaging, Barrie recruited the support of VCI's vice president of sales and marketing, David Wicks, to create awareness about the upcoming survey (Figure 2). By making the survey about improving "the quality and relevance of the training and support offered to BDMs," it took away the perception of an individual employee appraisal. Even with Wicks' letter, Barrie noted that communication could have been better. She admitted, "I think I should have done a better job up front explaining to people what the project was and why we were doing it. There were a lot of people who didn't have a clue what we were up to." Yet, Barrie received emails from a number of BDMs saying they found the survey very interesting and "how did you get this so right?" They also wanted to see the results.

Figure 2. Letter announcing Gap Analysis Survey

VW CREDIT, INC.

Date: January 11, 2012

To: All VCI Business Development Managers

VW Credit, Inc.
2200 Ferdinand Porsche Drive
Herndon, VA 20171

From: David Wicks

Subject :   BDM Training Needs Survey

VCI and VCI Academy know that it is essential to provide resources that help our Business Development Managers in the performance of their jobs. We are constantly striving to improve the quality and relevance of the training and support offered to BDMs.

VCI Academy has enlisted the professional services of [performance consultant], an award-winning company whose specialty is to help organizations make wise and effective investments in their people. [Performance consultant] has been working with several of our BDMs and SMSOs since November to develop an online survey to identify key targets for training and support.

Now we need your help!

As part of this effort, we also need your participation. In the next few days you will receive an email from [performance consultant] with the link to the survey. We would like each of our BDMs to provide their input by completing the online survey. The survey is completely anonymous; [performance consultant] will host the survey and analyze the data. Results will be delivered to VCI Academy in aggregate form - no individual data will come to VCI Academy. Since the survey is anonymous, I want to encourage you to be completely open and honest in your responses to the questions. The very best part of this process is that all the input comes from you and your colleagues. This is an opportunity for you to tell us what you need to perform at your best.

This is a very important project for VCI, for it will help us ensure that the training and performance support that the VCI Academy provides will be built upon activities known to be associated with success in your key performance measures. The survey will take about 30 minutes of your time and your investment in that time will yield a wealth of insightful information that will guide future training. I think you'll find the survey both interesting and thought-provoking.

Thank you in advance for your valuable contribution to this project.

Sincerely,

David Wicks   Paige Barrie
VP, Sales and Marketing   Senior Manager, VCI Academy

The online survey ran for two weeks, with the initial invitation and three reminders. By the end of the survey period, 100% of BDMs and 100% of their managers had responded. Figure 3 shows a screen shot of the survey. In addition to questions about the tasks, the survey included one open-ended question: "If VCI could provide you with one thing that would help you do your job better, what would it be?"

Figure 3. Screen shot of Gap Analysis Survey

BDM Training Needs Survey

Welcome and thank you for your participation. VCI Academy is continuously looking to improve the quality of their services, and is requesting your input.

Your responses to this survey will tell the Academy what sort of training and performance support will be most helpful to BDMs in achieving success.

This survey includes a series of short items. Each describes a BDM job performance activity. Your task is to assign two ratings for each item: one for importance, one for proficiency.

1. Read each item.
2. Assign a rating to indicate how important you think it is with respect to your job.
3. Assign a second rating to indicate how proficient (competent) you believe you are on this item.

Be honest -- your particular survey will never be shared with VCI management. All responses are confidential and your answers will be combined with those of all other respondents. If you are unable to complete the survey in one sitting, you may close it at the end of any page (after clicking "Next") and return to it later.

Thank you in advance for your thoughtful participation.

Build Trust Relationships with **DEALER PRINCIPAL**

1. Identify Dealer Principal's business goals and motivators.

	Very Low	Low	Average	High	Very High
Importance of Task	○	○	○	○	○
My Proficiency	○	○	○	○	○

2. Meet regularly with Dealer Principal to discuss dealership issues.

	Very Low	Low	Average	High	Very High
Importance of Task	○	○	○	○	○
My Proficiency	○	○	○	○	○

3. Review progress on goals with Dealer Principal.

	Very Low	Low	Average	High	Very High
Importance of Task	○	○	○	○	○
My Proficiency	○	○	○	○	○

Interpreting the Data

The consultants coached the Academy to look at the survey results in several ways:

- Differences between BDMs and their managers.
- Differences between high, medium, and low performing BDMs.

The consultants computed gaps for each audience by looking at the difference between the percentage of respondents who rated a task as important versus the percentage of respondents who rated themselves as proficient. In other words, if a task is important but you're not very good at it, it's a gap. Survey items were then organized by BDM performance level (high, medium, low) and the nature of the gap:

1. Manager and BDM concur there is a gap,
2. Manager sees a gap; BDM does not,
3. Manager does not see a gap; BDM does,
4. Manager and BDM concur there is no gap.

The first cut of the data holds the proverbial "low-hanging fruit." These are gaps recognized by everyone and ripe for a performance improvement solution. The second two cuts are crucially important as the discrepancy between manager and performer generally indicates a difference of opinion in either the importance of a task or the performance standards of the task. The Academy discovered that high performing BDMs put a much higher priority on some tasks than did their managers, suggesting that these BDMs may know better than their manager how to get the job done. Differences in priorities between high and low performers pointed to possible confusion about prioritization among newer or lower performing BDMs. The fourth cut served to reinforce that these areas were not gaps, and were already being addressed through existing training or BDM selection criteria. VCI recognized that prioritization of tasks should be explicitly addressed in initial BDM training.

The identified gaps formed eight categories of opportunities:

- Become a trusted advisor to the Dealer Principal,
- Monitor and build the wholesale business,
- Grow ancillary business,
- Develop a strategic plan for the district,
- Leverage Brand relationships to achieve mutual goals,
- Evaluate and improve dealer retail/lease and certified pre-owned performance,
- Expand knowledge base,
- Manage time.

The analysis pinpointed very specific opportunities for VCI. Knowing the size of each gap enabled the Academy to prioritize their plans for closing the largest knowledge and skills gaps first.

BDMs offered thoughtful responses to the mandatory open-ended question ("If VCI could provide you with one thing that would help you do your job better, what would it be?") Responses reinforced the quantitative findings and supported other issues and themes the researchers had heard during the high-performer interviews. Comments provided rich qualitative descriptions of the issues BDMs were facing in the field. Using textual analysis, responses were quantified into key themes. Below is a sampling of the results in order of frequency of mention:

- Systems and Technology
  ○ Reports – more accurate, easier to access, more timely
  ○ Better tools
  ○ Faster technology
- Communications and Expectations
  ○ Better field communications
  ○ Cross-company awareness of "who is the customer"
  ○ Transparent objectives-setting
- Training
  ○ VCI systems and reports
  ○ Ancillary products
- Incentives
  ○ More pay
  ○ More contests and bonus programs

Communicating Results

Having quantified the gaps noted in the eight categories above, the Academy was able to easily communicate specific curriculum adjustments. Yet the findings went beyond the specific knowledge and skills gaps. Integrating the maps with learnings from the high performer interviews, the gap analysis, and the open-ended survey question ("If VCI could provide you with one thing that would help you do your job better, what would it be?"), the consultants saw the story unfolding. To help communicate the findings, they aligned results with Gilbert's Behavior Engineering Model (Dean & Gilbert, 1997) and Binder's Six Boxes (2012) (Figure 4).

Categorizing findings in this way quickly communicated that factors other than training were blocking BDM performance. For example, many performers, both in interviews and on the survey, complained about inefficient systems and reporting tools, noting the hours it took them to manually compile dealer-facing reports. This

Figure 4. Communicating VCI's results based on an adaptation of Gilbert's Behavior Engineering Model (Dean & Gilbert, 1997) and Binder's Six Boxes (Binder, 2012)

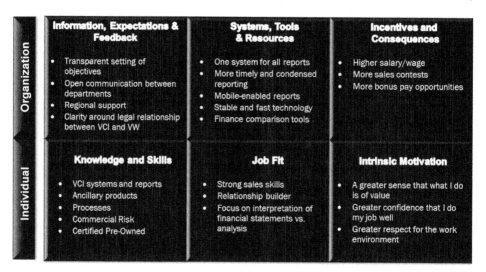

resonated in the Systems, Resources, and Tools box. Their request for more transparency around goal-setting and better communication between departments fell right into the Information, Expectations and Feedback box. Also in that box was a politically charged issue related to the legal relationship between VCI and the VW Brands. Looking at performance gaps in this way opened a lot of eyes, as all of VCI saw how performance improvement solutions needed to go beyond just the training department.

Action Taken

VCI Academy began the project to identify and prioritize knowledge and skills gaps to better inform their curriculum design. With results in hand, they quickly got to work developing a multi-year BDM curriculum plan. A major year-one initiative was revamping their financial analysis course. Traditional wisdom said a good BDM must have in-depth financial analysis skills. However, that was not what high performers said. They placed greater value on being able to read and interpret financial statements than on being able to do a deep analysis. The Academy took this finding to heart, and replaced the original offering with a new course from the National Auto Dealers Association University, titled "Through the Dealer's Eyes." Rather than training the skills to become a financial analyst, it teaches BDMs how to look at financial statements as a dealer would. This is now one of the Academy's highest rated courses.

Following the first year with the new curriculum, Barrie met with VCI regional management to discuss the BDM Certification program for the upcoming year. Typically, this annual meeting included an in-depth discussion about additional training needs and certification changes. This time, it was short and to the point as management said they wanted to "stick with what we have now, because it's clearly working." The only change requested was to accelerate the required time-to-completion from 36 months down to 18 months to get new BDMs up to speed faster. BDMs and management alike report that BDMs are now getting the training they need to succeed in their jobs. Certification is now very focused and stable, representing tremendous cost savings to VCI. They no longer need to build new courses every year, and even more importantly, the seasoned BDMs can stay in the field more rather than come in for unnecessary training.

As a result of this project, the Academy's approach to performance improvement now goes beyond training and involves HR and the business units. As the Director of HR had hoped, this project revealed more than curriculum gaps. He has embraced the project's findings and has begun taking actions from the "non-training" opportunities. For example, several gaps could be closed by improving BDM onboarding content and activities. This initial orientation has been enhanced to require a visit to a regional service center complete with a checklist of people to meet and things to observe while there, enabling the new BDM to build his or her support network.

The project also challenged thinking about the logical career path for a BDM where spending time as a credit or financial analyst had been viewed as necessary stepping stone. It turned out that most high performers were not analysts, but really salespeople. HR is changing the BDM job description, selection criteria, and career planning accordingly. Barrie says, "Our hope is that what we learned here and how we use it will improve the quality of our hires and improve the retention of talent and the performance of people in this role."

CURRENT CHALLENGES FACING THE ORGANIZATION

Tackling curriculum improvements was relatively straightforward for the Academy. Changes were largely within their own domain. The non-training issues were, by their nature, more systemic and broader reaching. The findings identified some serious barriers to performance that present organizational challenges to VCI. One, the systems and reporting issue, will require significant investment in design, programming, and infrastructure. It will also require intensive support from multiple departments, including Information Technology and Sales & Marketing. It will also require the political will to make the investment.

Another issue, largely unspoken until this project, is the natural tension between the finance arm (VCI) and the Brands (i.e., Volkswagen and Audi.) Federal law prohibits collusion, creating a fine line for cooperation between the BDM and the VW or Audi field representative. BDMs requested clarity and leadership by example to help them navigate these waters. The need for complete clarity on this is a broad organizational issue that the Academy has helped to surface.

The Academy stepped up and aligned the BDM certification with job success. It will take strong advocacy to drive for the removal of these other performance barriers. The challenge is: who is the advocate? Who, beyond the Academy, owns performance at VCI?

SOLUTIONS AND RECOMMENDATIONS

The Academy acknowledges that having quantitative evidence has helped bring broader organizational issues to light. It makes discussions more objective and productive. Rather than treat this as a "one-time project," the Academy anticipates continuing to use the findings to push to remove performance barriers. They are further advocating for developing performance maps for other key job positions. They may find that performance barriers are similar across job roles, lending even more weight to the need for change.

Unlike too many "research projects" where nothing happens, the Academy has leveraged their results and taken serious action. They also make it known at every opportunity that the changes are based on BDM input. By uncovering the issues that are truly blocking performance, the Academy has positioned itself as an advisor to the rest of the company. Leading with quantitative evidence, VCI Academy has gotten the attention of executive leadership and has presented facts that cannot be ignored.

REFERENCES

Adams, L. (2014, May). *Learning a new skill is easier said than done.* Retrieved May 31, 2014, from Gordon Training International: http://www.gordontraining.com/free-workplace-articles/learning-a-new-skill-is-easier-said-than-done/

Binder, C. (2012). *Get out of the training box! From training and development to performance improvement with The Six Boxes approach.* Bainbridge Island, WA: The Performance Thinking Network.

Bloom, B. (1956). *Taxonomy of education objectives.* Boston: Allyn and Bacon.

Dean, J., & Gilbert, T. (1997). Engineering performance with or without training. In J. Dean & E. Ripley (Eds.), *Performance Improvement Pathfinders: Models for Organizational Learning Systems*. Washington, DC: International Society for Performance Improvement.

Stolovitch, H., & Keeps, E. (2004). *Training ain't performance*. Alexandria, VA: ASTD Press.

ADDITIONAL READING

Boudreau, J., & Ramstad, P. (2007). *Beyond HR: The new science of human capital*. Boston: Harvard Business School Publishing Corporation.

Cascio, W., & Boudreau, J. (2008). *Investing in people: Financial impact of human resource initiatives*. Upper Saddle River, New Jersey: Pearson Education, Inc.

Colan, L. (2009). *Engaging the hearts and minds of all your employees: How to ignite passionate performance for better business results*. New York: McGraw Hill.

Edwards, J., Scott, J., & Raju, N. (2003). *The human resources program-evaluation handbook*. Thousand Oaks, CA: Sage Publications.

Fitz-Enz. (2010). *The new HR analytics: Predicting the economic value of your company's human capital investments*. New York: American Management Association.

Hubbard, D. (2007). *How to measure anything: Finding the value of intangibles in business*. San Francisco: John Wiley & Sons.

Huselid, M., Becker, B., & Beatty, R. (2005). *The workforce scorecard: Managing human capital to execute strategy*. Boston: Harvard Business School Publishing Corporation.

Lawler, E. (2008). *Talent: Making people your competitive advantage*. San Francisco: Jossey-Bass.

Lawler, E., & Worley, C. (2006). *Built to change: How to achieve sustained organizational effectiveness*. San Francisco: Jossey-Bass.

Ormrod, J. (2008). *Human learning* (5th ed.). Upper Saddle River, NJ: Pearson Education.

Overbaugh, R., & Schultz, L. (n.d.). *Bloom's taxonomy*. Retrieved May 31, 2014, from Old Dominion: http://ww2.odu.edu/educ/roverbau/Bloom/blooms_taxonomy.htm

Pease, G., Beresford, B., & Walker, L. (2014). *Developing Human Captial: Using analyitcs to plan and optimize your learning and development investments*. Hoboken: John Wiley and Sons.

Pease, G., Byerly, B., & Fitz-Enz, J. (2013). *Human capital analytics: How to harness the potential of your organization's greatest asset*. Hoboken: John Wiley & Sons.

Phillips, J., & Edwards, L. (2009). *Managing talent retention: An ROI approach*. San Francisco: Pfeiffer.

Stolovitch, H., & Keeps, E. (2002). *Telling ain't training*. Alexandria, VA: ASTD Press.

Stolovitch, H., & Keeps, E. (2005). *Beyond telling ain't training fieldbook*. Alexandria, VA: ASTD Press.

Van Tiem, D., Moseley, J., & Dessinger, J. (2012). *Fundamentals of performance improvement: Optimizing results through people, process, and organizations* (3rd ed.). San Francisco: John Wiley & Sons.

Vance, D. (2010). *The business of learning: How to manage corporate training to improve your bottom line*. Windsor, CO: David Vance.

KEY TERMS AND DEFINITIONS

BDM: Volkswagen Credit's Business Development Manager; the individual who sells VCI products and services to VW's dealer body.

Behavior Engineering Model/Six Boxes: The Behavioral Engineering Model (originally presented by Thomas Gilbert in 1978) and the Six Boxes Model (Carl Binder's practitioner revision of the BEM) present the variables affecting performance, categorized by environmental and individual factors. This model extends thinking beyond traditional skills and development.

Bloom's Taxonomy: A hierarchical classification of levels of intellectual behavior that represent the goals of the learning process.

Captive Finance Company: A subsidiary whose purpose is to provide financing to customers buying the parent company's product. In the automotive industry, their services include providing financing to consumers and dealerships. A captive finance company can be a source of significant profits for the parent organization.

Gap Analysis: A survey of job performers and their managers that investigates, task by task, the relative importance of each and the performer's proficiency at each. The term is often used to encompass both the survey and the analysis of the data.

High Performer: Individuals who consistently perform at high levels as determined by objective measures.

Performance Gap: A quantified gap on a particular task, computed as the difference between the percentage of respondents who rated a task as important versus the percentage of respondents who rated themselves as proficient. In other words, if a task is important but performers not very good at it, it is a gap.

Performance Map: A performance-based task analysis for a particular job function that starts with a definition of measurable success, as defined by high performers in that job. Each task is written using observable, action-oriented verbs. For each task, the map also includes inputs, outputs, tools, frequency, risk, and difficulty to learn. Performance maps often form the foundation for a curriculum plan and can be the basis for a gap analysis.

Chapter 2

Performance Improvement of a Sales Training Feedback System

Simone G. Symonette
Indiana University, USA

EXECUTIVE SUMMARY

This case study examines the analysis, design, development, implementation, and continuous improvement of a training feedback system. In this case, the system captured sales training participant feedback and distributed that data to stakeholders to analyze and to resolve problems within the learning experience. The intervention set presented in the case is intended for practitioners who have limited time and resources but are interested in creating a feedback system that meets ever changing business demands in a sales training environment.

ORGANIZATION BACKGROUND

In 2010, directors in a large pharmaceutical sales training department voiced concerns about the lack of usable feedback from learners to improve the overall learning experience. At the time, all company operating expenses were under scrutiny as a result of looming patent expirations and a shrinking US economy, leaving the department with limited resources to address any non-essential projects.

DOI: 10.4018/978-1-4666-8330-3.ch002

The sales training department provides several therapeutic businesses areas with product, disease state, selling skills, and leadership development training each year. This department supports approximately 2,970 sales representatives based in the United States. The role of a sales representative is to provide health care providers with exceptional customer experiences and product information. Training experiences consist of computer-based training modules, meetings, experienced-based learning, and live face-to-face training. Trainers ensure business unit curriculums are implemented and sales representative are prepared to enter the field and serve customers. Each trainer reports to a sales training director who is ultimately responsible for executing business unit sales training needs.

The US sales department accounts for approximately $2 billion in revenue for the global corporation, and an effective sales training program is a critical factor in supporting the business's goals. Preparing sales representatives to provide exceptional customer experiences and to adjust to changes in the business with minimal customer disruption is central to the mission of the department. Although a system was in place to capture participant feedback, leaders were dissatisfied with the system and the data were not used. Sales training leadership knew that feedback was an essential part of the business and instructional process, and without it they would not be able to make improvements and keep up with new business demands. Sales training leadership knew something had to be done to fix the broken feedback system. The question was how?

Through observation and inquiry, an internal performance consultant was able to uncover the root causes of the problem associated with the feedback system. This ultimately led to the system being upgraded to meet leadership's demand along with the redesign of internal workflow processes. Working in partnership with sales training leadership, the consultant was able to move the organization towards a greater emphasis on participant feedback instead of second-hand data as a source of feedback for continuous improvement. Collecting reactionary level 1 feedback on participants' engagement in training is important because it influences sales representatives' morale and their perceptions of future interactions with the sales training (Schultz, 2013). The core strategy behind the new feedback system was grounded in the Kluger and Denisi (1996) feedback intervention theory and Hysong, Best, and Pugh (2006) actionable feedback model. The feedback intervention theory explained how to focus the organization's attention on change (Larson, Patel, Evans, & Saiman, 2013). The four components of the actionable feedback model of timeliness, individualization, non-punitive, and customization were used to operationalize the feedback system (Hysong et al., 2006). By using these core principles as a guiding light through the design of the feedback system, the consultant was able to provide a more user-friendly, self-serviceable, actionable, and real-time feedback system.

SETTING THE STAGE

The performance consultant investigated the current state of the feedback system of the department. The goal to fix the feedback system seemed quite intuitive; however, barriers existed that prevented the feedback system from being improved and taking root in the sales training department. These barriers included the organization emphasizing centralized business goals at the expense of local business needs.

The feedback system was developed by an outside vendor who focused on producing corporate evaluation processes. However, direction on how the feedback system was designed and implemented came from a cross-functional Global Training and Development Council (GTDC) within the company. This group resisted the idea of customizing and localizing the feedback system and tended to side with a more centralized business approach that lacked consideration for local needs and changes in the business. The only solution provided by the council to meet US sales training desires for autonomy was to create customized reports for each request at a premium price. With a limited budget the customized solution was not a feasible option for the sales training department. Other departments within the corporation had similar concerns as the sales training department but were not aware of alternatives for capturing training feedback. The council's idea was to aggregate training data from across the company into one single analysis. The concept of aggregation across the company never materialized, leaving local business leaders frustrated with the feedback system.

CASE DESCRIPTION

Performance problems and concerns were revealed through the analysis phase of the project. For example, the feedback system did not yield valuable or actionable data, the data reporting delivery system had delays and was inconsistent, and the department's culture was focused on the number of people trained and not on the learning experience. Each of these performance problems included technology, management, and organizational concerns that had to be addressed. More detailed description of analysis findings are provided below.

Feedback System Not Yielding Valuable and Actionable Data

Sales training leadership's main problem with the centralization approach was that it lacked purpose. Local leadership did not understand why they were collecting training participant's data because the resulting data was so generic that it lacked meaning to the trainers and stakeholders. The centralized approach forced all departments to conform to a template-based list of questions when creating surveys. The process for changing the centralized questions was difficult, required additional cost, and getting approval was time consuming. As a result, individual departments were disengaged from the feedback system because they were left with data that was not useful or actionable.

Sales training leaders needed feedback data that had some quantitative measure that was easy to interpret and communicate to the department. The resulting data needed to be packaged so that mid-level managers, facilitators, and performance consultants could analyze the details in the qualitative open-end comments and quickly take action to make improvements before the next training experience. Problems identified that required more long-term and strategic solutions could then be documented and addressed by leadership. Sales training leadership wanted the feedback system to have rigor and solid research foundation; they did not want the questions, reports, or the general language around the feedback system to be communicated in academic and statistical terminology. Leadership and facilitator stakeholders wanted to view the data in a simple format that included the sample size, response rate, and participant responses.

Another source of disengagement in the feedback system revolved around the lack of ownership stakeholders felt in the learning experience. The old system did not allow trainers to get specific feedback on their performance from participants which led to a lack of facilitator ownership of the learning experience. Any customization to the survey or the process would cost additional funds that the department could not spare at the time. Survey data with responses rates lower than 30% was not consider useful or actionable and not worth the time and energy it took to review the feedback reports. As a result, stakeholders ignored the minimal feedback that was received.

Feedback Reports Delivered to Trainers and Directors Too Late to Take Action

The process for sending surveys to participants and receiving the data was not satisfactory. The feedback process started when the learning experience was completed and the participants received an online survey via email. Participants had a week to submit the survey. Once the surveys were submitted, administrative personnel would have to manually submit a request for the feedback report. The timing of this manual process was not consistent. Once the feedback report was ready, the administrative personnel would send it to someone in leadership to review. There was no standardized way to review and analyze the feedback data. By the time trainers received class feedback, plans for the next class were already solidified and no real changes could be made. There was not a user-friendly archival system in place to retrieve previous data if someone wanted to go back spot trending over time. Bureaucratic processes associated with receiving feedback data was another reason stakeholders disengaged with the process and overlooked participant feedback. To speed up the process, a few trainers resorted to creating their own paper versions of feedback forms which further diminished the centralized approach as participants were asked to complete two surveys: one paper-based and online.

Culture Focused on Quantity of Trainees Not on the Learning Experience

In addition to all the organizational, tool, and process barriers associated with the feedback system, a more critical cultural and awareness problem existed in the sales training department. The culture was one in which the trainers and sales training directors were not motivated to make changes to the learning experience because the metric the business focused on was the number of people trained and not the value of the learning experience to a sales representative's career development. The power of participant feedback in a training environment was not yet realized because of trainers and sales training directors were not able to see value in the data they were currently receiving. Theoretically, sales training directors knew participant feedback was important; however, they just could not see the value in the data they were receiving from the existing feedback system.

CURRENT CHALLENGES FACING THE ORGANIZATION

The Role of Leadership

The training department consisted of several businesses with competing priorities. The training department leadership knew that an effort to align the businesses to a common process or approach was not easy. Consensus on most projects in the department was seen as an attempt to force conformity and was often met with resistance. This created a culture of silos and reduced the probability of businesses learning from each other's successes and failures. The leadership team realized that they played a crucial role in the feedback process.

Lack of Common Goal

The problem leadership faced was identifying what their role entailed and how to execute their role to bring change. Using the feedback system was problematic because there was a lack of goals for the feedback system and no compass to guide how and why the training department should use it. Other initiatives in the department relied on scoreboards to publicly monitor progress towards goals while the feedback system did not have a mechanism for communicating progress.

Tightening of Budgets and IT Opportunity

In a year of tightened budget constraints, funding for additional projects that had not been budgeted for in the previous year were not seen as a priority. Although funding was limited, the Information Technology (IT) department started an initiative that made new business tools available to departments in an on-demand environment. The initiative fostered a collaborative and cross functional approach to learning new technologies across the company. Employees were empowered to explore technology resources that had companywide licenses to use at their discretion. The funding environment forced innovators to rely on what tools were available to them and to introduce new ideas into the work environment.

Trainer Turnover

The training department traditionally had high turnover with an average tenure of approximately two and one-half years for trainers before they moved on to other roles in the organization. As a result, any initiative that started in the department had to regain momentum at least once every year. In order for trainers to be engaged in the feedback system they had to recognize how the system could serve as a tool to help them in their career development. The feedback system and associated processes had to be simple to understand in order to accommodate the constant change. It also needed to be seamlessly integrated into business processes and the typical training experience.

Lack of Continuous Improvement Mindset

One of the biggest challenges with the feedback system was the attitude the department had towards continuous improvement. Typically, directors and trainer were satisfied when a training experience was delivered on time and reached the number of trainees required by the business. There was rarely any cohesive department-wide effort to bring lessons learned to the forefront so that training experience could be better for the next training class. The "one and done" approach needed to shift to a more continuous improvement mindset. This shift was nearly impossible with a broken feedback system.

SOLUTIONS AND RECOMMENDATIONS

The internal consultant faced several issues in the process of integrating the feed-back system into the department. The main issue dealt with figuring out a way to embed the feedback system into the larger training experience and sales training business workflow. The integration process needed significant support from the training department's leadership, specifically the Senior Director and the Director of Learning Strategies. These two executives championed the feedback system initiative and removed barriers as they were raised. For example, the Senior Director led the department to a more unified way of viewing participant feedback by the establishing a "♥ Love to Learn" goal that focused attention on and created excitement around achieving learning goals within all aspects of training. Establishing a common metric system and rebranding how the sales training department viewed the feedback system increased directors and trainers' engagement with continuous improvement. The Director of the Learning Strategy team within the department ensured that the internal consultant was empowered to try a different approach to capturing feedback in the company by using available technology to meet business needs.

The internal consultant used rapid prototyping as a methodology for educating the sales training leadership team throughout the improvement process. The rapid prototyping approach allowed the internal consultant to quickly and easily partner with leadership in the design, develop, and implementation phases of the process. By leveraging tacit performance improvement knowledge, business acumen, collaboration skills, and technical competencies the internal consultant was able to implement the intervention set that the training department continues to maintain to date. The final interventions included in the set are provided in detail in the next section.

Organizational Change

Leadership's vision and insight into the larger organization's strategic direction inspired the feedback system redesign process. Across the company, executives were charged to look for ways to make improvements with fewer resources, provide exceptional customer experience through customer feedback, and execute the concept of simplification on a daily basis. These company priorities gained momentum with the CEO and was acknowledged across the company all the way to the administrative assistants.

Sales training leadership and the internal consultant knew that in order for the new feedback system to take root in the department it had to be aligned with current company priorities and rebranded. The team realized that effective communication regarding the new feedback system was essential to ensure clarity that this new system was anchored to greater organizational goals. To gain acceptance into the sale training department, the first step in the rebranding process focused on shifting the perception of the feedback system from a traditional training evaluation system to a hybrid approach. The hybrid approach included the business elements of the training experience for the participants, trainers, and directors.

Rebranding

The new feedback system was positioned as a real-time performance support tool that allowed feedback stakeholders to receive participant feedback as soon as possible so they could take action to resolve issues discovered in the data. The framing also stressed that the change allowed the department to engage in a more business-friendly process as well as enabled the business to take advantage of more survey features in a manner that was less expensive and more efficient.

In the rebranding process, trainers were asked to be partners in the feedback system process by allotting time for participants to complete surveys towards the end of the training experience. In return, trainers would receive sufficient participant response rates, timelier reports, and make their classroom efforts more visible to their supervisors. The rebranding effort included communicating that the leadership team would have access to one central archive so that they could quickly access survey reports across all businesses and training experiences over time. Another highlighted feature of the feedback system was its ability to be embedded into Microsoft Outlook, the email and calendaring tool used by the company. Integration with Microsoft Outlook allowed the administrative staff to quickly generate the survey and place it into a Microsoft Outlook meeting invite or reminder so that the trainer responsible for the training experience could easily see the link and quickly send the Outlook meeting invite or reminder to participants to complete survey.

Establish Common Performance Metrics

To mitigate the problems associated with competing business needs, common performance metrics were established for the sales training department. Although the surveys used in the feedback system had multiple sections focused on an array of traditional items pertaining to the training experience, leadership adopted a single metric to drive the "♥ Love to Learn" goal. This metric was an adaptation of Reichheld's (2006) net promoter score (NPS). NPS was used because of its simplicity and ability to be modified for sales training purposes. While there were various metrics that could be used to measure aspects of training, NPS allowed for all metrics to be narrowed down into a single metric that was easy to monitor and communicate.

NPS was based on a single question that leadership used to gauge whether the training experience was meeting expectations. Over time the question evolved from, "How likely are you to recommend this learning experience to a peer on a scale of 1 to 10?" to "How valuable was the training experience to your development on a scale of 1 to 10?" Regardless of how the question was framed, the method used to calculate the score leadership wanted to observe stayed constant. The score served as a numeric representation of the standard that leadership wanted to observe as perceived by training participants. According to Reichheld's (2006) and Satmetrix's (2004) NPS calculation is the percentage of training promoters (or the percent of participants that rate training a 9 or 10) subtracted from the percentage of detractors (or the percent of participants who rate the training a 6, 5, 4, 3, 2, or 1). Participants who rate the training a 7 or 8 are considered passive and are not included in the calculation. Leadership decided to set the NPS goal at +45 to initiate the feedback system. Each year the NPS goal was also evaluated to ensure it was not only obtainable but also still a worthy goal for which to strive. The goal stabilized at +65.

While the intention of the NPS was to provide a simple method for tracking progress towards a departmental goal, the temptation for the NPS to be abused was a reality in a sales training environment. Leadership addressed stakeholder and employee opposition to and concerns about using a single question to sum up the learning experience. The main argument was that putting so much attention on a single score was potentially harmful. Learning consultants in the sales training department argued that multiple factors influence the training experience which could not be distilled into a single score. This fear rested on the competitive nature of the sales training staff. The learning strategy team argued that the trainers, who were formerly sales representatives, have been conditioned to use numbers as a behavior regulator, and as a result, would place more emphasis on obtaining a score than on learning. To help mitigate this concern, leadership drove the focus of the feedback towards the learner experience and not the NPS score. Also, some of the standard training questions remained on the new survey with minor adjustments to accommodate for the language of the training department and business priorities. The open-ended and closed-ended training questions along with knowledge assessments allowed trainers and directors to take actionable performance improvement steps. The NPS question simply served as a high-level monitoring metric. Intentional efforts were made by the sales training leadership to minimize the potential for competition or a culture of winning versus one of teamwork.

To uphold the ideal of collaboration and teamwork, specific mechanisms were implemented to mitigate the chances of the learning experience being overshadowed by the NPS score. First, leadership aligned and communicated that the feedback system was non-punitive. Business units that received NPS scores below the intended target were not reprimanded but encouraged and empowered to analyze the feedback so that they could make changes to improve. Second, it was reiterated at every departmental open forum that the focus of the feedback system was to learn and improve the learning experience. Leadership stressed that the objective was not to make changes to simply satisfy participants so that they could provide higher scores, but to continuously improve learning experience.

Reporting

The most strategic effort to encourage collaboration and reduce the chance of a competitive mindset was based on how the feedback data was presented and which reports were visible to whom. Feedback reports were electronically sent to the business unit director via a uniform resource locator (URL). After reviewing the reports, the sales training director in turn disseminated three reports to their specific business unit trainers. The first report was an overall departmental training experience report; this report did not differentiate data by business unit. The second report was filtered specifically for that particular business unit and only presented data based on participants who experienced that business unit's training. The third report provided individual trainers with data specific to their role in the training. Directors and trainers were instructed not to share their individual or business unit reports amongst their peers in order to reduce competition.

Directors and trainers were responsible for improving their specific business unit. By placing the onus of analysis and improvement recommendations on the business unit sales training directors and trainers, they felt a sense of empowerment because they were a part of the improvement process. If the business unit analysis revealed a structural problem with the training, the change would have to be proposed to the senior director of the sales training department before implementation. The goal of the self-analysis was to provide the business units with autonomy to make quick improvements and provide a sense of ownership in the feedback system.

Educating through Rapid Prototyping

The internal consultant used a rapid prototyping technique to aid in the explanation and visualization of the feedback system. Rapid prototyping allowed stakeholders to quickly conceptualize the ideas, tactics, and strategies necessary for the successful implementation of the feedback system. In addition, the technique increased awareness among leadership of the power and potential of the feedback system. This enabled them to be early adopters and champions for the new feedback initiative.

In the early stages, the rapid prototyping process was facilitated by quick survey design and development in Microsoft SharePoint. Although the survey features of SharePoint were limited, it served the purpose of demonstrating how the survey process would function and appear to the participants. More importantly, it allowed the internal consultant to systematically capture data and distribute to stakeholders. SharePoint also allowed the internal consultant to identify the limitations of the feedback system and make adjustments to strengthen the system. Rapid prototyping enabled the Internal Consultant to deliver the feedback system and at the same time eliminate kinks in the system before implementing to a larger audience and moving into a more sustainable technology for survey administration. Rapid prototyping also allowed the client and stakeholders to learn the process and experience the feedback system as the design and development occurred.

The rapid prototyping helped build a network of advocates of the feedback system throughout the process. Prior to the prototyping, certain aspects of the feedback system were unfamiliar to the audience as it was difficult for them to conceptualize through verbal explanation. For example, in the previous feedback system participants had to wait a few days to receive the survey in their email through an automated generated system once the completed class roster was entered into the system. Stakeholders were impressed with how easy the link process was and how it enabled learners to take the survey without having to wait. Embedding the survey link on a centralized location was perceived as easy and familiar, which increased the feedback process efficiency. SharePoint survey features also allowed the trainer to easily view the response rate by simply clicking on the survey link. This feature prompted the trainers to communicate how important participant feedback was to the department and ask that participants to complete the survey before leaving the training experience. During the early piloting of the feedback system, participants frequently left the experience without completing the survey and the response rate was significantly lower than if learners were given time to complete during the training experience.

Since the feedback system was in its piloting phase, the real time data reports were still rudimentary. Stakeholders could receive the data outputs but in an unsophisticated manner. It was simply an output of data with limited graphical depictions of the data. The intervention focused on reducing the amount of time it took before a report was distributed to sales training director, and trainers struggled until the new survey software was implemented into the feedback system. In the meantime, as desires for feedback data grew, so did the demand for more customized reports. Customized reports were manually generated from Microsoft Excel data outputs; however, they were not sustainable because of the time and effort they took to create.

Leveraging Technology and Analysis

During the prototyping, it became evident that automating administrative processes was necessary to increase the feedback system outputs. Although more advanced survey software would aid in the analysis of participant feedback, the internal consultant realized that it was also imperative to train directors and trainers on how to interpret the data gathered. The consultant introduced common methods and practices for analyzing and interpreting the training participant feedback data. This was done by assisting and teaching the sales training directors and trainers business unit how to content analyze the data until they were confident enough to conduct the analysis on their own and in turn the processes were ingrained in after action meetings. Some of the sales training directors and trainers had graduate degrees or exposure to data analysis, but for others, this was their first experience with inquiry.

The objective was to make the analysis and recommendation process as simple as possible for the stakeholders to maintain. The goal was to remove trainer's dependence on others to provide data analysis and recommendations and push them toward a state of empowerment and decision making. The internal consultant advocated the use of descriptive statistics for the quantitative data and simple coding or theming procedures for the qualitative data so the effort did not become too overwhelming. Including the trainers in the data analysis process gave them a sense of ownership and a responsibility to the success of the recommendations made.

CONCLUSION

The sales training feedback system eventually expanded beyond the sales training participant experiences to capturing area and district meeting participant feedback. Leadership realized that the feedback system allowed them to gauge business targets and adjust to meet needs. As time passed, the mindset of continuous improvement spread throughout the culture, which was observable in the demand for feedback surveys on additional projects. The following lessons were learned and serve as guidelines for the internal consultant and stakeholders as the feedback system grew and matured.

1. Change is inevitable in a business environment and a feedback system has to be flexible enough to adapt to the change quickly and intentionally. If the feedback system becomes too rigid it will become obsolete and thus defeat its intended purpose of supporting continuous improvement.
2. An internal consultant needs to be able to rapidly provide leadership with a prototype of the feedback system to enhance buy-in and communication. Rapidly designing, developing, and implementing a prototype allows the consultant to quickly define the process and document it. Early documentation of the process enables the process to be later used for job aid purposes as the system evolves and requires less administrative support.

3. Be patient with the adoption and integration of the feedback system into the business work processes. It takes time for behaviors and mindsets to change in an organization. Setback will occur but if a strong partnership between the internal consultant and the organization's leadership exist, progress will get back on track.

4. Do not underestimate the power of partnerships and collaboration with stakeholders at all levels of the organization, especially leadership. An internal consultant should allow leadership to remove barriers and bring others to consensus when necessary. Leadership can remove more hurdles in less time so maintain trust and appreciation in leadership's ability to remove seen and unseen barriers as well as energize their networks in support of the feedback system.

5. Scholars acknowledge that accountability and cultural diversity are current gaps in sales training evaluation research (Lassk, Ingram, Kraus, & Di Mascio, 2012). This case demonstrates that future research on feedback systems and evaluation also needs to focus on the difference between using metrics to facilitate the continuous improvement of performance versus proving the value of training. In addition, practitioners need to be aware of this difference in order to reduce possibility of metrics being misused within the organization.

These are the basic requirements for improving the performance of a sales training feedback system.

REFERENCES

Hysong, S. J., Best, R. G., & Pugh, J. A. (2006). Audit and feedback and clinical practice guideline adherence: Making feedback actionable. *Implementation Science; IS, 1*(9), 9–18. doi:10.1186/1748-5908-1-9 PMID:16722539

Kluger, A., & DeNisi, A. (1996). The effects of feedback interventions on performance: A historical review, a meta-analysis, and a preliminary feedback intervention theory. *Psychological Bulletin, 119*(2), 254–284.

Larson, E. L., Patel, S. J., Evans, D., & Saiman, L. (2013). Feedback as a strategy to change behavior: The devil is in the details. *Journal of Evaluation in Clinical Practice, 19*(2), 230–234. doi:10.1111/j.1365-2753.2011.01801.x PMID:22128773

Lassk, F. G., Ingram, T. N., Kraus, F., & Di Mascio, R. (2012). The future of sales training: Challenges and related research questions. *Journal of Personal Selling & Sales Management, 32*(1), 141–154. doi:10.2753/PSS0885-3134320112

Reichheld, F. F. (2006). *The ultimate question: For opening the door to good profits and true growth*. Boston, MA: Harvard Business School Press.

Satmetrix Systems. (2004). The power behind a single number: Growing your business with Net Promoter (White Paper). Retrieved from http://www.macu.ca/wp-content/uploads/2012/02/The-Power-Behind-A-Single-Number.pdf

Schultz, M. (2013). 7 keys for sales training with maximum impact. *T+D Magazine, 67*(3), 52.

ADDITIONAL READING

Addison, R. M., Haig, C., & Kearny, L. (2009). *Performance architecture: The art and science of improving organizations*. Silver Spring, MD: International Society for Performance Improvement.

Bichelmeyer, B. A., & Horvitz, B. S. (2006). Comprehensive performance evaluation: Using logic models to develop a theory-based approach for evaluation of humanperformance technology interventions. In J. A. Pershing (Ed.), *Handbook of human performance technology* (pp. 1165–1189). San Francisco, CA: Pfeiffer.

Brethower, D. (2006). Systemic issues. In J. A. Pershing (Ed.), *Handbook of human performance technology* (pp. 111–137). San Francisco: Pfeiffer.

Clark, R. E., & Estes, F. (2002). *Turning research into results: A guide to selecting the right performance solutions*. Atlanta, GA: CEP Press.

Conner, D. (1993). *Managing at the speed of change: How resilient managers succeed and prosper where others fail*. New York, NY: Villard Books.

Foshay, W. R., Moller, L., Schwen, T., Kalman, H., & Haney, D. (1999). Research in human performance technology. In H. D. Stolovitch & E. J. Keeps (Eds.), *Handbook of human performance technology* (pp. 895–915). San Francisco, CA: Jossey-Bass Pfeiffer.

Gilbert, T. F. (2007). *Human competence*. San Francisco, CA: Pfeiffer.

Hale, J. (2004). *Performance-based management: What every manager should do to get results*. San Francisco, CA: Pfeiffer.

Keiningham, T. L., Aksoy, L., Cooil, B., Andreassen, T. W., & Williams, L. (2008). A holistic examination of Net Promoter. *Journal of Database Marketing and Customer Strategy Management, 15*(2), 79–90. doi:10.1057/dbm.2008.4

Kirkpatrick, D. L., & Kirkpatrick, J. D. (2006). *Evaluating training programs: The four levels*. San Francisco, CA: Berrett-Koehler.

Mager, R., & Pipe, P. (1997). *Analyzing performance problems*. Atlanta, GA: Center for Effective Performance.

Mager, R. F. (1992). *What every manager should know about training*. Belmont, CA: Lake Publishing Company.

McGregor, J. (2006). Would you recommend us? *Business Week*, 30th January, 94. Retrieved from http://www.businessweek.com/stories/2006-01-29/would-you-recommend-us

Moseley, J. L., & Dessinger, J. C. (Eds.). (2010). *Handbook of improving performance in the workplace: Selecting and implementing performance interventions* (Vol. 3). San Francisco, CA: Pfeiffer.

Pershing, J. A. (2006). Human performance technology fundamentals. In J. A. Pershing (Ed.), *Handbook of human performance technology* (pp. 5–34). San Francisco, CA: Pfeiffer.

Piskurich, G. M. (2006). *Rapid Instructional Design: Learning ID fast and right*. San Francisco, CA: Pfeiffer.

Reichheld, F. F. (2006). The microeconomics of customer relationships. *MIT Sloan Management Review*, *47*(2), 73–78.

Robinson, D. G., & Robinson, J. C. (1995). *Performance consulting: Moving beyond training*. San Francisco, CA: Berrett-Koehler Publishers.

Rossett, A. (1992). Analysis of human performance problems. In H. D. Stolovitch & E. J. Keeps (Eds.), *Handbook of human performance technology* (pp. 139–162). San Francisco, CA: Jossey-Bass.

Rossett, A., & Schafer, L. (2007). *Job aids and performance support: Moving from knowledge in the classroom to knowledge everywhere*. San Francisco, CA: Pfeiffer.

Rothwell, W. J. (2005). *Beyond training and development: The groundbreaking classic on human performance enhancement*. New York, NY: American Management Association.

Silber, K. H., & Foshay, W. R. (2010). *Handbook of improving performance in the workplace: Instructional design and training delivery* (Vol. 1). San Francisco, CA: Pfeiffer.

Stolovitch, H. D., & Keeps, E. J. (Eds.). (1999). *Handbook of human performance technology* (2nd ed.). San Francisco, CA: Jossey-Bass Pfeiffer.

Van Tiem, D. M., Moseley, J. L., & Dessinger, J. C. (2004). *Fundamentals of performance technology: A guide to improving people, process, and performance* (2nd ed.). Silver Spring, MD: International Society for Performance Improvement.

Watkins, R., & Leigh, D. (Eds.). (2010). *Handbook of improving performance in the workplace: The handbook of selecting and implementing performance interventions* (Vol. 2). San Francisco, CA: Jossey-Bass.

Wile, D. (1996). Why doers do. *Performance & Instruction, 35*(1), 30–35. doi:10.1002/pfi.4170350209

KEY TERMS AND DEFINITIONS

Actionable Data: Data that are easily converted to information that are targeted and allow stakeholders to gain insight to change behaviors and processes.

Feedback System: An organized set of mechanisms that coordinate data input and output that are analyzed and used to influence change.

Intervention Set: A group of interventions working together as one to reduce to performance gaps.

Performance Metrics: Observable measures use to improve performance.

Rapid Prototyping: Quickly drafting a model or mock version of the intended end product.

Real-Time Data: Data that are accessible the moment they are entered into a system.

Rebranding: Communicating the new features and benefits of concepts and processes to change public opinion.

Chapter 3
Organizational Analysis Leads to Dissection of Recurrent Training Issues

Melanie E. Ross
Old Dominion University, USA

Jill E. Stefaniak
Old Dominion University, USA

EXECUTIVE SUMMARY

After consistently missing the contract's monthly-required staffing personnel re-quests, the senior director and senior manager of recruiting decided the day-to-day operations, procedures, and recruiting processes should be standardized within the recruiting section. The staffing department at Variant Data Systems, Inc. decided to move forward with instructional and noninstructional interventions to address incomplete biography submissions between the recruiters and the technical writer. This case study demonstrates how a layered organizational performance analysis was conducted to dissect recurring performance problems. The case also examines how an internal performance improvement consultant was utilized on the project to identify the performance issue and develop the expectations of the position, a communication plan, the formal instructional unit and knowledge management database, and accountability metrics to ensure it met the needs of the recruiting section in the staffing department.

DOI: 10.4018/978-1-4666-8330-3.ch003

ORGANIZATION BACKGROUND

Variant Data Systems, Inc. (VDS) is an information technology (IT) services company focused on providing individualized, innovative professional services for the analysis, design, development, delivery, implementation, and evaluation of information systems and networks in worldwide locations. VDS, Inc. serves as an independent organization that supports many external customers utilizing full-time and intermittent employees in domestic and overseas locations. VDS, Inc. also strives for improving efficiency and effectiveness, resulting in optimum productivity through aligning the organizations' IT strategy and goals to address the most important IT needs of ensuring the technology delivers what it promises.

VDS, Inc. is one of the United States leading information technology company's providing information technology infrastructures in austere locations worldwide. Based out of Denver, Colorado, four personnel are credited with starting VDS, Inc. Since then, the headquarters location has grown to support 232 full-time personnel; the company employs over 1,000 contract personnel in locations around the world. VDS, Inc. offers a wide variety of services, including initial security assessment of networks, vulnerability scanning plans, firewall management, wireless networking, and 24/7 performance monitoring.

VDS, Inc. is made up of several departments including operations, contracts, pricing, legal, human resources, and staffing. A senior director governs each department with additional senior managers serving as direct reports. The senior manager of recruiting serves as a direct report to the senior director of staffing and is responsible for managing three team leaders; two team leaders oversee a total of ten recruiters who support the Data Encryption Services (DES) contract in Iraq. Each department is integral in onboarding candidates through the four-month process and deploying to the specific contract location.

Throughout its existence, VDS, Inc. views its departments and employees through a combination of the traditional vertical view and the windowless silos view of an organization. The senior director employs managers that manage several sub-departments independently of one another, yet are interdependent among one another (Rummler & Brache, 2013). These views were believed to be an appropriate way to manage the organization during its inception and beginning years because everyone knew everyone's role and was able to work together cohesively to execute the mission.

Although VDS, Inc. has multiple departments that are interdependent of one another to onboard candidates throughout the lengthy process, the organization still functions in the traditional vertical view with windowless silos. This view severely limits the organization's ability to mature because managers work against each other rather than together; meetings between departments become activity reports rather than engaging partners in the battle against competitors (Rummler & Brache, 2013). Because of this, managers are often removed from handling high-priority tasks and competitor concerns, as they are required to handle lower-level issues that arise between the sub-departments. The mentality of the organization under this view revolves around each sub-department doing what is necessary to meet their personal goals and blaming any shortcomings and pitfalls on its interdependent parts, all of which are necessary to accomplish the mission (Rummler & Brache, 2013).

Utilizing a multi-layered analysis, such as the nine performance variable framework established by Rummler and Brache (2013), to combat the continuous use of the traditional vertical and windowless silos views at VDS, Inc. is necessary to understand the different parts of the organization at multiple levels. Employing the multi-layered approach will allow the organization to be viewed and analyzed through multiple lenses, which will provide insight into the ways sub-departments can be allies rather than enemies. Viewing the organization through multiple lenses will also assist in discovering the knowledge and skills possessed by its employees in the different departments and sub-departments regarding the organization, processes, and job in regards to the goals, design, and management. It will also allow for disconnects among the departments and sub-departments to be identified. Ultimately, dissecting the organization using the multi-layered approach will allow for a better understanding of the organization in addition to its individual parts that contribute to the system as a whole to accomplish the organization's goals and missions and how to posture the organization to mature and remove the traditional vertical and windowless silos view of the organization (Brethower, 2006).

SETTING THE STAGE

VDS, Inc. is nationally certified by the National Institute of Standards and Technology (NIST) and utilizes the NIST 800 Series as a standard for business. The NIST 800 Series is a set of documents that describe the United States government computer security policies, procedures, and guidelines (U.S. Department of Commerce, 1995). VDS, Inc. was recognized as a leading information technology services company in 2011, and has been the recipient of the IT Service and Support Award two years in a row.

The staffing department within VDS, Inc. is managed by the senior director and employs 25 personnel consisting of one senior director, two senior managers, one technical writer, three team leaders, recruiters, and staffing and deployment coordinators. Sixteen of the personnel serve within a recruiting capacity; ten are responsible for recruiting for the DES contract located in Iraq. The remaining individuals are responsible for staffing other contracts held by the company. Per contract requirements, candidates who wish to be considered for a position on the DES contract must have an approved biography packet from the customer. Each position requires its own biography packet approval. This serves as the customer's interview with the candidate to determine qualifications and eligibility to serve on the contract. Without an approved biography packet from the customer, the candidate is not eligible to serve in the position. The recruiters are responsible for submitting the biography packets on behalf of the candidate to the technical writer for review prior to being sent to the customer for approval or disapproval. The customer is responsible for approving or disapproving the biography packet, which will determine the candidate's eligibility for the respective position on the DES contract. When the DES contract calls for additional personnel that must be biography approved, each recruiter works with the technical writer to submit candidates with a completed biography containing all necessary supporting documentation.

In the summer of 2013, VDS, Inc. experienced reorganization where half of the department's recruiters were let go reducing the number of recruiters to six. Seven months later over the course of a month, VDS, Inc. restructured its staffing department and hired six additional recruiters; two started the same day and the others started individually. A former recruiter at VDS, Inc. was let go during the initial reorganization. Despite the layoffs, the recruiter who was initially let go due to poor performance was rehired into his previous recruiter position. The department continues to experience similar troubles from the recruiter during his initial employment duration. This is an example of one of the many performance problems occurring within the recruiting department at VDS, Inc., as qualified personnel have been identified as one of the critical factors that enable the company to successfully carry out and perform the necessary operations to deliver top-notch information technology services and support in stateside and overseas locations. Prior to the reorganization, the technical writer developed a one-hour, lecture-based instructional presentation highlighting many of the important aspects of the contract with an emphasis on what to include in the biography packet due to the robust requirements of the DES contract. An opportunity was provided for recruiters to ask questions following the presentation. A limitation to the training was that no application exercises were incorporated into the presentation for recruiters to practice specific tasks. Despite the attempt at increasing the accuracy of biography submissions, the recruiters continued to repeat errors when submitting biography packets.

Since much of the work completed by VDS Inc. is performance-based, it is necessary to seek qualified candidates. Each candidate is evaluated against verifiable, quantitative metrics set forth by the contract that must be supported by authentic documentation. If recruiters are unable to follow the contract's requirements and recruit unqualified personnel, the technical writer becomes inundated with additional work. For every person submitted by a recruiter, the technical writer conducts a thorough review of the biography packet to ensure all information is reported accurately and all supporting documentations verify the claimed experiences. When a biography packet is missing information, the technical writer compiles a thorough email to the recruiter of everything that is missing and/or needs to be corrected. When recruiters do not recruit personnel using the contract requirements and solicit unqualified personnel, the technical writer continues to expend resources by thoroughly reviewing the biography packet and supplying a detailed email of all pertinent information that is missing and/or needs correction. This slows down the technical writer's process and creates more work.

Administrative leadership at VDS, Inc. considered implementing a training program to address recruiter training within the staffing department. After the recent hires and continuous errors conducted by new and experienced recruiters on a variety of tasks, VDS, Inc. determined there needed to be standardization among its recruiters regardless of experience within the organization. A challenge with recruiter training is the lack of a formal training process to bring new recruiter's up to par with the vast systems, processes, methods of operations and procedures, and position requirements recruiters need to be successful in sourcing qualified personnel. Currently, very little time is provided to train the new recruiters. Recruiters who come to work at VDS, Inc. receive on-the-job training from another recruiter; recruiter length of service with VDS, Inc. is not an indicator as to who is selected to provide on-the-job training. Much of the learning experience for new recruiters occurs through trial and error as well as questions and answers. Without the implementation of a formal training unit and assessment, annual training is not provided to the experienced recruiters. This proves to be an additional challenge, as processes, procedures, methods of operations, and systems change. It is important that everyone on the team has a good understanding of the systems, processes, methods of operations and procedures, and position requirements needed to source qualified personnel to meet the contract requirement. It is also important that the recruiters have access to the most recent documents that outline the aforementioned information if ever needed to reference.

In summary, the following performance problems have continued to occur causing a delay in organizational productivity:

1.   The technical writer has noted that military documents, law enforcement letters of verification, and/or letters of employment verification are often not included, if needed due to the claimed experience.
2.   In addition, the technical writer has also noted that the biography is missing pertinent details in the description, as well as certificates required of the position to satisfy the position requirements set forth in the contract.

3. Recruiters do not know the position requirements for the respective positions being recruited.
4. There is a question of whether biography training is needed to address the abovementioned problem.
5. The process of submitting completed biography packets for customers to review has been slowed down due to incomplete packets.

Without clear expectations of duties, accountability metrics, clear communication, and knowledge of the requirements, processes, procedures, methods of operations, and systems, it will be difficult to promote change among the recruiters. To promote change among recruiter's efficiency and accuracy in locating qualified personnel, instruction and noninstructional interventions were developed. A formal instructional unit was created to provide the institutional knowledge needed by the recruiters to perform their daily job tasks; it provides an overview and the direction to the required resources. Noninstructional interventions including a communication plan, knowledge management database, accountability metrics, and an internal advancement plan were developed to provide recruiters access to the data required to source qualified personnel using the standardized process. The project consisted of the instructional and noninstructional methods to improve the recruiter's qualifications to recruit qualified candidates for the DES contract. All recruiters will be required to attend the formal training unit; recruiters specific to the DES contract will be required to attend additional training on the established knowledge management database where system manuals, process charters, position requirements, and procedures and operations reside. In addition, an internal advancement plan will be implemented to allow recruiters to become subject matter experts in a variety of position requirements, and is designed for easing recruiters into recruiting basic, intermediate, advanced, and expert level positions; recruiters will be required to demonstrate mastery of the positions at their current level before being promoted to the next level. Each recruiter's level will be determined by utilizing a separate performance analysis exploring reasons for kicked back biography packets.

An internal performance improvement technologist was brought onto the project to ensure the instructional and noninstructional interventions be customized to meet the specific needs of the staffing department. The performance technologist's role was to assist the senior director and senior manager of recruiting to create an instructional unit and knowledge management database that would focus on the skills needed to improve performance of the recruiters. A needs assessment and performance analysis was conducted that consisted of surveying staff involved in submitting biography packets for the DES contract, conducting interviews from various disciplines and levels, and direct observations of how team members carry out the day-to-day operations of sourcing qualified candidates. Utilizing this multi-layered approach rather than obtaining data from one source allowed the performance improvement technologist insight into the different parts of the organization, as well as the knowledge and skills possessed by each recruiter regarding the organization, processes, and job in regards to the goals, design, and management. All elements were used to recommend potential solutions and interventions to the leadership in the staffing department at VDS, Inc. The discovery analysis phase conducted by the performance technologist led to the identification and development of additional interventions and solutions.

CASE DESCRIPTION

The first day Lillian Rockwell was tasked to serve as an internal consultant for the recruiting department at VDS Inc., she was brought to the recruiters' weekly training meeting that was being held by the senior manager of recruiting, Sadie Altman. Lillian was notified that each week a new recruiter and/or team leader is responsible for providing instruction to the group as an attempt to cross-train all recruiters since each recruit for different contracts. When recruiters are hired, they are hired to recruit for a specific contract; however, as surges occur, recruiters are required to assist their colleagues. Lillian, carrying a legal pad of paper, took a seat next to the senior director of staffing, Lucy Hughes, and began observing each individual in the room in an attempt to demarcate each individual's role and position. With the help of Lucy, she was able to identify each individual and their respective role.

Two recruiters and one recruiting team leader walked to the front of the conference room to begin discussing the DES project located in Iraq. The purpose of the instruction according to Sadie was to provide a brief overview of the contract, living conditions, and any other vital information needed to attract candidates to work on the project. The recruiting team leader, Dez Whitman, introduced himself along with the three recruiters that would be assisting with the presentation. The first recruiter on Dez's team included Kelsey Parker who has been employed with the company for over three years. The second recruiter included Steven Peters who has been employed with the company for three years, but has only been serving in the recruiting position for six months. The third recruiter included Heather Beck who has been employed with the company for two and a half years. The team training began; however, it was noted that the focus of the team training shifted to discussing the positions that recruiters recruit personnel for on the DES contract. The team leader and recruiters each took turns reading the information on the power point slide one position at a time. At the end of each explanation, Lillian noticed the technical writer, Max Austin, had to continuously correct and elaborate on the position requirements. Different questions were brought up, and many looked to the technical writer, Max Austin, for the correct answer; Lillian made note of this on her legal pad. As the instruction continued, Lillian listened intently and watched the actions of each recruiter, team leader, and manager. As she continuously looked around, she paid close attention to each individual in the room and made note of the varying levels of attention. At the end of the instruction, Lillian asked Sadie if she could meet with Max to gain more insight into the corrections that were made, and she gladly agreed.

The next day, Lillian approached Max to discuss the training that occurred the previous day. The two went into a small conference room near Lucy Hughes' office to talk privately, and discussed in detail the issues. Lillian asked Max why there were so many interjections and corrections among the position requirements that were discussed. Max quickly explained that no one consulted him, the subject matter expert on all positions for the DES contract, prior to the training. He said he also felt recruiters did not understand the position requirements, as they often submit incomplete biography packets for review. Max continued to share that in order to employ someone on the DES contract, they had to have the 'bio' approved; the biography is similar to a resume, but is on a specific format provided by the customer. He stated the customer requires supplemental information including prior military documents, verification of employment documents, identity documents, and applicable course certificates. Max also shared that anytime a biography is submitted for review, he reviews it in its entirety and provides a detailed email to the recruiter articulating everything that is needed in order to qualify for the position, whether it is a qualification issue or a missing document issue. He finally stated that no matter how often he sends the biographies back, recruiters continue to submit incomplete biography packets. At this point, Lillian knew there was much more to the recruiters submitting incomplete packets, and she was determined to identify the root cause of the repeated performance issue.

Current Recruiter Onboarding

At VDS, Inc. recruiters do not go through formalized training during their onboarding sessions. Presently, recruiters who are hired sit through the mandatory benefits orientation and then are brought to their respective workplace. Each recruiter is introduced to the other team members and then told they will 'shadow' one of the current recruiters who are performing similar job tasks and duties. Recruiters are required to sit with their colleagues for one to two days maximum before being on their own; they are able to ask their colleagues questions as needed. Recruiters are also provided a recruiting handbook; however, the information is outdated and does not encompass every aspect of the job; job expectations are not included. Many forms and processes that are documented within the recruiting handbook are obsolete. In addition, recruiters are given the same handbook despite the contract they are assigned, so it is very generic.

When new recruiters begin at VDS, Inc. and are assigned to the DES contract, Max Austin sits with each and provides a reference book with the positions, position requirements, examples, the format, and a plethora of frequently asked questions. Even with these documents, recruiters assigned to the DES contract have difficulty submitting complete packets of qualified personnel.

The lack of formal training during the onboarding process for recruiters is proving to be detrimental to the success of the organization. Recruiters are seeking unqualified candidates and failing to submit complete biography packets within an efficient manner. In addition, the leadership at VDS, Inc. has identified other elements in which recruiters are not trained properly, such as the processes and procedures or the various systems used to capture personnel and imperative documents. In order to hand off a completed file for the DES contract, the customer must approve the biography packet and Max Austin must upload the approval to VDS, Inc.'s personnel system. Recruiters often attempt to hand off what they consider completed files prior to checking to see if the approval has been uploaded. Similarly, recruiters often fail to upload the candidate's packet including personal documents to the personnel system prior to handing off the file, which is required. These processes have been in place since the beginning of the DES contract acquisition in 2011, yet recruiters continue to demonstrate issues following the demarcated procedures.

The Committee

Later that week, Lillian was invited to her first meeting with the steering committee. The committee was comprised of the following individuals:

- Chelsea Bower, Senior Director of Operations;
- Lucy Hughes, Senior Director of Staffing;
- Sadie Altman, Senior Manager of Recruiting;
- Dez Whitman, Recruiting Team Leader (DES Contract);
- Max Austin, Technical Writer.

Ten minutes prior to the meeting starting, Lillian and Max were the only two individuals in the meeting room. Lillian decided to take this opportunity to informally interview Max to gain further insight into the performance issue. Lillian asked Max to be honest and share the frustrations that result from the performance issue.

Max began sharing how incomplete biography packets were received from new and seasoned recruiters and that he could not understand why. He recalled that Kelsey Parker was a recruiter who was let go during the reorganization. He stated, "Kelsey often submitted incomplete packets despite my emails including in-depth details of what was needed for the candidate to qualify. He also is the biggest repeat offender for submitting low-quality and unqualified personnel for review. This is a big waste of my time because I still have to provide an in-depth written explanation as to why the candidate is not qualified." Lillian continued to listen to Max as he continued to share frustrations about Kelsey.

Max shared "Kelsey walks around the office chit-chatting with others throughout the day often distracting others. When I've expressed my concerns to his manager, Dez Whitman, Dez responds that Kelsey is able to spit off the requirements for various positions without error. My response to Dez included "It is one thing to regurgitate the requirements, but if they cannot be applied when searching for personnel, there is a serious problem. There's also a serious problem when biography packets continue to get kicked back, yet it appears that improvements are not made. What I do know is that Kelsey forwards the email I send with the requests to the candidate and as information is received, he forwards it to me. All the other recruiters are also guilty of this too despite being repeatedly told to wait until all documents and updates are received so it can be reviewed in its entirety prior to sending to me for final review. This just leads me to believe that recruiters are not reviewing the documents and information they are receiving from their candidates. Rather, they are slinging documents and updates to me in a piece-meal fashion, indicating their lack of review. This further leads me to believe that changes will not be made because I continue to enable each recruiter, as they know that I will compile a completed biography packet with the piecemeal documents and updates they send me."

Max also shared "Every time I receive a document, I go to my tracker to review why I kicked back the biography. I review the biography again and send another email restating what is still missing. This increases the time it takes to process a candidate and takes up unnecessary time of mine when I can be reviewing other candidates. What the recruiters know, but do not seem to care is that I handle all biography packets for the entire DES contract including those who are currently on contract seeking position advancements, those who need to serve as instructors at the training facility, and all new hires that the recruiters submit. Although I know I enabled them, I feel as though a few of the recruiters have been empowered to do what they want without any repercussions." Lillian took note of all the elements Max shared regarding the recruiters and was able to hear the frustration in his voice. She continued to make note as others walked in for the meeting.

Once everyone arrived, the meeting immediately began. The group discussed recent challenges that had been unveiled when submitting biography packets. This led to Max speaking up about the constant repeated errors that were occurring as well as the interjections that occurred during the most recent DES contract training given by three recruiters and the team leader. Max also shared that he gave a presentation about two years ago to the recruiters who were here prior to the reorganization, yet errors still occurred. Although the presentation was lecture-based without a practical exercise, the recruiters had great questions and seemed to be paying attention. Performance issues improved for a limited amount of time before reverting back to old habits. Since a few things were done in the past with temporary improvement, Chelsea Bower and Lucy Hughes informed Lillian that she would need to construct interventions that placed special emphasis on the position requirements. If Lillian could focus the interventions on the position requirements, she was told, there would be fewer repeated errors when submitting biography packets because recruiters would know everything that was required.

The DES contract team leader became incredibly defensive of the accusations that the recruiters did not understand the position requirements. "Some of the recruiters have been recruiting for this contract for several years and can tell me the requirements for many of the positions!" exclaimed Dez. "Depending on the position, we cannot always determine what the customer will want from us each time!" Max chimed in and shared "While the customer has the ability to request additional documents, there are things that are required by contract standards. These are things that I continue to see issues with, not the new requests that come forward."

Lillian, picking up on the tension and disconnect between the individuals in the conference room, asked if it was possible for her to conduct a needs assessment to get a better idea as to the underlying root of the performance issue among the recruiters. Both Chelsea and Lucy stated that a needs assessment would only prolong the performance issue and that it was not needed. Dez stated "All the recruiters, despite the time spent working in the department, have been given the contract requirements for each of the positions. We know the recruiters are busy recruiting candidates and we have a technical writer who is able to determine what exactly is missing. It's clear the only problem we have is that the technical writer does not want to do the work." The committee seemed confused and frustrated by the back and forth and could not understand why the few things that had been tried were not successful in the long term. Lillian noticed the puzzled look at many of the committee members and stated that she was brought in to help the organization improve performance among all members. Given the information from the initial meeting, Lillian suggested conducting a needs assessment to identify the gaps by assessing where the organization currently stands and where they should be. To do this, Lillian also suggested conducting a multi-level organizational analysis to determine whether the root cause is due to personnel issue or infrastructure issue. By taking a closer look and examining the organization at multiple levels, perhaps the previously mentioned problems could be identified and corrected.

Conducting a Needs Assessment

Lillian knew the committee was frustrated with the performance of the recruiters despite efforts to improve performance through past presentations. Using the information gathered from meetings with Max Austin and the committee, Lillian decided it would be best to conduct a needs assessment. Lillian knew that conducting a needs assessment would provide data about gaps in performance and could be used as the framework for evaluating and implementing solutions to bridge the gaps (Kaufman & Lopez, 2013). Although she had heard banter back and forth between the technical writer and the recruiting team leader for the DES contract, Lillian wanted to get a clear picture of the current situation and the desired situation. Lillian wanted to make sure the task being set forth in front of her was feasible and conducting a needs assessment was the best way to do so. She also knows this is a crucial step in adding value to the organization's internal and external stakeholders, thus contributing to the success of the entire organization (Kaufman & Lopez, 2013).

In order to capture the current state, Lillian decided to take a holistic approach and utilize Geary Rummler and Alan Brache's nine variables of performance framework. The nine variables focus on the goals, design, and management at the organizational level, process level, and job/performer level (Rummler & Brache, 2013). Lillian developed the matrix and included pertinent questions to ask each recruiter, the senior manager of recruiting and recruiting team leader, and the senior directors involved in the functionality of the staffing department at VDS, Inc. Using the nine performance variable framework established by Rummler and Brache (2013) will allow Lillian to view the organization through multiple lenses to ensure each of the three performance needs including goals, design, and management is met at each of the three performance levels including the organization, process, and job/performer (p. 16). Using this multi-layered approach will also allow for a better understanding of the organization in addition to the individual parts that contribute to the system as a whole (Brethower, 2006). Table 1 provides an overview of the levels of performance that Lillian would follow during her assessment.

Lillian first met with Sadie Altman, the senior manager of recruiting to discuss the overall matrix. Since Sadie is responsible for overseeing the recruiters, Lillian wanted to ensure the questions were appropriate. She also asked permission to informally observe the recruiters as they complete their day-to-day functions including direct and indirect observations. Once approved, Lillian began meeting with

Table 1. Nine variables to be used during Lillian's assessment

	GOALS	DESIGN	MANAGEMENT
ORGANIZATION	Strategy, operating plans, and metrics. (Recruiters)	Organization structure and overall business model. (Senior VPs of functional areas, then Senior Recruiting Manager & Recruiting Team Leader) Relationship Map	Performance review practices and management culture. (Senior VPs of functional areas – specifically global staffing)
PROCESS	Customer and business requirements. (Process owners, then recruiters)	Process design, systems design, and workspace design. (Process owners in recruiting) Process Map	Process ownership, process management, and continuous improvement. (Process owners – specifically senior recruiting manager and recruiting team leader)
PERFORMER	Job specifications, performance metrics, and individual development plans. (Recruiters, individually)	Job roles and responsibilities, skill requirements, procedures, tools, and training. (Senior Recruiting Manager, then recruiters individually after matrix developed) Role/Responsibility Matrix	Performance feedback, consequences, coaching, and support. (Senior Recruiting Manager & Recruiting Team Leader)

each recruiter. With each recruiter, Lillian first explained the purposes of the interview and asked for complete honesty; it was approved that all answers would remain anonymous and that Lillian would be the only individual to see the names. Prior to sharing any information, Lillian would remove any identifying information. She first met with Kelsey Parker, the seasoned recruiter who was let go during the reorganization and then rehired. She began interviewing Kelsey and wrote down the answers to the questions. Forty-five minutes later, Lillian realized she was only half way through the questions and estimated all interviews not to exceed 30 minutes in length. Since she had another meeting to attend, she kindly asked Kelsey if she could email the remaining questions from the survey to complete. He quickly obliged and she emailed him the remaining questions. From there on, Lillian made the decision to meet with each recruiter for 20 – 30 minutes to explain the purpose of the interview, the different kinds of questions, and gain informal insight into their perspective on the overall situation. Lillian then emailed the questions to each recruiter as she met with them and gave them a deadline to return it within two weeks.

Next, Lillian met with Dez Whitman and asked if he would complete all survey questions from the matrix that were intended for the recruiting team leader. He kindly obliged and said he would get them back to Lillian as soon as possible. Similarly to the recruiters, Lillian requested the answers to the survey be completed within two weeks. Lillian then met with Sadie Altman to see if she would complete all survey questions from the matrix that were intended for the senior manager of recruiting. She obliged and said she would have the questions back to Lillian immediately.

During the two-week wait, Lillian began observing each recruiter directly and at a distance and recorded her observations. She noticed some recruiters constantly walked around the office while others frequently chatted with their colleagues. She also noticed some were frequently out of the office working from home. Lillian also observed some recruiters continuously asking repetitive questions about qualifications, documents, and other contract requirements to other new recruiters rather than asking Max Austin, the department's technical writer and subject matter expert. At the end of the two-week mark, Lillian had received the answers to the survey from all recruiters and Sadie, but had not received answers from Dez. Lillian immediately followed up with Dez via email to send a friendly reminder to send in the answers, but Lillian never heard back from Dez. After a week had passed, Lillian followed up with Dez again about the answers to the survey questions. He kindly replied, "I have not forgotten about you. I will get them to you as soon as possible, but I'm drowning over here." Lillian gave Dez another week to complete the answers; however, a week came and went and Lillian still never received the answers. Lillian then sent another follow-up email and offered to sit down with Dez to help him with the question; however, she never received a reply to the email. Over the course of the next two weeks, Lillian made repeated attempts in person and via email to obtain the answers from Dez. She continued to struggle with it, as emails were ignored and empty promises were made in person. Lillian continued making attempts for good practice; however, Dez failed to provide his answers to Lillian, thus providing her with this challenge. Although Lillian stumbled upon this challenge, she was still able to make her recommendations based on the information provided by the recruiters, her direct and indirect observations of the recruiters, and the information and conversations with Max.

The information that Lillian gathered from the survey questions and informal interviews and observations suggested that due to the changing environments of VDS, Inc., recruiters do not know the expectations of the position, there is a lack of accountability, communication among leadership and recruiters is limited, and recruiters demonstrate a knowledge deficiency of the DES contract position requirements. The survey questions provided verification that there is a lack of knowledge not only in the position requirements, but in many other aspects regarding the changing environments of VDS, Inc. including the markets, products, and services. The informal interviews from recruiters and leadership led to a discovery of lack of accountability metrics; although recruiters thought they were being measured on one thing, leadership was measuring recruiters in a different aspect. The informal observations provided insight that the biggest repeat offenders were the ones who were often away from their desk either chatting with colleagues or out of the office; these recruiters had the highest number of returned biography packets.

Upon completion of the needs assessment, a committee meeting was held to discuss the results. Lillian brought a report outlining her findings to share with the group. Prior to presenting her findings, Sadie expressed her gratefulness for having someone like Lillian come in with an unbiased perspective to help identify any potential issues. She stated, "Lillian, what did your needs assessment confirm?"

Lillian explained to the group the various ways she collected data during the assessment: interviews, informal observations, and the nine variables of performance survey questions. Lillian went on to report to the committee that information gathered from the multiple sources revealed the following challenges.

- There was a lack of clarity of position expectations for the recruiters. All recruiters reported that they never received a copy of their job description and they did not have one readily available.
- Communication methods were often unclear and unpredictable. Some recruiters said important information was disseminated in meetings and others said it was disseminated in emails or passing conversation; all agreed there was no standard method for disseminating information.
- There was a lack of knowledge and training units for the recruiters. Currently, recruiters are trained using on-the-job methodologies only without documentation for processes and procedures. All recruiters are given a brief training from the technical writer on completing a biography packet and given a copy of the position requirements.
- There was a lack of accountability measures in place to measure recruiter performance. Currently, the technical writer is responsible for making note of all missing documents and information and kicking it back to the recruiter. Leadership may be included on the email, but do not hold the recruiters accountable; they only measure recruiters performance in how many individuals get 'boots-on-the-ground,' which are identified as quality candidates. Due to the lack of accountability measures, recruiter numbers are low and quality has not improved.

Lillian suggested before jumping into any action to remedy the issue that the committee discuss the findings. Before she could identify and propose interventions, discussions would need to be held to determine how accountability would be measured, how communication would be handled, how training would occur, and how recruiters would know expectations of their job position.

CURRENT CHALLENGES FACING THE ORGANIZATION

Expectations of Position

Upon completion of the needs assessment, Lillian discovered there was a lack of clarity of position expectations for the recruiters. One set of questions from the survey was geared towards position expectations, and all recruiters reported that they never received a copy of their job description nor did they have one readily available. As Lillian interviewed and observed each recruiter, she noticed that everyone was doing things their own way; there was no consistency and no specific way to handle the required tasks. Before the committee could move forward with any interventions, recruiters would need to be provided a copy of their job description with clear expectations outlining their duties and responsibilities.

While it would be easy to determine and communicate to recruiters their roles and responsibilities, the greater challenge would be to determine who was actually responsible for what depending on their level of experience. Since VDS, Inc. employs recruiters of various experience levels from associate recruiter to senior recruiter, it is necessary to demarcate the duties, responsibilities, and expectations for each recruiter depending on their level, so accountability can easily be tracked. Recruiters cannot be expected to perform certain tasks and be held accountable if they are unaware of their duties and responsibilities. Recruiters must be provided clear and concise expectations that can be measured before being expected to perform in a certain manner.

Communication

Recruiters shared different responses in regards to how communication from leadership was disseminated. It was noted that communication methods were often unclear and unpredictable. Some recruiters stated important information was disseminated in meetings and others said it was disseminated in emails or passing conversation; all agreed there was no standard method for disseminating information from leadership to recruiters. This has proven to be detrimental to the group because more often than not, only some recruiters hear imperative information and do not pass it along. In addition, if information is passed along from recruiter to recruiter, it can easily become skewed. This can be likened to the telephone game where the end message is rarely ever the same as the beginning message, as individuals interpret and remember certain aspects of the message.

Over the course of the last five years, VDS, Inc. has started to shift its focus from overseas markets to domestic markets. With this, the company's mission has also evolved and appears to be a cause of the performance issue, especially with senior recruiters who have been serving with the company prior to the intended change in markets. Although the entire company meets once per year to discuss the strategic vision as well as the current and future state of the company, there is no clear communication strategy within the staffing department to identify when changes occur, how changes impact present performance, and the shifts that need to be made in order to keep the organization moving forward without interruption. A consistent communication strategy would need to be presented to the recruiters and other members of the staffing department to understand new guidelines were being put in place to streamline communication among leadership and all staffing department members, specifically the recruiters. Disseminating information to all members using a communication strategy allows for all recruiters to hear the same message at the same time; discussions for clarity should also be enabled to clarify any confusion.

Knowledge Management/Training

Without clear expectations or an appropriate communication strategy, the recruiters do not have a clear understanding of what they are supposed to be doing. Presently, recruiters recruit personnel without satisfying all requirements including qualifications and/or supplemental documentation and submit it to Max Austin, the technical writer, for review. Max does his magic and reviews each biography packet thoroughly providing a detailed description of everything that is needed to qualify for the position. Up to this point, recruiters have been able to skate by and recruit personnel successfully due to the help of Max. No matter how many times Max kicks back a biography packet for the same missing information and documentation, recruiters continue to submit incomplete packets; they are not using the kicked back emails as lessons to learn. They know Max will take care of whatever is needed. Max began including the managers on all of the kicked back emails for their knowledge. Recruiters still fail to learn how to submit a completed packet, which expends unnecessary resources and slows down Max's process. It has also been found that recruiters still have access to old forms that are not in use anymore. This is a huge problem that stems back to a lack of communication in when to begin using new forms.

VDS, Inc. currently offers one single day onboarding orientation regarding benefits for all new hires to attend despite the functional area where they will be employed. The staffing department currently does not have a separate recruiting onboarding orientation or training modules for recruiters to complete prior to working on their own. Current practices allow for on-the-job training where new recruiters will sit with a recruiter deemed appropriate by the senior manager of recruiting to gain insight into the contract as well as the practices and principles of VDS, Inc. and the applications necessary to be successful. The implementation of training modules would need to incorporate all aspects of the recruiting position including submitting a completed biography packet. All training modules should promote interactivity to provide ample opportunities for practice and assess learner outcomes. The training modules would hopefully mitigate some of the repeated errors from different facets of the recruiter's position.

Accountability

For a while, Max thought that the repeated errors were due to recruiters not knowing the position requirements for the DES contract. He made this very well known when talking with Lillian, the performance technologist. This was a big concern for Lillian who made it apparent to discuss this with the recruiters and leadership during the needs assessment phase. Lillian discovered that the recruiters knew the position requirements and had the position requirements readily available for reference. What was discovered was the lack of accountability of each recruiter. Currently, each recruiter is required to submit personnel for different positions on the DES contract. The recruiting team leader and senior manager of recruiting want to know how many personnel they recruit, how many are added to the system, and how many biography packets are submitted to Max. After that, accountability is out the window. Max repeatedly kicks back biography packets for missing qualifications and/or supplemental documentation. The recruiters then take Max's email and forward it to the candidate. Once documents are received, recruiters begin sending them to Max in a piecemeal fashion despite Max's repeated cries to wait until all requests have been satisfied. Max continues to receive documents and once every request has been satisfied, he reviews the biography packet again and submits it to the customer for review. The recruiting team leader of the DES contract states he reads all reasons for kickbacks; however, nothing has been done to remedy the issue for Max.

Presently, the only accountability recruiters are measured against includes how many personnel they submit into the system and how many biography packets they submit to Max each week. Without a targeted number of personnel needed to measure against, recruiters vary from zero biographies submitted each week to seven. Despite the initiative to remove quantity and submit quality, Max has expressed numerous times to both the senior manager of recruiting and recruiting team leader as well as the senior director of staffing that the quality of the product has not improved at all. In addition, for every person the recruiter gets deployed to the contract, they receive an incentive bonus. Unfortunately, there is nothing in place to penalize a recruiter for having biographies kicked back; therefore, since Max takes care of everything for the recruiter, there is no reason for the recruiters to change ways. The implementation of accountability metrics would need to identify all aspects of the biography packet submission including how many are received per day per recruiter as well as reasons for kickbacks. The senior director, senior manager of recruiting, and the recruiting team leader should enforce all accountability metrics with weekly or bi-weekly meetings including Max. The accountability metrics would hopefully provide insight into potential trends set forth by each recruiter; appropriate action can be taken to remedy constant individual and group performance issues.

SOLUTIONS AND RECOMMENDATIONS

Upon completion of her analysis, Lillian proposed several interventions to the steering committee to mitigate the identified performance problems. (Table 2).

Table 2. Summary of proposed interventions for identified performance problems

Performance Problems	Interventions
The technical writer has noted that military documents, law enforcement letters of verification, and/or letters of employment verification are often not included, if needed due to the claimed experience.	Checklist
The technical writer has noted that the biography is missing pertinent details in the description, as well as certificates required of the position to satisfy the position requirements set forth in the contract.	• Checklist • Point metrics system
Recruiters do not know the position requirements for the respective positions being recruited.	• Internal advancement plan • Revised job description
There is a question of whether biography training is needed to address the abovementioned problem.	Instructional training unit
The process of submitting completed biography packets for the customer to review has been slowed down due to incomplete packets.	• Daily/monthly metrics in conjunction with the point system metrics • Daily log • Rewards/repercussion performance chart • Communication plan

Expectations of Position

It did not take long for the committee to decide that all recruiters be provided a copy of their job description and that different levels of recruiter experience warrant different tasks and responsibilities. It took more time for leadership to identify what roles and responsibilities fell under each recruiting level. The four recruiting levels identified included associate recruiter, beginner recruiter, intermediate recruiter, and advanced recruiter. Once Lucy Hughes, Sadie Altman, and Dez Whitman were able outline the duties and position requirements for each recruiting level, Max Austin was able to develop a job description for each. The recruiters met with each of their managers individually to receive and discuss the job description for their respective level. This meeting also allowed the recruiter the opportunity to seek clarification regarding any questions, concerns, or discrepancies discovered within the respective job description. The development of the job descriptions will provide recruiters the written expectations of their position and will serve as an available reference.

Communication

More time was spent developing a formal communication plan to disseminate pertinent information to each recruiter. All recruiters and Max now attend a weekly meeting with Lucy Hughes where Lucy disseminates pertinent updates and other information about the organization. This meeting allows recruiters to hear the same information at the same time, eliminating the possibility for interpreting the information differently. In addition, Lucy and Max have been working together to update the department's individual website where updates can be provided daily, weekly, or monthly, and all updates can be archived for later retrieval. Again, recruiters will be able to read the updated information, but will also be able to seek clarification during the weekly meetings. The website will also serve as the department's knowledge management database where all documents including the biography format, the checklists, internal advancement plan, and training unit among other documents pertinent to the DES contract will be available. Documents will be managed through version controls to ensure only the most up-to-date documents will be available. By utilizing a formal communication plan, recruiters will know that when information is disseminated in the weekly meeting or updated on the website, they are provided the most up-to-date information and guidance to follow, thus ensuring all recruiters are on the same page as the organization's missions.

Knowledge Management/Training

To ensure all recruiters and managers were on the same page, Lillian removed all old documents from the department website that were no longer used to avoid confusion and using the wrong form. Lillian then met with Max to discuss what was done in the past as far as training recruiters. They spoke endlessly about what was done and how it did not work; recruiters were uninterested, not assessed, and knew they would have someone to pick up the pieces regardless. Max showed Lillian the previous presentation that was used as the training portion. Lillian carefully outlined a new training plan to include shorter segments with breaks in between for questions and comments. While the old presentation focused more on filling out the biography form, the new training unit focused more on the content to include within the biography to avoid undermining the recruiter's ability to fill out a form. At the end of the training piece, Lillian suggested that an activity occur to measure the recruiter's ability to submit a completed packet. Since the recruiters are required to submit completed packets on behalf of their candidates, Lillian thought it would be a great exercise if recruiters stepped into the role of the candidate and submitted all required documentation for the most basic position on the DES contract.

In addition to the training activity, Lillian suggested developing an internal advancement plan for recruiters to become subject matter experts for the various positions they recruit for on the DES contract. The internal advancement plan is designed for recruiters to advance their individual skillset at an individual pace. Since one of the identified performance problems includes recruiters not knowing the requirements for the various contract positions, Lillian believed developing an internal advancement plan would assist recruiters in becoming more knowledgeable at a pace that was conducive to each recruiter. The plan includes four levels – beginner, intermediate, advanced, and expert – and is divided into 15 stages. Positions within each level are based on difficulty of requirements and experiences needed to qualify. The basic level includes one stage and one position. The intermediate level contains four stages with two positions in each stage. The advanced level contains six stages; all stages have two positions except stage eight has one position and stage 11 contains all instructor positions. The expert level contains four stages with two positions in each stage except stage 15, which contains only one position.

All recruiters who are new to the company would begin at the beginner level. The recruiters who have been with VDS, Inc. would be assessed by their manager and the technical writer to determine the starting level for each recruiter; managers would assess the recruiter's ability to state the position requirements and the technical writer would assess the recruiter's ability to submit a completed biography packet for the various positions. Depending on the number of packets kicked back per position, the technical writer and manger would determine where each recruiter would start within the individual advancement plan. Once each recruiter had a starting point, assessments would occur quarterly to determine eligibility for advancement within the plan.

Accountability

After conducting the needs assessment, Lillian discovered that recruiters were not held accountable for their productivity levels. Each week recruiters had to report numbers about how many personnel they put into the system and how many biography packets they submitted for review, but the numbers did not mean anything and the management did not do anything with the reported numbers. She was baffled by the discovery and decided to include some accountability metrics to hold recruiters responsible for not only what they submit, but also the quality of the submittals.

First, Lillian wanted to see if what the recruiters were reporting to their manager was accurate to what Max was receiving each week in regards to submitted biography packets. She developed a daily/monthly metrics spreadsheet that tracks each recruiter on the y-axis and each day of the month across the x-axis. Lillian wanted Max to keep track of how many biographies were received per recruiter per day for each month. This would provide insight into the level of productivity for each recruiter, as well as a whole team for the entire month.

In addition, Lillian recommended that each recruiter keep a daily log articulating the number of resumes reviewed and number of phone calls made each day. Although the daily log is only as accurate and honest as the recruiter, the information gathered from the daily log in conjunction with the daily/monthly metrics will provide great insight into real recruiting numbers. For example, Recruiter A states he/she reviewed 25 resumes per day, called 8 people per day, and submitted two completed biography packets for the week; none were kicked back. Recruiter B states he/she reviewed 40 resumes per day, called 14 people per day, and submitted five biography packets for the week although three of them were kicked back. It would appear that Recruiter A took a bit more time to review each resume to determine qualifications before calling potential candidates and submitting completed packets. Recruiter B tried to review more resumes and call more people; therefore, potentially lost focus on submitting completed packets.

This information shows that while Recruiter B went through many more resumes, Recruiter A took his/her time to review each resume and find qualified personnel. Recruiter A also submitted only two biography packets, which appears low; however, they exuded quality and were complete without error. Recruiter B tried to submit as many as possible and ended up with more than half of the biography packets getting kicked back. This is the equivalent of only submitting two completed biography packets. Max is still required to review all five, but has to provide detailed emails for each biography packet that is kicked back explaining why it was kicked back, as well as what can be done to satisfy all requirements. This is one example of how submitting incomplete packets slows down the process of submitting completed biography packets for the customer to review. In addition, the information gathered from the daily log will hold each recruiter accountable for their daily, weekly, and monthly numbers of personnel recruited.

Second, with the assistance of Max, Lillian developed a checklist outlining all aspects of the biography including personal information, relevant experience, and applicable documentation. Lillian believed that although recruiters could recite various position requirements, the amount of information and documentation needed to submit a completed packet might be overwhelming. To alleviate any overwhelming feelings and risk for potentially submitting an incomplete packet, Lillian created a checklist to be filled out by each recruiter for each biography packet submitted. The recruiter is to sign the bottom of the checklist ensuring he or she went through each element of the biography packet. Lillian also added an additional section for a second review. Max, the technical writer, would serve as the second reviewer, and would be responsible for reviewing the biography packet in its entirety as normal. When the biography was ready to be sent forward for review by the customer, Max would sign off on the checklist prior to sending the biography packet. If the biography packet was kicked back, Max would wait to sign off on the checklist until all requests were satisfied.

Third, Lillian developed a point metrics system spreadsheet to capture every time a biography was kicked back. This metrics reporting system utilized a point system to determine quality. Each recruiter had a page dedicated to their candidates. Max would include the position, the candidates' name, when the biography packet was initially received, the date the corrected information was received, and the number of days it took to receive all requested items. Max would then be responsible for identifying all the reasons the biography was kicked back. Twelve categories were identified as common reasons biographies get kicked back and each were assigned a number of points it was worth. The more points the category is worth, the more important the information. The categories with their respective points listed in parentheses include:

1. **Biography Format (1):** There are two formats, one on a Microsoft Word document and one on a PDF document. The PDF document is what gets uploaded to the customer for approval, but sometimes candidates have a hard time filling it out and saving it without an Adobe program. All biography packets are now submitted to Max on the PDF form only.

2. **Personal Identifying Information (2):** In order to submit a candidate, the first step involves submitting the candidate's personal identifying information (PII) into the customer's site. Once approved, the biography packet can be submitted. This information includes full name, date of birth, place of birth, and social security number.

3. **DD-214 (4):** This is a military document that verifies any active duty military experience. The DES contract requires if someone served in the military, that this document be provided as part of the biography packet. All DD-214s demonstrating active duty service must be included.

4. **Narrative Reason for Separation Not Explained (2):** This is found on the DD-214. Sometimes individuals will be discharged from the military for various reasons. The customer requires an explanation for any reason other than 'sufficient for retirement' or 'completed required active service.' The explanation is brief, but should include what happened, when it happened, and the result, as well as if there are any lingering effects.

5. **Law Enforcement Verification (4):** The DES contract requires a letter of verification or a copy of the service record brief (SRB) to verify any law enforcement experiences. The verification should be written on department letterhead, include hiring and terminating dates, list any positions held if possible, and be signed by a higher-ranking official or human resources. Each department, if applicable, requires its own verification of employment.

6. **Verification of Employment (All Non-DES Contracts) (3):** For all non-DES contracts, law enforcement, or military experiences, the customer requires verification of employment for each claimed experience written on the biography. The verification should be written on company letterhead, include hiring and terminating dates, list any positions held if possible, and be signed by a higher-ranking official or human resources.

7. **Certificates (1):** The DES contract states if anyone wishes to claim any training courses completed, the candidate must provide the accompanying certificate for verification. For example, someone who completed an intro to IT course would need to provide a copy of the certificate as proof.

8. **Qualifications (5):** If Max receives a biography packet and the candidate does not meet the minimum requirements set forth in the contract, then the biography packet must be sent back to the recruiter with the qualifications that have not been satisfied. Max should not be receiving 'completed' biography packets where the candidate does not meet the minimum qualifications.

9. **Experience (5):** In order to qualify for the position, the candidate must articulate his or her duties and responsibilities in regards to the position requirements. If the candidate does not articulate the experiences appropriately, the customer may not approve the candidate for the contract.

10. **Dates (2):** Dates of experiences and certificates should match what is written on the verification of employment letter or actual training course certificates.
11. **Other (1):** Sometimes there are other things that are incorrect with a biography. For example, sometimes a candidate's social security number will be missing a number or the passport will be missing a number on the biography packet. Sometimes numbers will get inverted or the entire set of numbers is missing. This is where Max would note this error and correct it.

Once Max reviews a biography, and marks each reason the biography is kicked back, the total number of points will be automatically tallied to the right. Should the kickback reasons total twelve points or less, the score box will be highlighted white. Should the kickback reasons total 13 points, the score box will be highlighted yellow, and if more than 13 points, the score box will be highlighted red. This information can be used to identify trends over time or immediate instances where remedial training might be necessary. To the right of the score box is a place to include notes. This is where the technical writer can include a brief summary of the reasons for kickbacks as well as reference the email that was sent back to the recruiter.

Fourth, Lillian developed a performance chart outlining the number of successful submissions of each recruiter for all in the department to see. Although her intention is not to publicly humiliate any recruiters, she believes that individuals will slow down and take more time to review their biography packets before submitting them to have more successful submissions. This is aimed at eliminating the quantity versus quality mentality and providing motivation for each recruiter to aspire to be better than before, which will in turn make the review process more efficient for Max. Max will utilize the point metrics system to identify the number of successful submissions per recruiter each day.

CONCLUSION

In summary, conducting a multi-layered performance analysis provided Lillian with the necessary information that she needed to develop several interventions to address the organization from multiple positions. Dissecting the organization at three levels: organizational, process, and performer (Rummler, 2006) allowed Lillian to gather data from multiple representatives involved in the situation. The multiple data collection sources such as the interviews with the recruiters, conversations with Max and the steering committee, and document analysis allowed for the opportunity to triangulate the findings and establish commonalities between the data being reviewed.

By extending the needs assessment beyond the performance level, Lillian was able to obtain a clear picture as to the degree of support provided to the recruiters.

While it was evident from her findings that the technical writer, Max Austin, had attempted to make the necessary corrections to some of the performance issues, it was critical that the organization have the appropriate infrastructure to support the proposed interventions to ensure sustainability over time. Not only did Lillian have to confirm that the recruiters were trained and competent to perform their jobs, she also needed to ensure that the organization was able to support the recruiters through training and the necessary resources to be successful (Gilbert, 1978). After dissecting the organization using this multi-layered approach, Lillian identified the necessary resources needed to support the recruiters to successfully onboard individuals to VDS, Inc.'s DES contract.

This case presented several performance problems and the need for both instructional and noninstructional interventions. The complexity of the performance problem required that several interventions be developed and implemented in tandem in order to ensure organizational success. The purpose of this case was to highlight the challenges that can arise while conducting tiered performance analyses as well as how multiple levels of an organization need to be taken into consideration while developing and implementing performance interventions.

REFERENCES

Brethower, D. M. (2006). Systemic issues. In J. A. Pershing (Ed.), *Handbook of human performance technology* (3rd ed., pp. 111–137). San Francisco, CA: Pfeiffer.

Gilbert, T. (1978). *Human competence: Engineering worthy performance*. Amherst, MA: HRD Press, Inc.

Kaufman, R., & Guerra-Lopez, I. (2013). Needs assessment for organizational success. Alexandria, VA: American Society for Training & Development (ASTD).

Rummler, G. A. (2006). The anatomy of performance: A framework for consultants. In J. A. Pershing (Ed.), *Handbook of human performance technology* (3rd ed., pp. 986–1007). San Francisco, CA: Pfeiffer.

Rummler, G. A., & Brache, A. P. (2013). *Improving performance: How to manage the white space on the organization chart* (3rd ed.). San Francisco, CA: Jossey-Bass.

U.S. Department of Commerce. (1995). *Special Publication (800 Series)*. National Institute of Standards and Technology Retrieved March 15, 2014, from http://csrc.nist.gov/publications/PubsSPs.html

ADDITIONAL READING

Addison, R., & Haig, C. (1999). Human performance technology in action. In H. Stolovitch & E. Keeps (Eds.), *Handbook of Human Performance Technology* (2nd ed., pp. 298–318). San Francisco, CA: Jossey-Bass.

Addison, R. M., & Haig, C. (2012a). A walk on the human performance side: Part 1. *Performance Improvement, 51*(8), 37–41. doi:10.1002/pfi.21297

Addison, R. M., & Haig, C. (2012b). A walk on the human performance side: Part 2. *Performance Improvement, 51*(9), 6–9. doi:10.1002/pfi.21302

Addison, R. M., & Haig, C. (2012c). A walk on the human performance side: Part 3. *Performance Improvement, 51*(10), 21–25. doi:10.1002/pfi.21311

Addison, R. M., & Haig, C. (2013). A walk on the human performance side: Part 4. *Performance Improvement, 52*(1), 38–42. doi:10.1002/pfi.21320

Arthur, W., Bennett, W., Edens, P. S., & Bell, S. T. (2003). Effectiveness of training in organizations: A meta-analysis of design and evaluation features. *The Journal of Applied Psychology, 88*(2), 234–245. doi:10.1037/0021-9010.88.2.234 PMID:12731707

Austin, J., Olson, R., & Wellisley, J. A. (2001). The Behavior Engineering Model at Work on a Small Scale: Using Task Clarification, Self-Monitoring, and Public Posting to Improve Customer Service. *Performance Improvement Quarterly, 14*(2), 53–76. doi:10.1111/j.1937-8327.2001.tb00209.x

Brethower, D. M. (2006). Systemic issues. In J. A. Pershing (Ed.), *Handbook of human performance technology* (3rd ed., pp. 111–137). San Francisco, CA: Pfeiffer.

Carl, D. R. (2009). Cue representation and situational awareness in task analysis. *Performance Improvement Quarterly, 22*(1), 115–132. doi:10.1002/piq.20048

Crigler, L., Fort, A. L., de Diez, O., Gearon, S., & Gyuzalyan, H. (2006). Training alone is not enough. *Performance Improvement Quarterly, 19*(1), 99–116. doi:10.1111/j.1937-8327.2006.tb00359.x

Crowell, C., Anderson, D., Abel, D., & Sergio, J. (1988). Task clarification, performance feedback, and social praise: Procedures for improving the customer service of bank tellers. *Journal of Applied Behavior Analysis, 21*(1), 65–71. doi:10.1901/jaba.1988.21-65 PMID:16795713

Dean, P. J., Dean, M. R., & Guman, E. C. (1992). Identifying a range of performance improvement solutions through evaluation research. *Performance Improvement Quarterly, 5*(4), 16–31. doi:10.1111/j.1937-8327.1992.tb00563.x

Folsom, A. (2001). A performance approach to job analysis. *Performance Improvement Quarterly*, *14*(4), 37–44. doi:10.1111/j.1937-8327.2001.tb00228.x

Gilbert, T. (1978). *Human competence: Engineering worthy performance*. Amherst, MA: HRD Press, Inc.

Lane, M. (2010). HPT models: Performance aids. In R. Watkins & D. Leigh (Eds.), *Handbook of improving performance in the workplace: Selecting and implementing performance interventions* (Vol. 2, pp. 344–365). San Francisco, CA: Pfeiffer. doi:10.1002/9780470592663.ch33

Mager, R., & Pipe, P. (1997). *Analyzing performance problems*. Atlanta, GA: Center for Effective Performance.

Meyer, A. D., & Goes, J. B. (1988). Organizational assimilation of innovations: A multilevel contextual analysis. *Academy of Management Journal*, *31*(4), 897–923. doi:10.2307/256344

Nguyen, F. (2009). The effect of performance support and training on performer attitudes. *Performance Improvement Quarterly*, *22*(1), 95–114. doi:10.1002/piq.20047

Rothwell, W. J., Hohne, C. K., & King, S. B. (2007). The role of the analyst. In W. J. Rothwell, C. K. Hohne, & S. B. King (Eds.), *Human performance improvement: Building practitioner performance* (2nd ed., pp. 41–85). New York, NY: Elsevier. doi:10.1016/B978-0-7506-7996-1.50007-6

Rummler, G. A. (2006). The anatomy of performance: A framework for consultants. In J. A. Pershing (Ed.), *Handbook of human performance technology* (3rd ed., pp. 986–1007). San Francisco, CA: Pfeiffer.

Rummler, G. A., & Brache, A. P. (2013). *Improving performance: How to manage the white space on the organization chart* (3rd ed.). San Francisco, CA: Jossey-Bass.

Schaffer, S. P. (2000). A review of organizational and human performance frameworks. *Performance Improvement Quarterly*, *13*(3), 220–243. doi:10.1111/j.1937-8327.2000.tb00183.x

Schaffer, S. P., & Keller, J. (2003). Measuring the results of performance improvement interventions. *Performance Improvement Quarterly*, *16*(1), 73–92. doi:10.1111/j.1937-8327.2003.tb00273.x

Van Tiem, D., Moseley, J. L., & Dessinger, J. C. (2012). *Fundamentals of performance improvement: A guide to improving people, process, and performance* (3rd ed.). San Francisco, CA: Pfeiffer.

Watkins, R. (2007). Designing for performance, part 1: Aligning your HPT decisions from top to bottom. *Performance Improvement, 46*(1), 7–13. doi:10.1002/pfi.033

Watkins, R. (2007). Designing for performance, part 2: Selecting your performance technologies. *Performance Improvement, 46*(2), 9–15. doi:10.1002/pfi.102

Watkins, R. (2007). Designing for performance, part 3: Design, develop, and improve. *Performance Improvement, 46*(4), 42–48. doi:10.1002/pfi.124

Wedman, J., & Graham, S. (1998, Fall). The performance pyramid. *The Journal of Continuing Higher Education, 46*(3), 8–20. doi:10.1080/07377366.1998.10400352

Wilson, C., Boni, N., & Hogg, A. (1997). The effectiveness of task clarification, positive reinforcement and corrective feedback in changing courtesy among police staff. *Journal of Organizational Behavior Management, 17*(1), 65–99. doi:10.1300/J075v17n01_04

KEY TERMS AND DEFINITIONS

Accountability Measures: Standard units used to hold each recruiter responsible for the number of biography packets submitted for review and to ascertain the quality of each packet received.

Contract Employee: Employees that are intermittently used on the project when needed to fill a position.

Instructional Intervention: A program designed to teach recruiters a specific set of skills for reviewing and submitting completed biography packets to the technical writer. Instructional interventions serve interdependently with noninstructional interventions to improve performance.

Job Aid: Supplemental material used to direct and guide performance to support work activities.

Kickbacks: When a biography packet is considered incomplete due to missing supplemental information including prior military documents, verification of employment documents, identity documents, and applicable course certificates. A detailed email is provided to the recruiter articulating everything that is needed in order to qualify for the position, whether it is a qualification issue or a missing document issue.

Knowledge Management: The process of capturing, sharing, and effectively applying organizational information to produce quality products and services in order to achieve the organization's objectives.

Needs Assessment: The process of gathering information to identify a specific need that can be resolved through training or an educational intervention. This assessment identifies a gap between the desired state (the standard or goal) and the actual state (existing level of performance).

Nine Variable Performance Framework: A model (Rummler & Brache, 2013) used to conduct a needs assessment to understand the organization as an adaptive system utilizing a systemic approach. This framework focuses on the goals, designs, and management of the organization at the organization, process, and performer level.

Noninstructional Intervention: Organizational, job structure, communication, and documentation interventions designed to improve recruiter performance through aligning standard operating procedures and increasing motivation. Noninstructional interventions serve interdependently with instructional interventions to improve performance.

Onboarding: The orientation process for providing full-time and intermittent employees the knowledge, skills, and attitudes to be effective organizational members at VDS, Inc.

Organizational Analysis: A technique used to examine the efficiency of an organization to determine potential instructional and noninstructional interventions to improve efficiency.

Performance Analysis: A technique used to examine the performance of current employees to determine potential instructional and noninstructional interventions to improve performance.

Chapter 4
Solve the Problem…
So it Stays Solved!

Joe Monaco
National LIFTOR Licensing Systems, USA

Edward W. Schneider
Peacham Pedagogics, USA

EXECUTIVE SUMMARY

This case study explores how a performance management system was developed to address recurring health and safety issues in an organization. Performance improvement technologists were recruited to address the problem and ensure that it stayed solved. The authors describe the process that was used to develop a training program that eventually evolved to a full scale Performance Management (PM) System. Today, nearly three decades later, the PM System has endured with its original mission intact; it has influenced the international dialog on forklift operator safety; and it provides, through ongoing field research, insights into how a Performance Management system might endure past the first change in the management that championed it.

ORGANIZATIONAL BACKGROUND

Early in my career I had the good fortune to work for a large European, cosmetics company doing business in the USA. I started as an "operations trainer" in a recently acquired division, tasked with custom design of instructional systems for skilled and semi-skilled jobs in factories and distribution centers. Shortly after I was hired,

DOI: 10.4018/978-1-4666-8330-3.ch004

the Senior Vice-President of Administration, called me to his office, explained a situation that clearly caused him concern, and then he asked me the key question, "Can you help me to solve this problem...so it STAYS solved?"

What Was the Problem?

The Vice- President explained the situation: Four months ago, a 20-year-old woman was in a forklift accident. The doctors are still deciding whether they are going to amputate her leg. She was a temporary employee, not a forklift operator, and during her regular lunch break, decided to step onto an electric-powered, stand-on model that was parked with the power on.

At this meeting, I learned from our extensive discussion that he was personally concerned for the injured woman, and what might happen to others if he didn't take effective action. Although it was rare, this was not the first forklift related injury in the company's warehouses. He was hopeful that, with help, it would be the last. His immediate superiors were concerned with the negative fall-out from being publicly known as the company in the beauty/fashion industry that carelessly injures its young female employees...an image that contradicted a brand representing beauty, wholesome fun, sexy, high energy and youthfulness. Then too, the division was recently acquired by a European firm that was sensitive to possible national political resistance to its growth strategy of acquiring American companies. The firm was being extremely careful.

I replied that I understood his request, and was delighted to have such a project. I agreed to report back in two weeks with my recommendations.

During the ten years I was employed by this company, I was pleased to learn that its management committed a lot of resources to the engineering of worker health and safety to meet their own high standards. This worked for product quality and it would also work for industrial safety. The Performance Management (PM) System would eventually develop from an operator training program to a comprehensive Performance System that today is employed in a number of warehouse and distribution center venues. It has influenced the international dialog and government regulation on powered industrial truck (forklift) safety. Indeed, solving the problem was not enough! Keeping it solved has been the ongoing mission.

SETTING THE STAGE

Applied Systems Thinking: Forklift Safety Protecting Brand Investments?

I reported back to the Vice-President with the promised recommendations. I concluded from the "...STAYS solved" part of his request that he wanted a comprehensive, systemic solution that could be applied to his organization. I liked his "systems thinking" perspective. It would guide us to take a broad perspective, seeing the interrelationships between overall structures, patterns of behavior, and cycles in the system, rather than seeing only specific events. Besides, although he never mentioned the word "training" I knew that an instructional solution might be useful for forklift operators. It might also be useful for supervisors, too. Then there was the question of how to get the relevant department heads informed, so they might know how to support the new forklift PM System in their own organizations.

I learned from my investigation that forklifts were frequently in disrepair; supervisors, out of ignorance of the risk and/or budget pressure would not always give operators permission to get needed repairs and sometimes chastise them for asking; there were floor layouts and traffic patterns that were collisions waiting to happen; and only one in 10 front-line supervisors had ever operated a forklift. There were other issues that would take months, if not years, to show themselves. I could design, develop, and implement an effective instructional solution, but most of the issues would not be solved with just "training." Certainly the problem would not "STAY solved" just with training.

This was an opportunity to design and implement an enduring, systemic corporate policy around "forklift safety" as most would eventually see it. In reality, the presenting problem of forklift-related injury was only the face of my mission. The management, being intensely consumed with their brand image, made large investments in advertising, public relations, special promotions, market intelligence, creative design, etc. The investments fueled what the Chief Operating Officer (COO) would call The Spiral of Growth. By keeping the forklift injury problem solved, the new Performance Management System would be making its contribution toward protecting the company's brand image and future growth. It is noteworthy that the senior vice-president' was able to apply a systems thinking perspective to establish a relationship between forklift operator safety and a brand image. It was now up to me to recommend a solution that would endure for as long as it was needed.

Applied Performance Engineering

Where systems thinking would help us form a mental map of the problem to be solved, we still had to align the resources of our organization to actually solve the problem ...so it stays solved. I used a Performance Engineering (Gilbert, 1979; Rummler, 1980) vantage point because of its simple structure and easy-to-learn terminology. It was a simple way to explain to others what had to happen and why. The discussions turned to engaging dialogs that helped the others learn their role and where they fit into a system that included accomplishments, processing and sending systems, double-loop feedback, and positive as well as negative consequences.

From the outset, I was confident we could solve the problem of serious forklift injuries. They occurred at a rate of about 1.5 per year, spread across 10 different locations in three states. They were ugly events to watch, but most people who witnessed them, especially local managers, would eventually forget they even happened. With managers rotating in and out of the locations, they had no institutional memory of forklift injuries, or their causes, at their current location.

The "STAYS solved" mission was important, but because of the lack of institutional memory among managers, we needed to systematically track injuries, standardize methods of managing operator and supervisor performance, feedback the results to several organizational levels, and have an acceptable avenue for recommending next actions to local management authorities. This was a lot to ask of operations managers who might have only a vague recollection of hearing something about a forklift injury. There was certainly a place for training, and I eventually learned that the greater influences on safe and productive forklift operating were in the "organizational context." Training, or more specifically "instruction," was only one of the keys to keeping the problem solved. The context included all the influences on forklift operators including, among others, the good-or-not-so-good condition of the forklifts; the broken dock levelers, the budget for getting repairs; supervisors who failed to provide acceptable methods of continuous performance feedback and positive reinforcement, and whether everyone involved was crystal clear on what was expected. Based upon a systematic Front-End Analysis (FEA) model (Harless, 1990), a systematic approach to instruction (Mager, 1962), a general systems description (Gilbert & Brethower, 1976) we used United States government safety training research (Cohen & Jensen, 1984), and direct observations to evolve, combine, and derive our own custom performance system that continues to improve with each iteration.

Training-for-All: The First Iteration

From my original two-week investigation for the Division Senior Vice-President, I noted two important contradictions that I shared in the report:

1. To solve and keep the problem solved, we needed to identify, name, and use a complete set of organizational "influences" relevant to operator behavior. If not complete enough, I feared the problem of forklift-related injury would be viewed as solved, and the quick solution would become invisible over time until the next serious injury occurred. We had to break the cycle with a more comprehensive set of influences, including, but not limited to "training".
2. The managers had an overwhelming bias toward training. Their collective, prepared lists of recommendations were convincing when coupled with their enthusiastic support for it during the interviews.

How could I resolve the contradiction and not discourage the enthusiastic response for training? Obviously, training was going to be part of the ongoing solution, so I took this opportunity to leverage the enthusiasm, assuming it would help me get the kind of buy-in needed for later introducing a whole systems intervention. I would eventually learn to facilitate continuous improvement of the forklift PM system and not just problem solve each injury event as though it was isolated from the other system elements. (Weisbord, 1991)

To define the content for Operator Training, I solicited lists from the managers, and promised I would use them as I developed custom instruction. I soon found that when converting each recommendation into on-the-job behavior to be trained, the vast majority of the items had more to do with supervisor or manager job requirements inasmuch as they influenced safe and productive forklift operation.

Table 1 outlines a list of three (3) items originally offered by department managers as recommendations for a forklift operator training program, with their conversion to on-the-job behaviors that can be trained:

At the end of this Behavior-Conversion exercise, a comprehensive, categorized list of instructional objectives, along with copies of all their original lists of recommendations, were discussed with each department manager to gain their approval. The objectives were divided into four categories of training, each category having its own list of job-behaviors:

Table 1. Recommendations for forklift operator training

Recommendation	Behavior	Train Who?
1. Ensure that operators take their trucks out-of service when they need repair.	• Produce a simple written procedure and form for operators to use for requesting repairs. • Schedule a repair technician to stand-by to repair and PM forklifts on "written" demand. • When employees turn-in their forklift for lengthy repair, on written form, STOP assigning them "undesirable" jobs; and put them into a job of their choice, including going home without pay.	Supervisor with his budget-level manager
2. Train operators to turn-in their forklift key each day and check it out at the beginning of their shift.	• At time clock location, trade key for time card to allow punch-in and punch-out. • Alternately, replace key switch with "time-out" digital key pad and pin code known only to certified operators.	Under authority of manager, security guard or department staff person controls daily key and time card trade for each operator. Maintenance technician with budget-level manager.
3. Train operators in how to inspect their forklift for safety defects.	• Produce a job-aided set of questions specific to each make and model with a recording form for examining the forklift BEFORE using it each day. • Provide practice and on-truck test for operators in "How to Use the job-aided Daily/Shift Exam Procedure.	Supervisor with instructional designer, and experienced expert operator. Supervisor with operator.

1.   Operator Training,
2.   Front-Line Supervisor Training,
3.   Department Manager Training,
4.   In-plant Pedestrian Training.

All the department managers voiced their approval except for one category. None thought it necessary for them to be personally "trained". When I asked them to explain, each simply assured me that they would take the list I provided and take the required action to make it happen. To their credit, they were good for their word…and then some. This made it easy to conduct the training as the schedule of workshops immediately developed a wait list. Later I learned that the Vice President included discussions of the new forklift policies at all his staff meetings. "Training for All" was an important step in the eventual success of the mission: "…Solve the problem…so it STAYS solved."

Many front-line supervisors were reluctant to get involved, and politely but persistently found reasons for being conspicuously absent from workshops designed to turn them into classroom instructors and test examiners. For about the first year, except for the help of a few supervisors and as many operators who wished to become instructors, I systematically and regularly conducted operator workshops and one-on-one, on-truck operator testing for about 90 people. This first-hand knowledge gave insights that would eventually enhance the new PM System and improve its chances of enduring for the long term. The experience yielded important lessons that today influence how and why the forklift PM system works.

Due to the high demand, I needed back-up to conduct the classroom-type workshops and testing. I finally settled on two actions that would provide it:

1. Redesign the operator and supervisor workshops to remove unnecessary activities that did not directly promote both ease of instruction and speed of operator certification testing.
2. Recruit front-line supervisors to become instructors with the help of their department managers, who learned of this initiative at the Vice-President's staff meetings.

The original forklift operator instructional design was typical of any industrial training, except for the criterion-referenced instructional objectives used to guide on-truck coaching and testing. At the time, we used a generic "university education model", consisting of classroom activities such as, lecture, multi-media presentations, discussions, pencil & paper testing, etc. There was an OSHA rule mandating powered industrial truck (forklift) training, but it was so sketchy that it was useless to anyone attempting to develop effective, systematic forklift operator instruction. OSHA at 29 CFR 1910.178(l) stated:

Only trained and authorized operators shall be permitted to operate a powered industrial truck. Methods shall be devised to train operators in the safe operation of powered industrial trucks.

With my *move forward* goals in mind, I set out to redesign the operator and supervisor/instructor workshops, so everything was more attractive to supervisors and easier to learn and conduct. The following items were removed from the two day workshop classroom were:

- 50 of the 100 pencil & paper test items.
- The generic 20-minute video tape.
- A 40-minute slide show.

- The unlimited time for Question and Answer discussions.
- The round-robin discussion of every Learning Objective with a discussion of each of its standards. (Going forward, only three of approximately 30 behaviorally-stated learning objectives were discussed in the classroom with trainee operators.)

This reduced the classroom-type workshop training to one day for operators while preserving the time needed to get an operator to pass the on-truck test. For their part, the supervisors, gratified by the reduced training commitment, became easier to recruit as trainers. Front-line supervisors started to conduct nearly all operator training and on-truck testing. I started to back away from daily and weekly involvement, but occasionally monitored the system, and conducted occasional instructor or pedestrian workshops.

Training-for-all was only the first iteration of the whole system I envisioned, and I was waiting for the "shoe to drop"; telling me to move on to another project because some senior manager with clout thought the problem no longer warranted all those resources. I did move on to other projects, but the "shoe" never dropped on the forklift Performance Management System. Two years after the Performance Management System inception, I heard of a lost-workday injury due to a forklift accident at one of the distribution centers, and immediately went to investigate.

Another Serious Injury Causes a System Change

A forklift operator driving a counterbalance sit-down forklift with rear-view mirrors and without a load, collided with a steel I-beam. He was moving at full throttle when the left fork hit the beam about six inches off the floor. The forklift skewed and stopped abruptly, sending the operator headfirst into the left rear-view mirror. Caroming off the forklift, he slammed onto the concrete floor. He had not fastened his seat belt.

At the time of the incident, the operator was driving through an empty part of a large 500,000 square foot distribution center. While waiting for an ambulance to take him to the hospital, he told his supervisor that he did not see the I-beam. One day later, the hospital released him because they observed no concussion or broken bones. He had lacerations to the right side of his head, as it had hit and cracked the mirror and knocked its metal frame from its mounts.

During my investigation, the two front-line supervisors, who were certified instructors, dismissed the incident cause as "an accident-prone employee". I had not spoken to these supervisors for more than a year, and was not about to accept their conclusion. They clearly wanted me to cut my visit short, as they claimed to be deluged with operations problems needing to be solved. I told the more senior of the two that I would be on my way if he could send me off with the injured employee's forklift certification file. He handed me nearly 40 files of all the operators they certified during the prior two years. He commented that they did not have time to maintain training files and I should take them because it was not their job. I reviewed each carefully for evidence of some influence on the injured operator's behavior immediately before the incident. What I found would henceforth change my assumptions about effective forklift operator training.

Taped to the inside flap of each manila file folder was a photocopy of a badly-rendered wallet-size document labeled "Certified Operator", with the operator's name handwritten below it. I also found the original 4-page pencil & paper test completed by each operator who was certified. Missing was any documentation indicating that the operators were tested on-truck, and on-the-job, and measured against the criteria listed in the learning objectives. The learning objectives and test required that the operator perform to the original 1971 OSHA-mandated rule on powered industrial trucks, including:

29 CFR1910.178(n)(6): The driver shall be required to look in the direction of, and keep a clear view of the path of travel.

Missing was the on-truck test documentation certifying the injured operator knew how to perform this under working conditions. Every operator was trained and issued certification credentials but had no documentation showing they could safely operate their forklift in their workplace. What implications did this have as a possible cause for the operator injury?

One phone call to the senior supervisor convinced me that another major change to the forklift Performance Management system needed to be made. He declared that on-truck testing, averaging about 45 minutes per operator, was taking too much time to perform, and detracted from the operation of the distribution center. He and his superiors decided that they would not do the on-truck testing and would issue operator certification credentials when their employees finished the pencil & paper test at the conclusion of the classroom training.

It was obvious to me that the cause of the operator's injury had less to do with an "accident-prone" operator, and a lot more to do with a failure in the management system. It was not a malicious action on the part of the supervisors. The supervisors at this facility, and nearly everyone else, viewed the forklift system as a "compliance training" program; a low-value activity to assuage government regulators who rarely came to inspect the site. Because serious forklift-related injuries were rare occurrences, not using valuable resources to solve problems that did not exist every day was seen as a reasonable response by management. They typically were rewarded or punished daily for inventory-related activities. Inventory needed to be received, moved, sorted, stored, counted, recorded, picked, labeled, managed, and shipped - the faster, the better. For these supervisors, working in a building far removed from the place where the PM system was originally developed, forklift safety training was not a major factor in their reward or punishment scheme. Clearly, it was time to start shifting the dialog from a training program to a Performance Management System.

BACK TO THE ITERATIVE DRAWING BOARD

I had what psychologists call a Gestalt moment, an insight that surprises and delights at the same time. The Performance Management System failure was predictable! The so-called forklift training program needed to make better use of the natural order of things. The facts were staring me in the face.

1. The goal of any training is to achieve "transfer of training". Transfer occurs when one can observe a person who has acquired new skill through training - use that skill routinely and correctly on-the-job, without external prompting. Good forklift operator training will achieve such transfer. Ineffective operator training will not.
2. Transfer is a function of newly acquired skill/knowledge and the organization's on-job contextual influences on an operator's desired behavior (Broad & Newstrom, 1992).
3. Sitting in a classroom, taking pencil and paper tests, watching generic video tapes, and discussing forklift safety will not transfer any skills to the job because classroom behaviors are not on-job behaviors.
4. The injured operator's supervisor never tested him on an important behavior called "...keep a clear view of the path of travel" nor was he tested for "Wear the seatbelt". Prior to his injury, we could not be sure these required behaviors were in his skill set. After the incident, we can infer that the lack of these skills was clearly a cause of his injury.
5. Certifying operators solely on the basis of "classroom behavior" is rewarding the wrong behavior. This practice may be convenient, but it is unfounded, contrived, and artificial. On-the-job behavior and resultant on-job accomplishments of operators are linked to rewards and punishments for supervisors. It would be the natural order of things to stay with this on-job principle, especially during operator training.

Given the above, the Forklift Performance Management System changed:

1. Pencil and paper tests were eliminated from the training plan.

2.   Operators sitting in a classroom was eliminated from the training plan.
3.   All training and coaching was performed On-The-Job (OJT), with the forklift, and using materials, supplies, and equipment normally available on-the-job.
4.   Passing an on-truck, on-the-job test was the only way to earn operator certification credentials.
5.   100% of test items, listed as criteria in the learning objectives, had to be performed by each operator to get certified.
6.   Since management practices of supervisors had a major affect on operator action, a concerted effort was made to start recruiting front-line supervisors as Certified Instructor/Test Examiners. Non-supervisors (those with NO direct authority or accountability over forklift operators, e.g. peer operators, staff professionals, engineers, internal consultants, and human resources personnel) would perform that role only when the senior manager in charge of the entire distribution center made a strong case, and delegated authority for forklift safety training and safe on-job behavior.

With the emphasis on management practices of supervisors, and a solid on-the-job, on-truck instructional system, the move to a comprehensive performance management system was starting to take shape. A performance system vantage point was new to most participants and supervisors and the trainees were introduced to a performance model that would continue to evolve.

Figure 1 provides the Accomplishment Based Performance System model overview, also known by its now proprietary acronym, LIFTOR (Lift Truck Operating Resources) has evolved over time and now guides the Forklift Performance Management System installation and any of its components. Note that it has a systematically arranged set of elements, including a feedback link for system self-guidance. By definition, the elements of systems work together for a common purpose. In the model, it is important that the four categories of influence on the operator's behavior be interconnected to achieve the desired goals. All are made possible as a result of effective management practices, not limited only to training employees:

1.   Selection (operators and equipment),
2.   Skill/Knowledge (operators, supervisors, pedestrians),
3.   Engineering/Environmental,
4.   Incentives.

The following Performance Chain model shows the natural order of influences, the behavior(s) they cause, and their resultant accomplishments. All of this can be objectively measured. For this model, we define key terms as follows:

Figure 1. The performance system overview

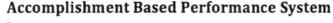

Accomplishment Based Performance System

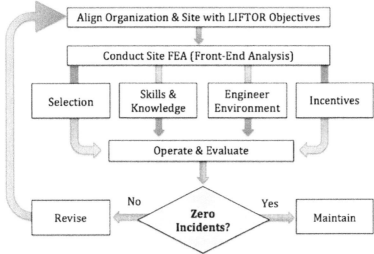

- **Influences:** Any condition, antecedent, or event that is both recognized by an operator and causes him/her to act in a particular way.
- **Behavior:** Any action that can be seen or measured in some other way.
- **Accomplishment:** A thing of value to another person using it to perform their job. Operators produce accomplishments, and use them to signal or "influence" the behavior of others.
- **Organization Objectives:** High level accomplishments that can describe the organization's purpose in service to its customers. Can also be used to describe the accomplishments of departments, or other work groups with a common purpose.

The performance sequence is clear in Figure 2. The influences need to be managed by front-line supervisors to make anything useful happen. For example, providing incentives to operators, as well as task-clarity, adequate equipment and feedback go a long way toward coordinating their efforts. Also, like everyone else, front-line supervisor behavior is influenced by its own set of contextual influences. For distribution/warehouse supervisors, whose incentives are heavily biased toward inventory control and valuation, it is typically not a priority to expend much energy

Figure 2. Links in the performance chain

Performance Chain

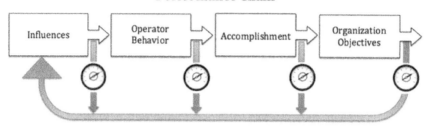

on managing the safe operator behavior of subordinates. Indeed, for the vast majority of these supervisors, providing an incentive for operator behavior would not be effective until they first learned how to recognize both safe and unsafe operator actions.

Notice that forklift operators need to be influenced to "behave" in the most useful way (Figure 3). Useful means their actions (on-the-job behavior) will produce desirable accomplishments that serve the organization's purpose. From the outset, the forklift Performance Management System was designed to intervene in the company's normal behavior patterns that caused serious injury, with far-reaching implications, about every one and a half years. Once solved by applying the correct mix of influences in a timely way, it would become a matter of fine tuning the influences so the problem would stay solved. From a Performance Chain vantage point, we knew that the influences were the important starting point for affecting the required on-forklift behavior of operators.

Figure 3. The influence link

Manage the Right Mix of Influences

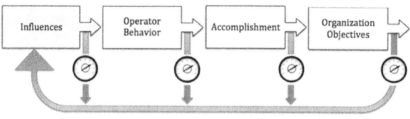

EXAMPLES
- Supervisor as Test Examiner
- Clear Expectations
- Authority to Take Truck out of Service
- Marked Walkways

The performance chain model tells us that the most important management action is to bring the right mix of influences to bear on operator behavior (Figure 4). Without the behavior, nothing moves. Nothing gets done. Examples of operator behavior are listed with the above diagram. It is the operator's behavior that causes important things to happen, namely the production of valuable things (accomplishments.) Those accomplishments signal the next person so s/he can start to act (behave). It is noteworthy that each accomplishment becomes one of the influences in the next person's work life. It is behavior that makes everything happen.

It was the operator's on-the-job accomplishments that were the links between the operator's on-job behavior and the company's purpose, stated in its objectives. Although operators had to produce many job accomplishments, as far as we could see, few of the required behaviors led to a serious injury. However, every accomplishment produced by the behavior affected the company's objectives in some way (Figure 5). This dual insight, recognizing that both the behavior and the resulting accomplishment were related in an important way, went unrecognized for its relevance to operator safety training and on-job performance. Then, after about year nine of the Performance Management System's inception, having the one serious head laceration injury during the interim, the systemic relationship among operator behavior, accomplishment, safety and productivity became obvious when two events converged to prompt the connection.

Figure 4. The behavior link

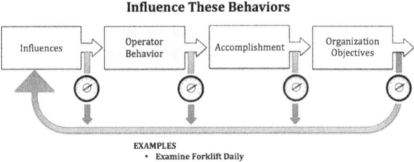

Influence These Behaviors

EXAMPLES
- Examine Forklift Daily
- Travel 3 Inches or Less
- If Pedestrian, Stop 3 & 1
- BEFORE Lift, UN-tilt Load

Figure 5. The accomplishment link

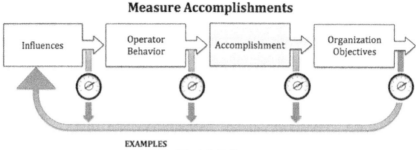

Measure Accomplishments

EXAMPLES
* Finished Goods in Trailer
* Daily Exam Record
* Triple Stacks in Bulk Area
* Pallet Load in Assigned Location

CURRENT CHALLENGES FACING THE ORGANIZATION

Event One: Supervisor Push-Back

Several supervisors and managers of forklift truck operators, who were certified as instructors and test examiners, started approaching me for answers to the conundrum they faced frequently. They took forklift operator safety somewhat personally as they trained, certified, supervised and had to "live with" their operator subordinates. This daily conundrum is common among conscientious front-line industrial supervisors who would share the same sentiments (paraphrased here):

I catch hell if I don't get the work done. My bosses get it too.
It's company policy. We never compromise safety for productivity. The policy is crap. We're behind in loading trailers, today. Its graduation night and my loader wants to leave early to see his son graduate high school. He says he can get all the trailers loaded on time if I tell him it's OK to ignore the safety rules. What the hell am I supposed to tell him?

It was time to thoroughly examine the company objectives and goals for insights into how to align them with actual performance in the field. When I examined the high-level objectives of participating manufacturing or distribution centers, they clearly included a reference to operating with zero-to-few injuries.

I was beginning to learn that using a periodic injury count was not an effective measure for pivoting decisions about how to manage and prevent any particular serious injury. Injury count was, after all, a trailing indicator; removed in time and space from the specific influences, causes, or antecedents to the behaviors that precipitated the serious injury event. You could count one only after each serious injury occurred. Yet, every instance of unsafe behavior did not precipitate a serious injury. It was becoming clear that measuring the trailing indicator, absent both its causal behavior and influences, did little to make effective changes to the conditions that precipitated it. If managers made it to the end-of-the-year with a zero injury count, they knew they were mostly just lucky. If not, they would take their licks like everyone else; knowing the punishment would pass as they got promoted or moved on to their next job.

The common practice of measuring trailing indicators of forklift injuries is slightly refined by the professional engineering practice of risk management (Daniels, 1999). The Forklift Performance Management System is better suited to managing the realities of human performance because it has a primary bias toward managing the application of all relevant "influences. With the Forklift Performance Management System, we make the transition from managing the theoretical, abstract concept of risk, and treat very real, predictable behaviors and accomplishments by timely applying the right mix of influences.

Event Two: An Injured Foot

The next serious injury to a novice operator's crushed foot, combined with the front-line supervisor's frequent conundrum (safety versus productivity), provided the urgency to perform a thorough analysis, starting with all company objectives and working backward to the misapplication of influences that were antecedent to it. About ten o'clock in the morning, I received a phone call from my favorite client; a woman director of one of the company's largest distribution centers in North America. She had inherited the Forklift Performance Management System from the person she replaced. She was an industrial engineer with an uncanny ability to understand and apply Human Performance Engineering methods to her organization. With the performance management system's engineered set of rules and principles, she was very effective in getting her subordinates to follow her lead.

"I have some good news for you…and some bad news" she said. "Which do you want to hear first?"

I said I would first like to hear the good news. At that point, she said "NO. I'm going to give you the bad news first, so the good news will be put into context." I didn't know what to expect.

She said that Anita, a back-up forklift operator, certified on a stand-on model, narrow aisle reach truck was in a serious incident. She was traveling at a fast pace with a double load trailing through the interior aisles of a pallet rack storage system. When she came to a 4-way, blind intersection, she failed to come to a dead-stop, started into a left turn, but wasn't fast enough to steer the forklift so it would make a clean turn. The 10,500-pound forklift, carrying a 3,000-pound load, headed for the corner of the metal rack system upright. She panicked, lifted her foot up to brace herself for the impact and it was crushed between the forklift and the metal upright. As her foot hung over the side dripping blood, it took the ambulance nearly 30 minutes to arrive.

"Do you want to hear the good news?" It was her way to pause during telephone conversations. I respected her enough to just shut up until she continued talking, but I was mentally feeling tortured by the news. My first thought was: "Anita's foot was crushed this morning."

Other thoughts followed quickly. I was dwelling on how bad the situation sounded. I would probably get sued over this, since I was the designer of the Performance Management System, used for training, testing and certification of forklift operators. I offered a conditional money back guarantee for instruction I delivered. There might even be some public humiliation. I'd lose all my clients. Worse yet, six months ago, the department manager hired me to personally train and certify Anita because she was a special case. She was to be a back-up operator. She had what the manager called a "nervous disposition", and she had never before operated a forklift. No matter how long it took, the manager wanted her to be available as a back-up in the event a regular operator was absent. With on-truck coaching for about a week, she learned all the safe maneuvers to standard, save one: she kept taking her foot out of the operator's compartment, putting it at risk from getting clipped by a passing forklift, or by a metal rack upright during a tight maneuver.

Except for this, she developed nearly flawless skill, as she could precisely and deliberately guide the forklift, or accurately maneuver the forks wherever intended. Because she drove slowly to allow time to mentally process everything she did, it took an extra week just to get her to keep her foot in the right place. Finally, she was able to pass the on-truck certification test; meeting every one of the precise standards in the learning objectives. When she finally earned her forklift certification card, I had a closing conference with both her and her manager; advising she should get much more practice before he let her drive as a back-up operator. The day she was injured was her first time on the forklift since that closing conference six months earlier.

"If that's all the bad news, the good news better be really, really good", I said. She replied, "I think you'll think it's really good, even under the circumstances."

She explained that the entire time Anita was waiting for the ambulance to arrive, face down, her chest was lying across the forklift so her foot, now bandaged by first-responder co-workers, could freely hang down as she winced in pain. Her rescuers helped her lay down on the concrete floor. The first-responders reported that Anita kept repeating the same words over and over again:

Oh my gosh! O my gosh! I did just what Joe told me not to do. I'm so sorry!

I was immediately relieved. My client wasn't going to ask for her money back. I probably was not going to be sued by Anita, and I never again harbored any thoughts that my training and coaching skills were, in some way, from a lesser god.

When Anita returned home from her hospital stay, having endured several foot operations to re-align her bones, I called her. She was still in pain. She spent nearly two hours crying, and frequently apologizing to me for her failure to keep her foot in a safe place. I was sad for her, and reminded her that she needed to get well and look forward to the future. Her surgeon told her that her foot would probably walk normally when fully healed. She attempted a moment of levity; reporting that she would also be able to predict the weather with the expected onset of arthritis.

At the time, I was un-nerved that the Forklift Performance Management System had not yet solved the problem, so that it stayed solved. Anita's forklift injury was a clear signal that:

- The forklift PM system substantially decreased the frequency from 1.5 years to about 8 year intervals between serious injuries, but
- There were yet unidentified influences requiring investigation so they might be addressed within the PM System.

What would they be? The latest forklift-related injury and the daily conundrum faced by front-line supervisors suggested some improvements.

Further System Improvements

After investigating Anita's forklift incident and a complete statistical study of forklift operator experience from performance management system inception and interviews with relevant managers, we discovered needed improvements in all four categories of System Influence:

1. **Selection:** Clearly, on the day she was assigned to operate the narrow-aisle reach truck, Anita was not the person for the job. She was ill-selected by her department manager who had been advised to avoid putting her on the forklift until she developed more confidence, and speed that would match the normally fast work pace of regular operators. In the six months she worked as a non-operator she lost most of the skill and knowledge she had gained to pass the certification test.

2. **Skill/Knowledge:** In nature, behavior analysts recognize there is a certain rhythm to repetitive behavior. Humming birds move their wings nearly 50

times per second to stay aloft and flit from one flower to another. Baseball players can see a ball hurled at them going 90 miles per hour, hitting it one of three times at bat to achieve fame and fortune. The percussionist in a band or orchestra can pace the exact beat of the other instruments so their sound becomes an auditory delight. So too, forklift operators safely load trailers at the pace required by their situation. Every skill known to humans has at least these two dimensions (Binder, 1996):

a.   A clear and precise pattern of behaviors, and

b.   A specific pace or speed at which the precise behaviors occur.

To analyze behavior, we must recognize both dimensions. This principle, that speed or pace cannot be separated from the precision of behavior tends to be ignored by those responsible for safety training. Nor is it recognized by trainers, who base their training criteria solely on government regulations or consensus standards.

When developing forklift operating skill and knowledge, it is routine for forklift operator instructors and supervisors to ignore on-job requirements for speed during training; teaching and learning only precise (safe) behavior. This is a misguided practice, unnecessary, and counterproductive. Teaching both precision (safety) and speed is a well-researched, documented, and practical approach (Binder, 1996) that treats the two important dimensions of safe behavior. Generative learning, precision teaching, mastery learning, and accomplishment-based instructional design are long-established examples of this. Why not establish it as a part of the forklift Performance Management Skill & Knowledge intervention? It would go a long way toward the "keep it solved" part of our forklift performance management mission.

Training for job mastery became the focus. This was driven by the insights gained from our analysis. The first "ah hah" moment came when I realized that forklift safety training could be better focused as On-Job-Training (OJT). With its on-truck training and testing, we had already moved in that direction. If it included both precise (safe) actions AND speed that matched the pace of the actual work, everyone gained something. It was the second ah hah moment. Operators would not have to choose between safety and productivity because they would be able to achieve both. Supervisors would be better able to measure, predict, and evaluate both the likelihood of forklift-related injury as well as group and individual productivity. Costs related to injury and operator productivity would be reduced accordingly. Perhaps the problem of forklift injury could be finally solved...so it stayed solved.

3.   **Environmental/Engineering:** When the on-site forklift technician was queried about the physical state of the forklift, I asked him about the status of the "dead-man" feature on Anita's forklift the day of the incident. When she lifted her foot from the pedal, it should have stopped the truck. The technician,

who I trusted for his exceptional skill and no-nonsense opinions, said that the "dead-man" was set within the manufacturer's specifications. Given the momentum with the near-capacity load she was carrying, even with the proper stopping procedure followed, the forklift was designed to stop gradually, to avoid throwing the operator. He estimated that she did not lift her foot until she was about three feet from the collision point. Given her estimated speed, this was not enough time for the loaded forklift to come to a complete stop.

About a month after the incident, the Director of Distribution told me that they were doing away with the 4-way in-rack intersections. Two months later, that entire section of the distribution center, about 175,000 square feet, was reconfigured. Pallet rack storage was reduced and re-distributed to other parts of the facility to alleviate congestion. The space was replaced by a new order-picking operation. These steps eliminated the possibility of a repeat injury under the same environmental circumstances. Additionally, "throughput", a key metric of warehouse efficiency, was improved. As it turned-out, the distribution center re-configuration plan had been on the approved project list months before Anita's injury. Afterward, it became an immediate priority.

4. **Incentives:** An incentive is an external influence that increases the likelihood of a person to do something specific; to perform specific actions. Incentives always originate from a source outside the person. Each from their own perspectives, managers and workers eventually ask: "Given the incentives available, will I/ you be willing (motivated) to do what is expected?" This question underscores the unseen side of organization and individual performance. People ask the question because of the inherent assumption behind offering incentives: "If I do not offer the correct type or amount of incentive, people will NOT do what I need them to do." The implication is that people need to be coerced into doing work because they find it unpleasant. McGregor (1960) calls this management view Theory X.

In the case at hand what were the incentive influences? Both Anita and her department manager knew, on the day she was expected to operate the forklift, she was not ready. Although the manager was new to the building, he had worked in a small warehouse outpost for the same company for 13 years. He was a reasonably responsible citizen. Both individuals were somehow compelled to do what they did, and the possibility of a serious, debilitating injury became a reality.

In my discussion with Anita, I asked her why she did not refuse to operate the forklift on the day of her incident. Anita replied that she "could not afford to get fired". She did not resist the assignment because she "did not trust how the department manager would react"; assuming he might find her objections to her assignment a cause for getting fired.

When I interviewed Anita's department manager, I found him to be an engaging, gregarious man with entertaining stories. When I asked him how he viewed Anita's injury, he characterized it as a normal cost of doing business. When I explained the mission and 10-year improvements within the Forklift Performance Management System, he asserted that such accidents were not preventable, no matter what your statistics show. I was disappointed to hear those words. About 6 months later, he was abruptly fired from his job for unrelated reasons. This was not the first, nor would it be the last time, I heard those words from a manager in a position of authority. This manager simply did not recognize a role for themselves in reinforcing safe forklift operating practices. The incentives to stay safe could not compete with the easier and more lucrative productivity incentives, just as they functioned for Anita.

Improvements: Ten years of PM experience, Anita's injury investigation, the statistical study, and associated learning all combined to prompt major improvements in the forklift Performance Management system practices. These improvements have become mainstays of the system's long-enduring success.

1. **Performance Speed:** A *speed* criterion was added to each operator learning objective describing a core distribution center task. Operators would now be trained in precision (safe) maneuvers and then over-train in the same maneuvers until they could consistently meet both precision and the speed criterion. Non-core tasks, or those containing maneuvers that where considered too dangerous for an on-job simulation, would not require any particular speed, and would be practiced at a lower level-of-simulation unlikely to injure anyone.

2. **Equipment-Specific Tests:** Instead of one generic check-list that doubled as learning objectives and test criteria covering all forklifts, we customized the learning objectives with a matching and separate test document for each make and model forklift in the facility.

3. Our study (See OSHA, USDOL Docket S-008) and empirical observations uncovered a pattern of unique performance. Over a 10-year period, one unique group of forklift operators, representing 668 operating years, experienced zero (0) serious injuries. Two other groups, (one much larger and one about the same size) studied over the same 10 years, at the same locations, had multiple (16) serious injuries. The difference was that the ZERO (0) group of operators were required to pass the on-truck certification test administered by a front-line supervisor based at the operator's work location. It became clear that *every* one of the 16 operators who had a serious injury either:

a.   Did not take and pass an on-truck certification test, and/or
b.   The test was administered by someone other than a front-line supervisor based in the same location.

The role of front-line management had emerged as an important element in the prevention of serious injuries among operators. We believed then, as we do now, that the most important influences on safe and productive operator behavior come from the organizational context made possible by local management practices. The last serious injury, nearly 23 years from Performance Management System inception, confirmed this assumption so well, that the System was not substantially changed in any way as a result of it.

Another Event, Another Iteration...

I received a call from the cosmetic company's newly hired Safety, Health, and Environmental Engineer. He was tasked with administering those programs at two distribution centers in the southern States; the one where Anita was injured years before, and a smaller display assembly center a few miles away.

This high-energy professional walked with an obvious limp. When I met him for the first time, he explained that he worked for the company in Chicago for some 20 years. When he was a forklift operator, he narrowly escaped with his life from a lateral tip-over of the forklift he was operating. When it tipped, his leg was momentarily caught under the body. Immediately before the five-ton forklift settled on its side, he was able to pull his leg out by standing up between the tipping forklift body and its overhead guard. He felt blessed that he escaped with only a permanent deformity in his leg. He wanted to become a Certified Instructor and Test Examiner under the forklift Performance Management System. He was diligent, a fast learner, and met every requirement for Certified Instructor/Test Examiners. I was pleased to include him as part of our community of certified instructors, even though he was not a front-line supervisor/manager.

When I heard his voice over the phone, he sounded nervous. He was calling from a conference hotel about a 30-minute drive to my office in New Jersey. All the company safety managers were meeting there, and it was his first meeting in his new role.

He said he wanted to report a lost workday injury. I asked how he got his information, as he has been in New Jersey for several days. "Chris called", he said.

I had known Chris for nearly 16 years. He was an exceptional Certified Forklift Instructor and Test Examiner. He thoroughly knew forklift safety and productivity. He was a front-line manager, accustomed to exercising his authority. He was keenly aware of the organizational context in which operators had to work. He knew when to get after a poorly performing subordinate, and he knew when to launch into coaching mode; helping an operator to perform with precision and speed after having been subjected to a different supervisor's lack of skill. Months before, he had been the senior supervisor at the injury site, but a promotion to manager relocated him to the main building. He occasionally visited the smaller building where he formerly spent two years certifying and supervising 18 operators. He knew how to investigate a forklift incident for its precise causes.

Faye was the accident victim. She had been standing next to an I-beam, waiting for her electric-powered forklift battery cells to be checked by an in-house maintenance technician. When he was done, he slammed down the battery cover. The forklift immediately spun its drive wheels, squealing and smoking in reverse, accelerating 12 feet across the floor to where Faye was bending over to scratch her ankle. She was pinned by her forklift against the I-beam; it broke multiple bones in her shoulder, ribs, and foot. The 5 ton+ forklift ran over her foot and stopped, pinning it under a rear wheel. The maintenance technician had to get the truck off of her foot by again driving over it. Had she not been wearing safety shoes, damage to her foot would have included her toes. This incident was so unusual that the company's European Safety Management sent engineers to the USA to investigate. With their US counterparts, they converged on the assembly center for a two-day flurry of activity.

It would be more than a year before the new corporate forklift safety policies were issued for worldwide implementation. Absent from the new policies would be any evidence that they relied on detailed, precise conclusions already investigated by Chris. He was clearly the resident expert on forklift safety, and had already written a detailed account of the incident causes and the organizational context that allowed them to exist.

When Safety Headquarters in Europe declared the new policies were ready for implementation, the solutions did not directly address the root causes of Faye's incident. I was distressed. This incident triggered the company to physically re-engineer all its facilities to ensure that no pedestrians would again be hurt by a forklift truck. They installed millions of dollars' worth of physical barriers and mechanisms along practically every pedestrian path in their warehouses. They painted a red stop line on the floor wherever a pedestrian path crosses a forklift path. They installed traffic lights at many of these crossings.

Yet, when you examine the forklift Performance Management System that was already in place when the rogue truck incident occurred, you discover the real causes of Faye's injury. It was not caused by a lack of 4-foot high physical barriers along pedestrian walkways. It was not caused because there was no red line on the floor. It was not caused by her failure to push a traffic light button.

Had the corporate engineers asked the local management, especially the on-site manager practiced in forklift operator supervision and systematic operating standards, they would have arrived at a precise and true set of causes, and a much more economical and effective solution:

1. The seat-switch with its mechanical spring should have automatically disengaged power to the forklift's transmission when the operator got off the forklift. It was broken many days before the incident. Faye, like nearly all operators in her building, stopped performing the standard forklift daily examination that included a simple procedure to verify seat-switch function, even though she daily signed-off that she did it. She earned her certification only after passing a rigorous test that included the simple seat-switch procedure among many others.
2. Her original supervisor, Chris, was promoted to manager months before the incident, and now worked in another location, occasionally helping the newer, much less experienced supervisor at his old location.
3. The most senior director in the building had made his sentiments toward precision forklift standards known to his subordinates. He repeatedly reminded everyone that the PM system's precision forklift standards were unnecessary. In doing this repeatedly, he confused, if not totally eliminated the clear expectations the forklift Performance Management System had instilled.

This was a clear example of management system failure. Faye's serious injuries had little to do with her skill, or the lack of pedestrian crosswalk engineering. Yet, management failed to identify or acknowledge the actual causes.

Writing about management effectiveness in *Breakthrough Performance*, William R. Daniels (1995) describes the supervisor's mission:

1. Provide clear expectations to workers.
2. Provide adequate resources to achieve the clear expectations.
3. Ensure the performer gets timely feedback on how well or poorly they are meeting expectations.

When a supervisor, manager, or a forklift operator systematically uses the above three principles, and performs them within the context of the Performance Chain, ordinary people can achieve extraordinary things. The Performance Management System that targeted forklift operator safety and productivity is a clear example of enduring management practices that have withstood the changes in management during a 30 year period. All stakeholders benefitted. Operators and pedestrians had nearly eliminated all serious forklift related injuries. Supervisors learned that they can make a difference if they apply fairly simple performance management principles. Finally, management, under the forklift Performance Management System, benefitted from an injury-free facility, lower costs, and the admiration of any who would see what they have accomplished.

SOLUTIONS AND RECOMMENDATIONS

If you are about to design and implement a Human Performance System, the forklift Performance Management System offers a model that has endured well past the original management that championed it. While the forklift Performance Management System targets the very specific problem of powered industrial truck (forklift) injuries, the approach and methods can be broadly applied.

Implementing a performance system is challenging. Based on the lessons from this case, here are our recommendations for creating a sustainable system:

1. **State an Explicit Purpose of the System:** Continue to restate the purpose in as many ways as possible, e.g. annual goals or objectives, budget line items, events to celebrate, and review team assignments. The goal is important because as long as there is a need for achieving it, the performance system will be able to endure. If the goal goes away, as it does in every project management system, then it is okay to stop.

2. **Agree on a Systems Model:** An important early requirement for establishing an enduring Performance System is to agree on a mental model for a comprehensive Human Performance System. The Accomplishment Based Performance System was adapted from the late Joe Harless' work at the Harless Performance Guild. There are others, such as the work of Carol Panza (1991) on organization mapping, or Rummler and Brache (1995) on performance improvement.

3. **Enlist a Champion:** The champion is a person who has a vision of some future outcome, and has access to the resources to ensure it is attained. Moreover, the champion is responsible for aligning the resources he has delegated to his subordinates to his/her envisioned outcome. Alignment means that those resources will actually be used to achieve the explicit purpose. The forklift Performance Management System had a champion at the beginning and continued to be financed by several champions, thereafter. Endurance of the Champion's influence = Endurance of the Performance System Championed.

4. **Set-Up a Monitoring System That Tracks Only Important Metrics:** Start with the only metric that matters (Croll & Yoskovitz, 2013). Don't try to measure everything. Vanity metrics are useless. You will find that the most important metric will change with the different stages of performance system

development. Having only the most important one can accelerate the early stages of development, as well as give you good data from which to make well-informed decision, also known as pivot points.

5. **Train the Participants, or "Bullet-Proof" Their Organizational Context:** For most Human Performance System start-ups, training will be needed to ensure learning. Ensure it is effective. After the initial training is complete, except for future new hires, find ways to diminish its costs. Instead of time-consuming training sessions, consider the use of job-aids and expert on-the-job workshops. Look to other interventions, such as: employee selection, engineering or environmental changes, or different ways to reinforce desired behavior (incentives). Failing to develop good training is a common error, but it isn't as fatal as failing to develop the proper incentives and other influences on behavior.

Incentives are an important influence on an employee's, and your own, behavior. The behaviors though are not the real mission. It's in the accomplishments, or things of value, that are the result of behavior. The Performance Chain tells us that that accomplishments define the organization's purpose and success. Finally, when you manage the influences, behavior, and accomplishments throughout, the business will deliver on its objectives and benefit all stakeholders accordingly.

6. **Use the Following List to Investigate a Comprehensive Set of Durability Factors:** These are factors that might influence the durability of your Performance System. By the time you have designed the first working iteration, it is likely time to modify or re-align resources and support facilities to improve the system's chances for survival. Consider which items might apply.
   a. Management and Quality Systems:
      i. Modify management practices to reflect changes required by the performance system.
      ii. Update quality systems documents (e.g., ISO 9000).
      iii. Update Operations Manuals to explain the performance system operation.
      iv. Designate a formal champion in upper management for the performance system.
      v. Appoint group to evaluate the performance system at regular intervals.
   b. Personnel Systems:
      i. Update new employee orientation to explain operation of the performance system.

      ii.   Update job descriptions to reflect the performance system responsibilities.

      iii.   Update job performance standards to recognize the performance system results.

      iv.   Update performance evaluation procedures recognize the performance system.

  c.   Training:

      i.   Update operator training courses to explain purpose and operation of the performance system.

      ii.   Update manager training courses to explain purpose and structure of the performance system.

      iii.   Brief impacted vendors and/or customers on the performance system.

  d.   Accounting:

      i.   Give direct costs for operation of the performance system their own line item.

      ii.   Account for time spent, maintaining the performance system.

      iii.   Add line items to operations and training budgets for the performance system.

  e.   Technical Support:

      i.   Train technicians to maintain the performance system programs and files.

      ii.   Update and distribute system documentation.

      iii.   Assign responsibilites and priorities for the performance system support.

  f.   Reporting and Communications:

      i.   Set schedule and distribution for periodic performance reports.

      ii.   Brief Communications and Public Relations Departments.

Finally, if you champion a performance management system for endurance, please know that most fail within a few years. There are reasons for this, most rooted in the resistance one normally gets when attempting to change the status quo.

The good news is that with focus and a systematic approach, you can end up with a long enduring performance management system. This chapter is an example of how it works. Focus your resources on the recommendations, the Performance Chain, the performance system checklist, and the other principles and practices described above. Then, even if your performance management system is faced with the inevitable change in upper management, it is more likely to endure until the need for it goes away.

REFERENCES

American Society for Safety Engineers (ASSE). (2009, January 1). *Criteria for accepted practices in safety, health, and environmental training* (ANSI/ASSE Z490.1-2009).

Binder, C. (1996). Behavioral fluency: Evolution of a new paradigm. The Behavior Analyst, 19, 163–197. PubMed PMID:22478257

Brethower, K. S., & Rummler, G. A. (1976). Evaluating training. Improving Human Performance Quarterly, 5(3), 103–120.

Broad, M. L., & Newstrom, J. W. (1992). Transfer of training: Action-packed strategies to ensure high payoff from training investments. Reading, MA: Perseus Books.

Cohen, H. H., & Jensen, R. C. (1984). Measuring the effectiveness of an industrial lift truck safety training program. Journal of Safety Research, 15(3), 125–135. doi:10.1016/0022-4375(84)90023-9 doi:10.1016/0022-4375(84)90023-9

Expert OJT. (n.d.). *JobAid Writing System.* Retrieved 1 May 2014 from www.http://www.expertojt.com/

Harless, J. H. (1990). Diagnostic Front End Analysis. ABCD (Accomplishment-Based Curriculum Development) System. Newnan, GA: Job Aid.

Industrial Truck Standards Development Foundation (ITSDF). (2009). *Safety Standards for Low Lift and High Lift Trucks* (ANSI/ITSDF B56.1-2009).

McGregor, D. (1960). The human side of enterprise. New York, NY: McGrawHill.

ADDITIONAL READING

Brethower, D. (2006). Systemic issues. In J. A. Pershing (Ed.), Handbook of human performance technology (pp. 111–137). San Francisco, CA: Pfeiffer.

Clark, R. E., & Estes, F. (2008). Turning research into results: A guide to selecting the right performance solutions. Charlotte, NC: Information Age Publishing.

Croll, A., & Yoskovitz, B. (2013). Lean analytics. North Sebastopol, CA: O'Reilly Media, Inc.

Daniels, W. R., & Mathers, J. G. (1997). Change-able organization: Key management practices for speed and flexibility. Mill Valley, CA: ACT Publishing.

Daniels, W. R. (1995). Breakthrough performance. Mill Valley, CA: ACT Publishing.

Galbraith, J. R. (1977). Organization design. Reading, MA: Addison-Wesley Publishing Company.

Gilbert, T. F. (2007). Human competence: Engineering worthy performance. San Francisco, CA: Pfeiffer.

Ketchum, L. D., & Trist, E. (1992). All teams are not created equal: How employee empowerment really works. Newbury Park, CA: Sage Publications, Inc.

Kirkpatrick, D. L., & Kirkpatrick, J. D. (2006). Evaluating training programs: The four levels. San Francisco, CA: Berrett-Koehler.

Mager, R., & Pipe, P. (1997). Analyzing performance problems. Atlanta, GA: Center for Effective Performance.

Mager, R. F. (1992). What every manager should know about training. Belmont: Lake Publishing Company.

Panza, C. (1991). Picture this ... your function, your company (2nd ed.). Morristown, NJ: CMP Associates.

Porter, M. E. (1980). Competitive strategy: Techniques for analyzing industries and competitors. New York, NY: The Free Press.

Pryor, K. (1999). Don't shoot the dog: The new art of teaching and training. New York, NY: Bantam Books.

Robinson, D. G., & Robinson, J. C. (1995). Performance consulting: Moving beyond training. San Francisco, CA: Berrett-Koehler Publishers.

Rummler, G. A., & Brache, A. P. (1995). Improving performance: How to manage the white space on the organization chart. San Francisco, CA: Jossey-Bass.

Senge, P. M. (1990). The fifth discipline: The art & practice of the learning organization. New York, NY: Doubleday.

Trompenaars, C., & Hampden-Turner, F. (2005). Riding the waves of culture: Understanding cultural diversity in business. London, England: Nicholas Brealey Publishing.

Weisbord, M. R. (1987). Productive workplaces: Organizing and managing for dignity, meaning, and community. San Francisco, CA: Jossey-Bass Publishers.

KEY TERMS AND DEFINITIONS

Accomplishment: A thing of value to another person using it to perform their job. Operators produce accomplishments, and use them to signal or "influence" the behavior of others.

Behavior: Any action that can be seen or measured in some other way.

Front-End Analysis: A method to determine the gap and cause of performance problems in behavior before interventions are selected or implemented; a method to uncover the underlying causes of poor performance.

Influences: Any condition, antecedent, or event that is both recognized by an operator and causes him/her to act in a particular way.

Organization Objectives: High level accomplishments that can describe the organization's purpose in service to its customers. Can also be used to describe the accomplishments of departments, or other work groups with a common purpose.

OSHA: Occupational Safety and Health Administration agency in the United States that serves as the main federal agency responsible for the enforcement of safety and health legislation.

Systems Theory: Theory that holds that systems in nature are holistic, interconnected and interdependent. If change occurs in one part of a system, other parts of the system are affected as well.

Chapter 5
User Design:
A Case Study in Developing Workplace Curricula

Robert Anthony Jordan
Independent Researcher, USA

Alison Carr-Chellman
Penn State University, USA

EXECUTIVE SUMMARY

This case describes how a federal government agency engaged in a user design process to design, develop, and implement a workplace learning curriculum to be implemented throughout several agency offices. While several offices had developed their own training program, there were inconsistencies and a lack of standardization. The authors describe how a user design process was utilized in the development of a standardized curriculum. User design shifts the responsibility of design from expert designers to frontline users and stakeholders. Several user-driven tools are available to organizations that adopt user design processes. Potential advantages of a curriculum developed through user design include better adoption and diffusion of the curriculum and improved engagement of the users in the workplace.

ORGANIZATION BACKGROUND

The case involves a federal government agency that collects, tabulates and reports statistical data related to the labor market. It employs approximately 2,500 employees who work in the Washington, D.C. national office and five regional offices spread across the nation. Economists comprise approximately 80% of the agency's workforce.

DOI: 10.4018/978-1-4666-8330-3.ch005

SETTING THE STAGE

The senior leadership at the agency expressed an interest in developing a learning curriculum for the agency economists. While some offices within the agency had developed their own training plans, other offices had no such plans for their employees. In addition, a lack of consistency characterized these office-specific curricula, and no general learning plan applicable across the agency had yet been developed. Curricula had been previously developed for new supervisors and agency mathematical statisticians using expert-driven curriculum development processes. The top leadership at the agency had indicated an interest to complete a curriculum for economists in the agency.

In addition, management hoped to link learning opportunities to the agency's economist competency model which had been developed some years before and had been previously used to assess the competencies of agency economists. Several years before, an agency team developed an economist "resource guide" that contained a list of suggested training courses and other developmental resources for economists, but it had not been updated in many years and was linked to unofficial Knowledge, Skills, and Abilities (KSAs). Senior management charged an interagency team comprised of economists to develop an economist curriculum that would meet the general learning needs of all economists across the agency as well as reflect office-specific learning programs. This team would be managed as an official agency project team but the key question that emerged was what sort of design *process* the team would adopt.

CASE DESCRIPTION

The agency senior managers assigned the project leadership to the agency's training and development branch located in it human resources department. An instructor designer within the branch was assigned as the leader for the project design team. The team was comprised of eight agency economists from the major program offices that employ economists. Team members were assigned to the team by each office. Some team members were supervisory economists, while others were not. The team had one year to complete the curriculum. Team members were expected to complete the work in addition to their normal work duties. In addition, no specific budget was provided for this project making the actual costs to the agency difficult to accurately calculate. The primary costs were the individual team members' work time. This varied by team member and we collected no data on the hours that individual team member's spent on the project, although no more than five hours a month per team member was anticipated at the beginning of the project and this proved to be the case. Neither the project sponsors nor other agency leaders required that a return-on-investment (ROI) calculation be provided by the team regarding the project. Unfortunately, no such data are currently available.

Given that the benefits of the curriculum are not linked to an easy-to-identify performance increase, such as increased sales, it might have proven difficult to calculate the dollar value of such benefits. In addition, the notion of user design is built on a premise of long-term returns that will take many years to realize as well as ease of implementation of this and other innovations, which is a difficult thing to measure within a short time after a user design has been undertaken. One of the primary benefits may be improved employee productivity that results from having an easily accessible program for professional growth and development but such a productivity increase would be difficult to calculate in robust ways even if such data could be easily collected. Isolating the percentage the curriculum would have contributed to a productivity increase would be problematic. Finally, the agency would likely not have approved the additional costs of collecting of such data since the curriculum was developed internally with existing resources not specifically earmarked for the project.

The team leader had seen previous efforts at developing curricula fail to be adopted and was seeking a different design approach that would more deeply engage the team members in the development process leading to an economist curriculum that better reflected their needs. He hoped that such a design process would improve adoption and diffusion of the resulting curriculum throughout the agency. User design provides such a process. It empowers frontline stakeholders, or users, to design their own systems and innovation by shifting the power and decision making to them and away from an expert designer. User empowerment leads to designs that reflect their needs and desires rather than those of the expert. Since users act as co-designers, it leads to designs that are more likely to be fully adopted by users. While user-*centered* design also accounts for the user needs, this user-centered approach does not engage the users in powerful ways. The agency was looking for a process that would really engage users in the hopes that it would produce a more adoptable final product. It is truly their design. Naturally, user design does not work for all design projects. The team leader needed to assess the probability of success for a user designed economist curriculum.

User Design Questions

Carr-Chellman (2007) posed seven questions for individuals who might be interested in utilizing a user design process. The project leader assessed the feasibility of developing the economist curriculum through user design. These questions may be used to ascertain whether user design might provide a suitable design process for an organization.

Is Leadership Secure? Are They Able to Consider Power Sharing?

There were two separate groups of leaders of concern to the team. The agency's Human Resources Governing Board (HRGB) sponsored the curriculum design project. The Associate Commissioners from each agency office comprise the HRGB and are the most senior agency leaders. The leaders from the HRGB that were most interested in the curriculum project were from the five agency offices that employ economists. The HRGB functioned primarily as a steering and oversight committee, although as the project unfolded they did provide important contributions. The HRGB expressed support for sharing power and allowing the team to conduct its design work without significant managerial interference or micromanagement. Organizational culture favored the prospects for user design. At the agency, interagency teams often conduct critical work rather than outsourcing such work to outside experts or consultants.

The leaders within the administrative and human resources offices for whom the team leader worked comprised a second group of leaders with whom the design team had to interact. This leadership group was more likely to interject into the working of the group. Early on in the process they had a direct impact through approval of the team's draft charter and recommendations of potential team members. They reserved the right to review ideas and the curriculum drafts that the team produced. In the case of both the HRGB and agency administrative and human resources offices, the team leader concluded that the leadership was generally secure with a user design approach. In addition, a culture of team-oriented design and problem solving was already well established at the agency.

Are Ready-Made Solutions Unlikely to Be Adopted?
What Is the History of Change in the Organization?

The agency had a recent history with curriculum design. A consultant had been engaged to develop a curriculum for new managers. He worked closely with agency subject matter experts, primarily new supervisors. The consultant has successfully created curricula at other federal government agencies in the past and applied lessons learned from those curricula to the agency's new manager curriculum. There had been a full rollout of the new curriculum but shortly thereafter it became apparent that adoption and diffusion was and continues to be poor. One possible reason was that the curriculum did not fully reflect the agency's culture or experiences with managerial training. Many of the training courses contained within the curriculum were courses with which the consultant was familiar. What may have worked well at other federal agencies did not necessarily resonate with new agency managers. The agency had demonstrated aversions to "ready-made solutions." Several processing systems, including a training registration system and conference room reservation system had been developed in-house rather than procured from vendors. At one point, consideration had been given to engaging an external consultant to assist with the development of the economist curriculum. As mentioned, the agency typically preferred to accomplish tasks through interagency teams and ultimately decided the curriculum would be developed with internal resources.

Regarding organizational change issues, the agency can initiate change when it is needed but might be considered by many to be conservative in this regard. Data users value the stability and reliability of the agency statistical data and the drive to maintain such stability has, at times, been reflected in a culture, which treads carefully when it comes to major changes. User design with its emphasis on bottom-up change initiated by front-line users was culturally well-aligned for the agency.

Is User Resistance High?

User resistance to innovations has often been high at the agency. This was even reflected at the design team's kickoff event where some of the team members expressed some skepticism to the actual need for an economist curriculum. The primary concern was that offices already had their own ways of training their economists and there was concern about usurping local office control. Why was a curriculum suddenly a priority? This skepticism was by no means a team consensus, however. Several team members thought it would be of benefit to the agency's economists.

Is the Problem Systemic?

Problems are systemic when they are holistic, interconnected, and interdependent. The development of the economist curriculum provided a systemic problem for the design team. Five offices were involved. Each of these offices offer their own training programs and informal learning opportunities and reflect their own organizational systems. The curriculum was an attempt to bring together these various systems as well as define interdependencies and common needs across the offices. One might therefore see the economist curriculum as a system connected by the office-level learning programs or supra-systems as Banathy (1968) described it. In addition to this agency-wide dynamic, there were other systems at work. The agency is an extension of the federal government and there are training policies maintained by the U.S. Department of Labor and the U.S. Office of Personnel and Management that in part drove interest in developing a curriculum for economists. Finally, there is the continuing need for reducing training expenditures as a result of budgetary limitations and pressures. This affected the design of the curriculum in that the team members wanted the curriculum to include low-cost and free learning opportunities. These considerations illustrate how interconnected issues were reflected in the curriculum design process.

Is There Sufficient Time (as a Resource and in Actual Deadlines) for the Protracted User Design Process?

The team was granted a year in the project plan to complete the development of the economist curriculum. As it happened this was more than enough time for the team to complete its work.

Are Users Engaged in Their Organization?

The users are engaged at the agency. As had been mentioned, the agency has had a legacy of using interagency teams to conduct substantive work that crosses boundaries, such as the curriculum. In addition, with regard to training and workplace learning many of the offices had already engaged in developing loosely organized training plans for employees. What was lacking was a consistency across offices and a curriculum that reflected general competency development rather than program-specific skills. The fact that the users had been engaged in previous efforts at defining learning opportunities provided a favorable environment for user design efforts to develop the curriculum.

Are Users Already Equipped or Motivated to Gain Design Skills?

A mix of the agency's economists and supervisory economists comprised the design team. Many team members had worked previously on designing or overseeing the design of systems. Two of the team members were responsible for designing training and learning opportunities within their own offices. Whether some of the team members were intrinsically motivated to design was doubtful. Most were asked by their office's leadership to participate on the team and did not volunteer. There was some initial skepticism expressed about the enterprise. When the team leader thanked the members at the kickoff meeting for agreeing to participate on the team a couple of the members quickly corrected him by replying that they had actually been asked by their office leadership to participate.

Shifting Power from Experts to Users

Carr-Chellman (2007) suggested that experts must be willing to accept the shift of power to users if they are to be successful at facilitating a user design group. This means they must release themselves from their own expertise, whether real or perceived. In the case of the agency, the team leader and facilitator was an expert instructional designer who had significant practical and academic expertise in the field. However, when he had previously participated in design teams, he often asserted his expertise and sometimes found that this was not always well-received by other team members. User design provided a way for his design skills to be useful to the team, but these skills would now have to be offered in the spirit of collaboration.

Letting go of the power that comes with expertise was not easy for the facilitator, however. Successful user design requires not only listening to the needs of users but also successfully engaging them to fully participate in the design process as co-designers (Carr-Chellman, 2007). The facilitator accomplished this by providing the resources and tools the team needed to make critical decisions but worked to not impose his own views on what should be in the curriculum or the direction it would take. He provided team members with access to previously developed agency curricula, including curricula designed for new supervisors and mathematical statisticians. Given that the team members did not have expertise in curriculum development, he provided some general articles on workplace curricula but was careful to provide minimal commentary so the team members could make up their own minds regarding the curriculum.

Another role the facilitator played was that of project management leader. He developed a formal project plan with schedule and certain basic ground rules but did not find this incompatible with introducing user design techniques to the design team. User design does not equate with haphazard planning. A user design team can have milestones and due dates and yet retain the creative design-oriented conversations that characterize a user design process. It is in the creative and innovative aspects of a team's work where user design can have its greatest impact.

The Role of Conflict in User Design

Managing differences of opinions is an important part of user design. In fact, conflict is to be expected and even embraced as frontline stakeholders are encouraged to advocate for their ideas and beliefs about the directions for the design (Carr-Chellman, 2007). The facilitator encouraged collaboration and openness of discussion and disagreement. One conflict that the team had to work through was whether to include a requirement status option for the metadata the team created for learning items within the curriculum. This data element would indicate whether a learning opportunity was mandatory, highly recommended, or optional. The facilitator believed adding these data might prove useful for curriculum users. In addition, the learning management system the organization used included a requirement status field. Team members had different opinions, however. Some team members believed it would prove too difficult to categorize what learning was mandatory and what was highly recommended since few offices actually had established policies dealing with this issue. Managers already had the right to assign learning to their subordinates—was there a compelling reason to now include a formal requirement status in the curriculum? Other team members believed it might result in mixed messages being sent to users. What if a course was categorized in the curriculum as mandatory or highly recommended, and then it was not offered, or there were no resources to provide it, or budget authorization to pay for it? There were others who thought it was a good idea to include it in the curriculum. It might provide useful information to the user in manage their career by indicating priorities in their individual learning paths.

In addition, some team members believed that the curriculum could be used to initiate a discussion on training requirements throughout the agency—a discussion that was long overdue in the minds of some team members. It was eventually decided by the team that since no written policy existed for most agency training, it would be best to not include it in the final curriculum. Considering the goal of the curriculum was not to establish new training *policy*, the team conflict surrounding the requirement status element may have resulted in creating fewer problems down the road. User design brings these potential difficulties to the surface and team members can directly address them in the early phases of design. As aforementioned, the facilitator initially thought the inclusion of a requirement status element was a good idea and if he had had the final decision as an expert, it may have ultimately been included in the curriculum.

Whole communities of users should be involved in user design processes extending beyond the design team itself as necessary (Carr-Chellman, 2007). Team members were encouraged to include potential users within their offices contribute directly to the curriculum. Several users were given direct access to the SharePoint site in which the curriculum would be housed to contribute learning items directly and edit existing information. There are advantages to encouraging this activity, especially regarding the fuller inclusion of indigenous knowledge, and disadvantages, such as inconsistency of style and less control over the users' contributions to the curriculum. The facilitator valued the indigenous knowledge that the users brought to the process over maintaining control and accepted the fact that there would be the need later to revise the curriculum lists to ensure consistency of data. This occurred with the economist curriculum. Maintaining tight control over content in the development process is counterproductive for those who intend to engage in user design. Style is less important than content and adoption.

In the case of the economist curriculum, there were areas in which user contributions needed to be revised for consistency of style. For instance, there was inconsistency in how hyperlinks to various online resources were presented in the curriculum lists. These were easy enough to revise and did not change the actual content. There were other areas of consistency in the data that the team had to deal with, including consistent assignment of the defined training type indicator. While these issues did result in additional time being spent revising the curriculum, the team was empowered and did, in fact, include more relevant and useful content in the actual training. User design requires more time than expert-driven design processes in which an expert designer controls all aspects of the design rather than engaging users as fellow co-designers, but the time spent during design phases can be more than made up for in effective and efficient adoption of a close-to-design solution.

User Design Tools

Carr-Chellman (2007) described five tools that are available to use by user design teams. These tools are not necessarily unique to user design but offer many advantages in producing a design. The five tools include ethnography, design-based research, scenario-based user design, cooperative design, and action research. The selection of which tool to use depends largely upon the design goals and what process will work best for the team in meeting those goals. Selection of appropriate tools is one area where a facilitator's knowledge might prove useful. One of facilitator's critical roles in user design is to introduce design tools to the team and assist them, as necessary, with the selection of the appropriate tool for the situation (Carr-Chellman, 2007). Ethnography emphasizes understanding the cultural interactions of participants in a group or culture (Wolcott, 2008). Ethnographers use techniques such as observation and open-ended interviews to assess these interactions. Ethnography can be particularly useful in user design for understanding workplace interactions or processes. Design-based research incorporates techniques of experimental research undertaken throughout the design process with an emphasis on measurement and refining the design as a result of what is discovered (Carr-Chellman, 2007). Design-based research engages users as co-researchers in the process of design and empowers them in ways not common in expert-driven design.

Scenario-based user design combines two streams of futuristic planning, scenario planning and scenario design (Carr-Chellman, 2007). User design teams work with stakeholders to plan out various scenarios for developing innovations. This tool is particularly useful when expansive stakeholder input is needed to map out a future for an organization. Such engagement provides user design teams with the ability to spot and address potential blind spots in a design (Carr-Chellman, 2007).While these three tools may have proved useful to the design team, the team leader working with the team decided that what they offered to the team did not directly address the team's user design objectives. It was the remaining two user design tools—action research and cooperative design— that proved more useful to the design team given its needs.

In the development of the economist curriculum, the design team used two of the five tools—action research and cooperative design. To analyze and evaluate what was needed in the curriculum, the team incorporated an action research approach. Action research is useful in that it provides a way to draw in information and ideas for moving forward that are bottom-up from the users, thus ensuring that their voices are heard and the direction is agreed upon (Park, 1993). Action research is a tool associated with an Organization Development approach and is differentiated from Human Performance Technology (HPT) which is largely expert-driven, relying on users serving primarily as subject matter experts rather than as co-designers in the process. It may represent a *user-centered* approach but is not a user design approach. As Carr-Chellman (2007) pointed out, user-*centered* design approaches should not be confused with user design—in user-centered approaches there is no fundamental shift in power away from an expert to the users.

The Process of User Design

Once the appropriateness of user design was determined and the likely tools scoped out, the facilitator entered the process with his design team with no preconceptions of how the design should unfold. Given that many of the team members, including the facilitator himself, had never designed a curriculum, there was initially a sense of discovery and sorting things out. The existing project plan mentioned an analysis phase but the details were left vague so the users themselves could work through the process and decide for themselves what they wanted to explore further. The facilitator provided team members with selected resources, including access to existing agency curricula and an article on curricula in workplace learning. In addition, there had been one ground rule established by the sponsors of the project—learning items in the curriculum had to be linked to the existing Economist Competency model. This model was provided to all team members as well as information on competency development. Team members would need to link all of their learning content with the twelve competencies found in the competency model.

As the discussion unfolded, it was discovered that most of the offices already had economist training plans available. Many offices had developed training plans as a requirement for a defunct program, the Federal Career Intern Program (FCIP). This program was designed to hire recent college graduates into the federal government as interns and provide them with extensive development opportunities, both formal and informal, during the two-year internship program. The team agreed that these FCIP plans would provide an initial, if somewhat incomplete, basis for the development of their individual office curriculum lists. Team members agreed to reach out to their offices to gather any existing FCIP plans to analyze and use.

Another issue that the team dealt with in their initial analysis was the scope of the curriculum. Previous curricula had focused on formal training opportunities, including internal training, external vendors, and academic coursework at local universities. The agency had a reputation for providing funding for external training and many of their economists had academic coursework funded by the agency. This generosity had been reflected in the curricula for new supervisors and mathematical statisticians with an emphasis on the inclusion of expensive academic and vendor courses. Some team members questioned this approach. First, some of the resources on workplace curricula development emphasized the importance of pathways to development within the flow of work as an important consideration in the development of workplace curricula. Second, some team members reflected upon the importance and inclusion of on-the-job training occurring within their own offices, including required readings, structured work activities, and coaching and mentoring. Similarly, team members recognized the wide array of more informal learning opportunities available at the agency, including seminars, conferences, user groups, project team activities, among others. Third, there was the issue of budget. At the time of design, the agency training budgets had been declining over that prior few years and they were unlikely to rebound. This reflected the larger systems that were at work in the federal government and needed to be reflected in the curriculum if it were to prove realistic. It would make little sense to design a curriculum consisting of expensive external training opportunities if there was going to be no money to pay for it. The team opted to design a curriculum with a more expansive scope than had been created previously that would reflect both what actually happens in their offices and emerging budget realities. The curriculum would be grounded in the current work in the offices, as opposed to reflecting an expensive training wish list or a new vision of what learning might be in a perfect world. The team would include both formal learning as well as informal learning already occurring in the offices and agency-wide.

An issue regarding scope was the organization of the curriculum itself and the individual learning opportunities that would be included in the curriculum. It was obvious from the team discussions that there was significant office-specific training occurring. Different offices maintained different requirements for its economists. In some offices, for instance, analytical and statistical skills were of prime importance, while in other offices writing skills might be paramount. The competency model was holistic regarding the range of skills needed by economists but did not necessarily reflect skills that were emphasized in each office. It was evident that the curriculum needed to reflect an office-centric and agency-wide approach. Thus the curriculum had to balance the needs of individual offices as well as the entire agency. The team decided that each office would have its own curriculum list. The team also believed that there were more general skills reflected in the competency model that all economists needed and crossed office boundaries, including writing skills, interpersonal skills, decision making skills, and oral communication. As a result, the design team determined that the curriculum should also reflect these agency-wide skills. At this point in the design process, the team opted to separate the curriculum between office-specific lists and an agency-wide list of learning opportunities. The user could then use both lists to meet their overall professional development needs.

In terms of data to include in the curriculum, the team began by assessing previously designed curricula. The facilitator introduced the Learning Management System (LMS) used by the agency for learning administration and management. There was not a legacy of its use at the agency but it did provide a list of useful metadata and with a possible push toward using the LMS at the agency level, it was seen by the team to be beneficial to incorporate some of its data elements into the curriculum. Some of the team members were not convinced about the benefits of drawing upon the LMS for data elements. One data element the team believed would be very useful was a "cost indicator" that would indicate whether a learning item cost money or was cost free. In the end, the team agreed upon a list of data to include, most of which was drawn from the LMS data elements. Some elements, such as the requirement status element mentioned previously, resulted in disagreement among team members and much discussion and further exploration of all of the systemic factors at work. It was this sort of in-depth conversation within the user design process that resulted in increased conflicts during the design stage, but better adoption rates later in the process.

Another topic discussed in the assessment phase that the team grappled with was the platform to be used to deliver the curriculum to the end user. They considered the new supervisors' curriculum, developed in Microsoft Word, and the mathematical statistician's curriculum, which was developed using Microsoft Excel. Given the shape of the curriculum with its lists of learning opportunities, one of the team members discussed her office's successful use of Microsoft SharePoint in creating lists of information. SharePoint had a presence at the agency but some offices used it more than others, so it was not immediately as familiar to all team members. The list function was not as familiar to the facilitator. The team member provided other members with access to the site to view. One thing it had in its favor was the ability to sort and filter data included in the lists. The team believed this ability would enhance the user's experience with the data, in that they would be able to better customize the information to meet their individual needs. For instance, if a user just wanted to view no-cost learning opportunities it could be filtered so only that element would display. This flexibility had considerable appeal to the team. For these reasons, the team opted to use SharePoint as the curriculum platform. The facilitator created a SharePoint site to house the curriculum and assigned team members as site "owners" who could add information to and revise the curriculum as they desired.

There was one other point during the assessment phase that several team members made clear— they asked for a plan to be included for maintaining the curriculum. They expressed concern that once the curriculum was completed, the learning data included in it would not be regularly maintained and updated. This had been the case with previous design efforts and had been the source of consternation for some team members. SharePoint would provide a good platform for regular updates. Unlike using Word or Excel there would be no versioning issues for the user. A maintenance plan would be developed by the team as part of the project, and it was included by the facilitator in the formal project plan.

Using action research methods, the team created a design plan for the economist curriculum. The process took about a month. It was a user-driven plan that incorporated user ideas, needs, and data directly into the plan that team members could eventually agree to. Furthermore, using action research allowed potential issues to be brought up for discussion early on in the design process rather than later. This created unforeseen efficiencies in the project plan. With the initial assessment completed and a design plan in place, the team shifted its focus to the development of the curriculum.

The facilitator provided the team members administrative access to the SharePoint site that would house the curriculum. This would empower the team members to develop their own office's curriculum lists. In order to provide development flexibility it was decided that development would occur in phases based on each office. Offices either had one team member or two depending on the size of the office. Team members worked with stakeholders within their own offices throughout the duration of the project. The team members estimated that each office would need approximately a month of development time to complete their individual office-level lists, and this was built into the overall project plan. Team members gathered information from their fellow co-workers on training and other learning opportunities, including the FCIP plans that existed within each office. The team leader took the lead in compiling the agency-wide curriculum list working closely with the team members. He also took the lead in compiling a list of resources that would be linked to a resources page. Team members were encouraged to review and make changes directly to the SharePoint lists as necessary.

In addition to Action Research, which the team members used to conduct the analysis and suggest the design for the project, the team utilized a cooperative design process in developing the curriculum in SharePoint. Carr-Chellman (2007) described the cooperative design process in user design as a process connected to software and information systems in which the users directly create the design using tools that are already familiar to them. In this respect, power shifts to the users from the expert designer. For example, SharePoint was suggested by a team member and many of the team members were familiar with the software. Cooperative design as a user design tool incorporates future workshops, mock-ups, and prototyping (Carr-Chellman, 2007). In this case, team members developed the curriculum directly into an empty SharePoint site established to house the curriculum.

Initially, access to the SharePoint site was limited to the team members. Eventually, however, team members asked that others from their offices be given access to both review and comment on the emerging curriculum as well as directly enter data into the lists. This expanded the pool of user co-designers beyond the individual team members. The facilitator believed this enhanced the benefits of user design by having the design in the direct hands of even more users. There were potential pitfalls in this approach as well. As it turned out, team members had to return to the curriculum and revise the data entered by those outside the team to ensure consistency. While this took time, it ultimately resulted in a final product that was better grounded in the indigenous knowledge of the end users. There was another benefit to having an extended group of end users actively participate in the design process and put their collective imprint on the final curriculum. It served to help market the curriculum and increase end user consciousness about its potential benefits and this ultimately proved useful in the curriculum's launch.

There were several ways in which the direction of the curriculum design was influenced by user design. Early on, the team had decided that each office would have its own "splash" page on the site. A description of the office would be provided on the page along with links to each curriculum list within the office, most of which were provided at the division level. About half-way through the design process, one of the team members recommended that each curriculum be linked from the home page of the site. The other members of the team agreed and further exploration indicated that links to each list could be linked to and from a dropdown menu on the top menu bar of the home page.

This led to a discussion about whether a splash page was needed or even desired or whether it would be more efficient to have users access the lists in a single click of the mouse. The result was the splash pages were eliminated and the lists were directly linked to from the site's homepage. This led to a more streamlined design that the users on the team all agreed was better for the end user.

Team members engaged directly in the process in other ways as well. The team leader had to brief the team's sponsor group comprised of senior leaders within the organization, twice during the development phase. In both instances, he brought a member of the team along to ensure that the leaders understood the importance of the team members to the process and the user driven nature of the development. In both instances, the team members spoke at the meetings, providing important input and context regarding the project. This active engagement by frontline users made a good impression on the organization's leaders who provided continuing support for the project. Even agency leaders participated in the design process. One such leader provided valuable input and specific recommendations for items to add to the curriculum. In one case, the leader provided the names of several agency advisory groups that regularly meet to discuss agency work. The scheduled meetings of these groups provided a great opportunity for employees to learn more about how outside organizations use the agency's data.

As the final curriculum began to take shape, the team members were encouraged to have co-workers within their offices review the draft curriculum and make further recommendations. The facilitator provided the reviewers with direct access to the draft SharePoint curriculum lists. In some cases, they provided feedback that could be incorporated later, and in other cases, the reviewers made revisions directly to the SharePoint lists. Team members reviewed the revisions for consistency, but allowing these users to access the curriculum engaged them directly in the cooperative design process.

The team developed a communications plan that was implemented as the final curriculum was released to the agency at large. One potential benefit of user design is improved adoption and diffusion of innovations (Carr-Chellman, 2007). Agency curricula that had been previously developed by external experts had languished. While a lack of effective marketing of those curricula may have been part of the problem, it was evident that the curricula had been developed from an outsider's perspective and did not necessarily speak directly to the experiences and needs of the agency's economists. These consultants had done their due diligence in working with subject matter experts to assess needs, but the resulting curricula did not fully reflect the indigenous knowledge and organizational culture of the users. In the case of the economist curriculum, it was found that since so many users had had direct and indirect input in its creation, there was a strong sense of ownership of the curriculum. Several examples given here support the finding that the curriculum at the agency that was engaged through user design better reflected the culture of the agency in both style and substance.

The Aftermath of the User Design Process

The curriculum has now been in use for over a year. Due to technical limitations in the installation of SharePoint at the agency, it has been difficult to accurately assess how many have actually accessed it. The agency intends to ask users about their familiarity and use of the curriculum on a future training needs assessment. However, anecdotal evidence exists that there had been significant and ongoing interest in the new curriculum. As soon as the curriculum was launched, several agency offices asked the office responsible for the curriculum to demonstrate the curriculum for their employees. When a focus group of supervisors was convened to discuss training and development during an audit, the topic they raised as wanting more information on was the economist curriculum.

Carr-Chellman (2007) pointed out that one of the disadvantages of user design processes is that on occasion negative issues may result. One issue that arose after the curriculum was launched was the lack of accessibility of the new curriculum for disabled learners. The facilitator was aware of the need to develop an accessible site and based on what he knew it was, but he also believed it needed to be looked at more closely by someone with more expertise in the area of accessibility. The agency employed an outside consultant to assess the accessibility and ultimately make changes to make the site more accessible. This was an instance where expertise in a specific area would have made a positive difference in the final design. The team should have perhaps solicited this expertise during the development phase. For future development projects, this will serve as a lesson learned. It is important to point out that while this expertise would have been useful, the resulting curriculum was easily fixed for this issue and the participation of an expert who would have focused on this issue throughout the process may have stunted the overall team process and their feelings of deep empowerment. Our sense is that while some experts may be consulted by a user design team during the process, it is best not to include them on the design team for fear that they may usurp the user design process.

While the overall conclusion reached by the facilitator was that user design worked well in developing the economist curriculum, it was not necessarily a perfect example of user design. There were various levels of interest among team members, not all were wholly engaged as co-designers. Carr-Chellman (2007) pointed out that sometimes users prefer a more passive role and are not excited about engaging in user design processes. Not all were necessarily ready from the beginning to assume the responsibility for design, although as the project advanced the team members gradually took ownership over the design of their own office curriculum lists. In some rare instances, the facilitator needed to provide more direction and support than he would have liked. Some of the team members were busy with their own work projects, and the facilitator assisted them when he could do so. While most of the design decisions were driven by the team members, there were instances where certain ground rules were established, including the notion that the curriculum be based on the economist competency model.

Finally, while the leadership was supportive of using a user design process, it was critical that enough time was provided to implement user design in this case. A formal project plan and schedule were developed and approved by the sponsors of the team and it is unclear whether significantly more time would have been available to the team if it had fallen far behind schedule in completing its work. Those who plan to incorporate user design into their development projects should ensure that they have enough time approved by their leadership from the start of the project. One of the benefits of user design is that it provides participants with interesting work to do and exposes them to new ideas and skills (Carr-Chellman, 2007). There were a few of the team members that were not necessarily initially keen to participate in the project. They had been assigned to the team by their offices. After the team had completed its work, some of these team members expressed to the facilitator how much they learned by working on the project.

Comparisons with Human Performance Technology (HPT)

There are similarities and significant differences between user design process and HPT. Carr-Chellman (2007) pointed out that both user design and HPT are systemic in nature, emphasizing interconnectness and interdependence, as well as putting the user at the center of innovations. The critical difference, however, is that in HPT processes there is no shift of actual power to the front line user with systems theory primarily serving as a way for the HPT consultant to understand the various connections that may help define performance gaps (Carr-Chellman, 2007). Users may be active participants in the HPT design process but ultimately important design decisions, from assessment to prescriptions, remain in the hands of the consultant. This may be an example of user-centered design that falls short of user design in that the power remains with the designer. In addition, Carr-Chellman (2007) argued that companies that are performance-oriented may not readily adapt to user design processes due to the fact that such companies may not want to invest the significant time it often takes to effectively employ user design and may eschew the conflict among users that often occurs. In addition, the leadership of such companies may not be secure in shifting power to users.

Other change intervention strategies are more similar in approach to user design. Organization Development (OD) emphasizes ground up change processes for instance. In OD processes, users themselves define gaps in performance and prescribe interventions to close those gaps or define new opportunities (Rothwell & Sullivan, 2005). Action research, and early OD process, is a tool that can be useful in implementing user design (Carr-Chellman, 2007). Other methods of OD, such as Appreciative Inquiry, emphasize empowerment of the frontline stakeholder to assess problems and design their own interventions (Cooperrider & Whitney, 1999). These types of interventions align more closely with user design processes than expert-driven approaches.

User design is also compared with other design processes, such as Instructional Design (ID). In the field of ID a great deal of emphasis is placed upon successfully working with subject matter experts (SMEs). The designer, while using the information that SMEs provide to inform the resulting designs, maintains control over the design and often it reflects the skills of the designer. ID processes tend to be more linear than user design although both processes can be iterative as well (Carr-Chellman, 2007). In user design much of the early stages are devoted to the team deciding what the design process may be instead of incorporating a pre-defined process such as ID.

Reflections of the Facilitator

The facilitator of the economist curriculum user design team was an instructional designer, who had designed training for many years. Switching to a user design process for the curriculum project represented a complete shift in perspective for the facilitator. He was used to controlling the project and took pride in his creativity as a designer as well as his ability to work productively with SMEs. Although he enjoyed and took great pride in his work as an instructional designer over the years, he recognized the limits of designing instruction for others. Having served on other teams charged with designing training, he had seen firsthand the resentment that some stakeholders experience when an expert designer, no matter how well-intentioned, pushes certain design concepts or processes on others. This often created a wall between designer and stakeholder. Conversely, when he recommended certain tools to the team that might be useful to overcome a design problem, the team would welcome such assistance. This reflected the user design facilitators' role as a provider of resources. For the facilitator, this meant giving up a certain amount of control over the design but still making use of his acquired skills to assist team members when he could.

The facilitator had also seen previous curricula designed by experts fail to be fully adopted by users. A few years before, a curriculum had been developed for new supervisors. A highly regarded consultant who had developed curricula for other organizations was brought in to develop the curriculum. The consultant worked closely with stakeholders and subject matter experts to develop a curriculum that would meet their interests and expressed a desire to put the users' needs at the center of his design. He clearly respected the priorities of the users. However, the users in this instance deferred to the consultant in allowing him to drive the design process. As a result, the curriculum may have reflected learning opportunities that had worked well in other organizations but did not necessarily reflect what was needed or would work at the agency. The curriculum contained several expensive courses that would ultimately prove difficult for many offices to afford under most circumstances. In addition, the curriculum was completely comprised of formal training opportunities, a fact about which a prominent stakeholder expressed concern. Once rolled out, the training office promoted the curriculum but it never really was adopted by users and continues to languish. On the surface, it was well-designed, with user input, but designed by an expert rather than by the critical stakeholders—the users. While a causal relationship cannot be established that this approach was the cause for a lack of adoption of the curriculum, the facilitator believed that it contributed heavily to the lack of adoption. For this reason, he opted for a radically different approach to design, and this led him to user design.

CURRENT CHALLENGES FACING THE ORGANIZATION

The curriculum has been available to economists for over a year. Whether it will eventually be fully adopted in the agency remains to be seen but initial assessments indicate that it has been more accepted that previous curriculum design efforts. A recent training program needs assessment conducted at the agency indicated that 15.8 percent of the agency's economists had viewed the economist curriculum with 73 percent of those respondents indicating that they found the information contained with the curriculum somewhat or very useful. Several comments provided by respondents indicated that the content is useful in their own professional development. Some respondents indicated that they would like more ways of tracking their progress in completing learning items contained within the curriculum. It is important to note we have not established a specific benchmark to compare the percentage of viewers with. The assumption is the curriculum is a tool that can be accessed on an as needed basis for development information. In this respect, we differentiate it from other types of performance support that would be accessed within the flow of work. We do not anticipate that most agency economists will regularly need to access the curriculum. Of more interest was the fact that 73 percent of those who did access the curriculum found the information to be at least somewhat useful to them. The response of agency *leaders* overall has generally been positive, although one senior leader indicated some confusion as to the ultimate purpose of the curriculum. As a result, there will be a renewed effort to provide information to supervisors and employees about the benefits of the curriculum as it applies to employee development.

One challenge the design team encountered concerned the SharePoint platform that was used to develop the curriculum. There was no feasible way in the agency's installation of SharePoint to track visits to the site, making tracking usage of the new system unfortunately difficult. Members of the design team insisted on putting a maintenance plan in place to accommodate changes and updates to the curriculum lists and resources. While updates have indeed been made as they have unfolded, a more systematic approach will likely be needed to ensure the ongoing accuracy and relevancy of the curriculum.

SOLUTIONS AND RECOMMENDATIONS

In the instance of maintaining the curriculum site, the facilitator recommended a regular maintenance schedule in which managers would be asked to review items in the curriculum and provide the facilitators with the necessary updates to keep the site current. Thus far, this procedure has not yet been implemented but updating has occurred when information has been provided by offices. There are concerns about burdening managers with such a task. Consideration was also given by the design team to create a maintenance team that would periodically review the site and provide updates. Eventually, the team opted against a maintenance team due to time burdens that may be placed upon team members. The curriculum site itself does provide contact information for those who want to request updates, and some in the offices have done just that. For instance, one unit that had their own curriculum list was eliminated due to budgetary reductions. The facilitator was informed by employees in that office and immediately eliminated the unit's curriculum list from the site.

Incorporating a user design approach to develop a workplace curriculum enabled the agency to complete the curriculum on time and with maximal input from stake-holders at each phase of the process, from assessment through design and launch. The process itself resulted in design-oriented conversations that built support from potential users at each step and uncovered potential problems that were addressed by team members as the curriculum was developed. Users throughout the agency were eagerly anticipating the launch of the curriculum in part because many of them had a direct input into its creation. For these reasons, user design provides organizations with a powerful alternative to expert-driven design processes.

REFERENCES

Banathy, B. H. (1968). *Instructional systems*. Palo Alto, California: Fearon Publishers.

Carr-Chellman, A. A. (2007). *User design*. Mahwah, New Jersey: Lawrence Erl-baum Associates.

Cooperrider, D. L., & Whitney, D. (1999). Appreciative inquiry: A positive revolution in change. In P. Holman & T. Devane (Eds.), *The change handbook* (pp. 245–261). San Francisco: Berrett-Koehler.

Park, P. (1993). What is participatory research? A theoretical and methodological perspective. In M. Brydon-Miller, B. Hall, T. Jackson, & P. Park (Eds.), *Voices of change: Participatory research in the United States and Canada* (pp. 1–19). West-port, CT: Bergin & Garvey.

Rothwell, W. J., & Sullivan, R. L. (2005). Organization development. In W. J. Rothwell & R. Sullivan (Eds.), *Practicing organization development* (pp. 9–38). San Francisco: Pfeiffer.

Wolcott, H. F. (2008). *Ethnography: A way of seeing*. Lanham, MD: AltaMira Press.

ADDITIONAL READING

Banathy, B. H. (1973). *Developing a system view of education: The systems-model approach*. Belmont, CA: Seigler/Feraron.

Banathy, B. H. (1991). *Educational systems design: A journey to create the future*. Englewood Cliffs, NJ: Educational Technology Publications.

Banathy, B. H. (1992). Comprehensive systems design in education: Building a design culture in education. *Educational Technology, 22*(3), 33–35.

Billett, S. (2006). Constituting the workplace curriculum. *Journal of Curriculum Studies, 38*(1), 31–48. doi:10.1080/00220270500153781

Boulding, K. E. (1985). *The world as a total system*. Beverly Hills: Sage.

Carr, A. A. (1994). Community participation in systemic educational change. *Educational Technology, 34*(1), 43–50.

Carr, A. A. (1995). Stakeholder participation in systemic change: Cornerstones to continuous school improvement. In P. Jenlink (Ed.), *Systemic change: Touchstones for the future school* (pp. 71–85). Palatine, IL: Skylight.

Carr, A. A. (1997). User-design in the creation of human learning systems. *Educational Technology Research and Development, 45*(3), 5–22. doi:10.1007/BF02299726

Carr-Chellman, A. A., Cuyar, C., & Breman, J. (1998). User-design: A case application in health care training. *Educational Technology Research and Development, 46*(4), 97–114. doi:10.1007/BF02299677

Carr-Chellman, A. A., & Savoy, M. S. (2003). Using the user-design research for building school communities. *School Community Journal, 13*(2), 99–118.

Checkland, P. (1999). *Systems thinking, systems practice*. Chichester, England: Wiley.

Hutchins, C. L. (1996). *Systemic thinking: Solving complex problems*. Aurora, CO: Professional Development Systems.

Jenlink, P. M. (1995). *Systemic change: Touchstones for the future school. Palatine.* IL: Skylight.

Jenlink, P. M., Reigeluth, C. M., Carr, A. A., & Miller, L. M. (1998). Guidelines for facilitating systemic change in school districts. *Systems Research and Behavioral Science*, *15*(3), 217–233. doi:10.1002/(SICI)1099-1743(199805/06)15:3<217::AID-SRES223>3.0.CO;2-N

Jordan, R. & Carr-Chellman, A.A. (2014). DIY design, *T+D*, 68(1), 54-58.

Miller, J. G. (1978). *Living systems.* New York: McGraw-Hill.

Ming-Fen, L. (2000). Fostering design culture through cultivating the user-designer's design thinking and systems thinking. Denver, CO: Association for Educational Communications and Technology. (ERIC Document Reproduction Service No. ED4557750).

Rapoport, A. (1996). *General systems theory: Essential concepts and applications.* Cambridge, MA: Abacus Press.

Rogers, E. M. (1995). *Diffusion of innovations.* New York: Free Press.

Rowland, G. (1993). Making change our friend: The design perspective. *Educational Technology*, *33*(7), 29–31.

Senge, P. (1990). *The fifth discipline: The art & practice of the learning organization.* New York: Doubleday.

von Bertalanffy, L. (1968). *General systems theory.* New York: Braziller.

Warfield, J. N. (1994). *A science of generic design: Managing complexity through systems design.* Ames: Iowa State University Press.

Yappa, L. (1996). Innovation diffusion and paradigms of development. In C. Earle, K. Mathewson, & M. Kenzer (Eds.), *Concepts in human geography* (pp. 231–270). Lanham, MD: Rowman & Littlefield.

Zemke, R. (1989). The systems approach: A nice theory but…. In C. Lee (Ed.), *Performance technology* (pp. 19–22). Lakewood Books.

KEY TERMS AND DEFINITIONS

Action Research: A participatory process in which stakeholders define gaps in performance and propose solutions to close gaps and manage organizational change.

Cooperative Design: A process in user design as a process connected to software and information systems in which the users directly create the design using tools that are already familiar to them.

Human Performance Technology: An expert-driven process used to assess whether performance gaps exist and the root causes of such gaps. Possible solutions for closing performance gaps are proposed.

Instructional Design: A systematic process of analyzing, developing, implementing, and evaluating instruction to facilitate learning and performance.

SharePoint: A website that houses the curriculum to be shared with end users.

Systems Theory: Theory that holds that systems in nature are holistic, interconnected and interdependent. If change occurs in one part of a system, other parts of the system are affected as well.

User Design: Design process rooted in systems theory that eliminates the role of an expert designer and places critical design decisions in the hands of frontline stakeholders and users of the resulting design.

Chapter 6

Improving Practice through Non-Instructional Technology Platforms:
A Case for Technology's Role in a Nonprofit Network

Allison M. Bell
University of Illinois at Urbana-Champaign, USA

Andrea Leigh Hernandez
Antioch University, USA

Wenhao David Huang
University of Illinois at Urbana-Champaign, USA

EXECUTIVE SUMMARY

This case study describes the processes and outcomes of intentional efforts to formalize and enable learning, communication, and collaboration in a network of nonprofit practitioners to enhance the capacity and effectiveness of member organizations. After identifying a need for nonprofits in Central Illinois to have increased awareness of others' efforts and work together to a greater extent, a technology-enabled Community of Practice (CoP) was formed to facilitate positive change. After a short period of implementation, an evaluation found that the virtual

DOI: 10.4018/978-1-4666-8330-3.ch006

CoP was valued by members as an important source of learning, networking, and finding resources. Further, intentional efforts to facilitate nonprofit network activities and productivity led to meaningful outcomes in this community and members' performance. This case study serves as a non-instructional Human Performance Technology (HPT) example for consideration by organizations seeking to support informal learning among nonprofit employees and stakeholders in order to improve and sustain members' performance.

ORGANIZATION BACKGROUND

With nearly one million public charities operating that account for 9.2% of all wages and salaries paid in the U.S. (National Center for Charitable Statistics, 2012), the nonprofit sector is being defined by a number of major trends. These trends include demographic shifts that are redefining participation, technological advances, networks that enable new ways to organize work, increased interest in civic engagement and volunteerism, and the blurring of sector boundaries (Gowdy, Hildebrand, La Piana, & Campos, 2010). The convergence of these trends has serious organizational and leadership implications. This case describes how a family foundation supported intentional efforts to formalize and enable informal learning, communication, and collaboration in a network of nonprofit practitioners through a technology-enabled Community of Practice (CoP) for the purpose of enhancing the capacity and effectiveness of member organizations.

The Lumpkin Family Foundation (hereafter the Foundation), based in rural Illinois, has a mission to support people pursuing innovation and long-lasting improvements in the environment, health, education and community access to the arts. They do this in a 16-county region where the wealth of the family was generated through a telecommunications company.

SETTING THE STAGE

As one of the larger foundations outside of the Chicago region, the Foundation realized that in order to make the most impact with their grant dollars, they needed to support capacity building efforts for their nonprofit grantees. Their theory of change was that a vibrant nonprofit sector was one where 1) nonprofits communicate, cooperate, and collaborate, 2) nonprofits have strong management, leadership, and governance, and 3) nonprofits are supported by an invested constituency.

The Foundation recognized the lack of affordable and appropriate professional and organizational development services in the region for nonprofits, including their grantees. In response, they founded the Nonprofit Excellence Program (NEP). Through the NEP, the Foundation offered trainings, conferences, and grants around areas related to nonprofit organizational leadership and development. As a grantmaking entity, however, they did not envision providing direct services for an extended period. The Foundation's intention from the outset had been to build a program whose value would be evident enough that a community partner could be attracted to take on the role of service-provider. After a few years of financially supporting and organizing these efforts internally, the Foundation turned its attention to this transition. They retained a consultant to determine how the NEP could be effectively embedded in the community.

The consultant recommended the creation of a nonprofit resource center to be located at a local university and endowed by the Foundation. Although the recommendation aligned with the Foundation's early expectations for the transition, the Foundation reached a different conclusion from the consultant's findings. The Foundation's board concluded that a focused investment in a single institution overvalued the underlying interest of the local university and failed to fully appreciate the resources and geographic reach of other organizations in the region that had started to provide capacity building services since the NEP was established. An alternative solution was desired that would better align with the Foundation's theory of change.

Four key concepts and trends converged to inform how the Foundation progressed toward their goal of achieving a vibrant nonprofit sector: 1) capacity building, 2) networked governance, 3) nonprofit collaboration, and 4) networked community of practice, shown in Figure 1. Each concept contributes to nonprofit effectiveness and influenced how the Foundation and their partners thought and acted as the project progressed.

Capacity Building

The Foundation sought to develop capacity mainly through trainings of nonprofits on topics of interest and microgrants to nonprofits in the region for staff or board development activities like trainings, strategy and marketing plans, or technology upgrades. Although previous definitions considered capacity building as organizational activities to improve and fulfill organizations' mission (Backer, 2000; Connolly & Lukas, 2002; Eisinger, 2002), recent findings broaden the scope to encompass the organizational knowledge, systems, processes, and people that contribute to the organization's ability to produce, perform, or deploy resources to achieve its mission at an optimal level (Kapucu, Healy & Arslan, 2011). Capacity-building activities can range from a small to large outcome, discrete internal visibility to explicit external

Figure 1. Nonprofit effectiveness performance opportunities

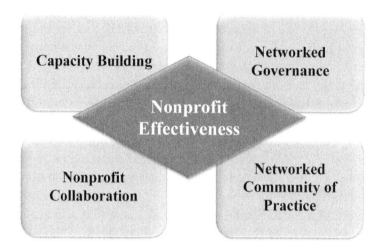

visibility, or short-lived versus long-term (Light & Hubbard, 2002). Milen (2001) identified several key factors for successful capacity-building programs including building ownership and self-reliance, practicing genuine and long-term partnerships, understanding the context of capacity, examining capacity from a strategic and systems perspective, and exercising process thinking in all phases of capacity-building. Further, effective capacity development should meet the demands of change (Milen, 2001). In this sense, capacity-building is multidimensional and an ongoing process of improvement that must fit the cultural, political, historical and economic context of the individual organization (Loza, 2004). Light (2004) divided capacity building activities into four groups:

- **External Relations:** Collaboration, mergers, strategic planning, fundraising, and media relations.
- **Internal Structure:** Reorganizations, team building, adding staff, staff diversity, rainy day fund, and fund for new ideas.
- **Leadership:** Board development, leadership development, succession planning, change in leadership, and greater delegation.
- **Management Systems:** Information technology, accounting systems, personnel system, staff training, evaluation, organizational assessment, and outcomes measurement.

These encompass areas identified by other researchers as needed for high performance nonprofits: mission, vision, and strategy; governance and leadership; administration; program delivery and impact; strategic relationships, resource development; program development, fundraising, human resources, systems and infrastructure, culture, and internal operations (Connolly & Lukas, 2002; Linnell, 2003; McKinsey & Company, 2001). By increasing organizational capacity, organizational performance is enhanced, which enables a nonprofit to more effectively and efficiently achieve its mission (Eisinger, 2002; Kapucu et al., 2011).

Networked Governance

During this time, the Foundation's staff and board were reading *The Spider & the Starfish: The Unstoppable Power of Leaderless Organizations* (Brafman & Beckstrom, 2008) which informed ways to best sustain the NEP. Nonprofit resource centers historically had relied on a single host (i.e., a "spider") and were funded narrowly to provide client service to a small audience, and elimination of funding led to program termination. Alternatively, a starfish approach is less dependent on any single participant or funder and values participants as users and providers of services through a network. Board members were inspired and interested in how they could apply the starfish / network approach to sustaining the capacity-building work in the NEP region.

Networks of organizations are becoming the new structure of governance for nonprofits as they bring more opportunities to increase community capacity (Gazley, 2008; Koliba, Meek & Zia, 2010; Provan & Kenis, 2008, Renz, 2010). Nonprofits have used a variety of structures including inter-organizational alliances, coalitions, collaborations and partnerships, and can be sector-based, location-based or issue/topic-based. Milward and Provan (2006) identified four types of public networks: 1) *service implementation networks* consisting of intergovernmental programs that provide services directly to clients, 2) *information diffusion networks* focused on sharing and disseminating information, 3) *problem solving networks* that solve a problem or crisis or lead to policy change, and 4) *community capacity-building networks* that build social capital to make communities more resilient. Regardless of the purpose or strength of these network linkages, value is derived (Granovetter, 1973).

Nonprofit Collaboration

Another concept that was informing the Foundation's decision making was nonprofit collaboration. Through a number of grants, the Foundation had brought together executive directors and mission-specific organizations to build their relationships between one another and work together collaboratively. One example was supporting three environmental organizations to pursue a joint fundraising initiative. Nonprofit collaboration is "what occurs when different nonprofit organizations work together to address problems through joint effort resources, and decision making and share ownership of the final product or service" (Guo & Acar, 2005, p. 342-3). Collaboration has a role in capacity building for nonprofits (Stone, Crosby, & Bryson, 2010). If nonprofit leaders are going to maintain and generate funding in an environment of rapid economic shifts, globalization, and other changes impacting nonprofit stability, they must not compete but collaborate and pull together resources to stabilize all those involvement (Mann, 2012). As nonprofits collaborate, build relationships, and discuss ideas, facilitation or resource sharing can happen.

The Foundation and the nonprofits they supported experienced at some level all of Austin's (2000) four categories of benefits of successful collaborations including: (1) cost savings, (2) economies of scale and scope, (3) synergies, and (4) revenue enhancement. Larger projects, programs, and goals may be accomplished at a smaller cost per organization within a group of nonprofits where the leaders are focused on collaborative efforts. Further, these collaborations will find access to greater resources and expertise. The synergy created among the diverse background of the collaboration leaders outweighs the risks. This potential shared risk and success that leads to higher satisfaction and revenue outweighs potential external pressures and loss. Collaboration has a clear impact on management, program and client outcomes (Selden & Sowa, 2006). For example, it can increase the resources available to a nonprofit from partner organizations (Cairns & Harris, 2011). The Foundation realized that in order to spur nonprofit collaboration on a wider scale, they needed nonprofit leaders to build relationships with one another and intentionally devote time and energy needed to develop nonprofit collaborations.

Networked Community of Practice

A final concept relevant to this case is networked community of practice (hereafter also abbreviated as CoP). Organizational and educational literature in recent years has emphasized social learning situated within a particular context of practice. The concept of CoP emerged from studies by Lave and Wenger (1991) who proposed that most learning is informal and situated in social interactions. Learning is driven by tasks and participation in an enterprise, and includes varying degrees of identity change as participants "become" what they are practicing (Jorgensen & Keller, 2008; Lave & Wenger, 1991). In this view, learning is emergent, based upon opportunities to participate in the practice of a community, and develop an identity with it, all of which enhance belonging and commitment (Handley, Sturdy, Fincham, & Clark, 2006).

Individuals belong to numerous communities of practice, which are of multiple sizes, visibilities, locations, organizational boundaries, and degrees of institutionalization (Wenger et al., 2002). Belonging in a CoP is a matter of mutual engagement, joint enterprise, and shared repertoire. Mutual engagement means that "people are engaged in actions whose meanings they negotiate with one another" (Wenger, 1998, p. 73). Members define and negotiate the joint enterprise through a process of ongoing interactions. Over time, a shared repertoire, which "includes routines, words, tools, ways of doing things, stories, gestures, symbols, genres, actions, or concepts that the community has produced or adopted in the course of its existence" (Wenger, 1998, p. 83). These communities "become informally bound by the value they find in learning together" (Wenger et al., 2002, p. 5), and social processes sustain and perpetuate practice (Retna & Ng, 2010). What tends to bring members together and sustain them over time is voluntary commitment to pursuit of common interests and learning embedded in work (Ellis, Oldridge, & Vasconcelos, 2004).

The nature of CoPs makes them prime spaces for informal learning among participants. In contrast with formal learning which is typically sponsored, planned, and intentional, informal learning is typically intentional but not highly structured (Marsick & Watkins, 2001). CoPs have enabled informal learning in several different settings including adult learning councils (Gray, 2004), business consultancies (Handley, Sturdy, Fincham, & Clark, 2006), public defender's offices (Hara & Schwen, 2006), and multinational corporations (Retna & Ng, 2011).

CoPs are a particular type of social network that support knowledge flow across the practice (Brown & Duguid, 2000), although not all social networks are CoPs as they may not share an identity or seek to learn and create knowledge about that practice (Wenger & Trayner, 2011b). Social network theory nonetheless provides insight into the relationships with others that people use to find information and solve problems, often informally (Cross, Borgatti & Parker, 2002). Relationships—according to social network theory—are depicted by a series of nodes and ties where nodes are the individuals within the network and ties are the connections between the actors (Kadushin, 2012). Connections can be useful to gain access to information from the direct connections with people as well as the connections available *through* one's direct connections. In its most simple form, a social network is a graphical depiction of all of the relevant ties between nodes. A network's structural properties help determine the network's usefulness to its members (Kadushin, 2012). A few examples of a network's structural properties are *density* (actual ties divided by all potential ties) and *centrality* (who or what in a network is most influential due to the number of connections) (Prell, 2012).

Networks exist when people interact with each other by communicating, sharing resources, working, learning or playing together, supported through face-to-face interaction as well as through the use of information and communications technologies (Haythornthwaite, 2008). Study of face-to-face social networks has a long history

(Kadushin, 2012), but more recent research has focused on technology-mediated networks, as offline and online social networks are distinct (Wellman, 2001). For example, the network with which a person interacts with via face-to-face contact may comprise different people, different duration, intimacy and reciprocity (tie strength) and different network reach than an online network. Online and offline networks thus complement one another (Zhang & Venkatesh, 2013).

Online social networks that span organizational boundaries (like the one in this case) can benefit individual and organizational performance. Research has demonstrated that social networks enable individual learning across boundaries (de Laat & Schreurs, 2013) and positively affect employee performance (Zhang & Venkatesh, 2013). Technology enables knowledge transfer among social networks between organizations (Retzer & Yoong, 2009), and ties among organizations have a significant effect on organizational behavior and performance outcomes (Zaheer, Gözübüyük, & Milanov, 2010).

Technology (and in particular social media) has removed physical boundaries previously associated with these types of networks, and introduced new ways that exchanges can occur (Ardichvili, Page, & Wentling, 2003; Wenger, McDermott, & Snyder, 2002). Networked CoPs—a dispersed group of people who work together in a virtual environment to achieve a specific objective—are becoming a basic work unit in our networked world (Restler & Woolis, 2007). Virtual spaces include websites, information and communication technologies, online repositories, or shared databases. Often, stewards of the community will select technology to be used based on community needs, and the community will adopt, adapt, or reject technology as the life of the community evolves (Wenger, et. al., 2005). Although technology can foster "togetherness" through time and space, members' comfort with the technology used, ability to monitor emotional responses, and a clear sense of community norms can either help or hinder participation (Guldberg & Mackness, 2009).

As CoPs increasingly rely on technology to collaborate and share, there is interest in understanding the value they enable which informs financial commitment to them (Fontaine & Millen, 2004). The need for evaluating technology effectiveness helps ensure that it supports desired organizational outcomes, and it is imperative to monitor its effects on stakeholders (individuals, groups, organizations, and communities). Because technology adoption has been rising in the nonprofit sector (Lohman, 2001), organizations are increasingly pursuing evaluation activities to monitor outcomes which may originate internally or come from external demands for accountability (Carman, 2009; Fine, Thayer, & Coghlan, 2000).

The concepts of capacity building, nonprofit collaboration, and networked governance all provide context for this case, as their convergence was informing key organizational actors and their decision making processes. Although the term networked community of practice was not being used by the organization at the time to describe their efforts, it emerged as the project continued to describe what was established.

Opportunity Analysis

The previous sections outline the Foundation's vision, strategies, and desired outcomes and opportunities for achieving nonprofit effectiveness that were informing discussion and decision making among the leadership team. However, outcomes at the time presented several gaps between the current and desired state. As discussed in earlier sections, capacity building was centralized with the Foundation and there was no opportunity for shared capacity building among multiple organizations. Communication and collaboration among nonprofits was ad-hoc and geographically isolated. Foundation staff found that many nonprofit board and staff members were using Facebook personally but most were not using Facebook, LinkedIn, or Twitter for their organizations. When asked where they found nonprofit resources and best practices, nonprofit board and staff members reported calling a colleague or searching Google.

Several factors were contributing to this existing state. As described earlier, there was insufficient access to centralized resources that nonprofit organizations could use for development. Existing governance was "spider-like" and centralized. Communication, cooperation and collaboration were either ad-hoc, unintentional, or non-existent.

The opportunity analysis is represented on the left area of Figure 2, which aligns with the Human Performance Technology (HPT) model ("What is HPT?," n.d.). A unique aspect of this case were the opportunities for building aspects of nonprofit effectiveness through networked governance, capacity building, communities of practice, and nonprofit collaboration, which may less relevant for for-profit organizations.

The iterative intervention design, implementation, and evaluation cycles that followed all were informed in varying ways (and at different times) by the opportunities identified. In the next section, each of the subsequent activities is discussed in detail.

CASE DESCRIPTION

Management and Organizational Concerns

The Foundation convened community nonprofit leaders to discuss the viability of a nonprofit network and they began work on creating a formal nonprofit network

Figure 2. Opportunity analysis and framework for design, implementation and evaluation

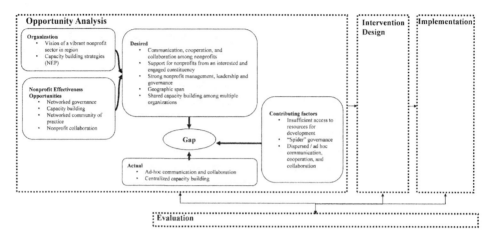

and virtual resource center. A governing body of organizations that were leading intermediaries (e.g., local United Ways, community foundations, libraries, University Extension) was established to connect the work of those interested in building nonprofit capacity. They established a vision for the effort and named it "Good Works Connect".

Their desired long-term outcomes served as a guide for design of early network initiatives, including a website which included resources and mechanisms for members to share and collaborate with one another. In-person gatherings were organized to facilitate discussion on member-driven topics of interest. The Lumpkin Family Foundation would support the start-up financially and with staff, then transition it into the community over a number of years.

The Good Works Connect leadership team consisted of approximately 20 region and statewide intermediary and nonprofit representatives. The network and online community would help link nonprofit leaders and would be the place for people doing good work to connect, communicate, and collaborate. Strategies focused on enabling three key outcomes in the sector: 1) Communication, cooperation, and collaboration among nonprofits; 2) Support for nonprofits from an interested and engaged constituency; and 3) Strong nonprofit management, leadership, and governance. These desired outcomes served as a guide for design of early network initiatives, including the website.

Good Works Connect functioned as a way to communicate immediately with a community of engaged nonprofit leaders. Through Good Works Connect, its members would be able to:

- Connect, share ideas, and network with the people, organizations and groups with common interests;
- Generate visibility and support for nonprofit trainings/events, job openings, and volunteer opportunities;
- Learn about resources and convening opportunities; and
- Find and apply for Microgrants—up to $1,500 for staff or board organizational and leadership development opportunities.

Technology Concerns and Components

Technology was a critical factor in effectively supporting communication, cooperation, and resource sharing between the geographically-distributed nonprofits. The leadership team determined that a website built using an open-source content management system (http://www.joomla.org/) would provide the features and functions needed to support the community. Using open source software, while not cost-free, reduced expenditures when compared with commercial technology solutions.

The website provided many features and functions to network members. To join the network, individuals registered (at no cost) and completed a member profile. Members were encouraged to add organizational profiles, and groups could be established to form smaller niche clusters if desired. The information entered in member, group, and organizational profiles enabled visibility of information about jobs, location, projects, and interests. Profile information facilitated finding like-minded individuals and groups, and the platform enabled direct and private communication between members. The website contained forums, which allowed members to post questions or discussion topics for the entire community to view and respond. A resources area allowed any member to upload resources such as checklists, guides, tips, or links to external information for others to view and comment. Members could post events to a shared calendar to promote visibility of training and other activities. The website enabled applications for professional development grants and viewing other grant opportunities. Finally, job postings and volunteer opportunities could be added by members. The website launched soon after the network's formation. In addition to the website, weekly email newsletters were distributed to members highlighting news or newly-added resources that might be of interest. Good Works Connect used popular social media to post announcements to their Twitter, Facebook, and later, LinkedIn accounts.

While the website provided several ways to network with others in the community, the group also utilized in-person gatherings. Good Works Connect—in partnership with local community foundations and nonprofit intermediaries—organized and promoted monthly nonprofit community gatherings on locally-determined topics in population-determined geographic regions. In partnership with its state nonprofit association, they organized and promoted annual in-person region-wide training events and a conference on nonprofit best practices.

Funding from the Foundation supported the initial construction and content population of the website. The website was maintained with the support of Foundation's program officer and part-time interns. Maintenance included developing content, moderating forums, updating social media, and developing and disseminating the weekly e-newsletter for members. In approximately two years, the online network grew to over 1,000 members.

Evaluation

After two years of facilitating the network, the Foundation sought to assess the value of the CoP to guide future endeavors with an eye toward making it financially sustainable. This coincided with a poor economic climate for nonprofits who were participating. Many of the nonprofits in the network had state contracts or grants had been adversely affected by drastic reductions in the state budget, making the need for a collective nonprofit voice even more important. The bleak economic climate had also heightened the need for nonprofits to collaborate and be resourceful in seeking free or affordable training opportunities. At the same time, community foundations in the state had continued to grow in asset size and were more committed to capacity building due in some part to another funder-based initiative. Statewide network partners had also emerged as possible partners to acquire and expand Good Works Connect. From a technology perspective, online nonprofit-focused resources had become more accessible through services like LinkedIn and Idea Encore Network (now 4good.org) and it was predicted that nonprofits would increasingly use social media (Kanter & Fine, 2010).

With the purpose of informing the next generation design of the website and guiding strategic planning through input from members and other stakeholders, the Foundation sought proposals from external entities to conduct an evaluation. External consultants (hereafter the evaluation team) conducted the evaluation through continual input from key stakeholders.

The study focused on the perceived value of network participation by members and if learning and changed practice had been achieved through participation. Stakeholders also wanted to assess how well the technology being used served the needs of members. With this in mind, the primary evaluation questions were 1) in what ways did technology enable learning and collaboration among community members? and 2) to what extent had Good Works Connect facilitated learning and changed practice in members? The evaluation also explored options for achieving financial sustainability, including possibilities for scaling the network to other regions.

Based on the opportunity analysis discussed earlier in this chapter (see Figure 2), the elements described in the preceding sections comprised the intervention design, implementation, and plan for formative evaluation shown in Figure 3. As noted in Figure 3, the focus of the evaluation was formative and predominantly focused on the technology-enabled aspects of Good Works Connect.

Data collection efforts sought to identify strengths and weaknesses of community activities, website design and features, and the strength, frequency, and value of member connections within the community. In addition, the evaluation team wanted to know if participation in Good Works Connect had induced changes within nonprofit community practice. With this in mind, the evaluation team con-

Figure 3. Intervention design, implementation and formative evaluation

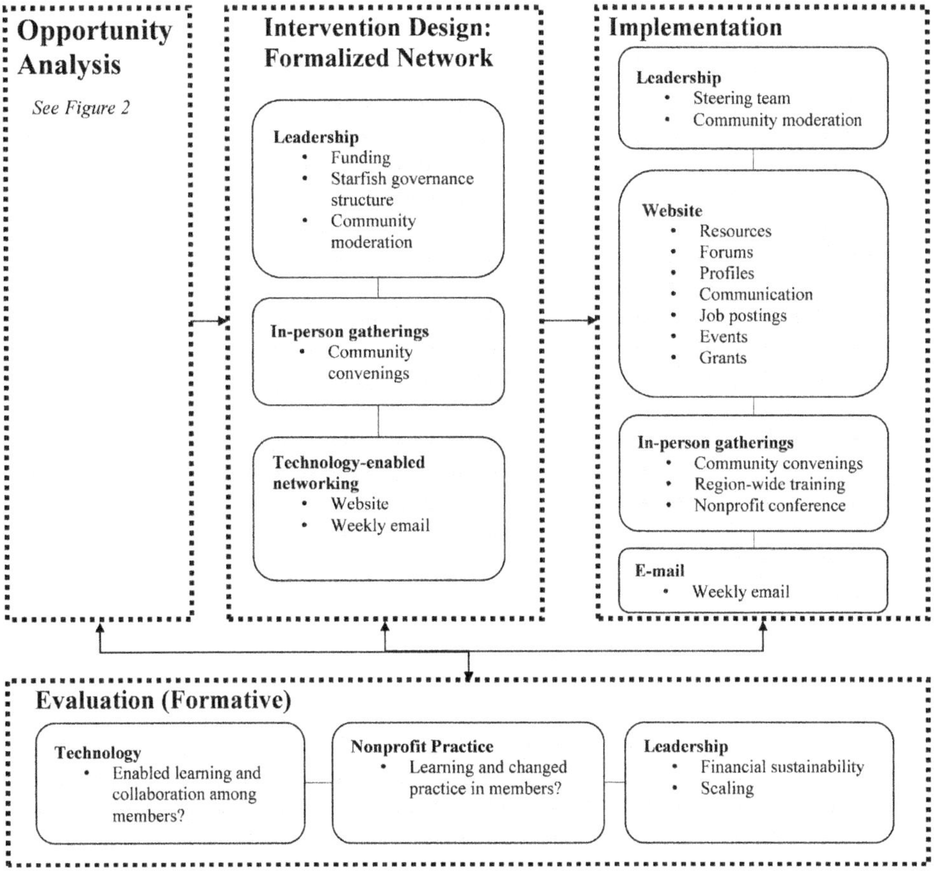

cluded that qualitative and quantitative data would help interpret findings from a holistic perspective and permit deeper inquiry about the meaning that a small number of members gave to participation and value (Creswell, 2003). While data collection occurred somewhat concurrently, quantitative data were collected first so that emerging patterns could be explored with qualitative methods as the study proceeded.

Data Collection and Analysis

Given that Good Works Connect utilized technology to a great extent to facilitate activities, it was appropriate to measure users' acceptance of information technology. The Unified Theory for the Acceptance and Use of Technology (UTAUT) was used (Venkatesh, Morris, Davis, & Davis, 2003). UTAUT identifies performance expectancy, effort expectancy, social influence, and facilitating conditions as four core factors that predict users' behavioral intentions in adopting information technology for work-related purposes. In addition, the survey included items from an Organizational Learning instrument (Templeton, Lewis, & Snyder, 2002) and Commitment to Organizational Change instrument (Herscovitch & Meyer, 2002) to identify the general readiness of change in its members' and if Good Works Connect enabled organizational learning. All members were invited to complete the online survey through email. Survey responses collected demographic data but were anonymous. Of the 69 surveys completed, 54 contained sufficient data to be included in the analysis.

Most people who participated in the survey were over 40 (73% over 40; 27% less than 40), female (74% female, 26% male), and served in upper management roles in their organizations. 35% of participants held executive level positions, 19% were administrative, 18% were program staff, and 13% were board officers with the remainder identifying as volunteers, external consultants, or interns. 66% had been involved with Good Works Connect for more than one year, with the other 33% having been involved for less than a year.

User traffic data on the website was compiled to identify potential networking and activity patterns among users. This included member posts, website hits, and other activity available through the website's administrative data. These data were reviewed for the period of the previous year.

After survey distribution, all members were invited to participate in individual interviews. Semi-structured interviews were used to elicit description and exploration of members' experiences. Questions probed the usability of the website (e.g. which features of the website are most / least helpful to you, and why?), their experiences and perceptions about participating in the community (e.g. describe how you have participated in the community), and any outcomes of participating (e.g. is there something you have learned or done differently in your work as a result of your participation in the community?). 20 interviews were conducted (18 by telephone and 2 in person), each lasting approximately 40 minutes. The evaluation team also conducted a face-to-face focus group to facilitate a collective discussion of perceptions and experiences. A semi-structured focus group protocol was used to inquire about members perceived value in participating, any outcomes they had experienced through participating, and the usability of the website. The focus group was conducted in a computer lab with a projection monitor and different areas of the website were displayed to prompt discussion about usability and the utility of features. Four members participated in the 2 hour focus group. With the participants' consent, all interviews and the focus group were recorded and transcribed.

The survey dataset was first processed with a series of reliability tests, to make sure that the survey items were consistent in collecting intended data points. Regression and correlation analysis were applied to identify underlying relationships among data variables. User traffic data on the website was analyzed to identify networking and activity patterns among users. Website hits, member counts, login activity, posts to forums, resources, and opportunities were analyzed for trends and patterns.

In order to triangulate with survey data, the transcribed interview and focus group data were first coded according to pre-defined codes based on the UTAUT and Organizational Learning constructs. Codes from the UTAUT included performance expectancy, effort expectancy, social influence, and attitude, while organizational learning codes included knowledge acquisition, information distribution, information interpretation, and organizational memory. The evaluation team also reviewed qualitative data to identify other emergent patterns. Finally, both types of data were consolidated and compared. The evaluation team identified areas where findings had mutual support from both types of data as well as where there was no support or disconfirming evidence from both data sources. This review resulted in a final inclusive set of findings.

Evaluation Results

Although members participated in the network both through the website and in-person activities, technology supported more frequent participation. Members engaged 3 times more frequently through features with high technology support (e.g., the website, webinars, and emails) than features with low technology support (e.g. in-person meetings or conferences). Despite more frequent participation in technology-enabled events however, some members reported that face-to-face interaction supported more in-depth networking. Said one member: "If I am going to network, I want to see a human being, not through a web site. But you do need to understand that younger staff members are comfortable [using technology] and that's their preferred learning style".

Website data and member user profiles showed that participation in the technology-enabled aspects of the community were similar to that of other virtual CoPs (Wenger, Trayner, & De Laat, 2011; Wenger & Wenger-Trayner, 2011), in that a core group of participants were most active and the majority were more passive. Key contributors were members in the "core" of the community. These individuals communicated actively and helped organize and carry out community activities, and it was within this group that engagement was most evident. The website features in which core participation was evident were the presence of sub-groups, resource postings by members, and an online presence indicator. Individuals in the middle strata exhibited milder participation by occasionally partaking in community activities and sporadically joining in the conversation if it was of interest to them, but rarely started a conversation. The online features of the website which demonstrated this level of participation included commenting on postings, adding a calendar event, posting a job, or rating a resource.

Finally, while members in the periphery had full access to opportunities and information, their participation was largely invisible. The website supported peripheral participation through distribution of a weekly email to members, the presence of individual profiles, downloads of online resources, and the ability to search the website. Other indicators of this were website statistics such as logins and page views. Figure 4 illustrates these strata of participation and how technology supported participation in each.

The distribution of the virtual CoP's participation aligns with the model of diffusion of innovations (Rogers, 1995), which suggests that up to 2.5% of total target users are considered "core" members and up to 50% of total target users could be considered as participating in the "middle". According to the website data, the CoP may have reached the "early adopter" threshold (approximately 16%) after two years in operation.

Technology Linking the Community and Making the Global Local

One of the primary ways in which the CoP enabled networking, sharing, and learning in its constituency was through the website. Use of the website enabled greater awareness of relevant opportunities and activities within the network, as shown in Figure 5. Respondents also indicated increased awareness in regional nonprofit

Figure 4. Technology support for network participation, Adapted from Wenger & Trayner (2011a). Slide: Levels of participation. Retrieved from http://wenger-trayner. com/resources/slide-forms-of-participation.

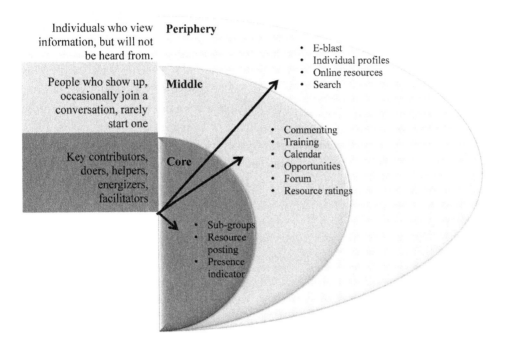

Figure 5. Awareness enabled by website usage

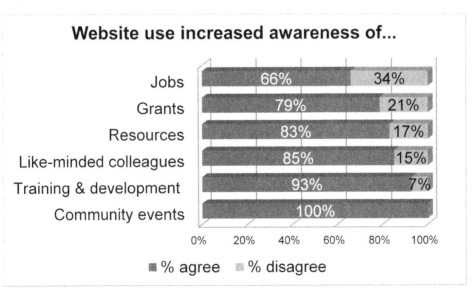

community events, training and development opportunities, and grant opportunities. Said one member, "there's no other [organization] pulling all that information together in one place".

Members reported a strong connection with the community, available resources, and other network members, as shown in Figure 6. Further, high levels of the quality, number, and frequency of contacts with other members were reported. Respondents indicated that these connections led to a high perceived closeness with other members. For example, one member noted "There is something about keeping the feeling of community close, so people can benefit from the shared sense of purpose and working together".

Although posted website resources were often from sources outside of the network (for example, a link to an external blog posting or news item), members perceived that it was more applicable to the community because other members posted it or commented on it. One participant commented:

There is something to be said about the fact that even if you don't add anything or comment on it, the fact that if [another member] thought it was worth reading, then it makes me think I had better take 5 minutes to read it. That recommendation goes a long way.

Indeed, one of the attributes valued most by members was the local focus on the non-profit community. One participant offered this perspective:

Figure 6. Perceived connection with community enabled by network participation

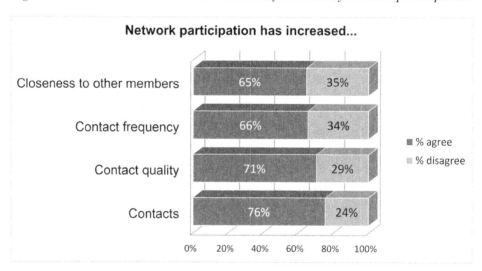

To me, the greatest value is the regional presence of [the CoP]. You know, when you start talking about big topics in nonprofit management or things like that, you can get that from endless numbers of national websites and information. But to me it's that local connection of what's going on here in our neighborhood…that's what draws me in the most, because I think the information's great, but everyone has that information. It's available in numerous ways. So to me, it's getting it with that local twist.

In the survey items related to technology acceptance, respondents reported a moderately high level of effort expectancy and attitudes toward the use of technology and a low level of anxiety. Participants also reported a high frequency of intention to use the website. Despite high ratings in effort expectancy (i.e., "I believe using the site is easy"), website usability was noted as a weakness in several interviews. Navigating the interface frustrated some users who wanted to find information in a quicker and more intuitive manner. For example, one member reported "It's a little overwhelming and busy in my opinion. When I get on it…lots of times my first response is 'OK, where do I need to go do this thing', like when I want to post a job". Noting usability challenges as well as sometimes duplicate information through all of their networking channels, one member noted redundancy with other social media tools:

[The CoP] should integrate the website into other social media tools…it is sometimes a duplication of posting. Nonprofits are busy people and you have to make it easier to use to get activity on the site. I'm on many social media websites and I can navigate them much more easily than the [CoP] site.

Emerging Changes to Nonprofit Practice

One of the goals of the evaluation was to determine if participation in the CoP activities enabled outcomes in nonprofit practice, such as an engaged constituency or strong leadership and governance. To address this question, the evaluation team adopted a scale to measure how the website facilitated the communication and interaction among members related to organizational learning. On average participants did not report a high level of organizational learning as a member of the CoP. The relationship between the perceived organizational learning and other measured constructs, however, revealed some significant findings. In particular, regression analysis indicated that perceived organizational learning can be predicted by the effort expectancy. In other words, the ease of using the CoP was a major factor to promote organizational learning within the community.

In terms of commitment to change, participants agreed that implementing the CoP was a beneficial strategy and served an important purpose. However, participants did not feel strongly obligated to utilize the CoP, which is further supported by a relatively low sense of duty to promote the CoP. When asked if they would feel uncomfortable not supporting the CoP, participants responded with a moderate level of confirmation. So while participants valued the community, the evaluation suggested that most members lacked a sense of ownership regarding the ongoing operation of it.

Similar to the findings on organizational learning, a significant regression model was also found between commitment to organizational change and technology acceptance. In particular, participants' attitudes towards technology (i.e., enjoyment from using the CoP website) and self-efficacy (i.e., the beliefs that one can use the CoP effectively to accomplish tasks) could predict the level of commitment to organizational change in this case study. The correlation analysis also revealed some interesting findings. Commitment to organizational change was correlated to all technology acceptance constructs, organizational learning items, and sustainability items. But the UTAUT constructs might be able to impact the perceived commitment to organizational change more than other measured constructs (for example, organizational learning and sustainability).

Findings from the survey regarding changes in practice were supported by member interviews and the focus group. While many members were optimistic about *potential* outcomes that might occur, reports of *actual* practice outcomes were isolated. However, the increased communication between nonprofit practitioners was in itself a change to nonprofit practice in the community. Sponsored events (in-person and online) provided exposure to others serving nonprofits through education and services. As one member noted, "There are people that I see because of the CoP that I wouldn't otherwise see regularly. I might email them or talk to them on the phone, but I might only see them once a year". This venue gave members an opportunity to become aware of one another's efforts and work outside of organizational silos. Some members noted that resources and training on social media presence made available through the CoP had directly contributed to an increased social media presence of their own organization. Others noted imminent changes to their organization's approach toward board development and retention based upon information attained through the community. She said "…so to me, that's huge, because it opened up a whole can of knowledge that I can spill on my organization".

Interviews indicated that the CoP membership gave credibility to potential network contacts and information. Having a space, both virtual and in person, where people can connect was noted as a "powerful model" by one member. Participants indicated that the CoP was a valuable mechanism to connect with nonprofits not just in the region, but throughout the state. Some stakeholders considered the CoP a strategic partner that that comprises a network of interconnected nonprofit practitioners. "I would consider [the CoP] to be an anchor institution in that if you've reached one, you've reached many at the same time", a member told us.

There was evidence of nascent but unrealized inter-organizational cooperation. Attempted joint projects and resource sharing arrangements showed limited success to date, but respondents noted that the lack of success had not deterred them from continued attempts. Others reported that advertising jobs on the CoP website had produced more favorable job applicants. One member noted that although some cooperative efforts had not yet materialized, initial attempts at doing so would not have happened without being involved with the CoP.

The evaluation also explored ideas to help it become financially self-supporting, including scaling Good Works Connect beyond the regions that it currently served. Interviewees were mainly positive toward scaling the operation and felt that scaling was "the next step" in the network's evolution given the interest and growth of the network size. Given the high value that members placed on networking and the perception of community proximity many interviewees reported that these features should be the central concern when considering what is scaled.

To address questions related to financial sustainability, the evaluation team solicited ideas about alternate funding models, including use of website advertisements, small transaction costs for downloading "premium" content, and a fee-based membership model. In the end, the evaluation team concluded that a more comprehensive analysis of funding models should be explored before implementing a model that imposed fees to members. Survey responses indicated that members were not in favor of the approach, and there was not enough compelling evidence warranting a need for this type of change that would likely alienate the member base. An alternative funding model was recommended by some stakeholders, whereby another more established entity would take primary responsibility for sponsoring Good Works Connect. In this approach, an organization with more statewide presence or strong presence in other regions would be the primary funder, while other organizations in the state (or region served) would contribute funds for programmatic activity and ongoing maintenance. This approach was particularly viable if the network decided to scale to regions beyond those served at the time.

In summary, the findings from the evaluation indicated that the network had hybrid levels and types of participation, and technology played an important role in community networking, sharing and learning. Despite some issues related to website usability, members reported value in the locally-relevant information and resources that the community provided. Although emerging, there was evidence of some changes to nonprofit practice in the community.

CURRENT CHALLENGES FACING THE ORGANIZATION

The evaluation provided several areas for the network's leadership team to consider. On one hand, several strengths were identified. It was clear that the resources and opportunities to learn and network with other members were highly valued. Technology was deemed integral for organizing the nonprofit community and providing mechanisms to host and disseminate information. Website users felt positive towards the online portal and reported a high frequency of intention to use it. Given its two-year presence during a period when use of social media had surged (Madden & Zickuhr, 2011; Van Grove, 2010), the findings suggested a strong preliminary stage. Participants considered the CoP as an instrumental means to support organizational learning and to enhance commitment to change among members in the region. The local sense of community enabled through the technology was valued, and there was general support to sustain the operation of the CoP.

In consideration of evaluation findings, the steering team noted some meaningful outcomes of the network's formation and subsequent work, including:

- Partnership with community foundations to provide small capacity building grants.
- Partnership with community foundations and other capacity builders to hold monthly nonprofit community convenings.
- Providing opportunities for members to engage in the grantmaking process.
- Ability to bring Chicago-based services downstate.
- Leverage of membership to attract national notice and resources.

Given these strengths, the evaluation identified opportunities for improvement. Respondents noted that improving the usability of the website would enhance users' experiences and may entice more passive members to engage more actively. The website's usability may have been affecting some of the outcomes of changes to nonprofit practice. Findings also suggested that there were opportunities to leverage popular social media to increase participation and reduce the cost associated with having community-specific website social applications.

Finally, the leadership team had some important considerations for the continued operation of Good Works Connect. There was some support for scaling it's operation beyond the region served which would make it more financially sustainable, but undertaking this effort would need to honor the aspects of the community that members valued most—namely that it was locally based and therefore more meaningful. Given these findings, recommendations were made for the leadership and steering team to consider, discussed in the next section.

SOLUTIONS AND RECOMMENDATIONS

First, the community of practice should be sustained as a mechanism to accomplish the interests of the network. There was ample evidence in the evaluation that supported sustaining online and offline endeavors. Although some members voiced differing opinions about the future direction of the community, there was no suggestion that the CoP should be discontinued or diminished. CoPs are keenly suited to address social concerns in for-profit and non-profit organizations alike (Synder & Wenger, 2010). Indeed, given trends in networked governance, capacity building, and nonprofit collaboration discussed at the beginning of this chapter, CoPs may be a viable HPT intervention in nonprofit organizations.

Second, forming an advisory committee of "core" members to provide insight into technology design and development is beneficial. This advisory committee could guide the redesign of the website, using the feedback on usability improvements as input. Core members who are leaders of the community will likely remain in the community if they have opportunities to be involved. An advisory group can help foster trust, cohesion, communication climate, and interaction frequency, factors paramount for "good" interaction and knowledge-sharing in virtual CoPs (Zboralski, 2009). This can enable the networked CoP to make decisions focused on activities that create value among members. Further, periodically rotating advisory group membership would disperse the decision making among different constituents in line with concepts of networked governance.

Third, allocating staff to the role of "community moderators" will keep the conversation and activity lively in the community. This role is vital in understanding the needs of the community, building and maintaining member relationships, and fostering growth within the community (Bourhis & Dube, 2010; Gray, 2004). Further, community moderators can serve an important role in addressing what Wenger and his colleagues called "the inventiveness of use" of technology (Wenger et al., 2005). Moderators can monitor how the community does or does not use its technological resources and discover unmet needs which will evolve with the life of the community. In this case study, a feature that members valued most was that online resources from various external sources were filtered for only the most relevant information to the community—a function performed by people centrally working in a moderator function. This recommendation can foster the networked community in consistent and meaningful ways.

Fourth, the community should reconsider how to integrate popular social networking applications such as Facebook and LinkedIn into network activities and the website. Members had mixed reactions towards the social networking aspects that were built into the website, with some suggesting there was too much redundancy of information between the website features and other social networking sites. As such, it is important to revisit if the website or popular social networking sites would be used for certain functions such as awareness of the network and enabling contacts between members. This will potentially reduce cost associated with maintaining additional functionality that was not used often, improve usability of the website by streamlining design, and leverage the popular social networking sites already being used by many members. This action would relieve financial resources that can be devoted to other capacity-building initiatives, and the community has increased possibilities of network reach due to the benefits of social media for non-profit endeavors (Kanter & Fine, 2010).

Fifth, the community should prioritize engagement mechanisms (e.g. rewards) to entice regular and diverse participation in the community. While many members were intrinsically motivated to learn and connect, external rewards may motivate passive users to engage more. Anticipated social recognition can be a strong motivating influence on knowledge sharing within the community (Jeon, Kim, & Koh, 2011). Capturing the interests of passive members can bring new knowledge and opportunities for learning or partnerships to the network. Another engagement mechanism to capitalize on intrinsic motivation is identifying professional development interests within the community and offering structured learning events, since learning has been cited as a strong motivating factor for individuals to participate in communities like this one (Baytiyeh & Pfaffman, 2010; Lakhani & Wolf, 2005). Members in this community valued that other members helped them make meaning of existing resources through content filtering and posting of available resources. To add additional worth, offering professional development opportunities can enhance this and distinguish value. Training and other development activities supports capacity building within member organizations. Shared decision-making on professional development goals and priorities can enhance nonprofit collaboration and also creates opportunities for cost and resource sharing. When professional development opportunities are meaningful, member engagement can be increased.

Sixth, the organization should implement regular analysis of the social network. An analysis of the social network in a CoP can reveal the flow of information, nurture valuable interactions, and enable innovation to gradually shift the community from being informal and ad-hoc to one that is value-producing (Cross, Laseter, Parker, & Velasquez, 2006). Social Network Analysis (SNA) can, for example, identify overly-connected members, identify invisible siloes within the network, and bring peripheral members closer to the core (Cross, et. al. 2006). The identification of network can make the existing governance structure visible as well as identify important governance gaps. The community can also be enhanced by identifying the strengths in members' ties that support learning.

Finally, it is recommended that to bring the vision of the community to scale, they should use information obtained in the evaluation to fully assess scaling to other regions, or to the state. The evaluation showed that the tools developed for grassroots organizing in geographic centers were scalable. Expanding would:

- Support expansion of services to members outside the region;
- Help the community market the works of members and enhance nonprofit capacity and programs; and
- Attract more partners (expand networked governance) and collaborations outside of the region for resources.

An action plan is recommended to support decision making about expansion, shown in Table 1.

Each recommendation supports the four dimensions of nonprofit effectiveness discussed at the beginning of this chapter, as shown in Table 2.

While some measures may only support one area, they may be more readily implemented. For example, introducing rewards to entice participation (such as giving a member credit to an online retailer for posting a resource) may require only a small amount of time, money, and work effort. Other recommendations support multiple dimensions but require intensive resources due to their complexity. For example, conducting a social network analysis can be a resource-intensive endeavor (Prell, 2012) but yield a wealth of information. Similarly, a comprehensive assessment of scaling to other regions would involve a longer time horizon in order to gather the necessary data for decision making. The combination of interventions, particularly if designed to work in concert with one another, can help improve performance over time by taking a systematic approach to problem-solving (Rosenberg, 1996).

From a human performance technology perspective, these recommendations represent multiple types of interventions for analysis, design, implementation, and evaluation. Some, like social network analysis and the assessment of scaling are other *analytical* endeavors which may inform the design of different interventions. Further, the *opportunity analysis* presented earlier in this chapter should be revisited as shifts in the structure and composition of the community may bring new opportunities to the fore. Other recommendations are squarely focused on *individual, group, and organizational learning* (as in structured professional development) or in modifying motivational systems (rewards to entice participation). Others cross multiple types of interventions and levels of impact. Implementing the roles of

Table 1. Big questions and action plan for network expansion

Information Needed	Action Steps
Need & Demand: What is the need and demand outside of the region? Who could we partner with/who would be interested in this?	
• Interest/need to nonprofits in possible target areas • List of stakeholders and strategic partnerships (for content and exposure) • Statewide organizations with replication models	• Develop list of stakeholders to do individual outreach • Survey nonprofits in target areas for their needs and interests • Solicit input via presentation to community foundations
Replication Packaging: What is the model/approach to expand? What do we replicate?	
• Refine website, community convenings, micograms, "connecting" • Specific cases / options for expansion model (e.g., statewide website, expand in-person community by community)	• Develop program descriptions and other communication about pending changes • Document how all activities are done now to support possible transition • Test the model in another community to learn lessons for refining model
Website Design: What should the website look like to support expansion?	
• Website needs / wants from members • Information about other web platforms to leverage • Needs assessment of alternate means of presentation (e.g., mobile, app)	• Review evaluation feedback • Create RFP for website redesign • Select design firm and provide input as developed.
Financial sustainability: Is this financially sustainable long-term?	
• Current budget/comparison • Potential revenue models (identified in evaluation) • Potential staffing models • Case studies of similar efforts	• Staff create budget documents • Determine revenue models to explore • Conduct case study interviews • Develop staff models
Structure: What leadership (staff and volunteer) is needed to make this happen?	
• Staff task and skills list • Various staffing models and partnerships	• Develop job description(s) • Review leadership team structure and make-up • Research and develop feasibility of staffing models for recommendation • Develop matrix of current volunteer leadership; determine recommendations for structure and changes needed for statewide focus.
Marketing: What do we tell as we expand?	
Value/benefits to the various stakeholders (need to keep community-based orgs in mind as well)	Internal: • Tell members about evaluation and strategy; ask for their input & support • Keep informed as changes emerge External: • Reach out to members outside the focus region with direct messaging • Use other nonprofit specific sector groups to share information • Writing article for sector; *Working Wikily*
Evaluation: How will we know if we are successful? What should we be measuring and reporting as the effort progresses?	
Qualitative and Quantitative information about the network and the website	• Review website metrics and determine ongoing opportunities • Review current analytics and determine indicators for network • Conduct a follow-up external user survey in 2-3 years

Table 2. Recommendations support for nonprofit effectiveness

	Networked Governance	Capacity Building	Nonprofit Collaboration	Networked CoP
Sustain CoP	✓	✓	✓	✓
Advisory committee	✓			✓
Community moderators				✓
Integrate popular social media applications		✓		✓
Prioritize engagement mechanisms		✓	✓	✓
Social network analysis	✓		✓	✓
Full assessment of scaling	✓	✓	✓	✓

community moderator and the advisory group are not just changes to *job design*, but should change the *processes* by which work is accomplished, how *knowledge is managed*, and *communication channels* within the community. These roles in particular may change the way in which *technical systems* are used to accomplish the work of the community. In summary, each recommendation aligns with one or more of the myriad HPT interventions aimed at improving performance at the individual, group, or organizational level (Pershing, 2006).

This case study illustrates the opportunities that nonprofit practitioners have to form and strengthen their networks of practice, especially through the use of technology. The findings from the evaluation suggested that the technology used to support this community of practice played an important role in enabling networking and learning among members. In this case, early indicators of enabling practice changes through the planned and intentional efforts of the CoP were evident.

While technology enabled activity and networking within the community, the study indicated that "the network" does not comprise "the online community". While technology was considered as an important asset by some stakeholders, the study revealed that the CoP was more than the online aspects of the community. Members found value in in-person opportunities to learn and connect, even if technology provided opportunities to connect more frequently. While some resources were also available elsewhere, the local sense of community was important to members. Through the planned, intentional efforts of this community, this network was able to collaborate, learn, and work in new ways. While it is too early to know if more transformational changes to nonprofit practice will take place, there are early indicators of this in the community.

REFERENCES

Ardichvili, A., Page, V., & Wentling, T. (2003). Motivation and barriers to participation in virtual knowledge-sharing communities of practice. *Journal of Knowledge Management*, *7*(1), 64–77. doi:10.1108/13673270310463626

Bates, I., Taegtmeyer, M., Squire, S. B., Ansong, D., Nhlema-Simwaka, B., Baba, A., & Theobald, S. (2011). Indicators of sustainable capacity building for health research: Analysis of four African case studies. *Health Research Policy and Systems*, *9*(1), 14. doi:10.1186/1478-4505-9-14 PMID:21443780

Baytiyeh, H., & Pfaffman, J. (2010). Volunteers in Wikipedia : Why the community matters. *Journal of Educational Technology & Society*, *13*(2), 128–140.

Botcheva, L., White, C., & Huffman, L. C. (2002). Learning culture and outcomes measurement practices in community agencies. *The American Journal of Evaluation*, *23*(4), 421–434. doi:10.1177/109821400202300404

Bourhis, A., & Dube, L. (2010). "Structuring spontaneity": Investigating the impact of management practices on the success of virtual communities of practice. *Journal of Information Science*, *36*(2), 175–193. doi:10.1177/0165551509357861

Brafman, O., & Beckstrom, R. A. (2006). *The starfish and the spider: The unstoppable power of leaderless organizations*. New York: Portfolio.

Brown, J. S., & Duguid, P. (2000). *The social life of information*. Boston, MA: Harvard Business School Press.

Carman, J. G. (2009). Nonprofits, funders, and evaluation: Accountability in action. *American Review of Public Administration*, *39*(4), 374–390. doi:10.1177/0275074008320190

Collins, J. (2005). *Good to great and the social sectors: A monograph to accompany good to great*. New York, NY: Harper Collins.

Creswell, J. W. (2003). *Research design: Qualitative, quantitative, and mixed method approaches* (2nd ed.). Thousand Oaks, CA: Sage Publications, Inc.

Cross, R., Borgatti, S. P., & Parker, A. (2002). Making invisible work visible: Using social network analysis to support strategic collaboration. *California Management Review*, *44*(2), 25–47. doi:10.2307/41166121

Cross, R., Laseter, T., Parker, A., & Velasquez, G. (2006). Using social network analysis to improve communities of practice. *California Management Review*, *49*(1), 32–61. doi:10.2307/41166370

De Laat, M., & Schreurs, B. (2013). Visualizing informal professional development networks: Building a case for learning analytics in the workplace. *The American Behavioral Scientist, 57*(10), 1421–1438. doi:10.1177/0002764213479364

Eisinger, P. (2002). Organizational capacity and organizational effectiveness among street-level food assistance programs. *Nonprofit and Voluntary Sector Quarterly, 31*(1), 115–130. doi:10.1177/0899764002311005

Fine, A. H., Thayer, C. E., & Coghlan, A. T. (2000). Program evaluation practice in the nonprofit sector. *Nonprofit Management & Leadership, 10*(3), 331–339. doi:10.1002/nml.10309

Fontaine, M. A., & Millen, D. R. (2004). Understanding the benefits and impact of communities of practice. In P. Hildreth & C. Kimble (Eds.), *Knowledge networks: Innovation through communities of practice* (pp. 1–13). PA: Idea Group Publishing Hershey. doi:10.4018/978-1-59140-200-8.ch001

Gowdy, H., Hildebrand, A., La Piana, D., & Campos, M. (2009). Convergence: How five trends will reshape the social sector. Retrieved from http://www.lapiana.org/downloads/Convergence_Report_2009.pdf

Gray, B. (2004). Informal learning in an online community of practice. *Journal of Distance Education, 19*(1), 20–35.

Guldberg, K., & Mackness, J. (2009). Foundations of communities of practice: Enablers and barriers to participation. *Journal of Computer Assisted Learning, 25*(6), 528–538. doi:10.1111/j.1365-2729.2009.00327.x

Handley, K., Sturdy, A., Fincham, R., & Clark, T. (2006). Within and beyond communities of practice: Making sense of learning through participation, identity and practice. *Journal of Management Studies, 43*(3), 641–653. doi:10.1111/j.1467-6486.2006.00605.x

Hara, N., & Schwen, T. M. (2006). Communities of practice in workplaces : Learning as a naturally occurring event. *Performance Improvement Quarterly, 19*(2), 93–114. doi:10.1111/j.1937-8327.2006.tb00367.x

Haythornthwaite, C. (2008). Learning relations and networks in web-based communities. *International Journal of Web Based Communities, 4*(2), 140. doi:10.1504/IJWBC.2008.017669

Herscovitch, L., & Meyer, J. (2002). Commitment to organizational change: Extension of a three-component model. *The Journal of Applied Psychology, 87*(3), 474–487. doi:10.1037/0021-9010.87.3.474 PMID:12090605

International Society for Performance Improvement. (n.d.). *What is HPT?* Retrieved from http://www.ispi.org/content.aspx?id=54

Jaskyte, K. (2004). Transformational leadership, organizational culture, and innovativeness in nonprofit organizations. *Nonprofit Management & Leadership, 15*(2), 153–168. doi:10.1002/nml.59

Jeon, S. H., Kim, Y. G., & Koh, J. (2011). Individual, social, and organizational contexts for active knowledge sharing in communities of practice. *Expert Systems with Applications, 38*(10), 12423–12431. doi:10.1016/j.eswa.2011.04.023

Kadushin, C. (2012). *Understanding social networks: Theories, concepts, and findings.* New York: Oxford University Press.

Lakhani, K., & Wolf, R. (2005). Why hackers do what they do: Understanding motivation and effort in free/open source software projects. In J. Feller, B. Fitzgerald, S. Hissam, & K. R. Lakhani (Eds.), *Perspectives on free and open source software* (pp. 3–22). Boston, Mass: MIT Press.

Leake, R., Green, S., Marquez, C., Vanderburg, J., Guillaume, S., & Gardner, V. A. (2007). Evaluating the capacity of faith-based programs in Colorado. *Research on Social Work Practice, 17*(2), 216–228. doi:10.1177/1049731506296408

Linnel, D. (2003). *Evaluation of capacity building: Lessons from the field.* Washington, D.C.: Alliance for Nonprofit Management. Retrieved from http://seerconsulting.com.au/wp-content/uploads/2009/09/Evaluation-of-Capacity-Building-Lessons-from-Field.pdf

Lohman, R. A. (2001). Editor's notes. *Nonprofit Management & Leadership, 12*(1), 1–5. doi:10.1002/nml.12101

Madden, M., & Zickuhr, K. (2011). *65% of online adults use social networking sites. Report for the Pew Internet & American Life Project.*

Mann, J. A. (2012). *Creating collaboration among small nonprofit leaders using an appreciative inquiry approach* (Doctoral dissertation). Retrieved from ProQuest, UMI Dissertations Publishing. (1516533)

Marsick, V. J., & Watkins, K. E. (2001). Informal and incidental learning. *New Directions for Adult and Continuing Education, 2001*(89), 25–34. doi:10.1002/ace.5

Milen, A. (2001). *What do we know about capacity building: An overview of existing knowledge and good practice.* Department of Health Service Provision, World Health Organization, Geneva, June.

Pershing, J. A. (2006). *Handbook of human performance technology* (J. A. Pershing, Ed.). 3rd ed.). San Francisco, CA: Pfeiffer.

Prell, C. (2012). *Social network analysis: History, theory and methodology.* London: Sage Publications Ltd.

Provan, K. G., & Kenis, P. (2008). Modes of network governance: Structure, management, and effectiveness. *Journal of Public Administration: Research and Theory*, *18*(2), 229–252. doi:10.1093/jopart/mum015

Renz, D. (2010). Reframing governance. *The Nonprofit Quarterly, Winter 2010*, 50-53.

Restler, S. G., & Woolis, D. D. (2007). Actors and factors: Virtual communities for social innovation. *Electronic Journal of Knowledge Management*, *5*(1), 81–96.

Retna, K. S., & Ng, P. T. (2011). Communities of practice: Dynamics and success factors. *Leadership and Organization Development Journal*, *32*(1), 41–59. doi:10.1108/01437731111099274

Retzer, S., & Yoong, P. (2009). Inter-organisational knowledge transfer and computer mediated social networking. In M. Purvis & B. T. R. Savarimuthu (Eds.), *Computer-mediated social networking* (pp. 76–85). Springer Berlin Heidelberg. doi:10.1007/978-3-642-02276-0_8

Rogers, E. M. (1995). *Diffusion of innovations* (4th ed.). New York: The Free Press.

Rosenberg, M. (1996). Human performance technology. In R. L. Craig (Ed.), *Training and development handbook* (4th ed., pp. 370–393). New York: McGraw-Hill.

Selden, S. C., Sowa, J. E., & Sandfort, J. (2006). The impact of nonprofit collaboration in early child care and education on management and program outcomes. *Public Administration Review*, *66*(3), 412–425. doi:10.1111/j.1540-6210.2006.00598.x

Shilbury, D., & Moore, K. A. (2006). A study of organizational effectiveness for national Olympic sporting organizations. *Nonprofit and Voluntary Sector Quarterly*, *35*(1), 5–38. doi:10.1177/0899764005279512

Snyder, W. M., & Wenger, E. (2010). Our world as a learning system: A communities-of-practice approach. In C. Blackmore (Ed.), *Social learning systems and communities of practice* (pp. 107–124). London: Springer London. doi:10.1007/978-1-84996-133-2_7

Templeton, G. F., Lewis, B. R., & Snyder, C. A. (2002). Development of a measure for the organizational learning construct. *Journal of Management Information Systems*, *19*, 175–218.

Van Grove, J. (2010). *Social networking usage surges globally*. Retrieved from http://mashable.com/2010/03/19/global-social-media-usage/

Venkatesh, V., Morris, M. G., Davis, G. B., & Davis, F. D. (2003). User acceptance of information technology: Toward a unified view. *Management Information Systems Quarterly*, *27*(3), 425–478.

Wenger, E., McDermott, R., & Snyder, W. (2002). *Cultivating communities of practice: a practical guide to managing knowledge*. Boston, Mass: Harvard Business School Press.

Wenger, E., Trayner, B., & De Laat, M. (2011). *Promoting and assessing value creation in communities and networks: a conceptual framework*. The Netherlands: Open University of the Netherlands.

Wenger, E., & Wenger-Trayner, B. (2011a). *Slide: Levels of participation*. Retrieved September 03, 2013, from http://wenger-trayner.com/resources/slide-forms-of-participation/

Wenger, E., White, N., Smith, J. D., & Rowe, K. (2005). Technology for communities. In *Work, learning and networked: Guide to the implementation and leadership of intentional communities of practice* (pp. 1–15). Quebec: CEFRIO.

Wenger-Trayner, B., & Wenger, E. (2011b). *Communities versus networks*. Retrieved August 08, 2014 from http://wenger-trayner.com/resources/communities-versus-networks/

Zaheer, A., Gözübüyük, R., & Milanov, H. (2010). It's the connections: The network perspective in interorganizational research. *Academy of Management Perspectives*, (February), 62–77.

Zboralski, K. (2009). Antecedents of knowledge sharing in communities of practice. *Journal of Knowledge Management*, *13*(3), 90–101. doi:10.1108/13673270910962897

Zhang, X., & Venkatesh, V. (2013). Explaining employee job performance: The role of online and offline workplace communication networks. *Management Information Systems Quarterly*, *37*(3), 695–722.

ADDITIONAL READING

Alliance for Children & Families. (2011). *Disruptive forces: Driving a human services revolution*. Retrieved from http://www.alliance1.org/form/download-free-copy-disruptive-forces-report

Arnstein, S. R. (1969). A ladder of citizen participation. *Journal of the American Institute of Planners, 35*(4), 216–224. doi:10.1080/01944366908977225

Austin, J. E. (2000). *The collaboration challenge: How nonprofits and businesses succeed through strategic alliances.* San Francisco, CA: Jossey-Bass.

Backer, T. (2000). Strengthening nonprofits: Capacity building and philanthropy. Encino, CA: Human Interaction Research Institute; Retrieved from http://www.nebhands.nebraska.edu/files/strengthening%20non-profits.pdf

Block, P., & McKnight, J. (2012). *The abundant community: Awakening the power of families and neighborhoods.* San Franciso, CA: Berrett-Koehler Publishers.

Cairns, B., & Harris, M. (2011). Local cross-sector partnerships: Tackling the challenges collaboratively. *Nonprofit Management & Leadership, 21*(3), 311–324. doi:10.1002/nml.20027

Connolly, P., & Lukas, C. (2002). *Strengthening nonprofit performance: A funder's guide to capacity building.* Saint Paul, MN: Amherst Wilder Foundation.

Crutchfield, L. R., & McLeod Grant, H. (2008). *Forces for Good: The six practices of high-impact nonprofits.* San Francisco, CA: John Wiley & Sons, Inc.

Dym, B., & Hutson, H. (2005). *Leadership in nonprofit organizations.* Thousand Oaks, CA: Sage Publications, Inc.

Gazley, B. (2008). Beyond the contract: The scope and nature of informal government-nonprofit partnerships. *Public Administration Review, 68*(1), 141–154. doi:10.1111/j.1540-6210.2007.00844.x

Gazley, B. (2010). Linking collaborative capacity to performance measurement in government - nonprofit partnerships. *Nonprofit and Voluntary Sector Quarterly, 39*(4), 653–673. doi:10.1177/0899764009360823

Granovetter, M. (1973). The strength of weak ties. *American Journal of Sociology, 78*(6), 1360–1380. doi:10.1086/225469

Guo, C., & Acar, M. (2005). Understanding collaboration among nonprofit organizations: Combining resource dependency, institutional, and network perspectives. *Nonprofit and Voluntary Sector Quarterly, 34*(3), 340–361. doi:10.1177/0899764005275411

Herman, R. D., & Renz, D. O. (2008). Advancing nonprofit organizational effectiveness research and theory: Nine theses. *Nonprofit Management & Leadership, 18*(4), 399–415. doi:10.1002/nml.195

Holley, J. (2011). *Network weaver handbook: A guide to transforming networks.* Athens, OH: Network Weaver Publishing.

Kanter, B., & Fine, A. (2010). *The networked nonprofit: Connecting with social media to drive change.* San Francisco, CA: John Wiley & Sons, Inc.

Kanter, B., & Paine, K. D. (2012). *Measuring the networked nonprofit: Using data to change the world.* San Francisco, CA: Jossey-Bass.

Kapucu, N., & Demiroz, F. (2013). Collaborative capacity building for community-based small nonprofit organizations. *Journal of Economic and Social Studies*, *3*(1), 83–118. doi:10.14706/JECOSS11313

Kapucu, N., Healy, B., & Arslan, T. (2011). Survival of the fittest: Capacity building for small nonprofit organizations. *Evaluation and Program Planning*, *34*(3), 236–245. doi:10.1016/j.evalprogplan.2011.03.005 PMID:21555047

Koliba, C., Meek, J. W., & Zia, A. (2010). *Governance networks in public administration and public policy.* Boca Raton, FL: CRC Press, Inc.

Krebs, V., & Holley, J. (2006). *Building smart communities through network weaving.* Retrieved from http://www.networkweaver.com/wp-content/uploads/2011/12/BuildingNetworks.pdf

Light, P. (2004). *Sustaining nonprofit performance: The case for capacity building and the evidence to support it.* Washington, D.C.: Brookings Institution Press.

Light, P., & Hubbard, E. (2002). The capacity building challenge. Washington, D.C.: The Brookings Institute; Retrieved from http://www.grantcraft.org/pdfs/capacitybuildingchallenge.pdf

Linnel, D. (2003). *Evaluation of capacity building: Lessons from the field.* Washington, D.C.: Alliance for Nonprofit Management. Retrieved from http://seerconsulting.com.au/wp-content/uploads/2009/09/Evaluation-of-Capacity-Building-Lessons-from-Field.pdf

Loza, J. (2004). Business-community partnerships: The case for community organization capacity building. *Journal of Business Ethics*, *53*(3), 297–311. doi:10.1023/B:BUSI.0000039415.90007.56

McKinsey & Company. (2001). *Effective capacity building in nonprofit organizations. Prepared for Venture Philanthropy Partners.* Retrieved from http://www.vppartners.org/sites/default/files/reports/full_rpt.pdf

Milward, H., & Provan, K. (2006). A manager's guide to choosing and using collaborative networks. *IBM Center for the Business of Government.* Retrieved from http://www.businessofgovernment.org/report/managers-guide-choosing-and-using-collaborative-networks

National Center for Charitable Statistics. (2012). *Quick facts about nonprofits.* Retrieved from http://nccs.urban.org/statistics/quickfacts.cfm

Scearce, D., Kasper, G., & McLeod Grant, H. (2009). Working wikily 2.0: Social change with a network mindset. Retrieved from http://www.workingwikily.net/Working_Wikily_2.0.pdf

Sobeck, J. (2008). How cost-effective is capacity building in grassroots organizations? *Administration in Social Work, 32*(2), 49–68. doi:10.1300/J147v32n02_04

Stevens, S. (2002). *Nonprofit lifecycles: Stage-based wisdom for nonprofit capacity.* Wayzata, MN: Stagewise Enterprises, Inc.

Stone, M. M., Crosby, B. C., & Bryson, J. M. (2010). Governing public-nonprofit collaborations: Understanding their complexity and the implications for research. *Voluntary Sector Review, 1*(3), 309–334. doi:10.1332/204080510X538310

Teegarden, P. H., Hinden, D. R., & Sturm, P. (2011). *The nonprofit organizational culture guide: Revealing the hidden truths that impact performance.* San Francisco: Jossey-Bass.

Wei-Skillern, J., & Marciano, S. (2008). The networked nonprofit. *Stanford Social Innovation Review.* Spring 2008. Retrieved from: http://www.ssireview.org/articles/entry/the_networked_nonprofit

Wilder Collaboration Factors Inventory. Retrieved from http://www.wilder.org/Wilder-Research/Research-Services/Pages/Wilder-Collaboration-Factors-Inventory.aspx

KEY TERMS AND DEFINITIONS

Capacity Building: The ability of individuals, organizations or systems to perform appropriate functions effectively, efficiently and sustainably; the goal of capacity building is to enable organizations to be adaptable and solve problems to achieve sustainability (Bates, Taegtmeyer, Squire, Ansong, Nhelma-Simwaka, Baba, & Theobald, 2011).

Collaboration: Nonprofit collaboration is "what occurs when different nonprofit organizations work together to address problems through joint effort resources, and decision making and share ownership of the final product or service" (Guo & Acar, 2005, p. 342-3).

Community of Practice: Communities of practice are groups of people who share a concern or a passion for something they do and learn how to do it better as they interact regularly (Wenger, McDermott & Snyder, 2004).

Informal Learning: Informal learning describes situations where the learner determines some or all combinations of process, location, purpose, and content; they may not be aware that learning occurred (Carliner, 2012). Informal learning contrasts formal learning which is typically sponsored by institutions, classroom-based, and highly structured. Although informal learning may occur in institutions, it is not typically classroom based or highly structured (Watkins & Marsick, 2001).

Learning Organization: An organization that changes and is supportive of learning, adaptation, and continuous improvement. It is one that acquires and transfers knowledge and uses evaluative inquiry to stimulate and support the ongoing process of asking questions, the collection and analysis of data, and using what is learned from an inquiry to act on important organizational issues (Botcheva, White & Huffman, 2002).

Networked Nonprofit: A networked nonprofit has a set of intentionally built trusting relationships and has systems and strategies that engage various stakeholders in meaningful conversations. They achieve their missions by developing strong partnerships where they invest in the goals of other organizations to mobilize resources for a common shared mission and values (Kanter & Fine, 2010).

Networked: Organizational power derived from intentional strategic and informal relationships that exist among those in leadership roles in the various centers of activity to cause action or support (Renz, 2010; Holley, 2011).

Nonprofit Organization: While the name applies to its tax-exempt status, a nonprofit is an organization that has a mission to have a positive social impact.

Nonprofit Organizational Effectiveness: This is a multidimensional social construct that is influenced by the Board of Directors. Effective nonprofits likely use correct management practice and are responsive (Herman & Renz, 2008). Nonprofit effectiveness is determined by organizations meeting their double-bottom line of financial solvency and advancing a social good (Collins, 2005).

Organizational Capacity: The ability for nonprofit organizations to fulfill their missions in an effective manner (Leake, Green, Marquez, Vanderburg, Guillaume & Gardner, 2007).

Organizational Effectiveness: The implementation of an idea, service, process, procedure, system, structure or product new to prevailing organizational practices (Jaskyte, 2004; Shilbury & Moore, 2006). Synonyms include effectiveness, performance, productivity, efficiency, health, excellence, quality, competitiveness, or success (Baruch & Ramalho, 2006).

Social Network: A social network is the set of relations between people. Theories of social networks have emerged from multiple fields such as anthropology, sociology, mathematics and psychology. The analysis of a social network can reveal a "helicopter view" of the interrelationships, that is, to rise above what one member sees from the point of view of their own network and view it from above. Social network analysis also can make the invisible attributes and relationships more visible (Kadushin, 2012).

Virtual Community of Practice: A community of practice enabled by information and communication technologies. Although virtual CoPs can rely on a wide range of technologies to support communication and collaboration such as websites, email, intranets, and web conferencing, some also use face to face meetings.

Chapter 7
Bringing Service Standards to Life

Julie Kwan
Hitachi Consulting, USA

Stephanie Clark
Learn on Demand, USA

Steven W. Villachica
Boise State University, USA

EXECUTIVE SUMMARY

This case study describes the efforts of performance consultants to improve the extent to which staff and volunteers at a nonprofit agency performed according to their customer service standards. After providing background information about the organization and its service standards, the case study describes the existing performance gap regarding the standards and the consultants' response to the client's initial request for training. The case study describes the performance analysis the consultants conducted, including the gap analysis, organizational analysis, environmental analysis, and cause analysis. The case study also describes the task analysis that the consultants conducted using the critical incident technique. The case study concludes with a description of how the consultants created the resulting training, and the effect of the training on the sponsoring organization.

DOI: 10.4018/978-1-4666-8330-3.ch007

ORGANIZATION BACKGROUND

Founded in 1972, the Teddy Bear Foundation (a pseudonym) is an international non-profit organization that provides temporary accommodations and financial support for families with a family member suffering from critical illness. The Foundation consists of a network of over 300 chapters, known as Dens (a pseudonym), which are located in various countries around the world. Guests are weary, emotionally taxed, and under extreme stress. The goal of a Den is to give support to these caretakers in their time of need.

Opened in 1988, the local Den is run by 13 paid staff and supported by 30 regular volunteers from the surrounding community. The Den may house up to 19 families at any given time. It provides private rooms, laundry facilities, meals, and other amenities. Families staying at the Den come from a variety of economic, social, and ethnic backgrounds. Guests may stay at the Den for anywhere from a few days to several months, depending on the length of their family members' hospital stay. To serve them, the Den ensures that two to four staff members and three to four volunteers are present each day.

This Den's leadership team consists of Daniel (Executive Director), Sarah (Director of Operations), and Kaitlyn (Volunteer Coordinator). They manage and direct the strategic and daily functions of the Den. Each has worked there for three to four years. In addition to the core leadership team, the Den also employs five weekend managers and one night manager. The managers watch over the property and tend to guests during non-business hours.

Working together, employees and volunteers support guests by answering questions, accommodating special requests, and providing necessary assistance. They serve on the Den's front lines to provide services to the guest families. Among other duties, volunteers check in and orient guests upon arrival. Volunteers also prepare meals, stock supplies, clean guest rooms, and perform light maintenance around the premises. They answer guest questions and provide a helping hand as guests share their needs and concerns, in many ways, acting as concierges. Many volunteers have been contributing their time and efforts at the Den for over ten years; they have the most interaction with, and act as the primary source of support for, the guests who stay there.

From a performance standpoint, these mission-critical interactions are *incredibly complex tasks* (Wulfeck & Wetzel-Smith, 2010). This knowledge work involves dynamic communications under complex conditions that are often unpredictable and novel. These interactions are highly variable and involve families dealing with high levels of stress, ambiguity, and uncertainty. Conversations can be emotionally charged and uncomfortable.

SETTING THE STAGE

Recently, the Foundation's international leadership directed all Den executive directors to push for excellence by improving customer service and fostering appropriate conduct by Den staff and volunteers. Daniel met with Kaitlyn and Sarah to discuss this directive and plan how they might fulfill it within their Den. Collaborating with key staff and volunteers, they developed a list of service standards for the Den. These standards provided staff and volunteers with a framework for appropriate conduct and engagement with guests and each other in this stressful environment. The standards consisted of behavioral statements grouped into four categories: Professional, Respectful, Compassionate, and Helpful. Table 1 provides examples of corresponding behavioral statements within each category of the service standards.

A few months after implementing the standards, Den leadership decided to collect data describing how well the standards were working. In formal meetings and informal individual conversations, staff and volunteers confidently reported that they met these service standards. However, leadership observations and a guest satisfaction survey indicated that guest services still needed improvement. Staff and volunteers were sometimes rude and judgmental. At other times, they were insensitive toward guests' backgrounds, situations, and needs.

Daniel, Kaitlyn, and Sarah quickly realized that staff, volunteers, and guests held differing views regarding the extent to which the Den met its own service standards. Other conversations indicated that staff and volunteers sometimes had no idea how to apply the service standards on the job—especially in stressful, highly emotional situations. This leadership team also realized that the service standards remained abstract, even though the behavioral statements provided examples for each category. In other words, the standards lacked contextual clues that could guide interactions

Table 1. Service standard categories and behavioral statements

Category	Example Behavioral Statements
Professional	• We respond to questions and/or concerns in a prompt and courteous manner. • We respect, support, and encourage each other, and work cooperatively as members of a team.
Respectful	• We protect our families' need to rest, relax, and sleep at any/all hours of the day. • When it is necessary to enter a guest's room, we respect the family's belongings and privacy. We give them prior notice before entering.
Compassionate	• We support and encourage guests, recognize when someone is in need of help, and assist appropriately. • We are open-minded, non-judgmental, and understanding of our families.
Helpful	• We are proactive and anticipate families' needs. • We provide a comfortable, safe, and reassuring environment 24 hours a day, 365 days a year.

with guests in any situation. For example, what one volunteer might perceive as responding to a guest question in a prompt and courteous manner, Kaitlyn, Sarah, or a guest might perceive as being curt or brusque. Daniel also knew that the Den's long-time dedicated volunteers were accustomed to certain pre-existing procedures. Although they had a sincere desire to serve the Den's guests, these volunteers had a tendency to resist new policies and procedures that Daniel and Kaitlyn had been trying to implement. Volunteers had outlasted the last leadership team. Some felt they would outlast this new team as well.

Den leadership recognized that merely communicating the service standards was not improving service itself. Because its guests were in the midst of highly stressful situations, employee and volunteer interactions with guests were often instinctive. Every situation was different. So, what did it mean to be professional, respectful, compassionate, and helpful when assisting these hard-pressed, afflicted families? The application of these service standards was unclear.

The Den needed help meeting the high standards it had set for itself. Leadership wanted employees and volunteers to act on the standards in a consistent manner. They wanted the service standards to become automatic to its staff and volunteers in every stressful, dynamic situation.

CASE DESCRIPTION

Defining the Need

Initial Client Meeting: Daniel, Kaitlyn, and Sarah decided that training would be the best approach to teach employees and volunteers how to meet the standards in their everyday dealings with guests and each other. To this end, Daniel brought in a team of performance improvement consultants.

The lead consultant asked Daniel, "What do you need staff and volunteers to do at the Den when they provide customer service?"

Daniel replied, "We need consistent customer service. There are many times when staff and volunteers interact with guests in ways that meet all of our service standards. There are other times, especially with guests that are already frazzled, when they don't. We need all of our staff and volunteers consistently responding to all our guests in a compassionate and kind manner that is aligned with our organizational values. We also need to implement our new service standards in a concrete, engaging manner that creates accountability for everyone that is involved in our program and daily operations."

The lead consultant asked, "What is it that you want your staff and volunteers to be doing on the job that they aren't doing now?"

Daniel responded, "My volunteers need to be less judgmental of our guests. I have heard them make insensitive comments about guest backgrounds and lifestyles. Comments like, 'No wonder his family is so unhealthy, they eat nothing but junk food', are never acceptable. I want them to be able to put themselves in other peoples' shoes, to be able to approach their interactions with others more compassionately. They need to be aware of how their words and actions affect others—especially when our guests are already vulnerable. I would also like for my staff and volunteers to be able to separate their personal concerns from their work. I need them to focus on our guests, not what they may have going on outside of our building. In addition, I need everyone to buy into our new service standards. I want to teach our staff and volunteers how to implement these standards well without sending the message that they're doing a bad job. I have ideas on how to implement the standards, but I want to make sure we do it the right way to make the best impact. I think what we really need is sensitivity and diversity training."

"Daniel," the lead consultant asked, "do you have any documents or information that you can share with us that will help us get to know the Den – planning documents for the service standards, policies and procedures, past evaluations or surveys, job descriptions, or guidelines for volunteers? The better we know your people and your organization, the better we will be able to design a solution that helps the Den consistently meet its service standards. To create any sort of training, we'll need access to the people in your organization that everyone turns to when they have questions. Our goal will be to create training that helps others at the Den act more like these key people. We'll also need access to your staff and volunteers. We need to learn more about where they are and what barriers may be getting in the way."

Daniel shared the data he and his leadership team collected on the impact of the service standards, including results of conversations with staff and volunteers, observations of Den employees and volunteers, and the guest satisfaction survey. He also promised to provide the consultants with the other documents and access to the individuals she requested.

Approach and Tools Selection: The lead consultant left the meeting feeling excited and relieved. She had been able to respond to the client in a way that he appreciated. She was able to get a commitment from Daniel to provide information the team would need to get started, as well as the people that the team would need to interview and survey. The lead consultant heard Daniel's prescription for sensitivity and diversity training. However, their conversation told the consultant that she needed to focus on improved performance and steer her client away from prescribing solutions without understanding whether there was a deeper cause. She knew that simply fulfilling Daniel's prescription might not solve the performance problem. Instead, it would be prudent for the consultants to start at the beginning.

The consultants opted to use Van Tiem, Mosely, and Dessinger's (2012) performance improvement model to guide their efforts. As depicted in Figure 1, they would conduct a Performance Analysis that would inform intervention selection, design, and development. This Performance Analysis would consist of the following:

- An Organizational Analysis to identify the Den's Mission and organizational goals, and how desired performance aligned with them;
- An Environmental Analysis to ascertain the existing performance and the various factors affecting it;
- A Gap Analysis to specify existing and desired performance, and to determine whether the gap was worth closing; and
- A Cause Analysis to determine the sources of the performance gap and corresponding solutions to close the performance gap.

Organizational Analysis: Accordingly, the consultants wanted to get to know the organization first. They knew that spending time upfront on understanding the Den's problem and its causes would help them be more efficient and successful in developing a solution. The first step in the Performance Analysis was an Organizational Analysis. The consultants reviewed the Mission Statement of the Teddy Bear Foundation, as well as the Statement of Values for the local Den.

The very essence of the Foundation's Mission was to provide a comfortable, supportive environment for families with members in hospitals receiving treatment for serious illness. The Statement of Values for the local Den emphasized service that should be friendly, supportive, respectful, and responsive to the families' needs. The service standards of being professional, respectful, compassionate, and helpful directly aligned with the organization's Mission and Statement of Values.

The consultants reviewed the documents that Daniel provided. These documents provided insight into the process that the Den leadership followed as they collaborated with their staff to create the service standards. The guest satisfaction survey illustrated guest perceptions of the performance level of staff and volunteers, supporting Daniel's concerns about his people lacking sensitivity and compassion for the Den's guests. One consultant on the team turned her focus toward analyzing the Den's environment, including the Den, its processes, and its staff and volunteers. She also wanted to assess Daniel's vision of desired performance. She met with Daniel to learn more.

The consultant asked Daniel, "What is the ultimate goal that you would like this training to achieve? How would you know that the training was successful?"

Daniel replied, "I want the standards to be a vehicle for us to become a strong team and to address the behaviors that interfere with our drive for excellence in hospitality. I want our people to be comfortable giving one another feedback – praise

Figure 1. The performance improvement model

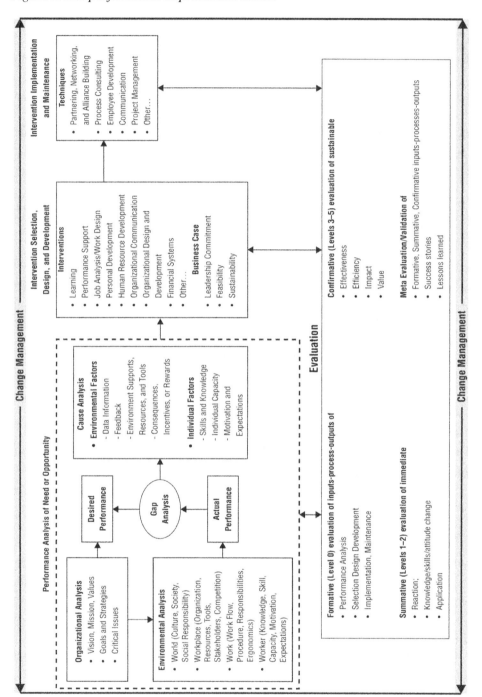

when they do something right and suggestions when they do something that does not conform to the hospitality excellence that we strive for. We need an environment where people know they will be called out in a supportive and helpful manner, not a punitive one. I am looking for excellence, but that requires agreement and consistency between everyone's idea of what excellence means and how to implement it."

The consultant asked, "If you had to realistically quantify this goal, what percent of the time will your staff and volunteers be doing this?"

Daniel leaned back in his chair and said, "Well, I would hope for 100% of the time. Realistically, I would say the staff and volunteers need to understand and communicate what the standards mean to them and demonstrate the appropriate behaviors listed in these standards 90% of the time."

"What would you say they're currently doing?"

Daniel sighed, "I feel they are demonstrating the appropriate behaviors about 75% of the time. Some areas could use a 25% improvement, such as maintaining confidentiality of information; respect, support, and encouragement of guests and each other; being open-minded and non-judgmental; and recognizing when someone is in need of assistance."

"Thanks, Daniel. I've had a chance to review the background documents you provided to us. They helped us follow your process of creating the service standards. In some of the notes, I saw that you performed a Strengths, Weaknesses, Opportunities, and Threats Analysis with your team. Could you tell me a little bit more about some of the weaknesses that your team identified? What led you to put them on the list of weaknesses? For example, the first one on the list is 'Inconsistent messages to guests'. Tell me about that."

Daniel responded, "There are times when a guest will ask the front desk volunteer a question and later ask a staff member. Often, the original answer is not accurate or causes confusion. We need to get everyone on the same page."

"Can you tell me about this next one, 'Impatient behaviors'?"

"Sometimes we have difficult guests. Sometimes we have difficult volunteers. I overhear our volunteers complaining about our guests and other volunteers, which means that some of our guests may overhear the same conversations. I also know that some volunteers lose patience with guests that take advantage of our resources. Maybe 30% of our guests use and abuse the system. It's hard to stand by and watch. I get it. But it is unacceptable for us to be impatient with guests or to try to police everything. I also want them to stop pointing out problems and start coming up with solutions to those problems. This also relates to handling difficult conversations. I know they're not going to be experts at this, but I want our staff and volunteers to be more confident in having difficult conversations with guests and one another. The big thing about this is listening and making the other person feel like they're being heard."

"That seems to be closely tied with the next item, 'Communication'."

"Yes. I think being able to handle difficult conversations is a large part of why communication was on our list of weaknesses. On top of that, it's also being able to clearly communicate rules with our guests and communicating with one another. Typically, there's some important note about a guest or need that doesn't get passed to others who need to know about it. There's sometimes a breakdown in the open communication that's necessary for us to serve our guests with top notch hospitality."

"Thank you, Daniel. That really helps me better understand more about what you want to achieve with the service standards and the work you've brought us in to do. From here, we would like to hear from your staff and volunteers so that we can gain a better sense of who they are and how we can more effectively help you meet your goals. We have written a short questionnaire that we would like all staff and volunteers to complete. Could we take a few minutes to review the questions together so that I can finalize it and distribute it to everyone in your Den?"

"Sure."

Environmental Analysis: The consultant and Daniel continued their meeting by reviewing the questionnaire. Daniel agreed to have his leadership team distribute it to the Den's staff and volunteers that week. In this questionnaire, the consultants hoped to learn more about staff and volunteer motivations, preferences, and attitudes. Figure 2 shows this survey.

Results of the questionnaire indicated that staff and volunteers had a high level of commitment to serving guests and were motivated to do what was best for the guests staying at the Den. To learn most effectively, participants would need to be reminded of their motivation for joining the Den and participate in interactive scenarios that demonstrate both exemplary and undesired application of the service standards.

The consultants also arranged to spend time observing the daily operations of the Den. During their observations, the consultants documented conversations, interactions, and activities they observed in the Den. The lead consultant even found herself interacting with one of the guests. As she walked into the kitchen, she heard the clanking of glasses and dishes. She observed a man trying to add dirty dishes into the dishwasher, which appeared to be full. He was visibly flustered. She knew she was supposed to be a quiet observer, but there were no volunteers in the immediate area.

"May I help you with that, sir?" The lead consultant asked.

"All I needed to do was put this stupid cup in the dishwasher, but it's so full, I can't find any room!" he shouted, slamming the cup onto the counter.

"You're right," she replied. "This dishwasher is super full. Why don't you grab one of those delicious cookies and rest on the sofa? I can get everything loaded in the dishwasher and then start the wash cycle."

Figure 2. Survey gauging staff and volunteer motivations, preferences, and attitudes

DEN STAFF AND VOLUNTEER QUESTIONNAIRE

1. What motivated you to volunteer/work at the Den and why?

2. Describe in a few words what you feel to be the Mission and Vision of the Den.

3. What do you find most interesting about serving guests of the Den?

4. What do you find most challenging about serving guests of the Den?

5. What would make your job easier in your daily interactions with our diverse population?

6. What is the most difficult part of your duties?

7. In what languages (other than English) are you conversational?

8. Please rate the following on a scale of 1 to 5 (1=strongly disagree, 5=strongly agree):

    a. The needs/concerns of the guests are easily communicated from one shift to the next.

    b. The duties of my position are made clear.

    c. I have received adequate training for my position.

    d. There is a high level of respect among the staff and volunteers.

    e. There is a high level of respect between staff and guests.

    f. When I care for guests, I am always confident that I am responding appropriately.

    g. It is important to put my personal beliefs aside when caring for guests, but sometimes it is difficult.

    h. I prefer interactive training activities as opposed to a lecture format.

    i. I can describe what it means to provide a comfortable, safe environment for guests.

"Great. I've got bigger things to worry about!" he said as he stormed out of the kitchen.

This brief interaction stunned the lead consultant. As she rearranged the dishes in the dishwasher and started it, she realized that this was exactly what staff and volunteers experienced every day. She felt how her reaction to the man's need was instinctive, and how the service standards didn't even cross her mind in that moment. She also felt a lack of appreciation from the man.

The lead consultant's interaction, along with the results of the questionnaire and observations, supported Daniel's concerns about implementing the service standards successfully. The consultants saw that implementing the service standards meant a culture shift for the Den. While the Den exhibited an overall culture of compassion and service for guests in difficult situations, the culture existing amongst its staff and volunteers needed a shift. They needed to be aware of how their actions affected others. To help foster this awareness, they also needed an open environment where staff and volunteers were encouraged to coach one another on their performance, reminding each other of the ultimate goal of providing excellent customer service to the Den's guests.

While the consultant focused on analyzing the Den's environment and administering the questionnaire, the lead consultant reached out to several other Dens within the Teddy Bear Foundation. She spoke with Den executive directors to learn about their operations and environment. She asked questions about various elements of the Dens, including demographics of staff, volunteers, and guests; daily operations; and efforts to improve customer service. She also spoke with a hospitality expert from a for-profit leader in the hospitality industry. All of this information would help the consultants learn about benchmarks and best practices within the Teddy Bear Foundation, as well as the hospitality industry.

The consultants planned their data collection efforts strategically. Illustrated in Figure 3, their observations, interviews, questionnaires, and document reviews contributed to various components of their Performance Analysis, as well as the Task Analysis that would follow. This strategic approach allowed the consultants to collect a large amount of data while minimizing their impact on the busy Den.

Figure 3. Consultants' observations, interviews, questionnaires, and document reviews

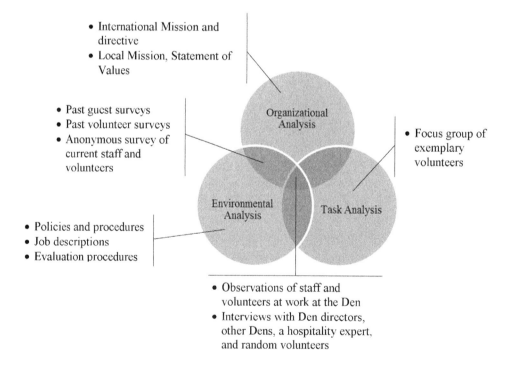

- International Mission and directive
- Local Mission, Statement of Values

- Past guest surveys
- Past volunteer surveys
- Anonymous survey of current staff and volunteers

Organizational Analysis

- Focus group of exemplary volunteers

Environmental Analysis

Task Analysis

- Policies and procedures
- Job descriptions
- Evaluation procedures

- Observations of staff and volunteers at work at the Den
- Interviews with Den directors, other Dens, a hospitality expert, and random volunteers

Examining the Systemic Factors of the Gap

Gap Analysis: Daniel wanted the staff and volunteers to apply the service standards 90% of the time while working at the local Teddy Bear Den. The data indicated that the current rate of service standard application was at 60% to 75%. A performance rate of 90% would indicate that the staff and volunteers are consistently treating the Den's guests with respect, support, and responsiveness. This would directly help the Den meet their Statement of Values, as well as comply with Teddy Bear Foundation's Mission and directive to improve customer service. Therefore, Daniel and the consultants confirmed that the performance gap was worth closing.

Cause Analysis: Once they determined the gap, the consultants continued to the Cause Analysis using Gilbert's (2007) Behavior Engineering Model, displayed in Table 2. As they reviewed the data they collected, the consultants looked for common themes and prominent pain points. For each item, they asked:

1. Does this pertain to the environment or the individual?
2. If it's environmental, does it relate to availability of data, resources, or incentives?
3. If it's individual, does it relate to the staff and volunteers' knowledge and skills, capacity to do the job, or motivation?

Putting their data into the Behavior Engineering Model, the consultants found that there were many causes for the Den's performance gap. They knew that a training solution would not address all of these causes. By nature, training solutions only

Table 2. Cause analysis using the behavior engineering model

Environment	**Data** • Service standards not prominently posted • No clear guidance describing how to apply the standards in daily activities • No feedback provided about extent to which volunteer performance met the service standards	**Resources** Faulty processes and tools hindered implementation of service standards	**Incentives** • Little recognition of exemplary performance • Few consequences for unacceptable performance
Individual	**Knowledge** • Poor communication skills with guests and other staff and volunteers • Inappropriate responses to guest needs • Staff and volunteers had a hard time applying service standards in uncomfortable, stressful situations	**Capacity** • Volunteers did not feel empowered to take action • Daily tasks assigned as needed, without consideration of skills	**Motives** Volunteers and staff wanted to help others in need

focus on individual knowledge and skills. The consultants knew that if the other causes were not addressed, the performance gap would not be completely eliminated with a successful training solution.

Despite Daniel's original prescription of sensitivity and diversity training, the consultants realized that the knowledge-related cause of the performance gap was actually a lack of skills in

- Effectively communicating with guests and other Den personnel, and
- Appropriately responding to guest needs, especially in stressful situations.

In other words, staff and volunteers couldn't meet the standards in these situations, even if their lives depended on it. They literally didn't know how to communicate with guests in ways that met standards.

Client Review: Before moving any further with the project, the consultants met with Daniel to review the results of the Cause Analysis and to propose the new subjects of the training course. The lead consultant started the conversation.

"Daniel," the lead consultant began, "thank you for taking the time to meet with us again and for allowing us to spend time with your people and in your Den. It has helped us tremendously in understanding your Den, your staff and volunteers, and your guests. We wanted to update you on the progress we've made. When we first met with you, we heard you say that you needed to implement and communicate the Den's new service standards. You expressed concerns over how your staff and volunteers might receive these changes. We also discussed the performance gap – you would like the staff and volunteers to apply the service standards 90% of the time, but they're currently performing at 60-75%. Through our questionnaires, observations, and interviews, we identified several causes for this performance gap." The consultant reviewed the Behavior Engineering Model (Table 2) with Daniel and explained the six different cells.

The lead consultant then continued, "You originally asked us to create diversity and sensitivity training. We believe training is a great solution for your Den. Industry experience tells us that training can directly affect the Knowledge area of this model. Everything listed in the top row of the table can be addressed by changes in the environment of the Den. An individual's capacity and motives are difficult for anyone other than the individual to change."

"So, because of that," the consultant added, "we believe that, rather than creating diversity and sensitivity training, we can help you have a greater impact by developing training that focuses on Communication and Responding to Needs."

The consultants paused while Daniel processed this information. He asked, "Tell me a little bit more about this new direction you want to take."

The lead consultant responded, "After spending time getting to know your organization, we saw that sensitivity and diversity are really just symptoms of a deeper problem. The very essence of the Teddy Bear Foundation's Mission and Statement of Values comes down to responding to guest needs. Part of responding well to guest needs is communication. We also know that these communications can be hard, and staff and volunteers need to be confident when they do this. We want to provide a safe, simulated learning environment where they can practice meeting the service standards in a variety of situations. When they pass an evaluation of their mastery of these skills, they should be performing more like the Den's best. When your people get these right, we believe that the sensitivity and diversity symptoms will disappear."

"I see what you're saying, and it makes sense. Let's keep going with this," replied Daniel.

Clarifying Exemplary Performance

Task Analysis Tool Selection: With the intervention selected and appropriate focus identified (see Figure 1), the consultants set out to create the training solution. The first question to answer was, "What does exemplary performance look like?" In order to train staff and volunteers on how to appropriately communicate with guests and respond to their needs, the consultants needed to define what meeting the service standards looked like in a variety of situations.

This would prove to be a challenge. Exemplary performance of the service standards could be fuzzy and bound to particular contexts. A response that met the service standards in one situation wouldn't meet it in another. The daily tasks of staff and volunteers varied, depending on the needs and situations of their guests. Furthermore, the standards and associated behaviors remained vague. Neither the volunteers nor the staff knew what the service standards actually looked like within the context of supporting a stressed family in need.

To create the performance-based training they had envisioned, the performance consultants would need to create a representation of exemplary performance. The typical procedural task analysis (Jonassen, Tessmer, and Hannum, 1999) would not work. Instead, the team used Flanagan's (1954) critical incident technique. They could use this technique to collect incidents involving exemplary and non-exemplary performance. The incidents equated to stories about performance in the workplace. The team could then use the incidents and stories in the design of activities for the training solution.

Data Collection for the Critical Incident Technique: To use this technique, the lead consultant conducted a focus group with three of the local Den's volunteers. She ensured them that pseudonyms would be used for the volunteers and that the data would be reported in aggregate to help protect their identities. She then asked them to share stories they had witnessed or experienced during their time volunteering at the Den. She asked for stories that were good, bad, funny, or stressful. For each story, the lead consultant asked three questions about the incident itself:

1. What was good/bad/funny/stressful about the situation?
2. What would the participant have done differently?
3. What, if anything, did the participant learn from this situation?

The lead consultant put these stories into a spreadsheet. The consultants then reviewed the data and notes they collected during the Performance Analysis to identify other stories and behavioral examples. They added these examples to the spreadsheet. The team analyzed each of the stories and statements in the spreadsheet by asking the following questions:

1. What is the key concept in this story?
2. To which targeted training area does this story relate: Communication or Responding to Needs?
3. What is the exemplary behavior being demonstrated?
4. Which service standard(s) are represented by this statement?

Exemplary Statement Development: Using a coding system, the team grouped the stories by their relevant training areas and the exemplary behavior(s) they demonstrated. From these groupings, the consultants derived a set of statements of exemplary behavior that defined performance for staff and volunteers at the Den. For each statement, the team wrote a rationale, which included supporting evidence for the statement and its related service standard(s).

There were 15 statements in total, and the consultants knew that it would be difficult to cover all of them in one training course. So, they reviewed the statements and their rationales and prioritized them by assigning a level of criticality to each statement:

1. The training *must* include discussion about the statement of exemplary behavior.
2. The training *should* include discussion about the statement of exemplary behavior, if time allows.
3. The training *will not* include the statement of exemplary behavior. It is better addressed using other solutions or later training, such as town hall meetings or evaluations.

This exercise helped the team identify the five most important statements of exemplary behavior that needed to be addressed in the training course. Table 3 shows a sample of statements of exemplary behavior, along with their criticalities and rationales.

Client Review: The team reviewed the prioritized list of statements with Daniel, explaining their process and criticalities. It was essential for Daniel to review the statements and agree on the criticality ratings because this would guide the design and development of the training course. They also explained to him that they would like to use the collected stories as the basis for the training activity scenarios.

Table 3. Sample of statements of exemplary behavior

Statement of Exemplary Behavior	Criticality	Rationale
RESPOND TO THE NEEDS OF GUESTS AND TEAM MEMBERS		
Offer assistance, without waiting to be asked, when you recognize a guest is in need.	1	During observations and interviews, the team observed some instances of lack of recognition for guests in need of help. Applicable Service Standards: • Helpful #4 • Compassionate #3
Be proactive in assisting each other with tasks and following Den standards.	1	When new volunteers arrived, the team observed that they were not given adequate assistance in where to sign in, store personal belongings, etc. until they asked. Also, interviews identified a need for staff and volunteers to support each other through both giving and receiving feedback. Staff recognized feedback as something all staff and volunteers should feel comfortable doing; volunteers viewed it as staff responsibility. Applicable Service Standards: • Professional #4
Review all possible solutions when assisting a guest with an unusual request.	2	Interviews indicated a general necessity for increased excellence in guest support. Staff and volunteers often exhibited impatience with guests or lacked focus for finding solutions. Applicable Service Standards: • Compassionate #3 • Helpful #4
COMMUNICATE WITH GUESTS AND TEAM MEMBERS		
When communicating with others, use a professional, respectful, and compassionate tone of voice.	1	Interviews suggested that volunteers sometimes did not respond professionally or respectfully when they were informed of changes to Den policy or rules. Also, volunteers demonstrated a lack of patience when interacting with difficult individuals. Applicable Service Standards: • Professional #1, 6 • Respectful #3 • Compassionate #1, 3
When appropriate, introduce yourself, including your name and role.	3	Observation and interviews indicated that staff and volunteers often did not greet guests immediately or by name. Applicable Service Standards: • Professional #1, 6

Daniel paused and then confided, "I'm a little concerned about protecting the anonymity of our people in the scenarios you are building into the training. I don't want anyone or any details in any of the stories you've collected to be easily recognizable by anyone else. It could upset participants, especially if the scenarios are used as bad examples."

The consultant replied, "I assure you, Daniel, that we will modify details and remove all names from the stories. They will not be recognizable, but the concepts behind the scenarios will be the same so that they will still be relevant to the group. For example, we collected a story about a staff member who confronted a volunteer in front of several guests about misplacing some important paperwork. We would change some of the details, perhaps to say that a volunteer provided guidance to another volunteer on how to correctly get a guest checked in."

"We'll also write some of the scenarios from scratch," added the lead consultant. "This way, the scenarios will feel familiar to participants. Staff and volunteers should be able to envision these scenarios happening in the Den, but be unable to point the proverbial finger to any specific instance. This is important in making the training course an authentic learning experience for your people. We will also send the library of scenarios to you for review before we include them in the training materials. Does that sound ok?"

"Yes. Thank you!"

Designing and Developing the Solution

The consultants wanted to address all of the causes of the performance problem. However, they also knew that this would be a far greater undertaking than that for which they were hired. Instead, the lead consultant suggested they develop a "Training+" solution. They would focus their efforts on developing a training course. They could even create a performance assessment tool for the training course that the Den leadership could also use in performance reviews and feedback sessions for staff and volunteers. And, to address the other causes, they would provide the Den's leadership with a list of recommendations and solutions. By addressing all of the causes, this "Training+" solution would have the greatest impact in helping the Den close its performance gap.

As they began work on an instructional plan for the training course, the consultants knew that the training would need buy-in and support from both the Den leadership and their staff and volunteers in order for it to be effective. They also knew that it needed to be short because volunteers were already giving their spare time to the organization. It would be difficult to consume any more of their time.

And, the training needed to be adaptable to the Den's changing needs. Should a new performance problem arise, the consultants wanted to provide a structure for the training that would allow Den leadership to create new training easily.

The consultants decided to create a two-unit, instructor-led training course for the Den. One unit would focus on Responding to Needs; the other unit would focus on Communication. The units could be delivered individually or together, based on needs and time constraints of the Den. Guided by Merrill's First Principles (2002), both units would follow the same basic structure, shown in Table 4.

Job-Focused Objectives: The consultants knew that clear, applicable objectives should be the first item in designing training. These objectives must reflect on-the-job behaviors to be relevant to the staff and volunteers. They also must include the criteria by which they would be measured and the conditions within which they would be performed. For each unit, the performance improvement team detailed the behavior to be learned and developed the criteria by summarizing the list of corresponding statements of exemplary behavior and their criticality rating from the critical incident technique.

Role-Play Activities: Another important design consideration for the training would be how to emulate on-the-job interactions that staff and volunteers have with guests. Given the uncertainty and abstract nature of interpersonal communications with guests, the consultants determined that the Demonstration and Application phases would use role-play activities. These activities would allow staff and volunteers to view these skills and practice them in context. Role-plays would also provide a safe environment to learn from mistakes that the participants wouldn't want to make

Table 4. Unit structure

Course Element	Explanation
Introduction/Activation	Promotes buy-in from the participants by reminding them of their prior experiences and reasons for working at the Den, and connecting them with the objectives of the training.
Demonstration	Includes a non-example and an example of exemplary performance. Introduces the Evaluation Checklist used as a performance assessment tool.
Application	Provides role-play activities that model on-the-job performance. Activities are based on stories collected using the critical incident technique. Uses the Evaluation Checklist to teach participants to provide peer feedback to one another.
Integration (During the training)	Asks participants to reflect upon their prior experiences and how they would be different now. Promotes transfer of the new skills to the participants' jobs.
Integration (Back in the workplace)	Uses the Evaluation Checklist to evaluate staff and volunteers on the job within a few weeks of training and provide coaching as needed.

with an actual guest and to provide feedback to one another. Providing constructive feedback during the course would, in turn, encourage them to provide feedback to each other in the workplace. Additionally, role-play activities during the training class required coaching (immediate error detection and correction) and feedback from training facilitators. This would be an opportunity for staff and volunteers to identify and discuss the small nuances inherent in the various role-play scenarios. By doing so, participants would better recognize contextual factors underlying appropriate service behaviors and gain confidence in applying them on the job.

The consultants based the training's role-play scenarios on the stories and observations they collected during the Performance and Task Analyses. To use these stories in ways that didn't violate confidentiality, the consultants removed identifying information from the stories they collected. The result was a collection of role-play scenarios that facilitators could use to facilitate the training. With this modular design, the facilitators and Den leadership could choose the scenarios that would appear in each training session in order to add variety to the training and address future Den needs as they arose.

Authentic Performance Assessment: Given their decision to use role-play activities, the consultants began designing the performance assessment tool. Their goal was to create an assessment packet that the Den could use in every training session and across different facilitators to reliably determine whether staff and volunteers met the performance objectives and their criteria. To make it sound a little less technical for the Den, they named it the Evaluation Checklist. As staff and volunteers completed several role-play scenarios depicting different guest and communication contexts, the facilitator would use the checklist to determine whether participants met the objective criteria. By tallying the number of "yes" observations, the facilitator could calculate a score used to determine a participant's mastery of the objectives.

The Evaluation Checklist would serve a variety of roles. Instructors would introduce it to staff and volunteers while modeling how to interact with guests during course Demonstrations. Then, participants would use it during practice exercises in the Application phase to provide feedback to each other on the role-play activities. The instructor could use the Checklist to determine whether each student met the mastery criteria in the training assessment. After the training was over, Den leadership could use the Checklist periodically to evaluate staff and volunteer performance on the job after the training. This Checklist had the potential to be used not only in the training course, but also in performance reviews. With the data collected from the Checklist, Den leadership could determine whether they were actually closing their performance gap relating to their service standards.

Client Review: With the design effort completed, the consultants once again met with Daniel to ensure he agreed on their recommended path.

"Daniel, we are making great progress on developing something that we believe will really help you implement the Den's service standards," the consultant said. "We wanted to take this opportunity to review our plan for the training course to ensure we still agree on how this course should look."

"Great! I'm excited to see what you have for me."

The lead consultant continued, "We know that the environment at the Den is full of complex situations. Your staff and volunteers typically have to react in the moment while consistently keeping with the service standards. We've also discussed that a job aid would be useless and hinder performance."

"And, the last time we met, we agreed that the Den needs a training course focused on two mission-critical objectives: Responding to Needs and Communication," said the consultant. "We have written a plan for the training course that will engage your staff and volunteers with plenty of practice applying the service standards and giving feedback to one another, in one guest-facing situation after another."

The lead consultant proceeded to walk Daniel through the instructional plan, role-play activities, and Evaluation Checklist.

Formative Evaluation: With Daniel's approval, the consultants proceeded to develop the training materials according to their instructional plan. They conducted a train-the-trainer session to prepare Daniel and Kaitlyn to deliver the training course. Then, the consultants coordinated a pilot session of the course, facilitated by Daniel and Kaitlyn. This pilot session included four staff and two board members.

The content and activities of the training course were well-received by pilot participants. Daniel and Kaitlyn successfully helped participants connect their motivations for working at the Den to the reason for the training course. Participants appreciated having the service standards illustrated for them in a variety of scenarios. The role-play activities, however, were the most impactful element of the course. Participants felt that the role-play scenarios were realistic. They experienced the scenarios from different points of view – volunteers experienced being guests and staff experienced being volunteers. In other words, the role-play activities asked participants to walk in someone else's shoes, which was a desire for his staff and volunteers that Daniel expressed during his first meeting with the lead consultant.

Based on other feedback from the pilot participants, the consultants made several minor modifications to the training materials before turning them over to Daniel. In addition, the consultants provided Daniel with the Evaluation Checklist, slightly modified, so that he and his leadership team could use it to conduct annual performance reviews for staff and volunteers. They gave him a role-play template that he could use to build new role-play scenarios as he collects stories from staff and volunteers about new situations that arise. The consultants also gave Daniel a template that he could use to create a new unit of training. Should a similar need for training arise in the future, he would be able to use the template as a structure for the new content.

To complete their "Training+" solution, the consultants compiled a list of recommendations, shown in Table 5, which would address the other causes of the performance gap that they identified during their Cause Analysis.

CURRENT CHALLENGES FACING THE ORGANIZATION

Since the completion of the project, the Den leadership team has conducted the training course multiple times in order to train all of its staff and volunteers. Feedback from participants has been very positive. After the initial rollout of the course, they determined that they would conduct the training twice each year. This would provide opportunities for established staff and volunteers to keep their skills sharp and new volunteers to learn how to properly apply the service standards while working at the Den. This decision also let the Den make decisions to update the set of role-play scenarios for each training session.

Although Daniel has not conducted a formal evaluation of the training course's effectiveness, he and his leadership team have seen marked improvement in staff

Table 5. Non-training causes and recommendations

Cause	Recommendation
Service standards not prominently posted	Display service standards on colorful posters throughout the Den for guests, staff, and volunteers to see
No feedback provided about extent to which volunteer performance met the service standards	Perform annual performance reviews of staff and volunteers
No clear guidance describing how to apply the standards in daily activities	Give timely, appropriate feedback when witnessing good and bad episodes in the Den
Faulty processes and tools hindered implementation of service standards	Change check-in procedures regarding rules – include them in the welcome packet and post them in guest rooms
Daily tasks assigned as needed, without consideration of skills	Design placement questionnaires to better match volunteers with tasks and volunteer positions
Volunteers did not feel empowered to take action	Encourage peer-to-peer feedback on a daily basis
Little recognition of exemplary performance; Few consequences for unacceptable performance	Highlight exemplary performance seen in the Den in a quarterly newsletter -And- Give quarterly recognition to exemplary performers based on staff and volunteer recommendations

and volunteer interactions with one another and with guests. They have seen volunteers offer one another help. They have observed coaching and feedback exchanges between staff and volunteers, and, they have witnessed far fewer incidents of poor hospitality toward Den guests.

The Den leadership team has also implemented several of the consultants' recommendations. First, they ordered poster-size prints of the service standards and posted them throughout the Den, particularly in common areas. They also began including a copy of the service standards in guest welcome packets to inform and encourage guests to behave similarly.

In the Den's quarterly newsletter, which is made available to staff, volunteers, and guests, the leadership team added a column to highlight and celebrate exemplary performers and examples of excellent hospitality. To encourage exemplary behavior, leadership placed a recognition box near the reception desk in which staff, volunteers, and guests could drop comments about the service they experience and observe.

Den leaders made conscious effort to provide their staff and volunteers with feedback on their performance. By setting the example, the leaders hoped to encourage an open culture of feedback and mutual support between staff and volunteers, regardless of their positions.

To address the recommended modifications to the guest check-in process, Daniel asked one of his staff members to review the process and its pain points. The primary concern with the check-in process was that it required the reception volunteer to walk guests through several documents, regardless of the guest's emotional state. The process needed to address the absolute essential paperwork upon guest arrival and allow some extra time for other check-in items, if necessary.

In the future, Daniel has plans to conduct a guest satisfaction survey, but lacks the resources. Due to recent economic downturn and increased healthcare costs, the Den has experienced a large increase in demand for guest accommodations. The Den has consistently been filled to capacity and maintains a long waitlist. This has increased the workload for staff and volunteers, and additional performance improvement initiatives have been placed on hold. The Den's leadership is determined to maintain the initiatives already in place but must focus all other energy on ensuring the Den has the resources and supplies it needs to serve its guests.

SOLUTIONS AND RECOMMENDATIONS

At the most recent Teddy Bear Foundation International Conference, the local Den earned the Standard of Excellence Award based on its training and performance improvement initiatives. Along with this award and recognition, Daniel and his team received a $15,000 unrestricted grant from the Foundation. The unrestricted grant award is significant for the local Den. Daniel and the Den's Board of Directors have allocated the majority of the award toward needed improvements and guest services. This is also an excellent opportunity to reserve a portion of the resources to implement other performance improvement initiatives that were placed on hold. While it is important to maintain daily operations of the Den, it is also important to maintain the culture of excellent hospitality and peer-to-peer feedback that the leadership team worked so diligently to create. Since winning the award, the Den's leadership team is preparing to present its performance improvement strategy and training materials to other Den leadership teams at the Foundation's next international conference.

Because the Den still lacks human resources and expertise to continue its performance improvement efforts, a team of consultants could conduct formative and summative evaluations. This would accomplish several objectives. First, the consultants could administer the guest satisfaction survey planned by Daniel. The survey, when compared against the previous survey, should indicate whether the Den's service level has improved. The consultants could also evaluate the impact of the training course. This should illustrate the transfer of learning that occurred in participants as a result of the training and changes in the Den's practices. And, in doing so, the consultants could assess whether other performance improvement initiatives, additional training, or modifications to the existing training course are needed. Through periodic evaluation of the Den's performance, the Den's leadership team will be able to identify initiatives and changes necessary to continually improve the Den's level of hospitality. It demonstrates the leadership's commitment to the service standards it has established.

ACKNOWLEDGMENT

The authors of this case would like to acknowledge that part of this case originally appeared in ISPI's Performance Xpress. The authors thank ISPI for its kind permission to expand the original piece into the case that appears here.

REFERENCES

Clark, S., Collins, A., Kwan, J., & Sesnon, A. (2012). Tales from the field: Making service standards real for families in need. *Performance Xpress* (August 1). Retrieved from http://www.performancexpress.org/2012/08/tales-from-the-field-making-service-standards-real-for-families-in-need/

Flanagan, J. C. (1954). The critical incident technique. *Psychological Bulletin*, *51*(4), 327–358. doi:10.1037/h0061470 PMID:13177800

Gilbert, T. F. (2007). Human competence: Engineering worthy performance (Tribute ed.). San Francisco, CA: Pfeiffer.

Jonassen, D. H., Tessmer, M., & Hannum, W. H. (1999). Procedural analysis. In *Task analysis methods for instructional design* (pp. 45–54). Mahwah, NJ: Lawrence Erlbaum Associates.

Merrill, M. D. (2002). First principles of instruction. *Educational Technology Research and Development*, *50*(3), 43–59. doi:10.1007/BF02505024

Van Tiem, D. M., Moseley, J. L., & Dessinger, J. C. (2012). *Fundamentals of performance improvement: A guide to improving people, process, and performance* (3rd ed.). San Francisco, CA: Pfeiffer.

Wulfeck, W. H., & Wetzel-Smith, S. K. (2010). Training incredibly complex tasks. In P. E. O'Connor & J. V. Cohn (Eds.), *Human performance enhancement in high-risk environments: Insights, development, and future directions from military research* (pp. 74–89). Santa Barbara, CA: ABC-CLIO.

ADDITIONAL READING

Addison, R. M., Haig, C., & Kearny, L. (2009). The performance architect's essential guide to the performance technology landscape. In J. A. Pershing (Ed.), Handbook of human performance technology (3d Edition ed., pp. 35-54). San Francisco: Pfeiffer.

Brethower, D., & Smalley, K. (1998). *Performance-based instruction: Linking training to business results*. San Francisco, CA: Jossey-Bass/Pfeiffer.

Butterfield, L. D., Borgen, W. A., Amundson, N. E., & Maglio, A.-S. T. (2005). Fifty years of the critical incident technique: 1954-2004 and beyond. *Qualitative Research*, *5*(4), 475–497. doi:10.1177/1468794105056924

Carliner, S. (2003). *Training design basics*. Alexandria, VA: American Society for Training and Development.

Christensen, T. K. (2008). The role of theory in instructional design: Some views of an ID practitioner. *Performance Improvement*, *47*(4), 25–32. doi:10.1002/pfi.199

Clark, R. C. (2008). *Developing technical training: A structured approach for developing classroom and computer-based instructional materials* (3rd ed.). San Francisco, CA: Pfeiffer.

Crossley, J., Johnson, G., Booth, J., & Wade, W. (2011). Good questions, good answers: Alignment improves the performance of workplace-based assessment scales. *Medical Education, 45*(6), 560–569. doi:10.1111/j.1365-2923.2010.03913.x

Dean, P. J. (2000). Editorial-the critical incident technique as a vehicle for voice. *Performance Improvement Quarterly, 13*(4), 3–5. doi:10.1111/j.1937-8327.2000. tb00187.x

Elsenheimer, J. (2006). Got tools? The blended learning analysis and design expediter. *Performance Improvement, 45*(8), 26–30. doi:10.1002/pfi.4930450806

Flanagan, J. C. (1954). The critical incident technique. *Psychological Bulletin, 51*(4), 327–358. doi:10.1037/h0061470

Flanagan, J. C. (1962). *Measuring human performance*. Pittsburgh, PA: The American Institute for Research.

Gulikers, J. M., Bastiaens, T., & Kirschner, P. (2004). A five-dimensional framework for authentic assessment. *Educational Technology Research and Development, 52*(3), 67–86. doi:10.1007/BF02504676

Hagera, P., & Butlerb, J. (1996). Two models of educational assessment. *Assessment & Evaluation in Higher Education, 21*(4), 367–378. doi:10.1080/0260293960210407

Hale, J. (2007). *The performance consultant's fieldbook: Tools and techniques for improving organizations and people* (2nd ed.). San Francisco, CA: Pfeiffer.

Harless, J. H. (1973). An analysis of front-end analysis. *Improving Human Performance. Research Quarterly, 4*, 229–244.

Holmes, T. A. (2004). Designing and facilitating performance-based diversity training. *Performance Improvement, 43*(5), 13–19. doi:10.1002/pfi.4140430505

Holsbrink-Engels, G. A. (2000). Designing role-plays for interpersonal skills training. *Performance Improvement, 39*(9), 32–39. doi:10.1002/pfi.4140390911

Kerka, S. (1995). *Techniques for authentic assessment: Practice application brief.* (ED 381 688). Retrieved from http://eric.ed.gov/?id=ED381688

Mager, R. F., & Pipe, P. (1997). *Analyzing performance problems: You really oughta wanna* (3rd ed.). Atlanta, GA: CEP Press.

Marrelli, A. F. (2005). The performance technologist's toolbox: Critical incidents. *Performance Improvement*, *44*(10), 40–44. doi:10.1002/pfi.4140441009

Pace, A. (2012). Sales training for the virtual interaction. T+D, 66(6), 18-18.

Robinson, D. G., & Robinson, J. C. (1990). *Training for impact: How to link training to business needs and measure the results*. San Francisco, CA: Jossey-Bass.

Robinson, D. G., & Robinson, J. C. (2008). *Performance consulting: A practical guide for HR and learning professionals* (2nd ed.). San Francisco: Berrett-Koehler.

Rossett, A. (2009). *First things fast: A handbook for performance analysis* (2nd ed.). San Francisco, CA: Pfeiffer.

Rothwell, W. J., & Kazanas, H. C. (2008). Selecting or designing instructional materials. In *Mastering the instructional design process: A systematic approach* (4th ed., pp. 257–287). San Francisco, CA: Jossey-Bass.

Rummler, G. A. (2006). The anatomy of performance. In J. A. Pershing (Ed.), *Handbook of human performance technology: Principles, practices, and potential* (3rd ed., pp. 986–1007). San Francisco, CA: Pfeiffer.

Stolovitch, H. D., & Keeps, E. J. (2011). *Telling ain't training: Updated, expanded, enhanced* (2nd ed.). Alexandria, VA: American Society for Training and Development.

Woolsey, L. K. (1986). The critical incident technique: An innovative qualitative method of research. *Canadian Journal of Counselling*, *20*(4), 242–254.

Wright, V.O. (1989). How to use (not abuse) role plays. *Performance + Instruction*, *28*(5), 16-21. doi: 10.1002/pfi.4170280505

Yi, J. (2005). Effective ways to foster learning. *Performance Improvement*, *44*(1), 34–38. doi:10.1002/pfi.4140440111

KEY TERMS AND DEFINITIONS

Authentic Assessment: An "assessment requiring students to use the same competencies, or combinations of knowledge, skills, and attitudes, that they need to apply in the criterial situation in professional life. The level of authenticity of an assessment is defined by its degree of resemblance to the criterion situation" (Gulikers, Bastiaens, & Kirschner, 2004, p. 69). "…involves interesting real-life or authentic tasks and contexts as well as multiple assessment moments and methods to reach a profile score for determining student learning or development" (p. 68).

Cause Analysis: "The process of determining the root cause of past, present, and future performance gaps" (Van Tiem, Mosely, & Dessinger, 2012, p. 624). Performance improvement practitioners investigate all potential environmental and individual causes of a given performance gap, along with their interactions. Environmental causes include a lack of information/data (standards, guidance, feedback), resources (processes, tools), and incentives (consequences for performance). Individual causes include a lack of skill/knowledge, capacity, and motivation. Anecdotal evidence indicates that environmental causes are more frequent (76%) than individual causes (Dean, 1997).

Critical Incident Technique: "…a set of procedures for collecting direct observations of human behavior in such a way as to facilitate their potential usefulness in solving practical problems and developing broad psychological principles. The critical incident technique outlines procedures for collecting observed incidents having special significance and meeting systematically defined criteria. By an incident is meant any observable human activity that is sufficiently complete in itself to permit inferences and predictions to be made about the person performing the act. To be critical, an incident must occur in a situation where the purpose or intent of the act seems fairly clear to the observer and where its consequences are sufficiently definite to leave little doubt concerning its effects" (Flanagan, 1954, p. 327). The critical incident technique can inform both components of the performance analysis and the task analysis that is typically part of intervention selection, design and development in the performance improvement process.

Environmental Analysis: "The process used to identify and prioritize the realities that support actual performance: organizational environment, world, workplace, work, workers" (Van Tiem, Mosely, & Dessinger, 2012, p. 627). Part of performance analysis.

Gap Analysis: "Describes the difference between current results and consequences and desired results and consequences" (Van Tiem, Mosely, & Dessinger, 2012, p. 628). Part of performance analysis.

Organizational Analysis: "Examines the organizational mission, vision, values, gold, strategies, and critical issues" (Van Tiem, Mosely, & Dessinger, 2012, p. 632). Part of performance analysis, an organizational analysis aligns the performance gap with strategic organizational goals and determine that the gap is worth closing. Savvy practitioners align their effort with both stated and unstated organizational goals that keep clients up at night.

Performance Analysis: After framing the performance gap, performance improvement practitioners conduct an organizational analysis to align the performance gap with strategic organizational goals and determine that the gap is worth closing;

an environmental scan to contextualize the performance gap within the work and the workplace; and a cause analysis to determine root environmental and individual causes of the performance gap.

Task Analysis: In performance improvement situations, task analysis can inform both performance analysis as well as intervention design, especially in the specification of performance requirements/objectives.

Training+: Clients and stakeholders often use the term "training" to mean any sort of performance improvement intervention (Villachica & Stepich, 2010). A "Training+" approach to performance improvement uses performance-based training to address skills and provide guidance in the form of job aids while creating a forum for the client to address other environmental, capacity, and motivational causes of the performance gap (Clark, Collins, Kwan, & Sesnon, 2012).

Chapter 8

Fostering Student Work-Based Experiences through Service-Learning

Jennifer Maddrell
Designers for Learning, USA

EXECUTIVE SUMMARY

This case study explains how a complete overhaul to the national high school equivalency test posed a significant organizational challenge to Grace Centers of Hope, a nonprofit based in Pontiac, Michigan in the United States. All adult clients participating in Grace Centers of Hope's one-year drug and alcohol recovery program who are without a high school diploma or equivalent are required to take in-house adult basic education classes to prepare for taking the high school equivalency test. Faced with the need to completely redesign their existing adult basic education program, Grace Centers of Hope reached out to Designers for Learning, an instructional design and performance improvement consultancy that matches nonprofits with instructional design students in service-learning projects. The resulting 100% virtual e-service-learning collaboration among volunteer college students, their faculty sponsors, and other advisors provided Grace Centers of Hope with educational resources to support the organization.

DOI: 10.4018/978-1-4666-8330-3.ch008

ORGANIZATION BACKGROUND

Grace Centers of Hope is a faith-based outreach to homeless and disadvantaged individuals and families. They offer a full recovery and rehabilitation campus for homeless men, women, and children who been abused or addicted to drugs and alcohol. Grace Centers of Hope is a registered 501(c)(3) nonprofit and is classified by the U.S. Internal Revenue Service as a public charity with $5.4 million in total revenue and support for the year ended 2012 (Grace Centers of Hope, n.d.). Their programs focus on total rehabilitation by meeting all of their clients' needs, including food, clothing, shelter, educational courses, daycare, job training, assistance in preparing resumes, substance abuse programs, medical care, and housing placement. Charity Navigator, a nonprofit organization that assesses the financial health, accountability and transparency of charities, deemed that Grace Centers of Hope exceeds industry standards and outperforms most similar charities, and recognized their exceptional status with the highest 4-star rating (Charity Navigator, n.d.). In addition, Grace Centers of Hope was acknowledged by Crain's *Detroit Business* as the 2012 Best-Managed Nonprofit (Welch, 2012).

Adult clients recovering from drug, alcohol, or other challenging issues who are without a high school diploma or equivalent are required to take Grace Centers of Hope's in-house adult basic education classes as a condition of staying in the recovery program. All learners enrolled in the education program live on-site in the Grace Centers of Hope shelter. Many in the program have minor children who also live on-site. While the learners range in age from 18 through adulthood, most are in their 30s or 40s.

The adult basic education courses aim to improve the learner's language arts, science, social studies, and math skills and knowledge for career and college readiness. Given the residency aspect of Grace Centers of Hope's recovery program, the adult basic education courses are held at their Pontiac location. The staff believes that completion of the education program provides their clients increased likelihood of passing the high school equivalency test, as well as obtaining a job or being accepted into college.

SETTING THE STAGE

U.S. Adult Educational Attainment

According to 2012 U. S. Census Bureau data, approximately 30 million adults over the age of 18 (13% of the total population within this age range) had not attained a high school diploma or the equivalent. To put this figure into perspective, the U.S.

Department of Education reported 55 million children were enrolled in grades PreK–12 in 2012 (National Center for Education Statistics, 2012). Therefore, if all adult Americans who had not reached high school equivalency entered the U.S. PreK-12 school system, enrollment would increase by 55%.

The U.S. Census Bureau data offered additional insight regarding the educational attainment levels of adults age 25 and over who have not completed high school. Table 1 summarizes the highest level of educational attainment for these 25 million adults. Of note is the need for educational opportunities at a range of levels, including for the 41% who concluded their formal education before completing the ninth grade.

Not surprisingly, the 2012 U.S. Census Bureau data reflected that high school completion was related to employment. While the unemployment rate reported in the census data was 6.2% among those who had not attained a high school diploma or equivalent, the unemployment rates were less among those who completed their formal education after receiving a high school diploma or equivalent (5.4%) and among those who completed a Bachelor's degree (3.5%).

High School Equivalency Test Changes

In 2014, the high school equivalency test was revised to conform with the College and Career Readiness standards released in 2013 by the U.S. Department of Education Office of Vocational and Adult Education as a guide for adult education programs that prepare learners for post-secondary college and career training (Hoffman, Wine, & McKinney, 2013; Pimentel, 2013). In addition to the inclusion of knowledge and skills that were not part of the prior test, the revised test is now only delivered on-

Table 1. Highest grade-level attained, no diploma

Highest Grade-Level Attained	(000)	%
Less than 1 year	796	3.15%
1st-4th grade	1,688	6.68%
5th-6th grade	3,504	13.86%
7th-8th grade	4,296	17.00%
9th grade	3,692	14.61%
10th grade	4,011	15.87%
11th grade	4,718	18.66%
12th grade	2,572	10.17%
Total	25,276	100.00%

line, which requires several technology skills not previously needed by test takers. While previous versions of the test were based on multiple-choice items, the new test items include drag-and-drop, fill-in the blank, as well as short and long essays.

Threats to Grace Centers of Hope's Education Program

Jean Richards, Director of Education and Career Development, administers Grace Centers of Hope's education program. Nancy Paulson, an Education Specialist, supports Jean. The number of Grace Centers of Hope clients participating in the education program fluctuates depending on who enters the one-year residency recovery program. On average, 10 to 12 clients are actively participating in the education program. However, the organization is growing, which means the numbers of learners is predicted to increase.

In 2013, Grace Centers of Hope's education program helped 18 clients successfully pass their high school equivalency exams. However, the announced high school equivalency test changes posed a significant threat to the program's ability to provide clients with instruction that matched the new testing requirements. Upon learning of the test changes, Jean feared that the existing instructional materials designed to align with the prior version of the test would no longer be applicable to new version.

Contextual Factors

Jean and her staff in the education program faced a range of factors that affected the redesign of their instruction. The following describes the critical contextual factors associated with the learners' skill and knowledge diversity, the tutored instructional approach, educational technology, and funding.

Learners' Skill and Knowledge Diversity

Learners in the education program work toward attaining required proficiency in the core adult basic education subject areas of English language arts, science, social studies, and mathematical reasoning. Upon entering the education program, learners take the Test of Adult Basic Education to determine their levels in math, reading, vocabulary, language, and mathematics. The results of the tests are used to develop individual learning plans. The learners vary in terms of their entry skills and knowledge in theses subject areas with some completing their formal education in elementary school and others in high school, but most are able to perform at a ninth grade level. Currently, there is no need to provide instruction in a language other than English.

Some learners have negative attitudes toward academic settings, and are apprehensive about the structured education program requirements. In addition, learners enter the program at different times, which affects the continuity of instruction. However, as adult learners, they have work and life experiences from which they can draw real-life application. While younger learners may be familiar with using the Internet to access social networking websites, many learners have little experience with computer hardware and software, particularly using a computer for education and testing purposes.

Tutored Instructional Approach

Tutors who work as instructors in the adult basic education courses are both Grace Centers of Hope staff and volunteers. The education courses are facilitated by the tutors in a combination of individual and small-group instruction. Some tutors involved in the education program have limited experience with this at-risk client population. In addition, the volunteer tutors enter or leave at varying points within the year, which can also hamper the continuity of instruction.

Educational Technology

Grace Centers of Hope education program works with older computer hardware and relatively slow Internet access. This problem is compounded when multiple users attempt to access the Internet at the same time. In addition, the education program does not have dedicated technical support staff to troubleshoot problems.

Even with these technology limitations, Jean and her staff used adult basic education software and other online programs. To prepare for the prior version of the test, the learners accessed these materials once or twice a week. The tutors recorded what the learners were working on, including how long each student was logged onto the program, and what lessons they were working on. These programs incorporated a variety of graphics, text, audio, and animation, and the learners seemed to prefer using instructional materials that utilized multi-media as opposed to primarily text-based instructional presentation. All of the computers used in the education program have speakers built into them, and clients liked using headphones to listen to audio as part of the instructional materials. However, Jean and the staff were concerned that their existing program were not well aligned with the new testing requirements and would be of limited value going forward.

Funding

While the unexpected need to update their instructional materials was a significant challenge facing Grace Centers of Hope, Jean was unable to spend beyond her existing operating budget. Therefore, purchasing new and unbudgeted adult basic education materials was not an option. Similarly, paying instructional designers to create new materials was also not feasible.

CASE DESCRIPTION

Management and Organizational Concerns

Jean was deeply concerned about Grace Centers of Hope's ability to provide their clients with instruction that matched the new testing requirements. When the high school equivalency test changes were announced in 2013, Jean reached out to Barbara Andrews, an instructional designer and curriculum consultant who volunteered with Grace Centers of Hope.

At Jean's request, Barbara conducted an analysis that examined (a) the planned changes in the test, (b) the current preparation materials, and (c) commercial instructional products available for purchase. Based on this review, Jean and Barbara knew that preparing Grace Centers of Hope's clients for the revised test would require new educational resources and approaches, but the available commercial options were not only beyond their budget, but also still under revision.

Desired Instructional Enhancements

Based on the noted concerns and contextual factors, Jean and Barbara considered their desired instructional enhancements, and their options for a solution. Given the residency requirement of the rehabilitation program, adult basic education courses held at off-site locations were not feasible for Jean and her team. Since clients joined the education program at different skill levels and at different times, Jean and Barbara knew the instruction and practice opportunities for the learners would need to remain tailored to the learner. In addition, since many learners entered the program with no experience in using computers for educational or testing purposes, Jean knew that the instruction would need to cover not only the core subject-matter, but also computer skills not previously needed when the high school equivalency test was administered by paper and pencil.

While Jean knew that all instruction must remain at the Grace Centers of Hope facility, she wanted to reduce the amount of time the staff spent creating instruction to conform to testing requirements. In addition, Jean was concerned about long-term sustainability, and her staff members' ability to update and adapt all created content. Therefore, design decisions needed to contemplate that Grace Centers of Hope's education program staff would assume the responsibility for updating or adapting the developed content.

Jean also needed educational resources that went beyond text-heavy instructional presentation to resources that contained engaging audio, video, and animation. The resources also needed to involve the learners in active practice opportunities. To that end, Jean wanted to explore ways to expand their use of online learning and other educational technologies to support their education program. However, without the budget to buy an off-the-shelf solution, or to hire an instructional designer, Jean and Barbara brainstormed on how they could secure the needed resources.

Performance Improvement through Service-Learning

Faced with the amended testing requirements and Grace Centers of Hope's unique needs and constraints, Barbara suggested that Jean consider engaging college instructional design faculty and students in a volunteer *service-learning* project. Barbara explained that service-learning is educational approach that combines community service, academic coursework, and work-based experiential learning (Bringle & Hatcher, 1996; Furco, 1996; Kenworthy-U'Ren, 1999; Kraft, 1996; Lehman & DuFrene, 2008; Mooney & Edwards, 2001). Barbara felt that engaging students in a service-learning project would be a win-win for both Grace Centers of Hope and instructional design students. Jean would receive no-cost volunteer instructional design help from the students, while the students could use the experience to fulfill classroom or internship requirements, and add an authentic instructional design project to their portfolios.

Based on a tip from a professor at a nearby university, Barbara reached out to Ann Fenner at Designers for Learning, an organization that matches instructional design students with nonprofits in service-learning projects ("Designers for Learning," n.d.). Following an exchange of emails discussing the project aims, Ann agreed with Barbara that a service-learning approach was a great solution to meet the challenges faced by Grace Centers of Hope. A conference call was held in which Ann described to Jean and Barbara the service-learning approach and her ideas for a project.

Why Service-Learning?

During the call, Ann explained why faculty and students would be interested in volunteering their time to offer help. She noted that fostering opportunities for authentic and engaging real-life application of the course content is a major challenge for college instructional design programs (Bannan-Ritland, 2001; Curtis & Nestor, 1990; Kenny, Zhang, Schwier, & Campbell, 2005; Larson & Lockee, 2009; Larson, 2005; Schwier & Wilson, 2010). Ann went on to explain how service-learning offers students *experiential learning* opportunities (Carver, 1997; Dewey, 1938; Giles & Eyler, 1994; Kolb, 1984; Kraft, 1996), and is used by instructors to engage the student in real-world authentic learning conditions (Correia, Yusop, Wilson, & Schwier, 2010; Herrington, Reeves, & Oliver, 2014). She also pointed out research findings that suggest service-learning can positively affect student academic achievement (Celio, Durlak, & Dymnicki, 2011; Conway, Amel, & Gerwien, 2009; Novak, Markey, & Allen, 2007; Warren, 2012; Yorio & Ye, 2012), as well as the community-based organization that is served, including added labor to fulfill their missions and access to resources (Bacdayan, 2008; Blouin & Perry, 2009; Bringle & Hatcher, 2002; Holland, 2001)

Similarly, Ann pointed out that volunteerism and civic engagement within U.S. higher education is strong. Between 2009 and 2011, the average college student volunteer rate by state ranged from 18.4% to 48.6% (U.S. Government, n.d.). Further, Campus Compact, a coalition of 1,200 U.S. colleges and universities with approximately 6 million enrolled students, reports that 95 percent of its membership offers service-learning courses (Campus Compact, 2013).

In addition, Ann also noted that the task of offering authentic experiences to the growing number of college students enrolled in online courses is an even greater challenge for faculty given the time and geographic separation of learners from the instructor and the college. However, this challenge for faculty represents a unique opportunity for Grace Centers of Hope. Ann recommended that Jean consider an *e-service-learning* approach in which the service component is conducted virtually (Dailey-Hebert, Sallee, & DiPadova, 2008; Waldner, Widener, & McGorry, 2012). In making her case, Ann noted that as of the fall 2010, 21 million students were enrolled in U.S. postsecondary degree-granting institutions, an increase of 18 percent from the fall of 2006, and enrollment is predicted to increase to 24 million by the fall of 2021 (Hussar & Bailey, 2013). Further, an estimated 30% of college students were taking at least one online course, an increase of 74% from 2006 (Allen & Seaman, 2013).

Formulating an E-Service-Learning Plan

Jean decided to move forward with the e-service-learning concept proposed by Ann and Barbara. Looking at this project as a chance to study the e-service-learning approach, Ann agreed to volunteer her time to facilitate a limited 11-week pilot service-learning project that would allow Jean a trial to decide whether this was the right solution for Jean's needs.

In working on this project, Ann had a performance improvement focus, and she integrated the principles of Human Performance Technology in her consultative approach with Jean. By starting with detailed discussions and examinations into the organization, the learners, and the adult basic education context, Ann took a systemic view of the problem. She also shared Jean's belief that the focus needed to remain on creating resources that helped the Grace Centers of Hope clients pass their high school equivalency test. That focus on results was paramount in order to establish a successful partnership.

To refine the need, Jean, Barbara, and Ann discussed the types of instructional resources required for the learners in the Grace Centers of Hope education program, as well as for staff and volunteers who work as tutors. All three agreed that the service-learning project would focus on the design of instructional materials and learning activities to meet the parameters of the college and career readiness standards.

In addition, Ann appreciated that it was important to respect the client's budgetary constraints by finding no-cost solutions in order to add value. While Jean and her staff continued to evaluate off-the-shelf commercial alternatives for student preparation and practice testing, finding solutions within their budget remained a key concern. Given the funding limitations faced by Grace Centers of Hope, Ann asked Jean if she had ever explored the use of *open educational resources*. Open educational resources are any materials used for instructional purposes that are openly licensed by the copyright holder, and do not require the user to request permission or pay for use (Butcher, Kanwar, & Uvalic-Trumbic, 2011). Jean indicated that while she often found materials on the Internet to incorporate into her instruction, she was not aware of good sources to find quality open educational resources. Ann suggested that they include an open educational resources exploration a part of the service-learning project. The resources found during this review would help Jean and her staff in the short-term, and offer a repository of vetted and openly licensed resources that the student service-learners could adapt within their customized instructional designs.

During several weeks of conference calls and email exchanges, Jean, Barbara, and Ann agreed to run the pilot service-learning project during the spring semester of 2014, and to target only college students currently enrolled instructional design programs. Ann formalized a draft project plan for Jean's review and approval. They agreed it would be exciting to attract multi-institution interest to tackle this need that was not unique to Grace Centers of Hope. Therefore, the Call for Volunteers that Ann agreed to facilitate would include students in all instructional design programs, rather than from only one college. This would open the project to students outside of Michigan, and tap into the thousands of students studying within online programs. Ann agreed to develop a website that would serve as the collaborative platform to facilitate the 100% virtual e-service-learning collaboration. All were in agreement that this project would be small in scale relative to the overall need, but would allow a pilot of the service-learning process and lay the foundation for future and larger scale design and development work. An evaluation at the end of the project's implementation would guide future iterations of the project.

Deliverables

Based on their conversations, Jean, Ann, and Barbara narrowed their focus a set of projects that could be completed by service-learners during the span of a semester. The follow deliverables became the agreed upon focus of the pilot service-learning project.

Deliverable 1

One student product team would conduct an extensive review of existing open educational resources. The service-learners would be responsible for collaboratively preparing a written report that identified existing open educational resources that align with the 2013 College and Career Readiness standards for both English language arts and literature, and mathematics. Given the alignment of College and Career Readiness standards to the Common Core State Standards (Pimentel, 2013), a project aim was to identify and adapt existing open educational resources developed for a K12 audience to an adult audience. Unlike the Common Core State Standards, the College and Career Readiness standards are bundled into five grade-level groupings: A (K-1), B (2-3), C (4-5), D (6-8), and E (9-12). The service-learners working on this deliverable would prepare a written report that focused on resources applicable to Group E.

Deliverable 2

Three student teams would design and develop instructional units that aligned with an anchor standard presented within the 2013 College and Career Readiness standards. Each unit of instruction would need to include all necessary content presentation, learner practice, and assessment materials for one hour of tutored instruction, as well as instructions for the tutor. The units of instruction will serve as prototypes for the design and development of future educational resources.

Deliverable 3

One student team would design and develop instruction that introduced learners to the use of computers for learning. The unit of instruction would include all necessary content presentation, learner practice, and assessment materials for one hour of tutored instruction, as well as instructions for the tutor.

Memorandum of Understanding

Once all of the parameters of the e-service-learning project had been discussed, Ann prepared a memorandum of understanding that served as the service-learning agreement between Grace Centers of Hope and Designers for Learning. The agreement summarized the overall instructional need, information about the client's operations, and the intended work to be completed on the project, including the deliverable requirements. A Scope of Services section clarified that the focus of the service-learning project would be the review of existing open educational resources and the design of instruction for college and career readiness. The agreement also included an overview of the service-learners' responsibilities, the project start date and the deliverable due date, and confirmation that was is a 100% virtual volunteer opportunity that would not require any volunteer to be physically present at any location.

The memorandum of understanding specified the service-learners' responsibilities, and what was expected within the deliverables. For the student teams designing a unit of instruction, the deliverable summary specified:

- The intended length of the instruction,
- What the unit of instruction must include, such as all necessary content presentation, learner practice, and assessment materials, and
- The licensing requirement that all work produced for this project would be licensed under a Creative Commons Attribution 3.0 license (Creative Commons, n.d.).

Online Collaboration Platform

As the first step in facilitating the e-service-learning project, Ann developed a website that served as the online collaboration platform for the project to share information and to facilitate communication among the team members working on the project. The primary website content areas included the detailed project description, an announcements section for ongoing project updates, an asynchronous project discussion board, and a project calendar. The website also linked to other online resources, including links to an online document sharing platform to coordinate the creation and sharing of project deliverables, and a social bookmarking site to aggregate and share relevant resources. To avoid web development costs, Ann developed the website herself using WordPress, open source web software ("WordPress," n.d.). In addition, she used only freely available online tools and social networking platforms.

While the online platform included many options to support asynchronous communication and collaboration, Ann felt it was important to include a synchronous option, as well. She selected a freely available web conferencing solution that allowed all participants to join in live audio, text, and video communication. The web conferencing solution also offered recording capabilities, which would allow participants who could not attend the live session the opportunity to view the recorded webinar from a link on the website.

Ann knew that the changes to the high school equivalency test affected not only Grace Centers of Hope, but also any organization that offered adult basic education courses. To encourage engagement, awareness, and input from people outside of the design teams who were interested in this topic, Ann took steps to reach out to the broader education community. To that end, Ann ensured that all content stored or linked from the website was open to public view, and she utilized her existing accounts and group spaces on social networking platforms (i.e. Facebook, Google+, Twitter) to post project announcements about the project with links back to the project's website. In addition, Ann encouraged participants to use a dedicated hash tag of #oerccr for the project, which allowed her to aggregate all social media posts related to the project.

Call for Volunteers

Once the memorandum of understanding and website were completed, Ann prepared the Call for Volunteers and posted it on the project website. The call linked to the project description, and offered information about how to apply, expectations and requirements of the service-learners and their faculty advisors, and key points on the project timeline, including the deadline to submit the service-learner application, the date the project team selection would be announced, and the project deliverable due date. In addition, the call confirmed that service-learners were required to collaborate remotely with the client and other volunteers on the project using phone, email, and other freely available online asynchronous and synchronous communication technologies.

Ann estimated that the total project hours to complete each of the three deliverable were approximately 120 hours. She also knew that many college students work while attending school and would only be willing and able to volunteer a few hours each week. Therefore, she included a requirement that each student must commit to volunteer a minimum of 30 hours during the 11 weeks from the project start date to the deliverable due date.

Within the call, Ann outlined the expectations and requirements for both the faculty advisor, as well as the student service-learner. To help with service-learner mentorship, the faculty advisors had to be willing to advise their students through the duration of the project, and commit to helping the service-learners complete all of their assigned deliverables. To ensure that the service-learners were qualified to complete the deliverables, only currently enrolled college students within instructional design program were eligible to apply.

Approximately 45 days prior to the project start date, Ann sent an email blast announcing the Call for Volunteers to approximately 200 faculty and students who had expressed interest in Designers for Learning service-learning projects. In addition, Ann posted the project announcement on several social networking platforms using the dedicated hash tag for the project.

Service-Learner Application

Ann facilitated the application process using a web-based survey platform in which candidates completed an online application form. Ann aggregated and shared the completed applications with Jean and Barbara. The volunteer service-learning application informed candidates that while Designers for Learning facilitated the project, service-learners were applying to be volunteers of Grace Centers of Hope. The application provided a link back to the online Call for Volunteers on the project website, and summarized the focus of the service-learning project. The application restated the expectations and requirements of faculty advisors, as well as of the service-learners.

The online application form required applicants to confirm that they were students currently enrolled within a college instructional design program. Applicants were asked to provide their complete contact information that included the student's full name, college or university, program, mailing address, email address, and phone number. Each student was also required to provide the contact information of the faculty member at the student's college or university who agreed to sponsor and advise the student on the project. The service-learners were informed that the faculty sponsors would be contacted to verify their agreement to sponsor and advise their students for the duration of the project.

The application included a section for students to rank the their interest level in volunteering to work on one of the three deliverables, ranging from not interested, somewhat interested, or very interested. A text box section asked the students to describe why they wanted to volunteer on the selected project in order to elicit information about their interest and experience with the topic.

Students were also asked to confirm the number of hours per week they were willing to commit to volunteering on the project between the start and end dates. A text box asked the students to describe their backgrounds, including an overview of their current academic level, instructional design work experience, and completed instructional design courses. Students were also asked to describe an example of at least one instructional design project that they had completed, including the process the student took to tackle the project, as well as a description of the outcome. In addition, the students were asked to consider how they would balance volunteering on this project with other commitments. A Likert-type scale (ranging from Strongly Disagree to Strongly Agree) response box asked the student to indicate the extent to which he or she agreed or disagreed with the following statements:

- I look forward to volunteering in a 100% virtual relationship with the client and other volunteers.
- I am comfortable using communication technologies such as email and on-line discussion forums.
- I'm able to meet at least once a month in live web conferences with other volunteers on the project team.
- My academic experience has prepared me for the requirements of this project.
- My work experience has prepared me for the requirements of this project.

An optional section asked students whether they would like to be considered for a volunteer project management role. Students indicating "yes" were given an additional roster of questions that asked the students to describe:

- At least one team project he or she managed in a work or school setting, including what the student did and the result,
- What the student believed were the key skills needed to develop and maintain successful professional relationships, including examples of how the student had demonstrated these skills in prior projects, and
- What the student believed were the key skills needed to guide others and successfully manage an instructional design project, including examples of how the student had demonstrated these skills in prior projects.

Service-Learner Selection and Agreement

With an estimated 120 hours to complete each project, and a 30-hour minimum time commitment from each student volunteer, Ann's goal was to form teams comprised of four service-learners. With five projects, Ann focused on securing 20 candidates. Fortunately, the number of applicants exceeded the number of available positions resulting in a larger pool of applications than expected.

After Ann reviewed each application, she provided a candidate summary to Jean and Barbara for their review and comment. As faculty in instructional design programs sponsored all of the student candidates, Jean and Barbara left the final selection decisions to Ann. Once Ann selected the top 20 candidates, she asked each chosen student to sign a service-learner agreement that confirmed the project's terms. The service-learner agreement confirmed (a) the scope of service that outlined the student volunteers' responsibilities to Grace Centers of Hope, (b) the reporting relationship between the service-learners and Designers for Learning, (c) the key deadlines, including the project start date, the deliverable due date, and key progress points on the projects, (d) that this was a 100% virtual volunteer opportunity that did not require any volunteer to be physically present at any location, and (e) the 30-hour minimum volunteer commitment. Regarding the ownership of intellectual property, the service-learner agreement confirmed that any work product created for Grace Centers of Hope under the terms of the Scope of Service would be licensed under a Creative Commons Attribution license 3.0. This provision allowed the students and others to reuse the resulting instructional materials in the future without the need for additional permission from Grace Centers of Hope.

Project Implementation

Approximately 50 participants volunteered their time on the service-learning project, including the service-learners, their college faculty sponsors, and other subject-matter expert and advisors who heard about the project and asked to help. By expanding the Call for Volunteers beyond only local Michigan colleges, the project team roster included service-learners and faculty from 14 different instructional design programs across the United States. Given that some faculty members sponsored more than one student, a total of 18 college faculty agreed to advise their students.

Project Kick-Off

The project kick-off was announced in an email blast to all project participants that included an invitation to the project's first live webinar. The announcement outlined the team composition and described the various roles on the project. Given the large number of service-learners, Ann decided to appoint team leaders to help coordinate activities not only within each project team, but also across the five different project teams. While the student team leaders had the same responsibilities as the other service-learners on the team, they were assigned the added responsibility of ensuring the team was making forward progress toward achieving the project's overall goals. In addition, one student service-learner was assigned as the Project Manager. The Project Manager was the primary client liaison, as well as the coordinator of the five project teams.

Communication and Collaboration

While the project discussion board was established to help facilitate communication with the client and across teams, the service-learners were encouraged to determine their preferred method of communication within their teams. The discussion board included threads for initial participant introductions, general comments or questions, questions and answers for the client team at Grace Centers of Hope, questions and answers for subject matter experts, and general comments and questions relevant to the project.

The teams worked independently from the project kick-off to the final deliverable due date, and the team leaders coordinated their activities with the student Project Manager using a combination of email and web conferencing. The teams relied on email for most of their communication, and used the provided online document-sharing platform to collaborate on deliverables and to post their work. Ann and the Project Manager communicated several times a week via email or web conferencing to discuss the project status.

Over the 11-week project, Ann facilitated seven webinars as a way to foster communication and collaboration across the teams. The client team from Grace Centers of Hope, the service-learners, faculty advisors, and others subject matter experts were invited to attend the live sessions. Those unable to attend the live sessions were able to watch the recordings that were posted on the project website after each webinar.

Project Outcomes

All five project teams submitted their deliverables to Ann on or before the due date. The service-learners presented their work to the Jean and her staff during a final webinar. The follow summarizes the project outcomes and impact of the service-learners' work.

Deliverable 1

The student project team that conducted the review of existing open educational resources documented dozens of resource collections with instructional materials for English language arts and literature, and mathematics. At Jean's request, the team also mined for science and social studies open educational resources. While most of the documented resources were originally developed for a K12 audience, the service-learners focused on openly licensed materials that could be adapted for use with adult learners. The service-learners created a spreadsheet to document the resource repositories that includes (a) the website address, (b) the subject area, (c) the major subtopics covered, (d) the grade level, (e) the resource sponsor, (f) the licensing terms, and (g) the strengths and weaknesses of each repository. These resources offer Grace Centers of Hope access to vetted instructional materials that can be immediately incorporated into their adult basic education program. In addition, the resources offer future service-learners a wealth of material to adapt for the specific needs of Grace Centers of Hope.

Deliverables 2 and 3

Three student teams designed and developed instructional units that aligned with an anchor standard presented within the 2013 College and Career Readiness standards. Given the wealth of existing math related open educational resources, the teams focused on designing instruction for English language arts and social studies. In addition, one student team designed and developed instruction that introduced learners to the use of computers for learning.

The instructional units included content presentation, learner practice, and assessment materials for one hour tutored instruction. Where feasible, the service-learners on these design teams incorporated open educational resources into their designs. The service-learners' deliverables will serve as prototypes for the design and development of future instructional units.

Online Home for Deliverables

As an added deliverable, one student service-learner took the initiative to create a website to display the project deliverables. While not an original part of the project, the website offers an online portal for the Grace Centers of Hope staff and clients to access the instructional materials. The website provided links to the open educational resource reports prepared by the service-learners, as well as the instructional materials prepared by the service-learning design teams.

Estimated Impact

While it is difficult to quantify the financial impact of the service-learning project, access to the thousands of open educational resources documented by the service-learners offers Grace Centers of Hope a no-cost alternative to the commercial instructional materials they were contemplating. A review of for-fee high school equivalency test preparation materials revealed a range of options, including print, software, and online alternatives. The retail prices of for-fee print or digital resources in a single subject area start at under $10. In contrast, the retail price of some multi-topic online access bundles exceeds $100. If Grace Centers of Hope is able to replace some of their free instructional materials with the no-cost open educational resources that were either documented or designed by the service-learners, the cost savings to the organization could be substantial. Assuming that Grace Centers of Hope serves 30 clients each year within their education program, a $100 per student savings on education resources would reduce the organization's annual expenses by $3,000.

While the service-learners were not required to keep a log of their work hours, Ann and the Project Manager assume their original 120 hours per project team estimate was a good representation of the actual time commitment of the service-learners. Therefore, across the five times, Ann estimated that Grace Centers of Hope received approximately 600 hours of instructional design work from the service-learners. This does not include the time Ann spent facilitating the project, or the time that Barbara, the faculty, and other advisors volunteered to help the student designers. Assuming an hourly rate of $25 per hour for a starting instructional designer, Ann estimated that Grace Centers of Hope received at least $15,000 of pro bono instructional design work from the service-learners.

CURRENT CHALLENGES FACING THE ORGANIZATION

Given that this service-learning pilot was intended to inform the design of future service-learning projects for Grace Centers of Hope, Ann incorporated an implementation evaluation into the design of the service-learning project to examine the success of the service-learning process, and to contemplate needed areas of improvement. Graduate students outside of the service-learning teams volunteered to conduct the evaluation. Working under the direction of their faculty advisor, the student evaluators collaborated with Ann to establish the parameters of the evaluation. Like all aspects of the project, the evaluation was conducted virtually using online surveys, phone conferences, and email. The evaluation protocols and instruments were prepared to capture feedback from the client team and the service-learners. The following describes the key challenges and problems that were uncovered during the evaluation process.

Service-Learner Attrition

While any volunteer endeavor will experience attrition, the steps taken to ensure faculty sponsorship, as well as the requirement that all student volunteers sign a service-learner agreement, did not prevent student attrition. Beyond reports of workload inequities common to group project work, four service-learners did not complete their responsibilities on project, including two service-learners who left the project with about five weeks until the final deliverables were due, and two others who did not complete their portions of the final deliverable. The departures meant an increased workload for the remaining service-learners who compensated for the lost contributions of the departed students.

Faculty Sponsor and Advisor Participation

The involvement of faculty ranged significantly across the project. While it was difficult to evaluate the amount of one-to-one interaction the faculty had with their students during the semester, only a few took an active role on the project as a whole. This was a disappointment to Ann as a goal of the project was to encourage cross-institution collaboration. Within their survey responses, the service-learners also reported disappointment that their advisors did not show much interest in the project, but the students noted that the lack of faculty participation did not negatively affected their performance.

Use of Collaborative Tools

The service-learners preferred working independently within their teams using email, phone, text, or other collaboration tools outside of the online collaboration platform. While many service-learners attended the live webinars, very few took advantage of using the audio and video capabilities to discuss the project during the live webinars. Instead the students joined the live session to passively listen to the webinar, or to add a few comments or questions in the text chat. While the webinars provided the service-learners with updates from the client, Ann, and the Project Manager, the students did not take full advantage of the synchronous forum to ask questions or to share updates about their individual projects. In addition, only a few service-learners discussed the project on social networking platforms, and fewer than 10 service-learners signed up for the Google+ community.

Online Home for Deliverables

Finding a no-cost online solution for the service-learners to house their deliverables for access by Jean and her staff, as well as the learners remains a significant obstacle. While the use of the website offered a temporary solution for this round of the pilot service-learning projects, Ann knows it is not a perfect long-term option. Further analysis will be required to assess potential alternatives.

SOLUTIONS AND RECOMMENDATIONS

Jean and Ann have agreed to run a second service-learning project during the fall semester of 2014 to capitalize on the success of the pilot. Ann will be making several program changes to overcome the noted challenges and to increase the impact of the service-learners' work. The following describes the solutions and recommendations she will be implementing.

Service-Learner Attrition

To help curb service-learner attrition, the next iteration of the service-learning cohort will include only 12 student volunteers working in pairs. Ann felt the student project teams in the initial pilot were too large causing some service-learners to become disconnected from the project. While a fewer number of service-learners will participate in total, the six project pairs will produce more design deliverables for Grace Centers of Hope than in the pilot that had only five project teams. Under this revised structure, Ann will eliminate the team leader and Project Manager roles. While each student will now be asked to commit to 40 hours of volunteer service, they will receive more one-to-one support and mentorship from Ann.

Faculty Sponsor and Advisor Participation

The inconsistency in the advisement of the service-learners by their faculty sponsors pointed to the need to adjust the student mentorship protocols. Dovetailing with the changes to the team structure noted above, Ann decided she needed to enlist the support of dedicated co-facilitators. For the upcoming project, Ann will co-facilitate with two instructional design professors. Rather than relying on ad hoc faculty advisement (i.e. when the students requested help), Ann and her co-facilitators will assume the responsibility of student mentorship from project kick-off to completion. In addition, a set of mentorship protocols is being developed that includes formalized student reflection to help the monitor the service-learners' process.

Use of Collaborative Tools

Given that the service-learners did not use some of the collaborative tools that were at their disposal, Ann decided to focus the facilitation efforts on the main project website, the asynchronous discussion board, and the live webinars. While the service-learners will still have access to the other collaborative options, important project announcements will be made only the project website and via email.

Online Home for Deliverables

Ann and her co-facilitators are planning an analysis of potential alternatives for the online home for the deliverables. This analysis will include an assessment of Grace Centers of Hope's needs, as well as the service-learner requirements.

REFERENCES

Bacdayan, P. (2008). Finding win-win forms of economic development outreach: Shared priorities of business faculty and community. *College Teaching*, *56*(3), 143–148. doi:10.3200/CTCH.56.3.143-148

Bannan-Ritland, B. (2001). Teaching instructional design: An action learning approach. *Performance Improvement Quarterly*, *14*(2), 37–52. doi:10.1111/j.1937-8327.2001. tb00208.x

Blouin, D. D., & Perry, E. M. (2009). Whom does service learning really serve? Community-based organizations' perspectives on service learning. *Teaching Sociology*, *37*(2), 120–135. doi:10.1177/0092055X0903700201

Bringle, R. G., & Hatcher, J. A. (1996). Implementing service learning in higher education. *The Journal of Higher Education*, *67*(2), 221–239. doi:10.2307/2943981

Bringle, R. G., & Hatcher, J. A. (2002). Campus–community partnerships: The terms of engagement. *The Journal of Social Issues*, *58*(3), 503–516. doi:10.1111/1540-4560.00273

Butcher, N., Kanwar, A., & Uvalic-Trumbic, S. (2011). *A basic guide to open educational resources (OER)*. Commonwealth of Learning/UNESCO. Retrieved from http://dspace.col.org/handle/123456789/428

Carver, R. L. (1997). Theoretical underpinnings of service learning. *Theory into Practice, 36*(3), 143–149. doi:10.1080/00405849709543760

Celio, C. I., Durlak, J., & Dymnicki, A. (2011). A meta-analysis of the impact of service-learning on students. *Journal of Experiential Education, 34*(2), 164–181. doi:10.5193/JEE34.2.164

Commons, C. (n.d.). *Creative Commons Attribution 3.0 License*. Retrieved from http://creativecommons.org/licenses/by/3.0/

Conway, J. M., Amel, E. L., & Gerwien, D. P. (2009). Teaching and learning in the social context: A meta-analysis of service learning's effects on academic, personal, social, and citizenship outcomes. *Teaching of Psychology, 36*(4), 233–245. doi:10.1080/00986280903172969

Correia, A.-P., Yusop, F. D., Wilson, J. R., & Schwier, R. A. (2010). *A comparative case study of approaches to authentic learning in instructional design at two universities*. Presented at the American Educational Research Association Annual Meeting, Denver, CO. Retrieved from http://files.eric.ed.gov/fulltext/ED509340.pdf

Curtis, R. V., & Nestor, D. (1990). Interpersonal skill-building for instructional developers. *Educational Technology Research and Development, 38*(2), 51–59. doi:10.1007/BF02298269

Dailey-Hebert, A., Sallee, E. D., & DiPadova, L. N. (2008). *Service-eLearning: Educating for Citizenship*. IAP.

Designers for Learning. (n.d.). Retrieved from http://designersforlearning.org

Dewey, J. (1938). *Education and experience*. New York: Macmillan.

Furco, A. (1996). Service-learning: A balanced approach to experiential education. *Expanding Boundaries: Serving and Learning, 1*, 1–6.

Giles, D. E., & Eyler, J. (1994). The theoretical roots of service-learning in John Dewey: Toward a theory of service-learning. *Michigan Journal of Community Service Learning, 1*(1), 77–85.

Grace Centers of Hope. (n.d.). *Grace Centers of Hope Financial Information*. Retrieved from http://www.gracecentersofhope.org/Financial.aspx

Herrington, J., Reeves, T. C., & Oliver, R. (2014). Authentic learning environments. In J. M. Spector, M. D. Merrill, J. Elen, & M. J. Bishop (Eds.), *Handbook of Research on Educational Communications and Technology* (pp. 401–412). Springer New York. doi:10.1007/978-1-4614-3185-5_32

Hoffman, A. M., Wine, M. P., & McKinney, J. S. (2013). *A GED test for a Common Core world: Understanding the changes coming in 2014*. Presented at the Annual Meeting of the American Education Research Association, San Francisco, CA. Retrieved from http://www.gedtestingservice.com/uploads/files/6c97b538e27804 91ee60d1d297d5d9f5.pdf

Holland, B. A. (2001). A comprehensive model for assessing service-learning and community-university partnerships. *New Directions for Higher Education, 2001*(114), 51–60. doi:10.1002/he.13.abs

Kenny, R. F., Zhang, Z., Schwier, R. A., & Campbell, K. (2005). A review of what instructional designers do: Questions answered and questions not asked. *Canadian Journal of Learning and Technology, 31*(1), 9–16.

Kenworthy-U'Ren, A. L. (1999). Management students as consultants an alternative perspective on the service-learning "call to action.". *Journal of Management Inquiry, 8*(4), 379–387. doi:10.1177/105649269984005

Kolb, D. A. (1984). *Experiential learning: Experience as the source of learning and development*. Englewood Cliffs, NJ: Prentice-Hall.

Kraft, R. J. (1996). Service learning: An introduction to its theory, practice, and effects. *Education and Urban Society, 28*(2), 131–159. doi:10.1177/0013124596028002001

Larson, M. B. (2005). Instructional design career environments: Survey of the alignment of preparation and practice. *TechTrends, 49*(6), 22–32. doi:10.1007/BF02763727

Larson, M. B., & Lockee, B. B. (2009). Preparing instructional designers for different career environments: A case study. *Educational Technology Research and Development, 57*(1), 1–24. doi:10.1007/s11423-006-9031-4

Lehman, C. M., & DuFrene, D. D. (2008). Achieving active learning through a service learning podcast project. *Journal of Business and Training Education*, 41.

Mooney, L. A., & Edwards, B. (2001). Experiential learning in sociology: Service learning and other community-based learning initiatives. *Teaching Sociology, 29*(2), 181–194. doi:10.2307/1318716

National Center for Education Statistics. (2012). *Digest of Education Statistics, 2012*. U.S. Department of Education. Retrieved from http://nces.ed.gov/programs/digest/d12/

Navigator, C. (n.d.). Charity Navigator Rating: Grace Centers of Hope. Retrieved June 5, 2014, from http://www.charitynavigator.org/index.cfm?bay=search.summary&orgid=5309

Novak, J. M., Markey, V., & Allen, M. (2007). Evaluating cognitive outcomes of service learning in higher education: A meta-analysis. *Communication Research Reports*, *24*(2), 149–157. doi:10.1080/08824090701304881

Pimentel, S. (2013). College and career readiness standards for adult education. Washington, DC: U.S. Department of Education, Office of Vocational and Adult Education; Retrieved from http://lincs.ed.gov/publications/pdf/CCRStandardsAdultEd.pdf

Schwier, R. A., & Wilson, J. R. (2010). Unconventional roles and activities identified by instructional designers. *Contemporary Educational Technology, 1*(2).

U. S. Census Bureau. (2012). *Educational attainment in the United States: 2012 detailed tables*. Retrieved from http://www.census.gov/hhes/socdemo/education/data/cps/2012/tables.html

Waldner, L. S., Widener, M. C., & McGorry, S. Y. (2012). E-service learning: The evolution of service-learning to engage a growing online student population. *Journal of Higher Education Outreach & Engagement*, *16*(2), 123–150.

Warren, J. L. (2012). Does service-learning increase student learning?: A meta-analysis. *Michigan Journal of Community Service Learning*, *18*(2), 56–61.

Welch, S. (2012, November 29). Data opens doors: Grace Centers develops system to better track clients, outcomes. *Crain's Detroit Business*. Detroit, MI. Retrieved from http://www.crainsdetroit.com/article/20121125/SUB01/311259995/data-opens-doors

WordPress. (n.d.). Retrieved from https://wordpress.org/about/

Yorio, P. L., & Ye, F. (2012). A meta-analysis on the effects of service-learning on the social, personal, and cognitive outcomes of learning. *Academy of Management Learning & Education*, *11*(1), 9–27. doi:10.5465/amle.2010.0072

ADDITIONAL READING

Andrews, C. P. (2007). Service-learning: Applications and research in business. *Journal of Education for Business*, *83*(1), 19–26. doi:10.3200/JOEB.83.1.19-26

Bacdayan, P. (2008). Finding win-win forms of economic development outreach: Shared priorities of business faculty and community. *College Teaching*, *56*(3), 143–148. doi:10.3200/CTCH.56.3.143-148

Becket, D., Refaei, B., & Skutar, C. (2012). A faculty learning community's reflection on implementing service-learning goals. *Journal of the Scholarship of Teaching and Learning*, *12*(1), 74–86.

Bernacki, M. L., & Jaeger, E. (2008). Exploring the impact of service-learning on moral development and moral orientation. *Michigan Journal of Community Service Learning*, *14*(2). Retrieved from http://quod.lib.umich.edu/m/mjcsl/3239521.0014.201?rgn=main;view=fulltext

Bringle, R. G., & Hatcher, J. A. (1995). A service-learning curriculum for faculty. *Michigan Journal of Community Service Learning*, *2*(1), 112–122.

Bringle, R. G., & Hatcher, J. A. (2002). Campus–community partnerships: The terms of engagement. *The Journal of Social Issues*, *58*(3), 503–516. doi:10.1111/1540-4560.00273

Bringle, R. G., & Hatcher, J. A. (2009). Innovative practices in service-learning and curricular engagement. *New Directions for Higher Education*, *2009*(147), 37–46. doi:10.1002/he.356

Butin, D. W. (2006). The limits of service-learning in higher education. *The Review of Higher Education*, *29*(4), 473–498. doi:10.1353/rhe.2006.0025

Cameron, M., Forsyth, A., Green, W. A., Lu, H., McGirr, P., Owens, P. E., & Stoltz, R. (2001). Learning through service: The community design studio. *College Teaching*, *49*(3), 105–113. doi:10.1080/87567550109595860

Carrington, S. (2011). Service-learning within higher education: Rhizomatic interconnections between university and the real world. *Australian Journal of Teacher Education*, *36*(6), 1–14. doi:10.14221/ajte.2011v36n6.3

Carver, R. L. (1997). Theoretical underpinnings of service-learning. *Theory into Practice*, *36*(3), 143–149. doi:10.1080/00405849709543760

Celio, C. I., Durlak, J., & Dymnicki, A. (2011). A meta-analysis of the impact of service-learning on students. *Journal of Experiential Education, 34*(2), 164–181. doi:10.5193/JEE34.2.164

Cooper, J. R. (2013). Ten years in the trenches: Faculty perspectives on sustaining service-learning. *Journal of Experiential Education.* doi:10.1177/1053825913513721.

Correia, A.-P., Yusop, F. D., Wilson, J. R., & Schwier, R. A. (2010). *A comparative case study of approaches to authentic learning in instructional design at two universities.* Presented at the American Educational Research Association Annual Meeting, Denver, CO. Retrieved from http://files.eric.ed.gov/fulltext/ED509340.pdf

Cress, C. M., Collier, P. J., & Reitenauer, V. L. (2013). *Learning Through Serving: A Student Guidebook for Service-Learning and Civic Engagement Across Academic Disciplines and Cultural Communities* (2nd ed.). Stylus Publishing.

Cundiff, N., Nadler, J., & Scribner, S. (2011). Teaching evaluation: A student-run consulting firm. *International Journal of Teaching and Learning in Higher Education, 23*(1), 109–113.

Dallimore, E. J., & Souza, T. J. (2002). Consulting course design: Theoretical frameworks and pedagogical strategies. *Business Communication Quarterly, 65*(4), 86–101. doi:10.1177/108056990206500408

Dave, A. (2009). Focus on teaching: Consulting by business college academics: Lessons for business communication courses. *Business Communication Quarterly.* Retrieved from http://bcq.sagepub.com/content/early/2009/07/07/1080569909340625.full.pdf

Dorado, S., & Giles, D. E. Jr. (2004). Service-learning partnerships: Paths of engagement. *Michigan Journal of Community Service Learning, 11*(1), 25–37.

Driscoll, A., Holland, B., Gelmon, S., & Kerrigan, S. (1996). An assessment model for service-learning: Comprehensive case studies of impact on faculty, students, community, and institution. *Michigan Journal of Community Service Learning, 3*, 66–71.

Eyler, J., Giles, D. E. Jr, & Braxton, J. (1997). The impact of service-learning on college students. *Michigan Journal of Community Service Learning, 4*, 5–15.

Flannery, B. L., & Pragman, C. H. (2008). Working towards empirically-based continuous improvements in service-learning. *Journal of Business Ethics, 80*(3), 465–479. doi:10.1007/s10551-007-9431-3

Furco, A. (2001). Advancing Service-Learning at Research Universities. *New Directions for Higher Education, 2001*(114), 67–78. doi:10.1002/he.15.abs

Guthrie, K. L., & McCracken, H. (2010). Making a difference online: Facilitating service-learning through distance education. *The Internet and Higher Education*, *13*(3), 153–157. doi:10.1016/j.iheduc.2010.02.006

Gygi, J., & Madsen, S. R. (2006). Collateral learning through service-learning: Developing competent business professionals. *International Journal of Management Education and Development*, *2*(1), 1–16.

Holland, B. A. (2001). A comprehensive model for assessing service-learning and community-university partnerships. *New Directions for Higher Education*, *2001*(114), 51–60. doi:10.1002/he.13.abs

Hynie, M., Jensen, K., Johnny, M., Wedlock, J., & Phipps, D. (2011). Student internships bridge research to real world problems. *Education + Training*, *53*(1), 45–56. doi:10.1108/00400911111102351

Johari, A., & Bradshaw, A. C. (2008). Project-based learning in an internship program: A qualitative study of related roles and their motivational attributes. *Educational Technology Research and Development*, *56*(3), 329–359. doi:10.1007/s11423-006-9009-2

Kapp, K. M., Phillips, T. L., & Wanner, J. H. (2002). A problem-based learning model for teaching the instructional design business acquisition process. *Performance Improvement Quarterly*, *15*(1), 25–46. doi:10.1111/j.1937-8327.2002.tb00239.x

Karakas, F., & Kavas, M. (2009). Service-learning 2.0 for the twenty-first century: Towards a holistic model for global social positive change. *The International Journal of Organizational Analysis*, *17*(1), 40–59. doi:10.1108/19348830910948896

Kecskes, K. (2006). Behind the rhetoric: Applying a cultural theory lens to community-campus partnership development. *Michigan Journal of Community Service Learning*, *12*(2), 5–14.

Keen, C., & Hall, K. (2009). Engaging with difference matters: Longitudinal student outcomes of co-curricular service-learning programs. *The Journal of Higher Education*, *80*(1), 59–79. doi:10.1353/jhe.0.0037

Kenworthy-U'Ren, A. L. (1999). Management students as consultants an alternative perspective on the service-learning "call to action.". *Journal of Management Inquiry*, *8*(4), 379–387. doi:10.1177/105649269984005

Kenworthy-U'Ren, A. L. (2008). A decade of service-learning: A review of the field ten years after JOBE's seminal special issue. *Journal of Business Ethics*, *81*(4), 811–822. doi:10.1007/s10551-007-9549-3

Lambright, K. T., & Alden, A. F. (2012). Voices from the trenches: Faculty perspectives on support for sustaining service-learning. *Journal of Higher Education Outreach & Engagement*, *16*(2), 9–46.

Larson, M. B., & Lockee, B. B. (2009). Preparing instructional designers for different career environments: A case study. *Educational Technology Research and Development*, *57*(1), 1–24. doi:10.1007/s11423-006-9031-4

Lester, S. W., Tomkovick, C., Wells, T., Flunker, L., & Kickul, J. (2005). Does service-learning add value? Examining the perspectives of multiple stakeholders. *Academy of Management Learning & Education*, *4*(3), 278–294. doi:10.5465/AMLE.2005.18122418

Madsen, S. R., & Turnbull, O. (2006). Academic service-learning experiences of compensation and benefit course students. *Journal of Management Education*, *30*(5), 724–742. doi:10.1177/1052562905283710

Novak, J. M., Markey, V., & Allen, M. (2007). Evaluating cognitive outcomes of service-learning in higher education: A meta-analysis. *Communication Research Reports*, *24*(2), 149–157. doi:10.1080/08824090701304881

Phillips, A., Bolduc, S. R., & Gallo, M. (2013). Curricular placement of academic service-learning in higher education. *Journal of Higher Education Outreach & Engagement*, *17*(4), 75–96.

Seifer, S. D., & Connors, K. (2007). Faculty Toolkit for Service-Learning in Higher Education. Scotts VAlley. CA: National Service-Learning Clearinghouse; Retrieved from https://www.nationalserviceresources.gov/files/he_toolkit_with_worksheets.pdf

Simons, L., & Cleary, B. (2006). The influence of service-learning on students' personal and social development. *College Teaching*, *54*(4), 307–319. doi:10.3200/CTCH.54.4.307-319

Steinke, P., & Buresh, S. (2002). Cognitive outcomes of service-learning: Reviewing the past and glimpsing the future. *Michigan Journal of Community Service Learning*, *8*(2), 5–14.

Turnbull, O., & Madsen, S. R. (2006). Beyond the classroom: Implementing academic service-learning. *Journal of Business Inquiry: Research, Education, and Application*, *5*(1), 65–71.

Waldner, L. S., & Hunter, D. (2008). Client-based courses: Variations in service-learning. *Journal of Public Affairs Education*, 219–239.

Waldner, L. S., McGorry, S., & Widener, M. (2010). Extreme e-service-learning (XE-SL): E-service-learning in the 100% online course. *Journal of Online Learning and Teaching, 6*(4), 839–851.

Waldner, L. S., Widener, M. C., & McGorry, S. Y. (2012). E-service-learning: The evolution of service-learning to engage a growing online student population. *Journal of Higher Education Outreach & Engagement, 16*(2), 123–150.

Warren, J. L. (2012). Does service-learning increase student learning?: A meta-analysis. *Michigan Journal of Community Service Learning, 18*(2), 56–61.

Zhang, G., Zeller, N., Griffith, R., Metcalf, D., Williams, J., Shea, C., & Misulis, K. (2011). Using the context, input, process, and product evaluation model (CIPP) as a comprehensive framework to guide the planning, implementation, and assessment of service-learning programs. *Journal of Higher Education Outreach & Engagement, 15*(4), 57–84.

KEY TERMS AND DEFINITIONS

Adult Basic Education: Instruction for adults that aims to improve the learner's language arts, science, social studies, and math skills and knowledge for career and college readiness.

E-Service-Learning: An educational approach that combines community service, academic coursework, and work-based experiential learning, and occurs when either the instruction or service components are conducted virtually.

Evaluation: A process to gather and analyze information to determine worth. In an instructional context, evaluation is used to identify the effectiveness, efficiency, and appeal of the instruction for the purposes of making improvements.

Experiential Learning: The process of learning through engagement in experiences and activities to help students develop their skills and knowledge in the subject area.

Memorandum of Understanding: An agreement between parties that specifies their intended actions.

Open Educational Resources: Any materials used for instructional purposes that are openly licensed by the copyright holder, and do not require the user to request permission or pay for use.

Service-Learning: An educational approach that combines community service and academic coursework.

Chapter 9
A Systematic Evaluation of a Soccer Club's College Advisory Program

Seung Youn (Yonnie) Chyung
Boise State University, USA

Colleen Olson
Boise State University, USA

Stacey E. Olachea
Boise State University, USA

Ben Davis
Boise State University, USA

EXECUTIVE SUMMARY

The College Advisory Program offered by Total Vision Soccer Club aims at providing young players with the opportunity to learn how to navigate the collegiate recruiting process, market themselves to college coaches, and increase their exposure to potential colleges and universities. A team of external evaluators (authors of this chapter) conducted a formative evaluation to determine what the program needs to do to reach its goal. By following a systemic evaluation process, the evaluation team investigated five dimensions of the program and collected data by reviewing various program materials and conducting surveys and interviews with players and their parents, upstream stakeholders, and downstream impactees. By triangulating the multiple sources of data, the team drew a conclusion that most program dimensions were rated as mediocre although the program had several strengths. The team provided evidence-based recommendations for improving the quality of the program.

DOI: 10.4018/978-1-4666-8330-3.ch009

ORGANIZATIONAL BACKGROUND

Human performance improvement (HPI) involves the use of systematic and systemic approaches to closing gaps in organizational outcomes by employing cost-effective solutions (Chyung, 2008; Van Tiem, Moseley, & Dessinger, 2012). The International Society for Performance Improvement (ISPI) is a leading organization that provides professional standards, principles, and ethical guidelines to the community of practitioners involved in various types of HPI processes. For example, HPI practitioners are expected to: 1) focus on results, 2) take a systemic view, 3) add value, 4) establish partnerships with clients and stakeholders, 5) determine needs or opportunities for improvement, 6) determine causal factors for performance gaps, 7) design solutions to close the performance gaps, 8) ensure solutions' conformity and feasibility, 9) successfully implement recommended solutions, and 10) evaluate results and impact of the implemented solutions (ISPI, n.d.). Among the 10 items, HPI practitioners often encounter barriers to conducting evaluations of implemented solutions or interventions, and thus evaluation is rather infrequently performed by HPI practitioners (Gordon, 2003; Guerra, 2003).

Evaluations conducted in the context of HPI involve investigations of the quality, value, and significance of the interventions that have been implemented to make improvements to current performance levels. The implemented solutions can be instructional programs such as educational or training courses, workshops, and e-learning programs, or non-instructional programs such as incentive programs, employee engagement programs, and electronic performance support systems. They can also be a combination of both. By referring to the solutions or interventions as programs, evaluations conducted in the HPI context can be characterized as *program evaluations*. The most popular evaluation model that HPI practitioners are aware of is undoubtedly Kirkpatrick's 4-level model of evaluation (1996), which is designed to evaluate training programs. However, since training programs are required only about 10% of the time (Dean, 1997), HPI practitioners also need to be equipped with knowledge of conducting evaluations on programs that are not training programs.

When conducting program evaluations, whether they are training or non-training programs, HPI practitioners need to follow a systematic process involving steps such as: 1) identify the program to be evaluated (a.k.a., evaluand), 2) identify the overall purpose and type of conducting the evaluation (e.g., formative vs. summative, and goal-based vs. goal-free), 3) identify stakeholders of the program, 4) review an existing, or develop a new, program logic model, 5) identify dimensions of the program to be investigated, 6) determine data collection methods, 7) identify or develop data collection instruments, 8) collect data, 9) analyze data against rubrics, and 10) synthesize dimensional results, draw conclusions, and make recommendations (Chyung, Wisniewski, Inderbitzen, & Campbell, 2013; Davidson, 2005; Scriven, 2007). This chapter describes a case evaluation study on a youth soccer club's college advisory program using those 10 steps. This 10-step procedure was established based on Key Evaluation Checklist (KEC) developed by Michael Scriven (2007), whose approach to evaluation is recognized as a consumer-oriented and needs-oriented approach. Other approaches to program evaluations include David Fetterman's (2001) empowerment evaluation, Robert Stake's (2004) responsive evaluation, and Michael Patton's (2012) utilization-focused evaluation [see Stufflebeam and Shinkfield (2007) for other program evaluation approaches and comparisons among them]. The evaluators of this chapter chose to use the KEC framework for its needs-oriented approach (i.e., assessing if the program is meeting the actual consumers' needs) and its explicit guidance for conducting comprehensive and systematic evaluations (Davidson, 2005).

SETTING THE STAGE

Identifying the Evaluand

Youth Soccer has become one of the most popular sports in the United States. According to an ESPN Sports Poll, "Soccer is America's second-most popular sport for those ages 12-24, outstripping the NBA, MLB and college football" (Bennett, 2012). High school soccer players have more than doubled since 1990 and the number of women's collegiate teams has increased by 115% (Belson, 2010). This huge growth has spurred the need for youth soccer clubs around the nation. Youth soccer provides youth ages 2-19 with the skills and knowledge of the game and exposure to college coaches. Many soccer clubs provide recruiting resources to their players; however, the benefits of these resources vary greatly.

A mid-size city in the Western United States has 18 soccer clubs, one of which is Total Vision Soccer Club (TVSC) (pseudonym). TVSC, a nonprofit organization, was founded in 1986 as a boys-only club; they have since added girls to their club and are now the oldest club in the state. The club remains highly competitive, winning more State Cup events than any other of the clubs combined. In 2012, TVSC partnered with Nike to become a Nike premier club. This partnership allows TVSC to use Nike's training curriculum methodology to assess, analyze, and improve output, to ensure their players are constantly learning and improving on the field. In addition, this partnership allows for special consideration for entry into many tournaments. These tournaments are a necessary resource in the college recruitment process.

TVSC offers a youth academy for ages 2-10 and a competitive program for ages 10-19. Their competitive training program develops the four areas of the game - technical, tactical, physical, and psychological. They believe that by doing this training, regardless of drive and ability, they will be able to develop every individual to his/her fullest potential. In addition to field training, TVSC offers college recruitment skills through their College Advisory Program (CAP).

The CAP provides a valuable resource to players and their parents. Due to the tremendous growth in high school soccer programs, high school coaches can only provide collegiate services to a marginal number of players. The college recruitment process is often a four-year process that begins and ends by players marketing themselves to college coaches. By teaching players/parents how to effectively market players to college coaches, providing them with a means to increase their exposure to college coaches, and aiding them in realistic goal setting, the TVSC CAP intends to meet a void present in the high school setting. Since 1986, TVSC has successfully aided in the placement of 300 players on college teams, approximately 7% of eligible registered players.

Determining the Purpose of Evaluation

TVSC shifted leadership of the program during 2013. With this shift, TVSC Director of Girls Coaching and TVSC Director of Boys Coaching requested a team of external evaluators from Boise State University's Organization Performance and Workplace Learning program to conduct a formative evaluation to determine how well the program aids players in finding the right college and to determine areas of improvement. They specifically requested this evaluation to reveal what areas of the program are contributing to players' failure to find collegiate placement. They felt there might be several reasons why more players were not being placed in college settings, including unrealistic player/parent expectations, lack of player/parent motivation to market themselves to college coaches, lack of player/parent knowledge of college and division requirements, and/or players/parents not realizing the CAP's existence.

During the initial phase of the evaluation project, the evaluation team conducted research to learn about the CAP in detail. TVSC offers the CAP to all players from 9th to 12th grade or age 19. This voluntary program assists club soccer players/parents in navigating the path to collegiate soccer programs. The CAP works with all players who have a desire to play soccer at the collegiate level or simply want to go to college to further their education. The program emphasizes finding colleges with the right academics, social interaction, and if desired, athletic fit for individuals. TVSC does this through requested one-on-one advisory sessions and through an annual information seminar. The seminar provides players/parents with an overview of the recruitment process, explains the various requirements of division schools, and provides each player with numerous written tools that include:

- General college admission requirements.
- National Collegiate Athletic Association (NCAA) Division I, II and III requirements.
- National Association of Intercollegiate Athletics (NAIA), National Junior College Athletic Association (NJCAA), and National Christian College Athletic Association (NCCAA) division requirements.
- Roles and responsibilities of the college advisors, club coaches, players/parents, and college coaches.
- Four-year timeline resource, starting in 9th grade that increases player exposure to college coaches.
- Tips and suggestions to aid in a positive outcome.

Furthermore, the CAP commits to training the TVSC coaching staff in college recruitment processes and strategies, emphasizing the differences between the various requirements found in each of the athletic divisions within collegiate sports, marketing TVSC club and players to college soccer programs, and researching potential tournament play to increase player exposure opportunities. College advisors are coaches as well; they value the importance of developing the players both on and off the field. Their goal is to build the character of players to shape the future.

Identifying Stakeholders

The evaluation team clearly identified upstream and downstream stakeholders of the program. Upstream stakeholders are the individuals who were involved in the development and/or operation of the program, whereas downstream stakeholders include immediate recipients who participated in the program and downstream impactees who would be further influenced by the immediate recipients (Davidson, 2005). Table 1 describes the three stakeholders groups of this program.

The evaluation team also became more familiar with the current resources available to the program in order to make a fair evaluative judgment about the quality of the program outcomes. The team understood that although TVSC is a non-profit organization, in order to provide their services, they require a budget that is sizable enough to meet program needs. TVSC's budget is reliant on revenue produced through club assessment fees, fundraising opportunities, sponsorships, and donations. TVSC relies heavily on parent volunteers' experience and expertise to ensure successful outcomes for their players.

Table 1. College advisory program stakeholders

Stakeholder Category	Members
Upstream Stakeholders	• TVSC President and Technical Director (n = 1). • TVSC College Advisors (n = 2). • TVSC Board of Directors (n = 10). • TVSC Coaches (n = 3 or 4).
Immediate Recipients	• 9th thru 12th grade TVSC soccer players who intend to play soccer at the collegiate level (n = 297). • TVSC players' parents (n = between 297 and 550).
Downstream Impactees	• TVSC players' parents (n = between 297 and 550). • TVSC Coaches (n = 42). • College Soccer Coaches (infinite). • TVSC siblings (n = between 275 and 700) (using the census of an average of 2.5 children per family). • High School Soccer Coaches (n = approximately 23). • Other club players/parents (n = infinite).

CASE DESCRIPTION

Developing a Program Logic Model

Evaluation involves consultative activities as much as investigative activities. After acquiring sufficient knowledge about the program, the evaluation team began consultative activities. Collaborating with the main upstream stakeholders and using W. K. Kellogg Foundation's guidelines (2004), the team developed a logic model of the program. As presented in Table 2, the program logic model outlines the resources and activities used by TVSC as well as the outputs, outcomes, and impacts they should achieve.

Determining Dimensions

One of the critical activities during an evaluation is to identify evaluative criteria or dimensions to investigate. To do this, the evaluation team sought to understand the true need(s) of the primary consumer of the program. Many high school athletes aspire to go to college with a sports scholarship. However, for most, it is rather difficult to do so. During 2010 -2011 academic year, there were 398,351 high school male soccer players, who had over a 25% chance of receiving a Division 1 college soccer scholarship and a 32% chance of receiving a Division 2 college soccer scholarship (Sports Scholarships, 2014a). In comparison, during the same year, there were 361,556 high school female soccer players, who had less than a 2% chance of receiving a Division 1 college soccer scholarship and a 40% chance of receiving a

Table 2. College advisory program logic model

Inputs	Activities	Outputs	Outcomes		Impacts
			Short-Term	**Long-Term**	

• General college admission requirements.
• Soccer players ages 14-19.
• Parents of soccer players.
• Certified coaching staff.
• College coaches.
• College advisors.
• CAP services and recruiting processes to the college advisors in their roles of collegiate advising.
• Facility and facilitators for program and meetings.
• Budget to accomplish informative or training meetings.
• Availability of college advisors to complete one-on-one sessions with players/parents.
	• Delegate roles and responsibilities to the college advisors.
	• Train coaching staff to be knowledgeable in:
	  - College recruitment processes and strategies, and division requirements.
	• Develop participant materials to explain the recruitment process.
	• Provide a yearly seminar to players/parents.
	• Provide one-on-one advising to players.
	• Network with college coaches to market TVSC players.
	• Research tournament opportunities.
	• Market the program to eligible participants.
	  - Recommend colleges that meet goals and satisfy eligibility requirements.
		• College advisors know their roles and responsibilities within the program and seminar.
		• Coaching staff is knowledgeable in the college recruitment process.
		• College coaches know of TVSC and look for their players during tournament play.
		• Players have varied opportunities to increase their exposure to college coaches.
		• Players/parents have the tools needed to follow a systematic collegiate recruiting process.
		• Players/parents have the knowledge and skills needed to navigate the collegiate recruitment process.
			• Matured College Advisory Program to include all eligible TVSC players with interest in a collegiate experience.
			• Increased collegiate exposure and placement of TVSC players.
			• Reduced finger pointing and hurt feelings.
			• Improved player GPAs.
			• TVSC achieves a united vision of what the program can offer to their players.
			• TVSC markets the CAP to potential players as a competitive advantage to other clubs.
				• Increased college coach interactions with TVSC players due to their knowledge of the recruitment process.
				• Increased player placement onto college teams by 15%.
				• TVSC is the club of choice through the results of their coaching staff and their college advisory program.
				• All TVSC players are aware of the college advisory program.
				• All players are informed of the process.
				• All players who want to pursue college feel supported and informed in their collegiate choices.
					• Players/parents make informed club play choices based on track record of college placement, knowledgeable coaching staff, and club support in meeting long-term goals.
					• Players graduate with college degrees and are contributing to society in a healthy, educated and informed manner.

Division 2 college soccer scholarship (Sports Scholarships, 2014b). Therefore, their true need is to have the tools and knowledge needed to navigate the college recruiting process to ensure a successful outcome. In order to address a realistic need for the consumers while meeting the needs of the program itself, the evaluation team used the following overall question to drive the evaluation:

Does the TVSC College Advisory Program aid players in college placement and are there areas for improvement?

To answer this question, the team needed to understand the various dimensions of the program. To do this, the team worked with selected upstream stakeholders, TVSC Director of Girls Coaching and TVSC Director of Boys Coaching, to draw on their knowledge of the program. While the team was developing the program logic model (Table 2) with them, both parties were able to identify and understand the various if-then relationships between means and outcomes. Focusing on the activities, outputs, and outcomes of the logic model, the team defined the significant dimensions of the program. After confirming the teams' understanding of the dimensions with the client, the team and client collaboratively determined that the evaluation should focus on two areas of process and three areas of outcomes:

1. **Program Design:** How well is the CAP designed (to provide services and tools) to aid players/parents in the college recruitment process?
2. **Marketing Design:** How well is the program marketed to eligible players/parents?
3. **Staff Knowledge:** How accurately are the TVSC coaches presenting the CAP and services to players/parents?
4. **Player/Parent Knowledge, Skills, and Abilities:** How prepared are the players/parents to navigate the collegiate recruitment process?
5. **College Placement Rates:** To what extent do the players using the CAP have a higher success rate in obtaining college opportunities?

The fifth dimension regarding college placement rates, however, was later determined that it could not be linked as an indicator of the quality of the CAP, because of insufficient data to determine outcomes on this dimension.

In order to determine the degrees of importance weighting among the multiple dimensions, the team used evidence from literature and consulted the knowledge of selected stakeholders (Davidson, 2005). The team conducted a literature review of recruiting techniques prior to the client meeting. The literature on the college recruiting process is vast; therefore, the team looked into other clubs who were governed by an affiliate of the US Soccer Association, focusing on their methods of college recruitment strategy. This review provided the team with important insights about what successful soccer clubs emphasize in their college placement programs, as well as how that aligns with evidence regarding successful recruitment strategies. As an example, the Richmond Strikers Soccer Club in Glen Allen, Virginia uses realistic goal setting for players/parents and provides convenient resources and reference materials to guide players through the college recruiting process (Richmond Strikers Soccer Club, 2014). Furthermore, the Richmond Strikers collegiate program emphasizes the importance of offering a program that supports the players/parents abilities to self-navigate the process. Their program focuses extensively on providing tools, information, and services that help the players/parents gain sufficient knowledge and abilities to achieve success. The Bavarian Soccer Club is another example. Founded in Milwaukee in 1929, the club follows the US Soccer Federation player development curriculum to develop young players through the levels of the National player development pyramid and to help them move into college and professional academy level play (Bavarian Soccer Club, 2014a). The Bavarian Soccer Club acknowledges that the college soccer recruitment process can be overwhelming to players and their parents, who often ask questions such as "When do I apply to College? How do I contact a college coach? How do I begin the recruitment process?" The concern regarding the players and parents abilities to navigate the process was further reinforced by NCAA guidelines. According to Sports Scholarships (2013), "NCAA guidelines also want the players to make first contact, so your first move is to send out an effective introductory letter that demonstrates your attributes." In response to this matter, the Club provides players and parents with step-by-step guidelines and college recruiting resources (Bavarian Soccer Club, 2014b).

These examples from the literature review supported an "extremely important" emphasis on the design of the program, as well as the focus on providing targeted knowledge and abilities to enable the players/parents to execute the process. This review also provided the team with an understanding of the degrees of importance for each dimension, allowing the team to make informed suggestions to the client. To solidify the importance weightings, the team recognized the importance of gaining client input given their extensive knowledge of the program. Both TVSC Director of Girls Coaching and TVSC Director of Boys Coaching worked together to provide a consensus on the importance weighting of dimensions. Table 3 identifies the results of the client's input and the rationale for the decisions.

Determining Data Collection Methods

The evaluation team used a goal-based, formative evaluation approach because the organization had a specific program goal of assisting aspiring student-athletes to

Table 3. TVSC dimensions of merit and weightings

Category	Dimension	Importance Weighting	Reasoning
Process	Program Design	Extremely Important	The upstream stakeholders believed that the program design was extremely important to the success of the program. They felt that the design would represent the foundation in which all efforts begin.
	Marketing Design	Important	This dimension was determined to be important because players/parents need to know the program is available, and how this program can benefit them as they strive to achieve their college placement goals.
Outcome	Staff Knowledge	Very Important	The upstream stakeholders determined staff knowledge to be very important given the staff's role and their abilities to influence positive or negative outcomes. They also felt that failure in this area could be easily remedied.
	Player/Parent Knowledge, Skills, and Abilities	Extremely Important	Because this program was designed as a self-navigation process for players/parents, the upstream stakeholders felt that this dimension was extremely important to achieve successful outcomes.
	College Placement Rates	Important	The upstream stakeholders felt that this dimension would be an important tool in answering the overall evaluation question, "Does the TVSC College Advisory Program aid players in college placement?"

find the right college fit in the following three key areas: academics, social interaction, and athletics, also based on the client's desire to determine improvements for the existing program. The process and methodology of this evaluation followed Michael Scriven's Key Evaluation Checklist (2007) to conduct the evaluation in a systematic manner that provided systemic results for the organization.

The evaluation focused on investigating two process-based and three outcome-based dimensions. To evaluate the process-based dimensions, the evaluation team concentrated on how well the program activities (or means) supported the program design and marketing of the program. For the outcome-based dimensions, the team focused on evaluating the outputs, outcomes, and impacts.

Using Donald Kirkpatrick's (1996) four-level evaluation model as a guide, the team incorporated Level 1 Reaction, Level 2 Learning, and Level 3 Behavior into the evaluation design. Specifically, Level 1 survey and interview questions identified the players/parents reactions to the program design and program marketing. Level 2 learning survey questions explored the players/parents knowledge of the self-navigation techniques provided by the program. Furthermore, Level 2 Learning and Level 3 Behavior survey and interview questions gauged the coaching staff's ability to accurately present their CAP knowledge.

The evaluating team used various research collection methods and sources for data collection. The priority on triangulation helped ensure unbiased results, having followed Scriven's (1999) advice on subjectivity. Furthermore, "good research practice obligates the researcher to triangulate that is to use multiple methods, data sources and researchers to enhance the validity of research findings" (Mathison, 1988, p. 13). Therefore, the evaluation team used the following data collection methods and sources to ensure triangulation:

- Reviews of existing data, including all program materials, processes, policies and guides, website materials, and literature review of relevant recruiting methods and other college advisory programs.
- Surveys of immediate recipients, downstream impactees, and upstream stakeholders to investigate awareness, knowledge, and reactions to the CAP.
- Interviews of upstream stakeholders and downstream impactees to further analyze the program's structure, marketing techniques, knowledge of CAP policies and procedures, use of knowledge and skills in the recruiting process, and collegiate opportunities.

Developing Data Collection Instruments

In support of the data collection process, the team developed interview procedures and questions, data review checklists, and electronic survey questionnaires. Specific data collection methods and sources that were used for each dimension are described in Table 4.

Collecting Data

Once the data collection instruments were developed, the evaluation team obtained approval from the main stakeholders for using the instruments and received their support for administering them, such as accessing existing documents and records to review and obtaining players'/parents' contact information to conduct surveys and interviews.

It is important to note that the timeframe available for data collection was short (about a month), requiring the simultaneous collection of data through various methods. Additionally, the team found existing internal data to be insufficient for two dimensions, preventing the completion of a thorough data review. This pertained

Table 4. College advisory program methodology

Evaluative Dimension	Data Collection Method	Instrument Used	Kirkpatrick Level
1. **Program Design:** How well is the CAP designed (to provide services and tools) to aid players/parents in the college recruitment process?	1-1. Existing data review of all program materials/processes and procedures used by the CAP staff	Document Review Checklist	N/A
	1-2. Web-based survey (297 households invited and 28 completed)	Electronic Survey Questionnaire	Level 1
	1-3. Interviews with upstream stakeholders and downstream impactees (n=5)	Interview Protocols	N/A
2. **Marketing Design:** How well is the program marketed to eligible players/parents?	2-1. Existing data review of website and extant materials to extrapolate the current marketing practices and tools	Data Review Checklist	N/A
	2-2. Web-based survey (297 households invited and 28 completed)	Electronic Survey Questionnaire	Level 1
	2-3. Interviews with upstream stakeholders and downstream impactees	Interview Protocols	N/A
3. **Staff Knowledge:** How accurately are the TVSC coaches presenting the CAP and services to players/ parents?	3-1. Existing data review of written documentation regarding the CAP's recruiting process and services	Data Review Checklist	N/A
	3-2. Web-based survey (13 U15-U19[1] coaching staff invited 4 completed)	Electronic Survey Questionnaire	Level 2 Level 3
	3-3. Interviews with upstream stakeholders and downstream impactees (n=5)	Interview Protocols	N/A
4. **Player/Parent Knowledge, Skills, and Abilities:** How prepared are the players/ parents to navigate the collegiate recruitment process?	4-1. Web-based survey (134 U16-U19 players/parents invited and 19 completed)	Electronic Survey Questionnaire	Level 2
	4-2. Interviews with upstream stakeholders and downstream impactees (n=5)	Interview Protocols	N/A
5. **College Placement Rates:** To what extent do the players using the CAP have a higher success rate in obtaining college opportunities?	5-1. Existing data review of client information regarding collegiate placement and scholarship awards	Data Review Checklist	N/A
	5-2. Interviews with upstream stakeholders and downstream impactees (n=5)	Interview Questions Protocols	N/A

[1]"U" in U15 or U19 stands for "under" – e.g., U15 means that the soccer age is under 15.

to data review for the staff knowledge and college placement dimensions, affecting the ability to triangulate information for the college placement dimension. Given that, the evaluation team removed college placement rates as a qualifying indicator of the quality of the CAP, and did not include it in the overall evaluation synthesis.

Analyzing Evaluation Results

Dimension #1: Program design (extremely important) - How well is the CAP designed (to provide services and tools) to aid players/parents in the college recruitment process?

As primary data, the evaluation team reviewed internal documents in order to evaluate the program's content and tools as it supports the program design. The team also used a survey with players/parents as a primary data source to gather additional insights from players/parents regarding their satisfaction with the CAP knowledge, tools and services, as well as explore how well the information and knowledge supports their abilities to navigate the college search process. Finally, the team conducted interviews, as secondary data, with a variety of TVSC personnel and players/parents to gather additional insights about the CAP design. The primary and secondary sources revealed the following information and results.

Document review: The evaluation team reviewed 11 TVSC documents focusing on seven criteria, including:

1. Accuracy.
2. Timeliness (i.e., are they current?).
3. Identification of roles/responsibilities for players, parents, coaches and college advisors.
4. Identification of college requirements.
5. Identification of eligibility requirements for student athletes.
6. Support for services' and tools' objectives.
7. Usefulness in a self-navigation process.

The evaluation team scored each document on the seven elements, applying a rating from 1 to 3 with 1 being not at all, 2 being somewhat, and 3 being mostly. The overall score was 15 out of 21.

Of significance, the data review revealed the following:

- Of those documents that were current, the information was accurate.
- The documents were aligned with the TVSC services and tools.
- The documents supported a self-navigation process, supporting the players/parents' abilities to navigate the college process with minimal support from TVSC.

Opportunities for improvement were also identified, including:

- While the documents highlighted players/parents' roles and responsibilities, there was little mentioning of the coaches and/or TVSC staff's roles and responsibilities.
- The documents inconsistently identified the college and/or student-athlete eligibility requirements. Some documents included the information, while others did not.

Survey: The team administered an anonymous, web-based survey with the players/parents. This included a group of boy and girl players ranging in age from 14 to 19 or on teams with the designations of U14 – U19. On behalf of the evaluation team, the Club distributed the survey to the players/parents and asked them to respond to the surveys together. A total of 297 households were invited to the survey, achieving a 9% response rate. Based on the responses, the survey identified only 49% of the respondents being either satisfied or very satisfied with the CAP design.

Of significance, the survey results identified the following strengths and opportunities for improvement:

- For self-navigation, 83% of respondents understood the self-navigation techniques identified in the CAP. Additionally, 42% of respondents identified the navigation techniques as satisfactory.
- While 42% of the respondents indicated they were satisfied with the CAP, none were very satisfied, and a combined total of 34% were dissatisfied or very dissatisfied.
- For support, 58% of respondents did not feel adequately supported through the CAP.
- For recommendations, 56% indicated they would not recommend the program to others.

Interview: The team conducted individual interviews with a small sample of downstream impactees and upstream stakeholders who have used or are currently using the CAP. The team used the insights gained from these interviews as secondary data to confirm or deny the data review and survey results, and to help identify improvements to the program. Insights were mixed with some interviewees satisfied with the program and some dissatisfied.

Of significance, the interviews identified the following strengths and opportunities for improvement:

- The program clearly explains the responsibilities of the players/parents to identify and seek out college opportunities.
- The use of a variety of materials and communication approaches was very helpful to comprehend the amount of information.
- Overall, the program could provide more support from coaches and TVSC. Accessing other experienced players/parents would be helpful.
- More individual attention rather than group session would be extremely valuable.

Triangulation: The evaluation team developed dimensional rubrics in collaboration with the main stakeholders. Based on this dimension's rubric presented in Table 5, the two primary data sources (data review and survey) indicated a difference in the quality of this dimension between *Good* (data Review score) and *Poor* (survey score). Then, the team used the interview data to make an adjustment to the overall dimensional rating to be *Mediocre*, because although the current information provided in the program design is accurate and it supports self-navigation, survey data and interviews confirmed the design of the program could be significantly enhanced to better align with the needs of players/parents. This includes an increased focus on individual advising sessions and providing more information about how to navigate the process, rather than just including academic/eligibility requirements. Interviewees noted that much of the provided information was common knowledge to those seeking college opportunities.

Table 5. Program design rubric

Excellent	Good	Mediocre	Poor
The data review achieves a score of 18 or greater, and 90% or more of players/parents are satisfied or very satisfied that the design of the CAP supports the college recruitment process.	The data review achieves a score of 15 to 17, and 75-89% of players/parents are satisfied or very satisfied that the design of the CAP supports the college recruitment process.	The data review achieves a score of 12 to 14, and 60-74% of players/parents are satisfied or very satisfied that the design of the CAP supports the college recruitment process.	The data review achieves a score of 11 or less, and less than 60% of players/parents are satisfied or very satisfied that the design of the CAP supports the college recruitment process.

Dimension #2: Marketing design (important) - How well is the program marketed to eligible players/parents?

The primary data for this dimension consisted of several years of past and present marketing flyers. The evaluation team also used survey results as primary data to determine the effectiveness of the current marketing tools (e.g., email flyers, website, and word of mouth). Interview data was compiled as a secondary data source to gather additional insights about the CAP marketing techniques and strategies and to confirm or deny data review results. The primary and secondary sources revealed the following information and results.

Data Review: The evaluation team reviewed seven internal documents focusing on the seven criteria as explained previously, by applying a rating from 1 to 3 with 1 being not at all, 2 being somewhat, and 3 being mostly. The overall score was 14 out of 21.

Of significance, the data review revealed the following:

- The information provided was accurate and appropriate for the delivery medium (email).
- The documents were appropriate for the marketing technique being used (email flyer).

Opportunities for improvement were also identified, including:

- The documentation failed to identify specific CAP services and provide specific contact information.
- The website needs to be updated to reflect accurate (as of 2013) information, including college placement rates.

Survey: The team administered an anonymous, web-based survey with the households of all boy and girl players ranging in age from 14 to19 or on teams with the designations of U14-U19. Among 297 households invited, 9% responded. Of those who responded, 67% of players/parents were aware of the program, 60% of those players had heard of the program through one or more source, and 42% had used one or more services.

Of significance, the survey results identified the following strengths and opportunities for improvement:

- More than 50% of players/parents surveyed were aware of the program.

- 76% of players/parents indicating they had heard of the program specified that they heard of the program through their team coach, indicating an active role by the coaching staff.
- 92% of survey respondents indicated they had heard of the program specified they had used the annual seminar; however, less than half used the written materials or individual advising sessions.

Interview: Individual interviews consisted of a small sample of downstream impactees and upstream stakeholders who have used or are currently using the CAP. The evaluation team used the insights gained from these interviews as secondary data to confirm or deny the data review and survey results, and to help identify improvement to the program. The data gathered from these interviews suggest that the coaching staff needed to take a more significant role in ensuring that players/ parents are using the program to its full potential.

Of significance, the interviews identified the following:

- Coaching staff needs to play a more proactive role in ensuring player attendance at the annual seminar, and their participation in the CAP services.
- Word of mouth seems to be the most useful marketing method.

Triangulation: The team analyzed the scores obtained from the two primary data sources (data review and survey) against the rubric as shown in Table 6, and determined the quality of this dimension as *Mediocre*. This result was supported by the interview data. Although the surveys indicated that most players/parents had heard about the program through coaching staff (word of mouth), the interviews revealed that the coaching staff is not reinforcing CAP strategies to ensure that players are engaged in the CAP.

Table 6. Marketing design rubric

Excellent	Good	Mediocre	Poor
The data review achieves a score of 18 or greater, and 90% or more of players/parents have heard of the program through 3 sources and are using all services provided through the CAP.	The data review achieves a score of 15 to 17, and 75%-89% of players/ parents have heard of the program through at least 2 sources and are using at least 2 services provided through the CAP.	The data review achieves a score of 12 to 14, and 60%-74% of players/ parents have heard of CAP through at least 1 source, are using at least 1 of service.	The data review achieves a score of 11 or less, and less than 60% of players/ parents have not heard of the CAP or used any CAP services.

Dimension #3: Staff knowledge (very important) - How accurately are the TVSC coaches presenting the CAP and services to players/parents?

As primary data, the evaluation team conducted an anonymous, web-based survey with the coaching staff responsible for coaching the target audience, players ranging in ages from 14-19, to explore the coaches' knowledge of the CAP, as their knowledge of the program is directly linked to their ability to accurately present the program to their players. The team gathered additional data through interviews with several downstream impactees and upstream stakeholders. These interviews were used as secondary data to help confirm or deny the results of the survey. While the team also considered a review of existing data for this dimension, research into TVSC's documents revealed that there was insufficient data that related to the staff knowledge of CAP. Therefore, a data review was not considered viable and was not used in deciding the quality rating of this dimension. The primary and secondary sources revealed the following information and results.

Survey: The team administered an anonymous survey to 13 coaching staff members, achieving a 31% response rate. This survey focused on assessing the coaches' level of knowledge about the CAP, as well as the actions or behaviors they exhibit to execute elements of the CAP.

Of significance in the survey results:

- Respondents indicated an understanding of their roles in the CAP process and what resources/tools are available, which includes their levels of involvement, the most commonly used resources, what they should not do for a prospect, and when players are most likely to commit.
- Only 35% of the respondents were clear about the types of advice they should provide to their players in order to secure college athletic opportunities.
- Only 55% of the respondents were clear about the academic requirements for each division.
- Respondents also indicated a lack of understanding in how to direct players to use supplemental player marketing opportunities, including the use of the internet and video.

Interview: To further explore the staff's knowledge of the CAP, the evaluation team conducted interviews with a small group of downstream impactees and upstream stakeholders.

Of significance, the interviews identified the following strengths and opportunities for improvement:

- Coaches have knowledge of the collegiate recruiting process and eligibility requirements; however, the knowledge is inconsistently shared. Additionally, minimal attention is currently placed on individual advising sessions.
- Coaches have access to resources to support the process that they can use to guide the players; however, players are inconsistently directed to these resources.
- Coaches view their roles as guides rather than directors, being resources for questions and advice and conducting follow-ups with college coaches as requested. In some cases, given this viewpoint, coaches are being more reactive than proactive in supporting the process.
- Coaches' knowledge levels and actions vary across the club, with some coaches offering more support, guidance, and information than others.

Triangulation: Based on the survey results analyzed against the rubric as shown in Table 7, the team rated the quality of this dimension as *Mediocre*. This rating was supported by the interview data.

Dimension #4: Player/parent knowledge, skills, and abilities (extremely important) - How prepared are the players/parents to navigate the collegiate recruitment process?

As primary data, the evaluation team reviewed internal documents to evaluate the resources provided to players/parents in order to increase their knowledge, skills, and abilities in navigating the college process. The team also used a survey of players/parents as primary data to gain a clear and thorough understanding of the players/parents' knowledge of the self-navigation techniques that aid in successful recruitment outcomes. As secondary data, the team conducted interviews with a variety of TVSC personnel and players/parents to gather additional insights about the players/parents' knowledge of CAP. The primary and secondary sources revealed the following information and results.

Table 7. Staff knowledge rubric

Excellent	Good	Mediocre	Poor
The group average score for the U14-U19 Staff Knowledge Survey is 90 or higher.	The group average score for the U14-U19 Staff Knowledge Survey is 75-89.	The group average score for the U14-U19 Staff Knowledge Survey is 60-74.	The group average score for the U14-U19 Staff Knowledge Survey is 59 or lower.

Data Review: The evaluation team reviewed 21 internal documents focusing on the following six criteria:

1. Accuracy.
2. Timeliness (i.e., are they current?).
3. Support the self-navigation process.
4. Material organization and ease of use.
5. Information prioritization.
6. Add value to the process.

Based on a rating from 1 to 3 with 1 being not at all, 2 being somewhat, and 3 being mostly, the overall score was 15 out of 18.

Of significance, the data review revealed:

- The information provided was appropriate for the delivery medium.

Opportunities for improvement were also identified, including:

- The documentation in some cases was not current.
- The material was not succinct and gave too much information.
- Navigation of information was often cumbersome or difficult.
- Materials were branded inconsistently leading to confusion and fragmentation in their intended message.

Survey: The team administered an anonymous, web-based survey focusing on exploring the players'/parents' knowledge of the college recruiting process and the CAP elements that support successful self-navigation. The survey was distributed to the households of all boy and girl players ranging in age from 16 to19 or on teams with the designations of U16-U19. A total of 134 households were invited, achieving a 14% response rate. The group average score of the survey was 38.

Of significance in the survey results included:

- Comments and free form answers given by players/parents within the survey indicated widespread confusion regarding the requirements and documentation needed during the college recruitment process.
- Almost half of survey respondents indicated confusion or wrote that they did not know what was required to navigate the process.

- Minimal information regarding strengths was uncovered through the administration of the survey.
- Overall, the survey data indicated that program was inadequately preparing and supporting players/parents for the college recruitment process.

Interview: Interviews involved downstream impactees and upstream stakeholders. Insights gained from these interviews were used as secondary data to confirm or deny the quality rating identified through the data review and survey results. The interview results revealed a significant cognitive load being placed on players/parents via the materials.

Triangulation: The evaluation team analyzed primary data (data review and survey) against the rubric as shown in Table 8. While the team found that the data review received a *Good* rating, with the materials identified as informative, the interviews were aligned with the survey rating of *Poor*. Due to this strong alignment between the interview and survey results, the evaluation team determined that the player/parent knowledge dimension reflects an overall rating of *Poor*. One of the significant challenges encountered by players/parents, as revealed through the surveys and interviews, is assimilating the knowledge necessary for navigating the college recruiting process. The team encountered several reports of "information overload" during the course of player/parent interviews, which was further manifested by the number of incorrect answers provided on the surveys. This condition is referred to as cognitive load, which is defined as, "the amount of work imposed on working memory" (Clark, 2008, p. 86). In the case of the CAP materials, the amount of information presented was creating an overwhelming burden on the working memory.

Table 8. Player/parent knowledge, skills, and abilities rubric

Excellent	Good	Mediocre	Poor
The data review achieves a score of 16 or higher, and the combined group average score for the U16-U19 Player/Parent Knowledge Survey, questions 15-24, is 90 or higher.	The data review achieves a score of 13 to 15, and the combined group average score for the U16-U19 Player/Parent Knowledge Survey, questions 15-24, is 75-89.	The data review achieves a score of 10 to 12, and the combined group average score for the U16-U19 Player/Parent Knowledge Survey, questions 15-24, is 60-74.	The data review achieves a score of 9 or less, and the combined group average score for the U16-U19 Player/Parent Knowledge Survey, questions 15-24, is 59 or less.

Dimension #5: College placement rates (important) - To what extent do the players using CAP have a higher success rate in obtaining college opportunities?

Overall, the primary interview data revealed that downstream impactees and upstream stakeholders felt that the CAP was *Mediocre* at supporting and guiding player opportunities to those individuals that were actively using the CAP services.

However, during the data review process, the evaluation team determined that the current data available was inadequate to support any determination of merit on this dimension because the recording of successful placement opportunities had stopped since 2009. Lack of data did affect analysis and the ability to triangulate the results. Therefore, the team determined that college placement results should be excluded from the overall synthesis.

Of significance, the dimensional analysis identified:

- TVSC has a robust college database to refer to, but that database is not current, potentially hindering college coach contact opportunities for the player.
- TVSC needs to update and begin recording college placements. This information will be a good asset in determining program outcomes.

CURRENT CHALLENGES FACING THE ORGANIZATION

Using multiple data collection methods from various sources associated with TVSC, the evaluation team found the quality of four dimensions of the CAP to be mediocre or poor. The following summarizes the rating for each dimension:

Process-related dimensions:

- The program design dimension was rated as *Mediocre* based on review of existing TVSC data, survey results from players/parents, with initial findings adjusted based on interview insights. While the program offers a variety of resources and information, they are not necessarily well designed to "aid" players in the college recruitment process.
- The marketing design dimension was rated as *Mediocre* based on review of existing TVSC data and analyzed survey results, as well as supported by interviews. The Mediocre score is aligned with data that identifies only 67% of players have heard of the CAP. Additionally, the data review received a score of 14 out of 21 (66.6%). The program needs to ensure that all eligible players have heard of the program, enabling them to make informed choices about using the program.

Outcome-related dimensions:

- The staff knowledge dimension was rated as *Mediocre* based on surveys completed by TVSC coaches, as well as supported by interviews. The Mediocre score is aligned with the limited accuracy and lack of consistency in terms of the way the program is presented to the players.
- The player/parent knowledge, skills, and abilities dimension was rated as *Poor* based on the review of existing TVSC data, survey results from players/parents, with initial findings adjusted by interview insights. Despite there being an immense amount of relevant information provided to players/parents via the TVSC documents, there is a clear lack of assimilated player/parent knowledge, which manifested through surveys and feedback from interviews. Since this is an extremely important dimension, this result is too significant to ignore.

Despite the Mediocre and Poor ratings of the four dimensions, the evaluation team identified several strengths for the program, as shown in Table 9.

While the evaluation revealed several strengths, it was evident that the program needed to make improvements on all four dimensions. Because the level of competition among youth soccer clubs in the region has increased, failure to address the areas to improve the program quality would likely result in losing players to other clubs.

Collected data revealed an eagerness by TVSC and its staff to help players achieve their collegiate goals. In contrast, the collected data also identified frustration amongst the immediate recipients/downstream impactees or the club's audience in successfully supporting their players in their pursuits. In part, data showed frustrations stemming from a misalignment in the club's goals for the CAP and the actual provided services. For example, the TVSC website identifies the CAP as a comprehensive support program and suggests that the program will walk you through the college process. The website suggests a personal and individualized service for each player that currently the CAP cannot and does not provide.

From a high-level, business outcome perspective, the evaluation team found a need for the program to review the CAP goals against TVSC's goals and desired outcomes. This review will help ensure tight alignment between what TVSC offers for a collegiate advisory program and how it implements the program to support long-term success. This could include limiting the focus of the program to players seeking collegiate soccer playing opportunities, rather than all players preparing to go to college. This review might be further enhanced by the development of a

Table 9. CAP strengths and reasoning summary

Strengths	Importance	Reasoning
Program Design: Accurate materials were presented in varied formats (i.e., written materials, annual meetings, and some individual advisory sessions) to meet the audiences' varied needs.	Extremely Important	Players/parents expect that the information they are receiving is accurate. Inaccurate information would diminish the program's validity. Using varied formats helps players/parents receive the information in various ways and at various times in the recruitment process.
Program Design: The players/parents' responsibilities are reasonably identified in the tools and information used during the recruitment process.	Extremely Important	This process needs to be driven by the players/parents with support provided by TVSC, so players/parents need to understand what and how to navigate the process.
Program Design: The tools and information were designed to support a self-navigation approach.	Extremely Important	Given TVSC's role is to support the players/parents; the provided tools should be designed to enable individual navigation.
Player/Parent Knowledge, Skills, and Abilities: Significant quantity of relevant information is provided through the materials.	Extremely Important	Information is essential to the program, and the documentation and presentation materials are full of a variety of information. These materials represent significant value, making them an asset to the program.
Staff Knowledge: Coaches exhibited a fair amount of knowledge regarding the recruiting process.	Very Important	Players/parents expect to receive accurate information about the college process. The delivery of inaccurate information, possibly through communication with coaches, diminishes the quality of the program.
Marketing Design: The program is using various means to disseminate information about the CAP services.	Important	TVSC currently uses email, their website, word of mouth, and flyers to notify players/parents of upcoming CAP events. Using various forms of outreach helps increase participation rates.

long-term plan, identifying 5-, 10-, and 15- year goals. A long-term plan would help the club further prioritize improvement opportunities and budget allocations from a variety of perspectives.

In addition, the collected data revealed that TVSC's CAP offers players/parents with significant information about the process, focusing on "what" players/parents need to know about the college recruitment process. However, it provides insufficient information about "how" to navigate that process, although respondents indicated a high value in receiving expert advice on how to navigate this complex process.

SOLUTIONS AND RECOMMENDATIONS

To help the program improve its quality, the evaluation team prioritized the recommendations for improvement according to the dimension's level of importance to the club, as well as the overall potential impact (see Tables 10, 11, and 12). Primary priorities were aligned with the dimensions that were identified as being "extremely important," while secondary improvements are focused on the dimensions identified as being "very important" and "important."

Primary Recommendations Regarding Program Design and Player/Parent Skills, Knowledge, and Ability

Based on the client's input and literature review, it was determined that the extremely important dimensions were program design and player/parent skills, knowledge, and abilities. It is the opinion of the evaluation team that focusing improvements on these two dimensions yields the greatest opportunities to strengthen the program (see Table 10).

Secondary Recommendations Regarding Staff Knowledge, Marketing Design, and College Placement Rates

Table 11 describes recommendations addressing performance gaps in staff knowledge, which was a very important area for the program. Table 12 provides additional recommendations addressing performance gaps in the important dimensions, marketing design and college placement rates.

Reflections

This case study evaluation showcases the use of systematic and systemic approaches to conducting a program evaluation. The evaluation team followed a 10-step procedure to analyze the types of evaluation, the overall evaluation question, and the stakeholders involved. The team also helped the client develop a program logic model, which helped them select evaluation dimensions, focusing not only on the program outcomes, but also the process that contributed to resulting in the outcomes. This is an example of taking a systemic view during evaluation practice. Then, the evaluation team, again in collaboration with the client, developed specific data collection methods that allowed them to collect evidence from multiple sources.

This careful evaluation planning stage helped the team and the client organization move quickly through the data collection phase and successfully complete this formative evaluation project. The team collected and used concrete evidence to

Table 10. Recommendation for extremely important CAP dimensions

Program Design and Player/Parent Skills, Knowledge, and Ability Recommendations and Explanations	
Improvement Opportunities	Explanations
Refocus design to emphasize individual advising sessions	Increasing the emphasis and resources on providing individual advising sessions will provide a stronger foundation for support and guidance throughout the process. Interview data demonstrated that players/parents need and desire more one-on-one aid throughout the recruiting process. The personalized attention will provide players/parents with additional opportunities to leverage the expertise of the coaching staff.
Align program content and materials with age-specific information	Given the long time horizon for the college recruiting process, program content and materials should be age-focused and extended to include U-12/13 players. By distinguishing the materials by age, players/parents will be able to focus on the highest priority actions for the players' age group. This will also help minimize information overload. Additionally, providing age-specific content, services and tools aligns with the club's commitment to players/parents. While the data confirmed the delivery of age-specific seminars, further review of the content revealed the majority of the information/tools were the same in each age group.
Develop "how to" learning tools and materials	Players/parents desire to obtain knowledge and tools that help them navigate the process. Although TVSC currently provides a wealth of information to players/parents, many viewed the content as common knowledge or information that they could easily access on their own. Therefore, the program would need to provide players/parents with "how-to" tips, which could address topic such as: • Resume writing. • Player profile development. • Camp selection to strengthen marketable skills. • Communicating and following up with coaches. • Video development.
Create a workbook tool	Players/parents suggested through surveys and interview data that the amount of information and tools was helpful, but overwhelming. Additionally, players/parents indicated they did use written materials (in some cases) as an on-going reference guide. By creating a workbook tool, players/parents will have a consolidated reference guide that supports their long-term recruiting process. To support self-navigation, this workbook tool should be designed to support ease of use and clarity of content. This includes factors such as: • Graphically appealing – with graphical icons to highlight extremely important content. • Quick reference guides – to support easy navigation and summaries of extremely important tips. • Prioritization knowledge/information – to highlight the most relevant information players/parents need to know. • Focus on "how-to" tips from TVSC experts – to leverage experience and advice from TVSC coaches, staff, and player/parent alumni.
Brand all materials presented through CAP	Branding of materials is necessary to ensure that players/parents can easily identify their TVSC resources. By branding all materials with the TVSC logo and contact information, players/parents will know that TVSC is a knowledgeable soccer club that is a reliable resource.

Table 11. Recommendations for very important CAP dimensions

Staff Knowledge Recommendations and Explanations	
Improvement Opportunities	Explanations
Provide CAP workshop to coaching staff	Evaluation data revealed inconsistencies in how coaches delivered services to players/parents. Additionally, no data was available to identify how coaches should provide the services or what knowledge, tools or abilities they should enhance. Developing a CAP workshop for the coaches would help ensure all coaches are providing consistent support that aligns with TVSC objectives. Specifically, this workshop should: • Provide instruction on "how-to" based learning tools and materials. • Provide lists of resources and phone numbers so that the players of newer coaches have the same advantages as players with a more seasoned coaching staff.

Table 12. Recommendation for important CAP dimensions

Marketing Design and College Placement Rates Recommendations and Explanations	
Improvement Opportunities	Explanations
Update and leverage website	Review of the TVSC website confirmed that the data listed on the site is not current, and is not designed to support the players/parents through the recruiting process. Program websites are an effective venue to promote players, as often done by other soccer clubs. This includes sharing player profiles, team stats, and tournament schedules. This type of information is limited on the TVSC site, and would be an excellent resource for interested college coaches. Finally, there is an excellent opportunity to communicate the club's accomplishments on player college placement via its website. However, the club website currently presents that TVSC has only placed 5%-7% of their players since 1986 ("College advisory TVSC," n.d.). The website is also presenting pictures of former TVSC college players of the year from 2008. Using out-of-date content potentially diminishes the message about the success of the program. As long-range opportunities, the club should consider using the website to host reference tools and templates for the players/parents. Sharing this information on a secured site (for player/parent only access) provides "just-in-time" access to resources and tools.
Brand all CAP materials for name recognition	Review of materials identified a lack of consistency in the presentation, content, formatting, and style of the TVSC written and annual seminar materials. Additionally, few materials reinforced the TVSC logo/brand. A redesign of the materials to align with the TVSC brand will provide a professional appearance that reinforces the brand's identity.
Track and share college placement results	The data review identified insufficient data on the college placement of TVSC players. Tracking and sharing these results will help confirm the club's ability to achieve success. This information could also be viewed as a benefit, helping attract potential players. This type of data will help the club measure future success against its goals.

identify areas for improvement and to generate recommendations. In doing so, the team again employed systematic and systemic approaches by triangulating results obtained from multiple sources including both upstream and downstream stakeholders to draw the most credible conclusions. Then, the team prioritized recommendations based on their overall potential impact on changing the process and outcomes of the program. Doing so will help the program achieve its goal, and satisfy the stakeholders' needs and values. Throughout the evaluation process, the evaluation team recognized that successful evaluations rely on effective collaboration between the evaluation team and the client and other stakeholders. Especially when using a needs-based approach to evaluations, it is essential to do planning and collaborating with stakeholders in a systematic and systemic way.

This systematic and systemic approach to conducting a program evaluation exemplifies practitioners' compliance to the HPT standards. In this project, all HPT standards, except #9 and #10, were addressed: 1) focus on results, 2) take a systemic view, 3) add value, 4) establish partnerships with clients and stakeholders, 5) determine needs or opportunities for improvement, 6) determine causal factors for performance gaps, 7) design solutions to close the performance gaps, 8) ensure solutions' conformity and feasibility, 9) successfully implement recommended solutions (the evaluation team did not get involved in implementing the recommendations), and 10) evaluate results and impact of the implemented solutions (the team evaluated the results of the program, but this project did not include a follow-up evaluation on the impact of their recommended solutions).

REFERENCES

Bavarian Soccer Club. (2014a). *Bavarian Soccer Club: Programs*. Retrieved August 15, 2014, from http://www.bavariansoccerclub.com/page/show/623023-programs

Bavarian Soccer Club. (2014b). *College recruiting resources*. Retrieved August 15, 2014, from http://www.bavariansoccerclub.com/page/show/623111-college-recruiting-resources

Belson, K. (2010, July 23). *Soccer's growth in the U.S. seems steady*. The New York Times. Retrieved from http://www.nytimes.com/2010/07/24/sports/soccer/24soccer.html

Bennett, R. (2012, September 20). *Soccer's big takeover*. ESPNFC. Retrieved October 8, 2013, from http://espnfc.com/blog/_/name/relegationzone/id/262

Chyung, S. Y. (2008). *Foundations of instructional and performance technology*. Amherst, MA: HRD Press.

Chyung, S. Y., Wisniewski, A., Inderbitzen, B., & Campbell, D. (2013). An improvement- and accountability-oriented program evaluation: An evaluation of the Adventure Scouts Program. *Performance Improvement Quarterly, 26*(3), 87–115. doi:10.1002/piq.21155

Clark, R. C. (2008). *Building expertise: Cognitive methods for training and performance improvement*. San Francisco: Pfeiffer.

Davidson, E. J. (2005). *Evaluation methodology basics: The nuts and bolts of sound evaluation*. Thousand Oaks, CA: Sage.

Dean, P. (1997). Thomas F. Gilbert, Ph.D. Engineering performance improvement with or without training. In P. J. Dean & D. E. Ripley (Eds.), *Performance improvement pathfinders: Models for organizational learning systems* (pp. 45–64). Silver Spring, MD: ISPI.

Fetterman, D. (2001). *Foundations of empowerment evaluation*. Thousand Oaks, CA: SAGE.

Gordon, D. (2003). *The development and formative evaluation of a human performance intervention evaluation model* (Doctoral dissertation). Florida State University, Florida.

Guerra, I. (2003). Key competencies required of performance improvement professionals. *Performance Improvement Quarterly, 16*(1), 55–72.

International Society for Performance Improvement. (n.d.). *What is HPT?* Principles of Human Performance Technology. Retrieved from http://www.ispi.org/content.aspx?id=54

Kirkpatrick, D. L. (1996). *Evaluating training programs: The four levels*. San Francisco: Berrett-Koehler Publishers.

Mathison, S. (1988). Why triangulate? *Educational Researcher, 17*(2), 13–17. doi:10.3102/0013189X017002013

Patton, M. Q. (2012). *Essentials of utilization-focused evaluation*. Thousand Oaks, CA: SAGE.

Richmond Strikers Soccer Club. (2014). *Playing college soccer and the recruiting process*. Retrieved December 7, 2013, from http://www.richmondstrikers.com/Travel/College/404879.html

Scriven, M. (1999). The fine line between evaluation and explanation. *Research on Social Work Practice*, 9(4), 521–524. doi:10.1177/104973159900900407

Scriven, M. (2007). *Key evaluation checklist.* Retrieved from http://www.wmich.edu/evalctr/archive_checklists/kec_feb07.pdf

Sports Scholarships. (2014a). *Men's soccer scholarship.* Retrieved August, 15, 2014, from http://sportsscholarship.com/womens-soccer-scholarships/

Sports Scholarships. (2014b). *Women's soccer scholarship.* Retrieved August, 15, 2014, from http://sportsscholarship.com/womens-soccer-scholarships/

Stake, R. (2004). *Standards-based & responsive evaluation.* Thousand Oaks, CA: SAGE.

Stufflebeam, D. L., & Shinkfield, A. J. (2007). *Evaluation theory, models, & applications.* San Francisco: Jossey-Bass.

Van Tiem, D., Moseley, J. L., & Dessinger, J. C. (2012). *Fundamentals of performance improvement* (3rd ed.). San Francisco: Pfeiffer.

W. K. Kellogg Foundation. (2004). *Logic model development guide.* Retrieved from http://www.wkkf.org/resource-directory/resource/2006/02/wk-kellogg-foundation-logic-model-development-guide

ADDITIONAL READING

Alkin, M. (2010). *Evaluation essentials: From A to Z.* New York: The Guilford Press.

Alkin, M. (2013). *Evaluation roots: A wider perspective of theorists' views and influences* (2nd ed.). Thousand Oaks, CA: SAGE.

Alliger, G. M., & Janak, E. A. (1989). Kirkpatrick's levels of training criteria: Thirty years later. *Personnel Psychology*, 42(2), 331–342. doi:10.1111/j.1744-6570.1989.tb00661.x

American Evaluation Association. (2011). *Guiding principles for evaluators.* Retrieved from http://www.eval.org/p/cm/ld/fid=105

Brinkerhoff, R. O. (2006). *Telling training's story: Evaluation made simple, credible, and effective.* San Francisco: Berrett-Koehler.

Clark, R. C. (2006). Evidence-based practice and the professionalization of human performance technology. In J. A. Pershing (Ed.), *Handbook of human performance technology: Principles, practices, and potential* (3rd ed., pp. 873–898). San Francisco: Pfeiffer.

Fain, J. A. (2005). Is there a difference between evaluation and research? *The Diabetes Educator, 31*(2), 150–155.

Fink, A. (2005). *Evaluation fundamentals: Insights into the outcomes, effectiveness, and quality of health programs* (2nd ed.). Thousand Oaks, CA: Sage. doi:10.4135/9781412984140

Fink, A. (2013). *How to conduct surveys: A step-by-step guide.* Thousand Oaks, CA: SAGE.

Fitzpatrick, J., Christie, C., & Mark, M. (2009). *Evaluation in action: Interviews with expert evaluators.* Thousand Oaks, CA: SAGE.

Fitzpatrick, J. L., Sanders, J. R., & Worthen, B. R. (2010). *Program evaluation: Alternative approaches and practical guidelines* (4th ed.). New York: Longman.

Holton, E. F. III. (1996). The flawed four-level evaluation model. *Human Resource Development Quarterly, 7*(1), 5–21. doi:10.1002/hrdq.3920070103

Joint Committee on Standards for Educational Evaluation. (1994). *The program evaluation standards.* Retrieved from http://www.jcsee.org/program-evaluation-standards

Kirkpatrick, D. (1996). Great ideas revisited. *Training & Development, 50*(1), 54–59.

Knowlton, L., & Phillip, C. (2012). *The logic model guidebook: Better strategies for great results* (2nd ed.). Thousand Oaks, CA: SAGE.

Lincoln, Y. S., & Guba, E. G. (1980). The distinction between merit and worth in evaluation. *Educational Evaluation and Policy Analysis, 2*(4), 61–71. doi:10.3102/01623737002004061

Mathison, S. (1999). Rights, responsibilities, and duties: A comparison of ethics for internal and external evaluators. *New Directions for Evaluation, 82*(82), 25–34. doi:10.1002/ev.1134

McDavid, J. C., & Hawthorn, L. R. L. (2006). *Program evaluation and performance measurement: An introduction to practice.* Thousand Oaks, CA: SAGE.

Morris, M. (2008) (Ed.). Evaluation ethics for best practice: Cases and commentaries. New York: The Guilford Press.

Preskill, H., & Catsambas, T. T. (2006). *Reframing evaluation through appreciative inquiry*. Thousand Oaks, CA: SAGE.

Rousseau, D. (2006). Is there such a thing as "evidence-based management?". *Academy of Management Review, 31*(2), 256–269. doi:10.5465/AMR.2006.20208679

Russ-Eft, D., Bober, M. J., de la Teja, I., Foxon, M. J., & Koszalka, T. A. (2008). *Evaluator competencies: Standards for the practice of evaluation in organizations*. San Francisco: Jossey-Bass.

Russ-Eft, D., & Preskill, H. (2009). *Evaluation in organizations: A systematic approach to enhancing learning, performance, and change* (2nd ed.). Cambridge, MA: Perseus Publishing.

Rycroft-Malone, J., Seers, K., Titchen, A., Harvey, G., Kitson, A., & McCormack, B. (2004). What counts as evidence in evidence-based practice? *Journal of Advanced Nursing, 47*(1), 81–90. doi:10.1111/j.1365-2648.2004.03068.x PMID:15186471

Scriven, M. (1991). *Evaluation thesaurus* (4th ed.). Newbury Part, CA: SAGE.

Shadish, W. R. Jr, Cook, T. D., & Leviton, L. C. (1991). *Foundations of program evaluation: Theories of practice*. Newbury Park, CA: SAGE.

Vogt, W. P., Gardner, D. C., & Haeffele, L. M. (2012). *When to use what research design*. New York: The Guildford Press.

KEY TERMS AND DEFINITIONS

Dimensions: Important aspects of the evaluand that are being investigated in order to draw a conclusion about its quality.

Evaluand: A thing that is being evaluated, such as a program, a project, or a process.

Evidence-Based Practice: An approach to making decisions based on empirical, supportive data.

Formative Evaluation: A type of evaluations conducted with an intention to provide recommendations to improve the quality of the evaluand.

Goal-Based Evaluation: A type of evaluations conducted to investigate the quality of the evaluand against the achievement of its goals.

Program Logic Model: An illustration of the overall structure of the evaluand outlining its inputs, activities, outputs, outcomes and impacts.

Stakeholders: Groups of people who were involved in the development and/or operation of the evaluand (i.e., upstream stakeholders) or who are directly or indirectly impacted by the evaluand (i.e., downstream stakeholders including immediate recipients and downstream impactees).

Triangulation: Drawing the most probable conclusions through analyzing consistency or inconsistency among data obtained from multiple sources (e.g., from different types of stakeholders and from extant data) or types (e.g., from surveys, interviews, and observations).

Chapter 10
Knowledge Management of Medical Information Resources and Tools

Misa Mi
Oakland University William Beaumont School of Medicine, USA

Jill E. Stefaniak
Old Dominion University, USA

EXECUTIVE SUMMARY

This case demonstrates how problem-based learning (PBL) was used as a teaching method to help medical students integrate their knowledge of basic sciences with a clinical application at a medical school. PBL promotes self-directed, problem-solving, and lifelong learning. In the PBL context, students sought out a variety of resources to tackle their learning issues and help them arrive at a solution to a patient problem. The existing strategy for curating resources was not aligned with the type of thinking and activities in the PBL process. Therefore, a knowledge management system was developed to provide an online knowledge base of medical information resources and tools easily accessible at the point of students' needs.

ORGANIZATION BACKGROUND

The Longdale University College of Medicine (LUCOM) is located in south Toledo, a city in northwest of Ohio. It is an accredited M.D.-granting medical school that provides four-year general professional education of physicians and prepares medical students for supervised practice during residency training. The medical school has

DOI: 10.4018/978-1-4666-8330-3.ch010

an annual enrollment of approximately 700 students. Once admitted to the study of medicine, medical students start two years of classroom-based coursework to learn scientific principles and acquire the foundation of formal knowledge of biomedical sciences on which clinical practice is based.

Foundational courses are followed by two years of clinical practice (clerkship or clinical education) that are organized into specialty blocks called clerkships. During the third year, students rotate through a series of required clerkships of core specialties such as family medicine, internal medicine, pediatrics, surgery, obstetrics and gynecology (Cooke, Irby, & O'Brien, 2010). The fourth year is primarily electives (rotations) that are designed to accommodate the diverse educational needs of students and to help them with career selection. In the fourth year, students have more freedom to choose electives that interest them. The electives provide them with the opportunity to further develop their medical knowledge, skills, and attitudes and prepare them for graduate medical education, residency in a variety of specialties. During their fourth year, students are also busy in making arrangements for interviews at multiple residency programs in their chosen specialty.

At LUCOM, the medical curriculum was presented in a discipline-based structure. The first-year curriculum comprised courses (organized as separate blocks) focused on normal structure, functions, and processes of the body in disciplines such as anatomy, physiology, microbiology, histology, and biochemistry; during the second year, students learn pathophysiology and disease management. The curricular structure and content of such a model reveals a lack of coordination or reference to clinical relevance. As a result, students may fail to construct conceptual understanding and to understand and appreciate the interconnectedness and integration of knowledge. When students arrive in the clinical setting, they may be unable to access and apply all the knowledge to patient care (Cooke et al., 2010).

The medical curriculum incorporated PBL and case-based discussion into a longitudinal course—*Clinical Decision Making* (I & II) during the preclinical years (first and second years). The PBL method addresses domains of performance or skills that are ignored in the discipline-based curriculum. These performance and skills include synthesis, integration, evaluation of information, as well as interviewing, communication, and physical exam skills. One of the Liaison Committee on Medical Education (LCME) standards stipulates that a medical education program provide instructional opportunities for active learning and independent study to foster the skills necessary for lifelong learning (Liaison Committee on Medical Education, 2013). The PBL experience in the curriculum infused traditional instructor-led didactic lectures with active learning opportunities and created the "lens of situated learning" or a clinical context for preclinical education that trained students for problem-solving, critical thinking, self-directed, and lifelong learning. The course provided students with an opportunity for integrated learning--integrating formal scientific knowledge with clinical medicine through PBL group discussion on unique patient cases. One objective of the course was to develop students' ability to apply scientific knowledge to solve clinical problems and to build students' basic skills related to the process of lifelong learning, specifically the ability to identify learning needs and locate evidence to resolve learning issues and inform clinical decisions about a patient problem.

SETTING THE STAGE

The PBL process in the course required first-year medical students in a small group of 10-12 students to meet for 2 hours weekly to work on a simulated patient case over a course of three weeks. At group discussion sessions, students in each group engaged in a series of learning activities such as patient history taking, physical examination, generating hypotheses, ordering laboratory tests, and identifying learning issues related to the patient case. Students were expected to spend time out of class in independent and self-directed learning to tackle the learning issues by searching and consulting various information resources. When they returned to their PBL group discussion, they shared their knowledge and findings pertaining to the identified learning issues. The process of information sharing, collaborative learning, and knowledge construction helped them adjust and revise their hypotheses and eventually, reach a joint decision on a possible solution to the patient problem.

In the face of the challenges in making decisions about a patient problem and identifying resources to tackle learning issues, students must determine what information was needed and relevant, where and how the information was located, and how different pieces of information were put together to solve the problem. To promote students' self-directed, problem-based learning, tools and sources of information became essential, and they contributed to rich learning environments conducive to their successful learning performance. The environments must be information rich (Richey et al., 2011), because PBL (or active learning) "involves interacting with information at a high level, elaborating upon this information, and interpreting it in light of one's knowledge and experiences" within the context of solving "real-life" patient cases (Driscoll, 2005; Jonassen, 1999).

For first-year medical students, they may not possess sophisticated information seeking and evaluating skills. With an exponential growth of biomedical knowledge, sifting through and filtering a wealth of diverse and abundant information resources to obtain the most appropriate and relevant information seems to be a daunting task for many students. With heightened information availability, students do not seem to become more informed. Instead, they may develop information overload and get frustrated when there is a great deal of information that does not tell them what to do. In the PBL environment, students' ability to locate and use appropriate information resources may affect their knowledge construction, understanding of learning issues, active participation in the problem solving process, and arriving at a solution to a clinical problem.

A wide array of knowledge-based medical information resources were acquired and made available to medical students on the Northhill Health Science Library website at LUCOM. Examples of these resources included:

- AccessMedicine
- ClinicalKey
- Cochrane Library
- DynaMed
- Micromedex
- VisualDX
- UpToDate

However, the usage tracking system inherent in these resources indicated under-utilization of these resources. An examination and review of the existing knowledge base of medical information resources and tools on the library website revealed a less than optimal way of organizing and managing these resources. On the website, all information resources available for students in health professions programs on the LU health campus were organized vertically in an alphabetic order. Dornan (2011) pointed out that simply making learning resources available to learners will not guarantee any kind of result unless the resources are incorporated into educational activities.

How these resources were organized on the website failed to support the kind of thinking and activity structures that facilitated problem solving in the PBL process. Simply linking the resource list in a course management system (e.g., Blackboard) or pointing the list to students in an information literacy instruction session may "provide serious distractions to thinking necessary for solving the problem" (Jonassen, 1999). In light of the resource intensiveness within the PBL context and requirement of independent study time to prepare for case discussion, there was a dire need for a mechanism for managing the knowledge base of online resources and tools to support students' learning and enhance their performance in PBL activities. During PBL discussion sessions, it was observed that students had the proclivity to use Google when researching learning issues associated with a patient case. The students' undue reliance on general Internet search engines for answers to their clinical questions gave rise to certain concerns.

Clearly, students' learning outcomes from PBL could hinge on their ability to leverage authoritative resources to support their decision making process in complex cases. A knowledge management project was initiated to support students' critical thinking, clinical reasoning, and problem-based learning activities and to enhance their skills in selecting and accessing high-quality information resources for their clinical questions about clinical cases. For this project, knowledge management (KM) is described as acquiring, identifying, classifying, storing, disseminating, managing access to bodies of knowledge to improve learning and performance. At its core, KM entails the process of making information known and available to all who need it (Rosenberg, 2007).

The project was developed within the framework of a human performance technology (HPT) model (Gillbert, 1996; Van Tiem, Moseley, & Dessinger, 2001). Though the model has been widely used in business and industry to improve people, process, and performance in a workplace environment (Van Tiem et al., 2001), it has a practical application in medical education with a strong focus on outcome-based or performance-based learning outcomes expected of learners across the continuum of medical education. Based on the HPT model, selection of a valid intervention must be based on a systematic conduct of environmental analysis by examining the organizational environment, work environment, work itself, and the worker (Rossett, 1999; Van Tiem et al., 2001). Following the environmental analysis are cause analysis, intervention selection and design, intervention implementation and change, and evaluation. "Analysis is the systemic basis for decisions about how to influence performance" (Rossett, 1999, p. 64). The analysis for the KM project in the context of medical education comprised different levels of analysis corresponding to those in the HPT model. Table 1 highlights key tasks for the project as well as a framework based on the HPT model in which any decision on the KM project was grounded.

A study on organizational learning culture reveals that organizational learning culture had significant influences on both job satisfaction and motivation to transfer learning and had an indirect impact on employees' turnover intention (Egan, Yang, & Bartlett, 2004). Increases in job satisfaction and reduction in turnover have been found to increase organizational productivity (Trevor, 2001). The results from the study by Egan et al. (2004) underscore the importance of learning culture and related impacts on employee learning and performance. The authors contend that efforts are needed to support organizational learning cultures because they have positive benefits for employees.

KM as a performance support system affects organizational learning cultures. Since KM uses a systematic process of analyzing and responding to individual, group, and organizational performance issues, KM can influence job performance at the

Table 1. Tasks for the KM project corresponding to the phases of the performance technology model

Environment Analysis	
Organizational Environment	Longdale University College of Medicine
Work Environment	Medical Students' Learning Environment
Work	Problem-based Learning Activities and Performance
The Worker	Medical Students
Cause Analysis	
Lack of Environmental Support	Information, resources, tools
Lack of Repertory of Behavior	Skills and Knowledge
Intervention Selection and Design	
Performance Support Systems	• Instructional Performance Support System • KM System of Medical Information Resources and Tools
Intervention Implementation and Change	
Communication & Alliance Building	Providing Student Development through Information Literacy Instruction; Promoting the System via Different Venues; Getting Buy-in from Administrators
Evaluation	
Formative Evaluation	Conducted throughout the Phases of Analysis, Design, and Development of the KM System
Summative Evaluation	Evaluation Measures Embedded in the KM System
Confirmative Evaluation	Future Plan

levels of work environment, work, and worker. KM promotes knowledge sharing, collective learning, and individual workers' lifelong and self-directed learning, all of which are vital in fostering organizational learning cultures and improving the bottom line of the organization. KM improves the work environment by integrating workplace learning and job performance. KM also improves the work since it provides easy and efficient access to knowledge-based resources and tools that workers need to perform their job and achieve their goals. Moreover, KM addresses individual needs; as an enabler, it improves the worker by saving his or her time in locating and using the right information at the point of needs and maximizing use of knowledge.

In an academic setting of a medical school, KM efforts can be initiated to facilitate medical students' success in developing key capabilities and core competencies expected of medical students as future physician. A KM system is to support student learning of new knowledge and enhance student performance in information seeking, critical thinking, and problem solving in a PBL environment. A majority of medical students belong to the millennial generation. Being digital natives and growing up with the technology, they know how to use the technology; however, they may not have developed necessary skills in evaluating and managing information. The KM system can help students recognize the value of quality medical information, assimilate it, and apply it to create new knowledge and capabilities.

The KM project was developed as an information portal to curate scattered proprietary information resources as well as other quality information resources available on the Internet, so that medical students could easily retrieve, access, and use these resources at the point of their needs in solving clinical problems in the PBL environment. The HPT process was applied in conducting a systematic analysis of LUCOM, the medical curriculum, the specific course, PBL activities, and medical students. As a result of the analysis, it was determined that the KM system would best address the performance issues that had been identified:

- First-year medical students tended to use Google or other Internet search engines to search for information that may be inaccurate, unreliable, and outdated.
- A wide array of medical information resources provided by the health science library was underutilized. How the resources were categorized, organized, and disseminated on the library website hindered effective and efficient use of these resources for their PBL activities.
- First-year students were technology savvy, but they may lack sophisticated information seeking skills in identifying, selecting, and using authoritative information resources.
- Students' use of Internet search engines did not foster the development of skills in finding, evaluating, and applying information in clinical decision making about patient care—an important lifelong learning skill as physicians.

It was anticipated that the KM system would develop students' information proficiency, improve their learning process, and support their performance in critical thinking, clinical reasoning, and problem solving in the PBL context.

CASE DESCRIPTION

Technology Concerns

A list of medical information resources and tools previously resided on the LUCOM Northhill Health Library website. These resources were essential to students in their investigation on learning issues in PBL activities. However, the website was static and had to be updated by a librarian with web development skills. Due to the stagnant nature of the site and a large number of resources amalgamated together, students hardly utilized the resources intended for them as they were unaware of their existence, content coverage, scope, utility, or relevance.

The LU libraries already had a general website constructed as a gateway to information services and online resources in support of learning, research, and teaching in over 300 undergraduate, graduate and professional programs at 17 colleges. Online books, journals, databases, multimedia resources, websites, online instructional tutorials, other learning, teaching, and research tools and aids comprised the library virtual environment—its KM system. With the digital information landscape in so constant a flux, the static website created for storing and managing the knowledge base of all the rich resources became very restricted and confined. The existing KM system that served the purpose of information storage and retrieval restricted thinking about how knowledge can be used to harness knowledge and add value (Rosenberg, 2007). In mid 2009, the libraries licensed LibGuides from Springshare to create dynamic and interactive websites to organize, manage, and curate discipline- and subject-based resources, course integrated information guides, other research and instructional materials and support tools.

Technology Components

Libguides, an online content and document management tool or online web development platform, enabled users to create and customize websites. Using LibGuides, information professionals were able to organize and present information services and knowledge-based resources tailored to different user groups in a user-friendly format. LibGuides featured searching, linking, and browsing functions, all of which were essential in finding high-quality information in a reasonable amount of time. It allowed customers to create dynamic content web pages embedded with videos/audios, podcast feed, RSS feed, and instant messaging widgets. Other features of LibGuides included Comment Box for users' input, Suggestion Form, a resource ranking capability, and Interactive Poll for instant feedback, all of which contributed to its interactive function. LibGuides also possessed the capacity to link seamlessly to information (holding records) from an online library catalog so that information seekers or end users could access and interact with a rich collection of information resources stored and classified in a library system (see Figure 1). Since it did not take sophisticated, technical skills, expertise, or intensive training to create a website with LibGuides, information professionals at LU found it quick and efficient to create websites to market their services, expertise, information resources in disciplines where they served as liaisons.

Figure 1. Linking to library items

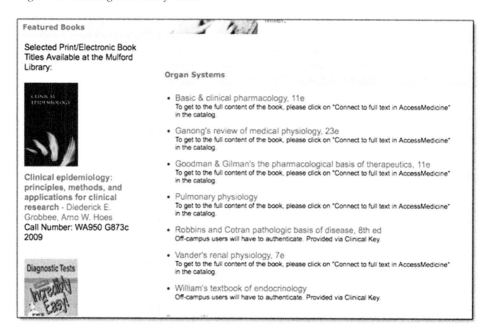

KM system is characterized by three components: people, technology, and content (Van Tiem et al., 2001). In the context of medical school, medical students are the "people" or end users of the KM system. Technology is an enabler for the KM system. In light of the significant resources required for PBL activities, the KM project was designed and developed to:

1. Serve the purpose of supporting students' performance in PBL activities;
2. Create a portal or gateway to a knowledge base of information resources easily accessible at the point of students' needs during their four year medical education; and
3. Develop their proficiency and skills in identifying, searching, and using biomedical information resources.

HPT is concerned with improving people, process, and performance by using a systematic approach. The KM project was attempted as a systematic approach to curating and managing access to a wide array of knowledge-based information resources and tools. The three target goals for the project aimed to improve the student learning environment, individual learning process, and performance in PBL activities. The resultant KM system would make a wealth of quality medical information resources explicit and known and available to all students. As these resources were made easier to access and navigate, they could improve students' process of finding information for clinical decision making and problem solving about a clinical case on hand and enhance students' performance as an individual or a group in the PBL environment.

While the KM system was intended to support students' independent, interdependent, and integrated learning desired for the PBL process in the *Clinical Decision Making* course, it was also developed to support students' learning of information skills that could enhance their efforts to integrate all forms of knowledge and a large volume of information acquired in the discipline-based medical curriculum. The ultimate goal of the web-based KM system via LibGuides was to contribute to the rich learning environment conducive to students' learning and performance as well as their accomplishment of learning tasks over the course of the preclinical and clinical years.

It was not enough to package all the rich information resources on the website created with LibGuides, because students would not know where the information they needed was located or how to find it. LibGuides as a content management technology does not produce a successful KM system because it does not address the process issues of who, when, where, how and why (Haney, 2006). The design of the web-based KM system took into account the developmental nature of medical students' learning as well as their varying abilities in searching and evaluating information. Therefore, the KM project was planned and undertaken in several phases and through multiple tasks:

- Examining the medical curriculum as well as a number courses to get a better sense of the structure and areas of content covered;
- Reviewing and analyzing LibGuides websites on the Internet for examples of a good practice in KM and web design;
- Identifying all the functions and unique features of LibGuides to determine an effective way of employing them for effective design and development of the KM project;
- Collecting input and analyzing needs of students, faculty members, and medical educators through different venues (e.g., classroom settings, committee meetings, and conversations); and
- Creating an inventory of resources licensed by the health science library; identifying, gathering, and selecting quality web resources, tools, and multimedia objects on the Internet, that could be beneficial and relevant to medical students during their preclinical and clinical years.

Management and Organizational Concerns

The heart of a good knowledge management system is in the content itself (Barclay & Murray, 2000). If the KM system did not provide end users with timely and relevant information or connect them to quality resources and tools, students would not realize the full value of the KM system. Facing all the rich medical information resources from varying sources and representing multimedia formats, decisions had to be made to organize, codify, curate, and annotate the resources appropriately. Otherwise, the KM system could be simply an amalgamation of information with a minimum impact and less utility and relevance to students. The unique features inherent in LibGuides and flexible integration of various emerging technologies and gadgets into the KM system website had potential for drawing students to the site and increasing its utility. Nevertheless, the features, technologies, and gadgets, if not used properly, could be perceived as added "bells and whistles" that were likely to diminish the effect of the website as a KM intervention to support students' PBL activities.

The KM project was an informational approach to enhancing students' performance in PBL activities, other learning and research efforts. At the same time, the project as an instructional performance support system had added value by serving as a guide to instruct students about how to use the knowledge-based resources in an e-learning environment. "Blending KM into a learning strategy significantly enhances the options available to improve performance" (Rosenberg, 2007, p. 162). The KM system added a new dimension to traditional library information literacy training programs. In the "crowded" medical curriculum, there were a limit number of contact hours for information literacy instruction and insufficient opportunities for students to practice searching skills and receive guidance in using a variety of knowledge-based resources and tools. The KM system complemented and supplemented what was covered in formal information literacy instruction integrated in the medical curriculum. The KM system also served to reinforce students' learning in a face-to-face classroom setting and aided them in effective and efficient use of information resources at the point of needs anytime and at any place. It was hoped that the added value could steer students towards different types and formats of credible information resources.

The content of the KM system was comprised of explicit knowledge including online full-content textbooks, specialty databases, online instructional tutorials, websites, documents, downloadable software application programs, audio and video materials, links to library-owned items, and other media. A KM system can quickly become overwhelmed if "access to knowledge is haphazard, difficult, or time consuming". The key for effective KM is to "synchronize all the knowledge into a well-defined common access strategy, where users or information seekers can quickly find what they are looking for" (Rosenberg, 2007, p. 159). A successful KM must be tailored to fit students' needs and support students. For that reason, all the resources were organized and classified by acknowledging students' varying abilities in searching and evaluating information, the developmental nature of their learning, and learning needs in acquiring different types of knowledge over the course of their four-year medical education. For example, the resources for students to use during their preclinical years were located under the tabs of Home, Year 1/Year 2, and Diagnosis respectively (see Figure 2). These resources included online full-text textbooks, dictionaries, differential diagnostic tools, lab tests, calculators, and other reference materials, that students needed to consult for background information or general knowledge on a specific health topic. There was also a specific tab for Clerkship where students could find learning resources related to their clinical rotations during the clinical years. Other categories of knowledge on the KM system included multimedia resources, prep resources for board exams, and resources for clinical research.

There are nine major activities that contribute to an effective KM (Van Tiem, et al., 2001). These include:

Figure 2. Tabs for different categories of medical information resources

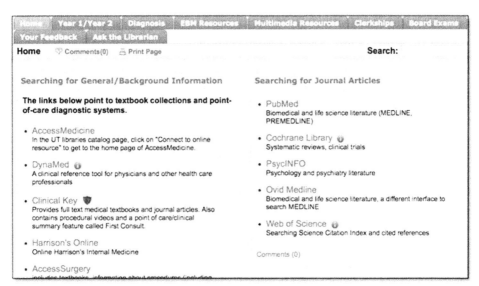

1. "Identifying the organization's knowledge assets, both explicit and tacit.
2. Capturing and explicitly recording the tact knowledge within an organization.
3. Codifying (cataloging, mapping, linking) knowledge assets for easier retrieval.
4. Storing knowledge assets in a central area where all members of an organization who need to know have access to it.
5. Transforming knowledge by making connections among pieces of information.
6. Generating new knowledge to help achieve competitive advantage.
7. Disseminating knowledge to people when, where, and how they need it.
8. Sharing best practices and technology to enable all of the activities listed above.
9. Managing the processes, people, and technology that enable these activities" (p. 29).

One of the activities involves disseminating knowledge to people when, where, and how they need it. However, there is potentially a danger that making more knowledge to more students could lead to information overload (Van Tiem et al., 2001). A well-designed KM system minimizes information overload (Paul, 1999). Given its e-learning instructional nature of the KM project, design decisions on the KM system necessitated the incorporation of the evidence-based practice derived from the principles of multimedia learning resulted from high quality research findings (Clark & Mayer, 2011). These principles, to a great extent, shaped the design and organization and presentation of resources and tools to promote active learning on the KM system. A few examples provided below demonstrate the application of several principles of multimedia learning in design decisions about the KM system.

Coherence Principle. People learn better when extraneous words, pictures and sounds are excluded rather than included. Adding interesting but extraneous words or including excess verbiage on the limited screen real estate of individual text boxes of each web page on the KM system would be distracting and interfere with students' use and learning about these resources. Therefore, a basic, concise scope note, description, or summary was provided to introduce and annotate resources as illustrated in Figure 2. The resulted clarity and simplicity avoided elaborated or embellished textual descriptions for these resources, which typically characterize a lot of websites of knowledge-based resources developed for students.

Segmenting Principle. People learn better from a multimedia lesson presented in user-paced segments rather than as a continuous unit. Multiple text boxes on each web page on the KM system were used to create a page layout characterized by segments of information (chunking of information). Each box was given a title for a subcategory of resources. Students could quickly and easily view each page without the need to scroll up and down a long list of information resources under a particular category or component.

Multimedia Principle. People learn better from words and pictures than from words alone. Multimedia resources were identified and presented to students to aid their learning. Students could find instructional videos, podcasts, and medical images on the KM system. To draw students' attention to new book titles related to their courses, images of book covers were inserted along with basic textual information to showcase these books. Links to detailed information about the books were provided to indicate their availability and location in the library online catalog system.

Signaling principle. People learn better when the words include cues about the organization of the presentation. A number of carefully selected tabs were created to help students explore and navigate the KM system and cued them to choose different components or categories of information based on their learning needs. These tabs offered students "conceptual scaffolding" to guide them in selecting resources relevant to their questions and learning issues they encountered in solving a clinical problem in PBL activities.

Typical resource guides or pathfinders from libraries tend to be a compilation of resources arranged vertically by categories of information services, journals, databases, and other web resources that reflect the mindset of information professionals or the nature of their work environment. The KM system website designed with LibGuides was an attempt to break the usual pattern or practice in the design of an online knowledge base of information resources. The resulting knowledge base of information resources and tools (the KM system) included meaningful components and categories for easy navigation and quick access, and it supported the type of thinking and inquiry involved in PBL activities. When students used the KM system, they learned to be better knowledge seekers and researchers. The system prompted students to select resources based on their types of questions (e.g., background and foreground questions) and learning needs (e.g., using prep resources for board exams). Furthermore, the interactive feature of the website encouraged students to offer input and suggestions, submit comments, and rate resources. If they needed help when getting stuck in their navigation or search effort, they could contact a librarian immediately through Meebo embedded on the website (a social media platform used for instant messaging).

CURRENT CHALLENGES FACING THE ORGANIZATION

Though the KM system created with LibGuides was well received among medical students, there are still challenges and barriers in successful implementation and maintenance of the system and retention of higher usage, content currency and relevancy of resources on the system. Once a learning resource is being implemented and used, it should be evaluated; improvements or changes are made based on the results of the evaluation (Ellaway, 2011). Evaluation is also one important phase according to the HPT model. Evaluation of a performance support system or solution includes formative, summative, and confirmative evaluation (Guerra-López, 2008; Van Tiem et al., 2001). For the KM project, formative evaluation was conducted at the start of environmental analysis and throughout the design of the project; thus, it shaped the ongoing activities in the design and development process for the project.

Summative and confirmative evaluation methods were used to gather information to judge the value and to examine immediate and enduring effects of the KM system implemented. Summative evaluation tools inherent in LibGuides were used to gauge the effectiveness of the KM system website through usage tracking, a feedback form, and an instant poll (see Figure 3). Multiple measures of the effectiveness of the KM system and how they would be used are yet to be determined. Confirmation or follow-up evaluation of the KM system is needed to determine the long-term effect of the system on student performance in PBL activities or other learning experiences in the medical curriculum.

Currently, one area of concern is the ubiquitous influence of Internet search engines. Although Google, Yahoo, and other general search engines are easy to use and provide breadth, many proprietary online medical resources and databases such

Figure 3. Instant poll in LibGuides

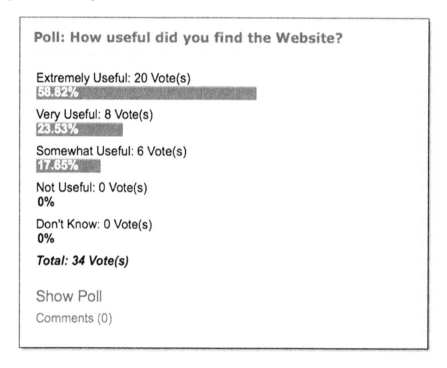

as UpToDate, AccessMedicine, and DynaMed are not publicly searchable with any Internet search engine. End users can only access them through subscriptions or licenses. When students rely on the Internet search engines for information or new knowledge to inform their decisions about a clinical problem, the information retrieved may be inaccurate, outdated, or even harmful if they do not have the skills in evaluating or filtering the information.

Librarians often provide one-time, stand-alone instruction sessions integrated into courses where the KM system is introduced to students as an access point for creditable information resources. It still remains a challenge to identify time slot or space throughout the curriculum where learning activities or experiences in courses are provided for students to learn and use the KM system. As students progress through their education, they may not be involved in learning activities, experiences, or tasks that require the use of the resources. Without continuous reinforcement of their acquired knowledge and skills in using the resources within the context of problem solving, students may relapse into their old habit of using Google for information. One time promotion of or instruction on the KM system may not make the message stick. Students would be less likely to remember the KM system unless they use it to meet their information needs and fill their knowledge gaps. Like the necessary repeated reinforcement of students' acquired knowledge and skills in other domains, efforts in promoting the use of the knowledge-based resources should be continued.

Another challenge is to sustain the KM system over time. In the information era, the lifetime of electronic resources is quite short; the resources have become more ephemeral (Ellaway, 2011). Content of free web resources on the Internet can become obsolete or even inappropriate. Internet resources are constantly changed, which result in different web addresses and even websites removed or taken down. Biomedical knowledge is constantly in a state of flux. Knowledge needs to be constantly updated, changed, added to, deleted, or replaced (Haney, 2006). With an exponential growth of research data in health sciences and the new development and advances in the knowledge base of basic sciences, resources that contain factual knowledge will inevitably become increasingly outdated. To sustain the currency and factual accuracy of resources, publishers produce and sell new editions of electronic books and create new versions of online resources. Therefore, health sciences libraries face the burden of purchasing new editions/versions of resources and encounter the challenge of providing resources access with a flat or lower library acquisition budget. As a result, subscriptions or licenses for some online resources may discontinue; access to specialty- or discipline-based databases may be affected. When any of the aforementioned situations occurs, it is difficult to sustain the consistence and continuity of the knowledge-based resources.

SOLUTIONS AND RECOMMENDATIONS

The KM system was well received by students, medical educators, and administrators at LUCOM. Since its debut of the website over 5 years ago, it has remained the most popular and visited website among all medical students. The high usage, positive feedback, and comments from end users were all an indication of the impact of the KM system in supporting students' PBL activities in the *Clinical Decision Making* course and other courses and clerkships in the curriculum. One of comments made by a medical student summarized the positive reactions and viewpoints that were shared by a majority of students:

Oh my goodness, this website is so refreshingly easy to access and find information!! It has everything that we need the most at our fingertips. I really like the tabs at the top, they organize the different years extremely well and are complete in what we as students find most important like Boards and Clerkships. I wish this was available to us 1st and 2nd year too!! Thank you so much for this. (Medical student of Class 2012)

Medical educators and administrators at LUCOM also recognized the effect of the project. An associate dean for medical education sent an email to acknowledge the efforts in creating the KM website for medical students:

On behalf of the Office of Medical Education I would like to thank you for all your efforts and hard work. Your medical student website page is excellent and a great resource for them. I am very grateful for your interest and help in making the course a success as well. (Harding, 2010)

In summary, a number of factors contributed to the determining impact on the efficacy of the knowledge base of learning resources. These factors included:

- Alignment between the use of resources and the PBL activities;
- Consideration of the developmental nature of medical students' learning;
- Organization of resources in an intuitive, meaningful way to meet students' needs in information seeking, critical thinking, and problem-solving;
- Appropriate use of LibGuides features and tools to create an interactive website of a KM system;
- Application of the best practice and multimedia learning principles in design and development of the web-based KM system;
- Obtaining the buy-in and support from medical educators and administrators.

These factors embodied principles of HPT applied in guiding the improvement of learning performance within the PBL environment in a medical school setting. These principles encompass the steps including performance analysis, cause analysis, intervention selection, design, development, intervention implementation, and evaluation. In conducting performance analysis, an environmental analysis was undertaken at different levels: institutional (medical school), medical curriculum, course, PBL activities, and medical students. The analysis shed light to learning expectations and requirements for students, their information seeking behaviors, and existing gaps in students' ability to identify, use, and access quality information resources. The analysis also helped determine what attributed to the gaps: lack of one centralized area for a wealth of information resources to support student learning. In selecting, designing, and developing an intervention, the KM project as a performance support system was carried out to enhance the students' learning environment; therefore, students' learning needs, use of technology, and multimedia design principles were taken into consideration in the process of design and development to maximize outcomess of the KM project. When implementing the KM system, the purpose and use of the KM system were communicated with medical educators and administrators at LUCOM. They offered suggestions for improving the web-based KM system, recommended information resources for the system, and helped promoting the system among medical students. Their support contributed to the successful implementation of the KM system. Evaluation efforts were important to ensure the intended results of the intervention; multiple evaluation tools inherent in LibGuides were utilized to assess the effect of the intervention and to continually improve the system.

To overcome the challenges and barriers presented in the preceding section, certain measures or actions are recommended for continuous improvements to the KM system and maintaining its sustainability and utility. Knowledge can be perceived as something with a lifecycle that grows, changes, and has different phases. Since change to knowledge is a constant, the KM system requires continuous maintenance efforts. Given that the KM system will evolve to keep pace with the change, maintenance activities are necessary. These activities involve monitoring, tracking, measuring, and evaluating (Haney, 2006, p. 627). LibGuides provided basic measurement tools as part of its inherent features. However, it would be useful to determine what important evaluation questions should be asked, what to be measured, and how to be measured to collect complete and relevant data to answer the evaluation questions (Guerra-López, 2008). Data collection methods such as interviews, surveys, questionnaires, and observations are some alternatives for collecting evaluative data from a large sample of medical students to demonstrate the value and immediate and long-term impact of the KM system.

Instead of shunning away from Google, students need instruction on how to use Google or other search engines properly, its strengths and weaknesses, unique features, and differences in search results between search engines and proprietary knowledge-based information resources. Students could learn how to use several approaches for more in-depth searching and how to use appropriate resources based on the information they desire. The results of using the KM system in combination with general search engines may provide complementary search results (Haney, 2006, p. 627).

It is important to help students develop a good habit of using the knowledge-based resources for learning and critical thinking involved in PBL and other learning and research activities. Repeated opportunities to use information in different contexts would enhance the formation and cultivation of a good habit. Given limited contact hours available for reinforcing their learning and skill development in information literacy, librarians can work in collaboration with basic science and clinical faculty to identify learning opportunities through a project or task assigned to students so that students consult reliable resources to complete a given task. To increase the value and utility of the KM system to students, informal learning opportunities and non-instructional interventions could be also identified and utilized to help students integrate the knowledge base into their individualized and independent learning process. The KM system could be promoted to students through one-on-one consultation or tutorial sessions on information literacy or library research skills. Bookmarks, library information brochures, flyers, and other promotional giveaways including the URL of the KM system could be distributed to students during their orientation and library visits. Another strategy is to educate faculty about the KM system and to facilitate their use of the resources to enhance their teaching. It would also be beneficial to students if the link to the KM system is integrated into course websites in a course management system (e.g., Blackboard).

There is a great potential for using social media or emerging technologies as a means to promote or increase the use of the KM system. Students could be encouraged to interact with the website content by submitting their feedback, rating the resources, recommending web resources, or participating in instant polling. The URL of the website could be embedded in Facebook pages, blogs, or Tweeters, of the students, library, or medical school.

In light of curricular changes or reforms and fluidity of online knowledge-based resources attributable to many factors mentioned above, special attention is needed to ensure there is continuous access, availability, currency, and relevancy of learning resources on the KM system website. It is vital for knowledge-based developers to:

1. Remain aware of any requirements from external sources;
2. Stay proactive in reaching out to medical students;

3.   Forge alliance with faculty members and administrators at the medical school; and

4.   Embed or integrate themselves into the entire curriculum.

Such efforts could potentially lead to a higher level of alignment of knowledge-based learning resources with the medical curriculum and students' developmental and progressive learning needs over the course of their preclinical and clinical years.

Where health information professionals are most likely charged with a task of developing and maintaining such a knowledge base of medical information resources, it would be useful for them to develop a working knowledge of different educational approaches and instructional methods commonly adopted in medical education such as problem-based learning and team-based learning. The knowledge would help them in creating projects to foster active learning and acquiring resources that would contribute to rich learning environments essential for implementing such an approach or method. Another important activity for information professionals or any KM system developer is serving on medical education curriculum committees and attending professional conferences for medical educators. The involvement would help health information professionals and KM developers (or performance technology practitioners) get first-hand information on end users' needs and current educational concerns and help them stay abreast of the trends, hot topics, and development in medical education.

All of the aforementioned recommendations and solutions to the issues and problems challenge health information professionals, KM system developers, and performance technology practitioners to think and move beyond their traditional roles. In developing a KM project such as the one illustrated in this chapter, it is necessary to build the project with the guide of multimedia learning principles to enhance the impact of the project and at the same time, to take into consideration the changing landscape of the virtual environment, external drives for medical curricular reforms, as well as students' information needs in arriving at desired outcome-based performance in different settings. The resulting project as a KM intervention had an added value by reaping the benefit of serving students as a primary tool for disseminating knowledge and as an e-learning and instructional performance support system integral to the resource intensive PBL environment.

REFERENCES

Barclay, R. O., & Murray, P. C. (2000, May 27). *What is knowledge management?* Retrieved from http://www.providersedge.com/docs/km_articles/what_is_knowledge_management.pdf

Clark, R. C., & Mayer, R. E. (2011). *E-learning and the science of instruction: Proven guidelines for consumers and designers of multimedia learning* (3rd ed.). San Francisco, CA: Pfeiffer. doi:10.1002/9781118255971

Cooke, M., Irby, D. M., & O'Brien, B. C. (2010). *Educating physicians: A call for reform of medical school and residency.* San Francisco, CA: Jossey-Bass.

Dornan, T. (2011). Developing learning resources. In T. Dornan, K. Mann, A. Scherpbier, & J. Spencer (Eds.), *Medical education: Theory and practice* (pp. 265–281). Edinburgh: Elsevier.

Driscoll, M. P. (2005). *Psychology of learning for instruction* (3rd ed.). Boston: Pearson Allyn and Bacon.

Egan, T. M., Yang, B., & Bartlett, K. R. (2004). The effects of organizational learning culture and job satisfaction on motivation to transfer learning and turnover intention. *Human Resource Development Quarterly, 15*(3), 279–301. doi:10.1002/hrdq.1104

Ellaway, R. H. (2011). Developing learning resources. In T. Dornan (Ed.), *Medical education: Theory and practice* (pp. 263–281). Edinburgh: Elsevier.

Gillbert, T. F. (1996). *Human competence: Engineering worthy performance.* Washington, DC: The International Society for Performance Improvement.

Guerra-López, I. (2008). *Performance evaluation: Proven approaches for improving program and organizational performance* (1st ed.). San Francisco, CA: Jossey-Bass.

Haney, D. (2006). Knowledge management, organizational performance, and human performance technology. In J. A. Pershing (Ed.), *Handbook of human performance technology: Principles, practices, and potential* (3rd ed., pp. 619–639). San Francisco, CA: Pfeiffer.

Jonassen, D. (1999). Designing constructivist learning environments. In C. Reigeluth (Ed.), *Instructional-design theories and models: A new paradigm of instructional theory* (Vol. 2, pp. 215–239). Mahwah, NJ: Lawrence Erlbaum Associates.

Liaison Committee on Medical Education. (2013). *Functions and Structure of a Medical School: Standards for Accreditation of Medical Education Programs Leading to the M.D. Degree.* Retrieved from http://www.lcme.org/functions.pdf

Paul, L. (1999). Thinking together. *Inside Technology Training, 3*(8), 18-22.

Richey, R. C., Klein, J. D., & Tracey, M. W. (2011). *The Instructional design knowledge base: Theory, research, and practice.* New York, NY: Routledge.

Rosenberg, M. J. (2007). Knowledge management and learning: Perfect together. In R. A. Reiser & J. V. Dempsey (Eds.), *Trends and issues in instructional design and technology* (2nd ed., pp. 156–165). Upper Saddle River, N.J.: Pearson/Merrill Prentice Hall.

Rossett, A. (1999). Knowledge management meets analysis. *Training & Development*, *53*(5), 62–68.

Trevor, C. (2001). Interactive effects among actual ease of movement determinants and job satisfaction in the prediction of voluntary turnover. *Academy of Management Journal*, *44*(4), 621–638. doi:10.2307/3069407

Van Tiem, D. M., Moseley, J. L., & Dessinger, J. C. (2001). *Performance improvement intervention: Enhancing people, processes, and organizations through performance technology*. Silver Spring, MD: International Society for Performance Improvement.

ADDITIONAL READING

Alavi, C. (1995). *Problem-based learning in a health sciences curriculum*. New York, NY: Routledge. doi:10.4324/9780203428023

Azer, S. A. (2011). Introducing a problem-based learning program: 12 tips for success. *Medical Teacher*, *33*(10), 808–813. doi:10.3109/0142159X.2011.558137 PMID:21942480

Baets, W. R. J. (2005). *Knowledge management and management learning extending the horizons of knowledge-based management*. New York, NY: Springer.

Baptiste, S. (2003). *Problem-based learning: A self-directed journey*. Thorofare, NJ: SLACK.

Barrows, H. S., & Tamblyn, R. M. (1980). *Problem-based learning: An approach to medical education*. New York, NY: Springer Pub. Co.

Carlile, S., Barnet, S., Sefton, A., & Uther, J. (1998). Medical problem based learning supported by intranet technology: A natural student centered approach. *International Journal of Medical Informatics*, *50*(1-3), 225–233. doi:10.1016/S1386-5056(98)00073-2 PMID:9726516

Colliver, J. A. (2000). Effectiveness of problem-based learning curricula: Research and theory. *Academic Medicine*, *75*(3), 259–266. doi:10.1097/00001888-200003000-00017 PMID:10724315 de Leng, B. A., Dolmans, D. H., Muijtjens, A. M., & van der Vleuten, C. P. (2006). Student perceptions of a virtual learning environment for a problem-based learning undergraduate medical curriculum. *Medical Education, 40*(6), 568–575. doi:10.1111/j.1365-2929.2006.02484.x PMID:16700773

Easterby-Smith, M. L. M. A. (2003). *The Blackwell handbook of organizational learning and knowledge management*. Malden, MA: Blackwell Pub.

Egan, T. M., Yang, B., & Bartlett, K. R. (2004). The effects of organizational learning culture and job satisfaction on motivation to transfer learning and turnover intention. *Human Resource Development Quarterly, 15*(3), 279–301. doi:10.1002/hrdq.1104

Eisenberg, M., Lowe, C. A., Spitzer, K. L., & Spitzer, K. L. (2004). *Information literacy: Essential skills for the information age* (2nd ed.). Westport, CT: Libraries Unlimited.

Frenkel, S. (1999). *On the front line: Organization of work in the information economy*. Ithaca, NY: ILR Press.

Frost, A. (2014). *Knowledge management tools*. Retrieved from http://www.knowledge-management-tools.net/

Hawkins, S., Hertweck, M., Goreczny, A., & Laird, J. (2013). Student expectations of problem-based learning (PBL). *Medical Teacher, 35*(6), 525. doi:10.3109/0142159X.2013.772963 PMID:23464897

Hommes, J., Van den Bossche, P., de Grave, W., Bos, G., Schuwirth, L., & Scherpbier, A. (2014). Understanding the effects of time on collaborative learning processes in problem based learning: A mixed methods study. *Advances in Health Sciences Education: Theory and Practice, 19*(4), 541–563. doi:10.1007/s10459-013-9487-z PMID:24469109

Jacobs, J., Salas, A., Cameron, T., Naguwa, G., & Kasuya, R. (2005). Implementing an online curriculum management database in a problem-based learning curriculum. *Academic Medicine, 80*(9), 840–846. doi:10.1097/00001888-200509000-00011 PMID:16123464

Jain, P. (2013). Knowledge management in academic libraries and information centers: A case of university libraries. *Journal of Information & Knowledge Management, 12*(4), 1–13.

Jantz, R. (2001). Knowledge management in academic libraries: Special tools and processes to support information professionals. *RSR. Reference Services Review, 29*(1), 33–39. doi:10.1108/00907320110366778

Jennex, M. E. (2007). *Knowledge management in modern organizations.* Hershey, PA: Idea Group Pub. doi:10.4018/978-1-59904-261-9

Karimi, R. (2011). Interface between problem-based learning and a learner-centered paradigm. *Advances in Health Sciences Education: Theory and Practice, 2,* 117–125. PMID:23745083

Kearsley, G. (2000). *Online education: Learning and teaching in cyberspace.* Belmont, CA: Wadsworth Thomson Learning.

Kerfoot, B. P., Masser, B. A., & Hafler, J. P. (2005). Influence of new educational technology on problem-based learning at Harvard Medical School. *Medical Education, 39*(4), 380–387. doi:10.1111/j.1365-2929.2005.02105.x PMID:15813760

Koenig, M. E. D., & Srikantaiah, T. K. (2004). *Knowledge management lessons learned: What works and what doesn't.* Medford, NJ: Information Today, Inc.

Kovalchick, K., & Dawson, K. (2004). *Education and technology: An encyclopedia.* Santa Barbara, CA: ABC-CLIO.

Krasne, S., Stevens, C. D., & Wilkerson, L. (2014). Improving medical literature sourcing by first-year medical students in problem-based learning: OLUCOMes of early Interventions. *Academic Medicine, 89*(7), 1069–1074. doi:10.1097/ACM.0000000000000288 PMID:24826850

Lee, H. W. (2005). *Knowledge management and the role of libraries.* Retrieved from http://www.white-clouds.com/iclc/cliej/cl19lee.htm

Lytras, M. D., Russ, M., Maier, R., & Naeve, A. (2008). *Knowledge management strategies: A handbook of applied technologies.* Hershey, PA: IGI Publishing. doi:10.4018/978-1-59904-603-7

Mala, M., Abdullah, A., & Abas, Z. W. (2011). Appreciation of learning environment and development of higher-order learning skills in a problem-based learning medical curriculum. *The Medical Journal of Malaysia, 66*(5), 435–439. PMID:22390096

McKnight, S. (2007). *A futuristic view of knowledge and information management.* Retrieved from http://bid.ub.edu/19mcknig.htm

Metcalfe, A. S. (2006). *Knowledge management and higher education: A critical analysis.* London: Information Science Pub. doi:10.4018/978-1-59140-509-2

O'Neill, P. A. (2000). The role of basic sciences in a problem-based learning clinical curriculum. *Medical Education, 34*(8), 608–613. doi:10.1046/j.1365-2923.2000.00629.x PMID:10964207

Preeti, B., Ashish, A., & Shriram, G. (2013). Problem based learning (PBL): An effective approach to improve learning outcomes in medical teaching. *Journal of Clinical and Diagnostic Research, 7*(12), 2896–2897. PMID:24551668

Rossett, A. (2002). *The ASTD e-learning handbook*. New York: McGraw-Hill.

Rumizen, M. C. (2002). *The complete idiot's guide to knowledge management.* Indianapolis, IN: Alpha.

Schwartz, D. G. (2006). *Encyclopedia of knowledge management.* Hershey, PA: Idea Group Reference. doi:10.4018/978-1-59140-573-3

Srikantaiah, T., Koenig, M. E. D., & Srikantaiah, T. K. (2000). *Knowledge management for the information professional*. Medford, N.J: Information Today, Inc.

Townley, C. T. (2001). Knowledge management and academic libraries. *College & Research Libraries, 62*(1), 44–55. doi:10.5860/crl.62.1.44

University of North Carolina School of Information and Library Science. (n.d.). *Introduction to knowledge management.* Retrieved from http://www.unc.edu/~sunnyliu/inls258/Introduction_to_Knowledge_Management.html

Veale, P. (2007). Prospective comparison of student-generated learning issues and resources accessed in a problem-based learning course. *Medical Teacher, 29*(4), 377–382. doi:10.1080/01421590701509712 PMID:17786754

KEY TERMS AND DEFINITIONS

Background Questions: Questions that ask about general information and background knowledge about a condition, disease, or treatment.

Foreground Questions: Questions that ask for information to inform clinical decisions about a specific patient. They are raised in practicing evidence-based medicine.

Knowledge Management: It is about managing knowledge and making it available to all who need it. It is a systematic and integrated approach to identifying, archiving, organizing, managing, and effectively disseminating valued information and resources that are easy to use and access.

LibGuides: An easy to use content management system used by libraries. Information professionals use it to organize and present knowledge and share information by creating and authoring websites and guides to resources on any topic, subject, course, or any process.

Performance Support System: An integrated system that provides users with resources, tools, guidance, advice, and learning experiences wherever and whenever they need it to perform a task.

Performance Technology: A field of study that is concerned with improving people, process, and performance by using a systematic approach—a set of methods, procedures, and interventions to improve performance and productivity.

Principles of Multimedia Learning: Principles based on the science of how people learn and how the mind works and also derived from scientifically valid research studies on multimedia learning. The principles are used to guide effective instructional design for multimedia learning or e-learning.

Problem-Based Learning: An instructional method or a student-centered approach in which students gain disciplinary knowledge and learn both clinical reasoning and critical thinking within the context of solving a patient problem. In the PBL environment, learners work collaboratively, set up their learning goals and objectives, identify and use resources to investigate their learning issues, share and apply their knowledge and findings to arrive at a viable solution to the problem at hand.

Wiki: It refers to either a website or a web application (software) used to create the site that comprises collective and collaborative work by many authors. Wiki allows people to create, add, edit, or delete content easily and quickly by using a browser interface.

Chapter 11
Implementation of Semantic Search to Support Clinical Decision-Making

Andrew Tawfik
Northern Illinois University, USA

Karl Kochendorfer
University of Illinois-Chicago, USA

EXECUTIVE SUMMARY

The current case study is situated within a large, land grant hospital located in the Midwestern region of the United States. Although the physicians had seen an increase in medical related human performance technology (HPTs) within the organization (e.g. computer physician ordered entry) some challenges remained as the hospital sought to improve the productivity of the electronic health record (EHRs). Specifically, physicians had difficulty finding information embedded within the chart due to usability problems and information overload. To overcome the challenges, a semantic search within the chart was implemented as a solution for physicians to retrieve relevant results given the conceptual semantic pattern. The case study will discuss many elements of the implementation based on our experience and feedback from clinicians. The case will specifically highlight the importance of training and change agents within an organization.

DOI: 10.4018/978-1-4666-8330-3.ch011

ORGANIZATION BACKGROUND

The University of Missouri hospital system is a comprehensive health care organization that serves the community through a variety of medical initiatives and clinics. To improve the quality of patient care, the University hospital system has worked with other organizations to implement various technologies. In particular, the university collaborated extensively with Cerner, an international healthcare information technology company based out of Kansas City, Missouri (United States). Cerner currently has approximately 10,000 employees that serve over 6,000 clients across the world.

Although Cerner had begun to implement various technologies within the University of Missouri healthcare systems, both organizations contemplated how to maximize patient care through effective use of human performance technologies (HPTs). One important issue in previous HPT projects was that Cerner did not have access and permission to authentic patient data in a real world setting, which was essential for accurate usability testing of their product. Although the 'dummy data' they employed was relatively easy to generate by the information technology department, it was often difficult for Cerner to accurately replicate the human-computer interaction between user and HPT without actual patient data. This, in turn, compromised the ability to accurately assess the impact of the HPT to support physician tasks, such as decision-making.

SETTING THE STAGE

To advance the quality of health human-performance technologies (HPT), the University of Missouri-Columbia and Cerner collaborated to create the Tiger Institute for Health Innovation. The goal of this research and development suborganization, entitled the Living Lab, was to develop HPT innovations that would improve patient healthcare using theoretical and practical experience from health informatics. As part of the agreement, the University of Missouri School of Information Science & Learning Technologies (SISLT) was also included within the collaboration. Specifically, the SISLT research lab, entitled the Information Experience Lab, provided graduate students to conduct usability and user-centered design research on various products for healthcare, education, and other technologies. The goal of the partnership was that these three organizations would collaborate to provide medical expertise, (University of Missouri Healthcare), software development expertise (Cerner), and evaluative human-computer interaction research (University of Missouri Information Experience Lab) to develop HPT solutions that would meet the needs of physicians and nurses.

Within the broader context of healthcare, hospitals and other medical organizations across the country have made an effort to improve patient care through effective use of human-performance technologies (HPTs) and electronic performance support systems (EPSSs). One measurement of effective application of HPT initiative includes the Health Information and Management System Society (HIMSS), which ranges from Stage 0 to Stage 7 to explain the EHR adoption model. The HIMMS model is an important measurement because it describes various stages an organization's maturity and ability to employ technology within healthcare. The low end of the spectrum, Stage 0, describes sharing information resources through artifacts such as paper records or message notes. Alternatively, the higher end of the spectrum, Stage 7, describes efficient sharing of patient data for performance, improved patient safety, and patient care using electronic resources. Prior to the initiative, the MU Healthcare system was at a Level 2 on the HIMMS index. This set the stage for the Tiger Institute and need for HPT initiatives as the hospital sought to achieve a higher HIMSS rating.

CASE DESCRIPTION

Cognitive Load and Physician Problem-Solving

In order to problem-solve, physicians are required to assimilate information from various resources. In previous years, the information resources often consisted of paper patient charts, colleagues, textbooks, and direct patient communication. However, this placed a strain on working memory and cognitive load (Meyer, 2003). In order to improve efficiency, the electronic health record (EHR) was proffered as a human-performance technology (HPT) to congregate these information resources into a single source. The belief was that if physicians were given a central resource to access pertinent medical information, their performance would increase in terms of efficiency and clinical decision-making.

As the scope of the EHR has increased, so has the information available within the HPT. Despite the potential of the EHR as an important resource, research has produced mixed results regarding its effectiveness as an HPT. For instance, research has shown that nearly 30% of EHRs have failed to support physician performance contexts due to human-computer interaction problems (Saitwal, Feng, Walji, Patel, & Zhang, 2010; Smelcer, Miller-Jacobs, & Kantrovich, 2009). Additional research suggested that navigation and the information seeking process alone may account for 20% of the diagnosis time (Lin, Harris, & Zalis, 2010). It is likely that this number will grow as additional practitioners seek to further integrate EHR into clinical practice. If usability and the human-computer interaction is not a priority during the design, the HPTs may inadvertently present misleading information (Bath, 2008), reduce the quality of patient care (Natarajan, Stein, Jain, & Elhadad, 2010), and add to the physician workload (Saitwal et al., 2010).

Physicians are often required to solve complex, ill-structured problems when presented with a patient. The decision-making of physicians often require them to integrate various information sources in order to problem-solve for the variables embedded within the problem (Boshuizen, Wiel, & Schmidt, 2012; Hmelo-Silver, 2013). To understand how HPTs support the decision-making process, previous models of medical informatics have approached systems design from an information-processing perspective (Hazlehurst, McMullen, & Gorman, 2007); we argue that additional factors such as usability and human-computer interaction are needed to understand the interaction between the EHR and physicians. Specifically, theories of cognitive load and information overload help describe the interaction between the physician, information resources, and decision-making.

Cognitive load theory suggests that the mind is at work on various levels during problem-solving. Germane load is the processing required for schema construction within the mind. The processing consists of both intrinsic and extraneous load. Intrinsic working memory describes the inherent complexity of the problem. In the context of a healthcare organization, intrinsic memory relates to the difficulty to resolve a patient problem given their medical history, extant symptoms, and context (living conditions, etc) (Baddeley, 1992; Hollender, Hofmann, Deneke, & Schmitz, 2010). By itself, intrinsic memory may present a challenge for a physician depending on the complexity of the problem and interconnectedness of the variables.

Extraneous load describes the additional cognitive effort required to process the information given the design of the materials. When a physician is presented with a problem, the additional navigation and unnecessary clicks within the HPT may tax working memory in addition to the pertinent variables of the patient. In the context of HPTs, research has shown that extraneous and germane load are significantly impacted by the design of an interface (Moreno & Valdez, 2005; Paas, van Gog, & Sweller, 2010). This lack of usability therefore strains cognitive resources because physicians must focus on navigation in conjunction with the patient diagnosis. Moreover, research suggests the additional cognitive effort posed by the extraneous cognitive lead to errors in diagnosis (Hollender et al., 2010). Designers of EHR interfaces thus need to investigate how to reduce the cognitive strain in order to effectively facilitate intuitive decision-making using the HPT.

Another important source of extraneous cognitive load within an HPT may stem from the information retrieval process (Natarajan et al., 2010; Savolainen, 2007). Research by Savolainen (2007) argues that physicians often overlook important information due to information overload within the system, which leads to additional cognitive effort for navigation. Specialties such as gerontology and family practice, which support chronic conditions, may be especially susceptible to information overload as the information is frequently updated within the EHR as the patient condition changes (Natarajan et al., 2010). The patient handoff procedure also confounds the process as various practitioners and medical personnel update the EHR (Wohlauer, 2012; Wohlauer et al., 2012). As such, advances in information retrieval with the EHR are required to better support the information and decision-making needs of the physicians (Holden, 2010; Smelcer et al., 2009).

Implementation Project Concerns

One of the main challenges of an electronic health record is that it is frequently updated by various medical personnel. When in a hospital, patients are frequently provided care by multiple physicians depending on the time of day or specialty. While this extends the care of the patient, it presents a potential problem for the electronic health record because the health is not used consistently. For instance, similar terminology may be used differently depending on the specialty; therefore, the information resources may be updated in an inconsistent manner. Moreover, the physician must constantly take into account this new information as s/he resumes care for the patient. To overcome the cognitive load and information overload issue, Cerner and the Living Lab worked to develop a semantic search system as a way to navigate the electronic health record interface. Specifically, this HPT would allow physicians to search on clinical terms (i.e. – cardiac arrest) and retrieve similar results based upon related indices and a semantic pattern (i.e. – heart attack). Ideally, the ability to search and retrieve information within the complex EHR would better allow the HPT to support clinical decision-making.

At the outset of this HPT implementation project, there were multiple concerns from a technological standpoint. The first concern of the semantic search related to the somewhat limited scope of the beta technology and its impact upon decision-making. The semantic search system was initially designed to only search for information embedded within notes, imaging studies (e.g. x-rays) labs, and reports. That is, the initial version of the proposed HPT solution did not extract information from other pertinent sources, such as medical orders or across patients. As such, it was unclear what information would not be present in the retrieval results. There was therefore the possibility the physician may construct their mental model based on a limited subset of the information. In doing so, they may unknowingly proffer erroneous solutions for the problem based on incomplete information.

The initial iteration of the HPT also highlighted the importance of trust in the early version of the technology. As noted earlier, the semantic search extracted information from specific areas of the EHR and some physicians were unclear about the scope of the technology. As such, there was ambiguity as to what information was left out of the search results. For those that assumed that the search retrieved all the relevant information, it provided a false sense of security. Therefore, they questioned whether the technology could be trusted to reliably retrieve all the information that would be pertinent to their decision-making. This, in turn, delayed the adoption of the system.

Another concern of the HPT related to its impact on workplace productivity. While the introduction of the semantic search was proffered as a means to extract meaningful information, there were concerns from the implementation team that the time to 'crawl' the production system would take too long as additional searches were performed. Specifically, there was a technical concern that as the semantic search adoption expanded among users, the additional queries would slow down other aspects of the EHR system, therefore reducing productivity across the organization. From a user adoption perspective, it was important not to alienate users by disrupting other aspects of the EHR. Alternatively, if the users were unhappy with the retrieval time of the semantic search, there was a concern that they may deem the new HPT as inferior to the current methods of browsing the EHR (Figure 1). The concern about these tertiary effects was reiterated during the usability testing that was conducted with physicians. Instantaneous search results, with little wait time, was thus a priority during the implementation of the HPT.

Figure 1. Standard EHR interface

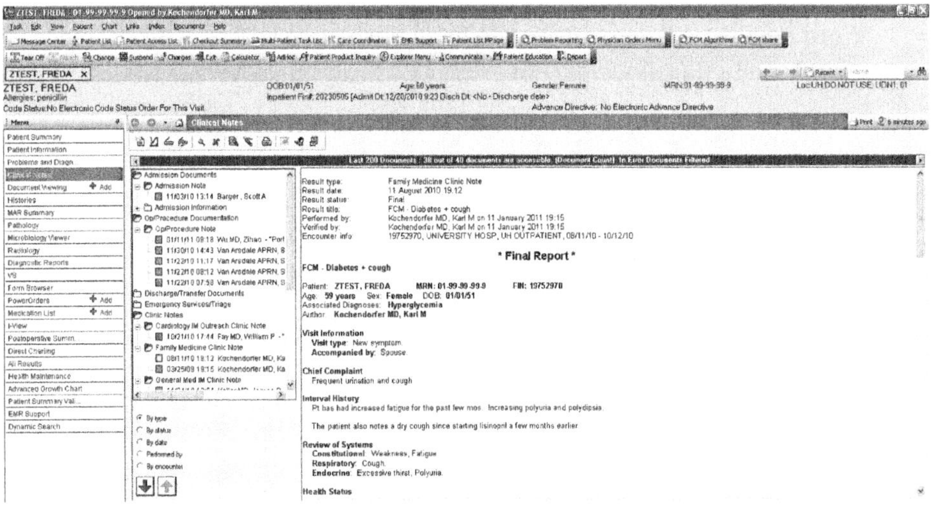

How Semantic Search Works

The field of medical informatics has begun to explore various HPT designs to support problem-solving in medical contexts. Semantic search within EHRs allows users to submit queries by typing keywords related to a clinical concept and repeatedly adding in multiple indices to build a semantic pattern. In doing so, the individual is able to not only search on one term (e.g. heart attack), but a set of related terms (e.g. heart failure, cardiac arrest). This is especially important in a medical context where multiple variables are present and referenced using differing terminologies. In the current case study, semantic search is defined as a cloud-based service for clinicians to perform structured searches of unstructured text anywhere in a patient's chart by using clinical vocabularies.

By allowing indexing of related terms (e.g. heart attack, cardiac arrest), the HPT is able to make relationships within the medical record. In doing so, the HPT is able to retrieve information that is relevant to the task at hand and thus more accurately support physician decision making. Many semantic search tools (Figure 2) contain three primary features:

- **Concept Search:** Allows searchers to find information based on the clinical concepts that occur in the record. For example, a search for "heart attack" would be able to find a document containing the medical term "myocardial infarction." Similarly, a term such as "obesity" could find related terms "overweight."
- **Word Search:** Allows searchers to find information based on the presence of specific non-clinical words. For example, "heart attack pizza" would be able to find a document that contained both the medical concept of myocardial

Figure 2. Semantic search interface

infarction as well as the non-medical word "pizza". A search that looked for the terms "motorcycle accident" and "leg fracture" could also be performed by the physician.

- **Smart Ranking:** Brings the most important search matches to the top of the list of search results. Semantic search understands the context and the usage of each concept and thus attempts to promote documents that are most pertinent to the user.

In order to perform the search, the HPT consists of the following stages: data normalization, concept recognition, semantic expansion, and generation of a clinical significance score. The last stage, clinical significance score, is a particularly important aspect because it calculates the score on a number of factors such as when and how the term was used ("Reason For Visit" vs. "Associated Symptoms"), temporality ("past history of… " vs. "presents with…"), subject context ("patient presents with…" vs. "family history of…"), negotiation and uncertainty ("…confirmed" vs. "rule out…" vs. "…ruled out"). Collectively, these factors ensure the physician is provided the most pertinent information for solving the extant problem of the patient given the search and patient context.

Management and Organizational Concerns

From an organizational and project management perspective, there were multiple issues to consider during the implementation of the HPT. Within any organization, the introduction of an HPT often requires the users to restructure their workflows to accommodate the new tool. Although the normalization process may be beneficial in the long term, this integration into the daily workflows of physicians may lead to diagnostic errors until users become familiar with the system. Based on some of these concerns, the rollout employed various means to communicate the benefits and features of the technology. For instance, short multimedia videos were provided to instruct physicians about the availability and embedded functionality within the existing EHR. Directed e-mails were also provided to the entire hospital staff (physicians, nurses, social workers, etc) as a way of informing them of the semantic search capability.

To overcome some of the project management concerns, the implementers of the project also employed more personal means such as physician product champions and change catalysts. The implementers targeted early adopters of previous technologies for multiple reasons. Moreover, the product champions were used to convey how the semantic search might be beneficial to solve specific problems related to their subspecialty. In addition, they provided feedback for any potential usability or implementation issues.

The implementation team also focused on usability as a key towards the success of the project at the early stages. Because we wanted to provide an authentic experience during usability testing, the early stages employed actual, real-world clinical data. If we had used 'dummy data', we would have received feedback that focused on usability issues related to navigation, aesthetics, or terminology. However, data based on actual patients provided extensive feedback about decision-making processes within clinical contexts. By understanding how the user might employ the system for problem-solving, we were able to address issues that might preclude adoption by the physicians (America Institute of Medicine, 2013).

Real-time, user-centered data was also essential as we sought to address management and organizational concerns. For instance, the system included a feedback function when the HPT was deployed in the production environment, which allowed users to comment on the system at the time of the search. Because there was a fear that we would not gather in situ feedback, the feedback provided a mechanism for the user to convey instantaneous feedback to the developers as they encountered issues or identified potential limitations of the semantic search. This feedback, coupled with the actual user logs, served as critical data that helped the developers construct user interaction patterns.

CURRENT CHALLENGES FACING THE ORGANIZATION

Hospitals are under increasing pressure to reduce expenses to counteract the rising costs of healthcare. To date, healthcare costs comprise a $2.7 trillion dollar industry, which accounts for 18% of the United States gross domestic product (GDP). Estimates suggest that $750 billion of that is wasted due to inefficiencies and errors. One way to reduce this waste is through the effective use of human performance technology as a way to facilitate productivity. However, one of the challenges of EHRs as an HPT is that they risk a diminishing return on value over time. As the EHRs are inundated with additional information, the data poses a strain on cognitive load, which become potential obstacles to clinical decision-making and problem-solving in a hospital context.

Some preliminary data has been gathered to ascertain the quality of the solution within the University of Missouri healthcare system and beyond. After just 1.5 years, the semantic search capability was implemented and launched at approximately 100 healthcare organizations across the country. The HPT currently has 2 billion documents and over 48 billion results indexed. More importantly, the search rate includes over 1 million searches (not searchers) per year, many of which have been performed by physicians. The majority of searches are now performed by nursing staff, Health Information Management staff, pharmacists and other healthcare workers.

Although there were some positive outcomes of our implementation, there are opportunities for improvements. Results of the pilot testing found that approximately 20% of the clients were conducting greater than 80% of the searches, with many of the searches being generated from the University of Missouri – Columbia. These findings from our pilot may be interpreted in multiple ways. First, it is positive that the earliest client among the sites was still employing the technology. The first client had several champions that helped to promote the HPT within the organization using real-world success stories. These success stories and case examples were used by other users within the organization as a practical framework to employ the HPT. As such, the rate of growth is favorable because the earliest organization has generated the most interest. At the same time, an effort is needed to promote the HPT across the country and reach those in other settings. To date, it is unclear if the lack of usage stems from a lack of knowledge about the system or issues that relate to workflow problems.

From a technological standpoint, it is somewhat of a challenge to keep up with the amount of indexed terms. As noted previously, data continues to increase at rapid pace within the organizational EHR, so the capability of the semantic search must keep pace with the amount of information. If the users perceive that the technology cannot be trusted to retrieve the most current information, the organization risks the possibility of medical errors.

Similarly, the functionality must also keep pace with the changing nature of the organization. The need for semantic search stemmed from the expanded application of the EHR. While the EHR was originally designed to be an information gathering tool, it has evolved into an HPT that plays a significant role in physician decision-making (Fowler et al., 2014; Middleton et al., 2013; Musen, Middleton, & Greenes, 2014; Oshima Lee & Emanuel, 2013). As an HPT becomes further integrated into an organization, individuals will co-evolve with the technology and leverage the HPT to support other areas of performance. Therefore, the scope of the semantic search may extend to cross-patient chart searches, expanded ranges of indexed content, and additional semantic search subject areas. Users may also look to the HPT to support collaborative activities among patient, pharmacists, and other subspecialties. However, designers of the HPT must understand how to avoid "scope creep", while also planning for the future expectations of the ever-evolving HPT within a hospital.

SOLUTIONS AND RECOMMENDATIONS

Based on our experience, there are multiple implications for others that seek to improve organizations through human-performance technology. The first implication relates to the importance of human-computer interaction and usability for these systems. Many physicians noted that the HPT was easy to understand because it had a 'Google-like' interface. Although the underlying queries within a semantic search are different than other search tools, it was intuitive enough for users to quickly understand the HPT. Moreover, the feedback that the HPT was 'Google-like' design suggested the interface had a frame of reference for which to understand the novel technology. This familiarity may have precluded some of the initial barriers by making the goal of the technology clear to the users.

Integration into the current workflow of physicians was also key to the success of the project. At the outset of the project, we underwent extensive user testing to understand the role the semantic search might play in supporting physician workflow. Based on the feedback, it was clear the product needed to be a 'just-in-time' resource that could be easily accessed as physicians progressed in their diagnosis and solution of the patient (Gegenfurtner, Veermans, & Vauras, 2013). As such, the solution would most likely have been less successful if physicians navigated to a development server or if the user had to exert additional effort to access the system. If the technology is designed to fit within the current workflow, users will be more likely to adopt it because they find it productive to accomplish their workplace goals.

Another important aspect was that the semantic search added to the existing EHR, but did not replace or significantly modify the existing EHR. That is, physicians were not forced to employ the new HPT and thus radically alter their workflow. The feedback gathered at various stages helped to underscore that the solution needed to be simple, clear, and easy to understand. Moreover, the feedback helped us understand the role the technology would play in their workflow. As noted earlier, the technology was accessed as physicians would have questions. If a physician needed additional information in order to diagnose the problem, they were still allowed navigate the EHR as they normally would. As physicians became more adept at using the semantic search features, they were also allowed the freedom to alternate between the semantic search and traditional browsing methods. By giving users freedom, they were allowed to employ the system to meet their needs as their expertise evolved and their trust with the system grew.

Trust in the semantic search was another important element from our experience. In the initial iterations of the HPT, the semantic search only searched within certain aspects of the EHR. Because physicians problem-solve by creating a mental model of the patient, it may be problematic if they assume they make decisions based on the entirety of the information resources rather than just a subset of the available information. In our experience, some physicians were unclear about what information may be missing from the search results, which resulted in some initial apprehension about how much they could trust the technology to support their decision-making. If a development team communicates the scope of the technology at the outset, users may be able to better understand the intent of the HPT. Moreover, it may also be beneficial for development teams to communicate additional features that are planned so users understand how the tool intends to grow over time.

Another important aspect was to understand how the performance technology fit within the broader context of the existing HPTs. In the current case, the development team made an effort to ensure the infrastructure could support the additional 'crawling' required of the newly integrated semantic search. This helped to ensure that the introduction of a new technology did not interfere or reduce the effectives of other performance technology initiatives within the health organization. It was also important to understand how the technology fit within the context from a social and personnel perspective. For instance, physicians operate and execute decisions alongside nurses, pharmacists, clerical workers, and other healthcare workers. Our experiences found that these other groups expressed an interest to employ the HPT to support their work functions and utilize the EHR to collaborate more effectively. Similarly, other organizations should understand how performance technologies are designed for individual decision-making, but also scale to support collaborative problem-solving in future iterations.

REFERENCES

America Institute of Medicine. (2013). *Best care at lower cost: the pat to continuously learning health care in America*. National Academy Press.

Baddeley, A. (1992). Working memory. *Science*, *255*(5044), 556–559. doi:10.1126/science.1736359 PMID:1736359

Bath, P. A. (2008). Health informatics: Current issues and challenges. *Journal of Information Science*, *34*(4), 501–518. doi:10.1177/0165551508092267

Boshuizen, H. P. A., Wiel, M. W. J., & Schmidt, H. G. (2012). What and how advanced medical students learn from reasoning through multiple cases. *Instructional Science*, *40*(5), 755–768. doi:10.1007/s11251-012-9211-z

Fowler, S. A., Yaeger, L. H., Yu, F., Doerhoff, D., Schoening, P., & Kelly, B. (2014). Electronic health record: Integrating evidence-based information at the point of clinical decision making. *Journal of the Medical Library Association: JMLA*, *102*(1), 52–55. doi:10.3163/1536-5050.102.1.010 PMID:24415920

Gegenfurtner, A., Veermans, K., & Vauras, M. (2013). Effects of computer support, collaboration, and time lag on performance self-efficacy and transfer of training: A longitudinal meta-analysis. *Educational Research Review*, 8, 75–89. doi:10.1016/j.edurev.2012.04.001

Hazlehurst, B., McMullen, C. K., & Gorman, P. N. (2007). Distributed cognition in the heart room: How situation awareness arises from coordinated communications during cardiac surgery. *Journal of Biomedical Informatics*, 40(5), 539–551. doi:10.1016/j.jbi.2007.02.001 PMID:17368112

Hmelo-Silver, C. E. (2013). Creating a learning space in problem-based learning. *Interdisciplinary Journal of Problem-Based Learning*, 7(1), 143–156. doi:10.7771/1541-5015.1334

Holden, R. J. (2010). Physicians' beliefs about using EMR and CPOE: In pursuit of a contextualized understanding of health it use behavior. *International Journal of Medical Informatics*, 79(2), 71–80. doi:10.1016/j.ijmedinf.2009.12.003 PMID:20071219

Hollender, N., Hofmann, C., Deneke, M., & Schmitz, B. (2010). Integrating cognitive load theory and concepts of human–computer interaction. *Computers in Human Behavior*, 26(6), 1278–1288. doi:10.1016/j.chb.2010.05.031

Lin, A., Harris, M., & Zalis, M. (2010). Initial observations of electronic medical record usage during CT and MRI interpretation: Frequency of use and impact on workflow. *AJR. American Journal of Roentgenology*, 195(1), 188–193. doi:10.2214/AJR.09.2946 PMID:20566815

Middleton, B., Bloomrosen, M., Dente, M. A., Hashmat, B., Koppel, R., Overhage, J. M., & Zhang, J. (2013). Enhancing patient safety and quality of care by improving the usability of electronic health record systems: Recommendations from AMIA. *Journal of the American Medical Informatics Association*, 20(e1), e2–e8. doi:10.1136/amiajnl-2012-001458 PMID:23355463

Moreno, R., & Valdez, A. (2005). Cognitive load and learning effects of having students organize pictures and words in multimedia environments: The role of student interactivity and feedback. *Educational Technology Research and Development*, 53(3), 35–45. doi:10.1007/BF02504796

Musen, M. A., Middleton, B., & Greenes, R. A. (2014). Clinical decision-support systems. In E. H. Shortliffe & J. J. Cimino (Eds.), Biomedical Informatics (pp. 643–674). Springer London; Retrieved from http://link.springer.com/chapter/10.1007/978-1-4471-4474-8_22 doi:10.1007/978-1-4471-4474-8_22

Natarajan, K., Stein, D., Jain, S., & Elhadad, N. (2010). An analysis of clinical queries in an EHR search utility. *International Journal of Medical Informatics*, (79): 515–522. doi:10.1016/j.ijmedinf.2010.03.004 PMID:20418155

Oshima Lee, E., & Emanuel, E. J. (2013). Shared decision making to improve care and reduce costs. *The New England Journal of Medicine*, *368*(1), 6–8. doi:10.1056/NEJMp1209500 PMID:23281971

Paas, F., van Gog, T., & Sweller, J. (2010). Cognitive Load Theory: New Conceptualizations, Specifications, and Integrated Research Perspectives. *Educational Psychology Review*, *22*(2), 115–121. doi:10.1007/s10648-010-9133-8

Saitwal, H., Feng, X., Walji, M., Patel, V. L., & Zhang, J. (2010). Assessing performance of an electronic health record (EHR) using cognitive task analysis. *International Journal of Medical Informatics*, *79*(7), 501–506. doi:10.1016/j.ijmedinf.2010.04.001 PMID:20452274

Savolainen, R. (2007). Filtering and withdrawing: Strategies for coping with information overload in everyday contexts. *Journal of Information Science*, *33*(5), 611–621. doi:10.1177/0165551506077418

Smelcer, J. B., Miller-Jacobs, H., & Kantrovich, L. (2009). Usability of electronic medical records. *Journal of Usability Studies*, *4*(2), 70–84.

Wohlauer, M. (2012). Fragmented care in the era of limited work hours: A plea for an explicit handover curriculum. *BMJ Quality & Safety*, *21*(Suppl 1), i16–i18. doi:10.1136/bmjqs-2012-001218 PMID:23173183

Wohlauer, M., Arora, V. M., Horwitz, L. I., Bass, E. J., Mahar, S. E., & Philibert, I. (2012). The patient handoff. *Academic Medicine*, *87*(4), 411–418. doi:10.1097/ACM.0b013e318248e766 PMID:22361791

ADDITIONAL READING

Cresswell, K., Bates, D. W., & Sheikh, A. (2013). Ten key considerations for the successful implementation and adoption of large-scale health information technology. *Journal of the American Medical Informatics Association*, *20*(e1), e9–e13. doi:10.1136/amiajnl-2013001684

Cresswell, K., & Sheikh, A. (2013). Organizational issues in the implementation and adoption of health information technology innovations: An interpretative review. *International Journal of Medical Informatics, 82*(5), e73–e86. doi:10.1016/j. ijmedinf.2012.10.007 PMID:23146626

Duftschmid, G., Rinner, C., Kohler, M., Huebner-Bloder, G., Saboor, S., & Ammenwerth, E. (2013). The EHR-ARCHE project: Satisfying clinical information needs in a shared electronic health record system based on IHE XDS and archetypes. *International Journal of Medical Informatics, 82*(12), 1195–1207. doi:10.1016/j. ijmedinf.2013.08.002 PMID:23999002

Häyrinen, K., Saranto, K., & Nykänen, P. (2008). Definition, structure, content, use and impacts of electronic health records: A review of the research literature. *International Journal of Medical Informatics, 77*(5), 291–304. doi:10.1016/j.ijmedinf.2007.09.001 PMID:17951106

Hsu, W., Long, L. R., & Antani, S. (2009). SPIRS: A framework for content-based image retrieval from large biomedical databases. *International Journal of Medical Informatics, 78*, 13–24. doi:10.1016/j.ijmedinf.2008.09.006

Hyppönen, H., Saranto, K., Vuokko, R., Mäkelä-Bengs, P., Doupi, P., Lindqvist, M., & Mäkelä, M. (2014). Impacts of structuring the electronic health record: A systematic review protocol and results of previous reviews. *International Journal of Medical Informatics, 83*(3), 159–169. doi:10.1016/j.ijmedinf.2013.11.006 PMID:24374018

Koopman, R. J., Kochendorfer, K. M., Moore, J. L., Mehr, D. R., Wakefield, D. S., Yadamsuren, B., & Belden, J. L. (2011). A diabetes dashboard and physician efficiency and accuracy in accessing data needed for high-quality diabetes care. *Annals of Family Medicine, 9*(5), 398–405. doi:10.1370/afm.1286 PMID:21911758

Krug, S. (2009). *Rocket surgery made easy: The do-it-yourself guide to finding and fixing usability problems* (1st ed.). New Riders.

Lanham, H. J., Leykum, L. K., & McDaniel, R. R. (2012). Same organization, same electronic health records (EHRs) system, different use: Exploring the linkage between practice member communication patterns and EHR use patterns in an ambulatory care setting. *Journal of the American Medical Informatics Association, 19*(3), 382–391. doi:10.1136/amiajnl-2011-000263 PMID:21846780

Li, J.-S., Zhang, X.-G., Chu, J., Suzuki, M., & Araki, K. (2012). Design and development of EMR supporting medical process management. *Journal of Medical Systems, 36*(3), 1193–1203. doi:10.1007/s10916-010-9581-1 PMID:20811768

Lin, A., Harris, M., & Zalis, M. (2010). Initial observations of electronic medical record usage during CT and MRI interpretation: Frequency of use and impact on workflow. *AJR. American Journal of Roentgenology*, *195*(1), 188–193. doi:10.2214/AJR.09.2946 PMID:20566815

Ludwick, D. A., & Doucette, J. (2009). Adopting electronic medical records in primary care: Lessons learned from health information systems implementation experience in seven countries. *International Journal of Medical Informatics*, *78*(1), 22–31. doi:10.1016/j.ijmedinf.2008.06.005 PMID:18644745

McAlearney, A. S., Robbins, J., Kowalczyk, N., Chisolm, D. J., & Song, P. H. (2012). The role of cognitive and learning theories in supporting successful EHR system implementation training: A qualitative study. *Medical Care Research and Review*, *69*(3), 294–315. doi:10.1177/1077558711436348 PMID:22451617

Norman, D. A. (2002). *The design of everyday things*. Basic Books.

Rogers, Y., Sharp, H., & Preece, J. (2011). *Interaction design: beyond human – computer interaction* (3rd ed.). Wiley.

Saitwal, H., Feng, X., Walji, M., Patel, V., & Zhang, J. (2010). Assessing performance of an electronic health record (EHR) using cognitive task analysis. *International Journal of Medical Informatics*, *79*(7), 501–506. doi:10.1016/j.ijmedinf.2010.04.001 PMID:20452274

Schaffer, S. P., & Kim, H. (2012). Responsive evaluation as a guide to design and implementation: Case study of an e-health learning system. *Performance Improvement Quarterly*, *25*(2), 9–25. doi:10.1002/piq.21119

Tawfik, A. A., Belden, J., & Moore, J. (2013). Agile management of a mobile application development project for surgeon workflows. In A. D. Benson, J. L. Moore, & S. Williams van Rooij (Eds.), *Cases on Educational Technology Planning, Design, and Implementation: A Project Management Perspective*. IGI Global. doi:10.4018/978-1-4666-4237-9.ch014

Tawfik, A. A., Kochendorfer, K. M., Saparova, D., Al Ghenaimi, S., & Moore, J. L. (2014). "I don't have time to dig back through this": The role of semantic search in supporting physician information seeking in an electronic health record. *Performance Improvement Quarterly*, *26*(4), 75–91. doi:10.1002/piq.21158

Thyvalikakath, T. P., Dziabiak, M. P., Johnson, R., Torres-Urquidy, M. H., Acharya, A., Yabes, J., & Schleyer, T. K. (2014). Advancing cognitive engineering methods to support user interface design for electronic health records. *International Journal of Medical Informatics*, *83*(4), 292–302. doi:10.1016/j.ijmedinf.2014.01.007 PMID:24503391

Wakefield, D. S., Mehr, D., Keplinger, L., Canfield, S., Gopidi, R., Wakefield, B. J., & Kochendorfer, K. M. (2010). Issues and questions to consider in implementing secure electronic patient–provider web portal communications systems. *International Journal of Medical Informatics*, *79*(7), 469–477. doi:10.1016/j.ijmedinf.2010.04.005 PMID:20472495

Zalis, M., & Harris, M. (2010). Advanced search of the electronic medical record: Augmenting safety and efficiency in radiology. *Journal of the American College of Radiology*, *7*(8), 625–633. doi:10.1016/j.jacr.2010.03.011 PMID:20678732

KEY TERMS AND DEFINITIONS

Cognitive Load: Amount of processing required to accomplish a tax. Cognitive load usually consists of extraneous, intrinsic, and germane cognitive load.

Electronic Health Record (EHR): Technology used to store pertinent information about the history of a patient.

Electronic Performance Support Systems (EPSS): Technology employed to make a task more efficient.

Extraneous Cognitive Load: Additional processing required because of the manner in which the content is provided to the individual.

Germane Cognitive Load: Processing required for understanding information and constructing schemas.

Human-Computer Interaction (HCI): Understanding of the interaction between a technology and user.

Intrinsic Cognitive Load: Inherent difficulty posed by a particular task.

Semantic Search: Queries by typing keywords related to a clinical concept and repeatedly adding in multiple indices to build a semantic pattern. By allowing indexing of related terms (e.g. heart attack, cardiac arrest), the HPT is able to make relationships within the medical record.

Usability: Degree to which the human-computer interaction is intuitive to the user.

User-Centered Design: Design philosophy that emphasizes on the user needs throughout the design.

Chapter 12

A Competency–Based Performance System in a Health Care IT Setting

William L. Solomonson
Oakland University, USA

Tomas R. Giberson
Oakland University, USA

EXECUTIVE SUMMARY

DiversiCorp Communications grew extremely fast to support Red Oak Health System's enterprise IT needs. Often promoting strong performers from within, DiversiCorp leadership recognized that their directors and managers needed enhanced support to maintain their expected level of service to their health care client. Two performance consultants were engaged who facilitated DiversiCorp leadership through a systematic organizational development process that culminated in the creation of an organizational "competency operating system." This competency/behavioral-based system took as key inputs existing relevant company competencies and was developed with stakeholder involvement using a critical incident approach. Additionally, it was the core mechanism that then drove performance improvement through improved hiring practices, behavioral interview training, job tools and performance support, enhanced job descriptions, and aligned performance expectations and appraisals.

DOI: 10.4018/978-1-4666-8330-3.ch012

ORGANIZATION BACKGROUND

DiversiCorp Communications is a provider of health care IT services, including communication networks (e.g. secured hard-wired and wifi internet), application support and implementation (e.g. electronic medical health care records), phone networks, IT consulting, as well as a staffed IT "Help Desk." It is part of a conglomeration of business entities that contribute to a $100B (US) global organization.

For the past several years DiversiCorp has provided these services to Red Oaks Health System, which is a network of approximately 10 regional hospitals, 40 medical centers, and 30 pharmacies. Red Oaks Health System (ROHS) is a not-for-profit corporation with approximately 20,000 employees. With annual revenues of over $4B US, ROHS has approximately 3 million out-patient visits and 100,000 patient admissions annually. ROHS has an estimated regional economic impact of over $6B US.

ROHS relies greatly upon the IT support services offered by DiversiCorp, not only for their basic IT infrastructure, but also for immediate IT support that underpins patient care and outcomes. The business relationship is often high-pressure, time-sensitive, and complex. Additionally, the outcomes of the relationship impact the likelihood of the renewal of multi-year service contracts between ROHS and DiversiCorp.

SETTING THE STAGE

DiversiCorp has adopted the ITIL approach to service management. ITIL (Information Technology Infrastructure Library) is a widely-used set of best practices in the IT service field and is based upon the service lifecycle of service strategy, service design, service transition, and service operation (Arraj, 2013). As DiversiCorp focused on continuously improving its services for ROHS, it looked to ITIL as a key component of this effort.

Over the course of the business relationship, the number of DiversiCorp employees who serviced the ROHS account has grown quite rapidly. Three years ago there were approximately 80 employees on the DiversiCorp-ROHS team; today there are over 260. This growth has provided opportunities for professional advancement for individuals at all levels. DiversiCorp has promoted several individual contributors to the manager ranks, and some managers to the director level. The 20 managers and 8 directors on the DiversiCorp-ROHS team have varying levels of skill and experience in managing and directing. As might be expected in a fast-growing organization, several individuals were promoted based upon performance and potential without much support in developing the competencies required for success at the next level.

Both DiversiCorp and ROHS had existing models for the purposes of leadership development. DiversiCorp has its own internal leadership initiative based around "leadership dimensions" and ROHS had an existing "leadership competency model." Both of these models were sound organizational development (OD) tools that aligned to each company's vision, mission, and values, but were not utilized because of lack of resources (i.e, time) and did not offer a specific set of competency-based behaviors that were vital to the success of DiversiCorp-ROHS managers and directors. Thus, developing management and leadership competencies for these 28 managers and directors represented the next phase of service improvement for DiversiCorp and their on-going partnership with ROHS.

The core team that was involved with the project included an independent performance consultant who specialized in organizational development and training, Robert Opecki, in addition to the following key DiversiCorp employees, all of whom were exclusively focused on their ROHS client:

- Thomas Burnet, Executive Director; responsible for the overall DiversiCorp-ROHS function and the business relationship with ROHS.
- Gretchen Piperia, Director of IT Group; responsible for quality assurance and ITIL processes.
- Margaret Templeton, Senior Business Analyst; responsible for talent management, recruiting, and hiring.
- Janet Tourbaden, Program Manager; responsible for service improvement initiatives and an internal trainer.

CASE DESCRIPTION

Project Engagement

Margaret Templeton was the DiversiCorp employee who reached out and engaged Robert as a performance consultant for DiversiCorp. The first two meetings were conducted via conference calls, and served the multiple purposes of a "meet and greet," providing Robert with an initial overview of the situation, as well as an initial collection of needs assessment data. Thomas Burnet, Janet Troubaden, Margaret, and Robert participated on these initial calls.

Margaret and Janet both described an emergent issue around the performance of managers, and some directors, and said that they felt there was a need for training to bridge those performance issues. Though the perceived needs by stakeholders should be taken cautiously, many needs assessment experts maintain that this early data collection can still offer meaningful data (Guerra-Lopez, 2007).

The DiversiCorp team's perceived needs for IT managers included:

- How to conduct sound, legally-defensible interviews (training);
- How to impact employee engagement (employee development);
- How to deal with personnel issues (training);
- Soft skills, such as written and verbal communication (training);
- Translating technical to "business speak" (communication);
- Business skills: Less function specific, more systems awareness (training);
- Performance improvement planning (performance management/ improvement);
- How to deliver performance reviews (coaching and mentoring).

Thomas spoke of DiversiCorp's rapid growth in response to ROHS's needs in the IT area. DiversiCorp had seen nearly 225% growth in the number of employees to satisfy this need over a three-year period. The number of managers and directors had a similarly rapid growth rate. This tremendous growth also came with growing pains. One of the challenges was that external hiring of managers and directors was difficult, as the pool of qualified external candidates was very small. Also, philosophically, DiversiCorp liked to promote from within. These two facts led to the result of promoting good performers. Of these 28 leaders, 8 were at the executive level (directors), and 20 were managers, most being at their job for only weeks to a few months.

Margaret said that she felt many of the employees who had been promoted had a "difficult transition from employee to manager." Due to the nature of their business these people were generally very good "technical people," and since that is what they knew, and were both good at and rewarded for, that is where they often focused their energy as managers. But now they needed to be "business people," which includes learning HR skills such as recruitment, interviewing skills, and selection. Many managers were aware of their shortcomings, and had asked Margaret for help in hiring. Jim added that "leaders are empowered to act, but may not know what it looks like." Margaret felt that the transition of employee to leader with a focus on the maturity of a manager over time was vital.

Janet, who was the internal trainer at DiversiCorp, added that although these managers were well-trained technical experts, they needed this technical expertise to be augmented with a management education and training program.

The DiversiCorp team had spent time thinking about such a program, and its initial vision included:

- A focus on managers,
- A potential quarterly or annual "Leadership Conference,"

- A curriculum developed around the perceived needs with an initial focus on soft skills,
- Skilled trainers to deliver the training,
- A potential tie-in to "ITIL Certification,"
- A Communication Plan.

Janet pointed out that they have had a robust training program in place for several years around the ITIL framework. Her hope was to have ITIL play a role in whatever end program or solution the core team came up with. In this way, ITIL would in a meaningful way provide a structural and process "backbone" of the organization. The initial years of ITIL training focused on "education and awareness" of ITIL for DiversiCorp employees, but DiversiCorp was now at a stage of "alignment and maturity" and ready for ITIL to be integrated into more daily work and new initiatives such as the one we were now focusing on.

An Integrated OD Approach

The types of performance issues addressed here are common in situations like the one DiversiCorp found itself in. Top employees were promoted to another level due to their performance in their current one. In essence, performers were placed in situations without the necessary support needed to perform (Gilbert, 1978; Rummler, 2006). It was highly likely (and would be confirmed later with the additional data collected) that DiversiCorp needed to develop management and leadership capabilities of its existing and future management team. This was true for the DiversiCorp team's desire for interview training, but the ideal approach would integrate not only training and development, but also should help to improve future hiring efforts, performance management, and promotion decisions.

The first step was to identify the behaviors and related competencies that were important to the organization. DiversiCorp was a mature company with a framework of Leadership Dimensions already in existence. Similarly, ROHS had its own Leadership Standards of Excellence, which DiversiCorp wanted to internalize into its own organizational practices to best serve ROHS and to minimize a sense of separateness from ROHS. So, as a starting point, the approach was to integrate a variety of strategic inputs, including not only DiversiCorp's Leadership Dimensions and the ROHS Leadership Standards of Excellence, but also the ITIL Management and Leadership Competencies.

These inputs had clear implications for managing and leading at DiversiCorp; however, they each had limitations that prevented them from providing direct guidance for management and leadership development. For example, the DiversiCorp Leadership Dimensions were fairly vague and did not provide clear guidance on desired behaviors *within the DiversiCorp-ROHS group*. Similarly, ITIL outlines competencies specific to ITIL, but does not provide clear interpretations *within the DiversiCorp-ROHS group*. Thus, the ideal solution would enable not only enhanced management and leadership performance, but also would provide the basis for improvements in hiring, promotion, and performance evaluation at DiversiCorp-ROHS.

Competency-Based Performance System

In order to achieve these ends Robert proposed a competency-based system for developing the DiversiCorp management team, and enhancing DiversiCorp's overall human resource performance. A competency-based approach is a flexible, powerful, best practice approach that in this case, ties together critical company and customer values, leadership dimensions, and ITIL requirements through specific behaviors (or *performance requirements*) required for success. A competency-based approach essentially provides an "operating system" which supports the development and integration of a variety of "applications," including training and development, hiring, promotion, and performance evaluation.

The approach to develop such a system follows a logical, proven method. The development process includes participation by individual contributors, managers, and directors at DiversiCorp. Participation in developing the system has two goals: first to identify the "right" competencies and performance requirements, and second, to begin building buy-in and support for the changes and improvements that inevitably follow. Additionally, for this project this approach was customized to fit into the ITIL process phases of *strategy*, *design*, *transition*, and *operation*.

The *Strategy* phase was already in motion at DiversiCorp as the core team first met. The first strategic decisions were to focus on ITIL implementation. The decision to develop an integrative management/ leadership development effort based upon ITIL, and key ROHS and DiversiCorp leadership dimensions, represented the next evolution of this strategy.

The *Design* phase focused on developing the core system comprised of the competencies and performance requirements expected of managers and leaders, as well as identifying DiversiCorp system-level support needs (such as development needs, improving hiring, promotions, and evaluations). This was the most critical and time-intensive phase.

At the juncture of the *Design* and *Transition* phases, the specific competencies and performance requirements become the foundation for developing various applications. For example, a key group-level need was interviewing candidates which was addressed through a group-based instructional intervention. In the case

Figure 1. ITIL leadership competencies lifecycle process

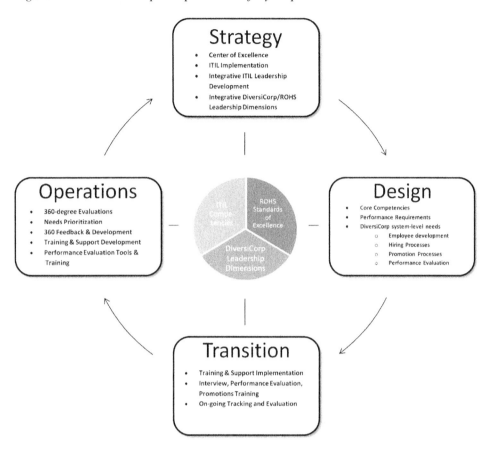

of unique individual needs, these can be addressed within individual development plans through a variety of individually-driven development methods, such as coaching, external training, and developmental assignments. Thus, toward the close of the *Transition* phase, the various applications (such as training and performance evaluations) were developed with leader, manager, and individual contributor input, and prepared for roll-out.

During the *Operations* phase, the various applications were rolled out. Training and other group-level development efforts were then scheduled and rolled-out. Similarly, other applications, such as behavioral interviewing, and recommendations for promotion systems and performance evaluations were rolled-out with supporting tools.

Robert intentionally embraced the existing framework used by the client (ITIL) and synthesized the solution within that familiar framework (see Table 1), which

Table 1. ITIL phases, process steps, and team involvement

	Step	**Involvement**	**Timing**
Strategy	1. Start of work meeting • Set goals for effort, including calendar timeline	Thomas, Gretchen, Margaret, Janet, Robert	Week 1
Design	2. Review existing inputs & develop initial interview tools	Robert	Week 1
	3. Conduct initial interviews • Initial prioritization of competencies	Focus group(s) of managers and directors, Robert	Week 3
	4. Develop focus group, interview, and survey tools	Robert	Week 4
	5. Review existing hiring, promotion, performance evaluation processes and tools	Robert	Week 4
	6. Conduct focus groups, interviews, surveys • Identify specific leader and manager performance requirements for the prioritized competencies	Robert, directors, managers, individual contributors	Week 6
Transition	7. Conduct 360	Robert, directors, managers, individual contributors	Week 8
	8. Prioritize individual and group development needs and support mechanisms • Identify & prioritize group-level development needs • Agree to training and non-instructional development methods	Robert, Thomas, Gretchen, Margaret, Janet	Week 9
	9. Conduct 360 feedback & development planning sessions • Small groups of directors, managers to understand individual results and to create development plans	Robert, directors, managers	Week 9
	10. Develop training and non-instructional interventions	Robert	Week 10
	11. Develop behavioral interview and performance evaluation tools & training	Robert	Week 12
Operations	12. Roll out training and non-instructional interventions	Robert, Thomas, Gretchen, Margaret, Janet	Week 6, 12
	13. Roll out behavioral interview, performance evaluation, and promotion processes and tools (training)	Robert, Thomas, Gretchen, Margaret, Janet	Week 13
	14. Support roll out with tracking and evaluation mechanisms	Robert, Thomas, Gretchen, Margaret, Janet	Week 14 onward

helped to build buy-in to the competency-based performance system process, and also to reinforce the commitment of Robert to his client's history, previous efforts, and decision-making. This can help to garner credibility, trust, and long-term commitment to the consultative relationship (Solomonson, 2012).

Competency Analysis

Robert facilitated DiversiCorp individual contributors, managers, and directors through a structured process to identify and prioritize manager and leader development needs at the competency level (e.g., Leadership Dimensions, ITIL competencies, Leadership Standards of Excellence). Again, it should be emphasized that Robert's job was specifically *not* to formally assess the validity of the competency sets that were in existence at the time of project. Rather, it was to integrate them with practical tools to help with the immediate organizational needs of hiring, employee engagement, and performance management. However, the process of data collection and analysis, and specifically the attempt to align critical incidents to existing competencies, helped to informally suggest the appropriateness and comprehensiveness of the previous work identifying competencies.

Data were collected from multiple sources and levels within the DiversiCorp-ROHS organization. Additionally, Robert collected both quantitative and qualitative data to ensure reliability, validity, and richness. Table 2 describes the data sources for the analysis.

During each individual interview, the 8 directors ranked the importance of 10 ROHS competencies, and then ranked the strength of both directors and managers in these competencies. Similarly, the directors ranked the importance of 11 DiversiCorp competencies towards IT success, and then ranked the strength of directors, managers, and individual contributors in these competencies. Directors then described examples of directors and managers demonstrating their top three ranked ROHS competencies. In this way, Robert was able to: 1) rank director perceptions of relative competency importance; 2) determine the perceived strength and weaknesses of each competency by job level; 3) prioritize which competencies should be focused on to maximize value to the organization; and 4) build examples of "effective" behavioral examples of key leadership competencies within the DiversiCorp-ROHS

Table 2. Data sources, participation level, sample size, and type

Data Source	Participation Level	Sample Size	Method/Type
Directors	100%	N=8	Interview/Qualitative
Directors	100%	N=8	Focus Group/Qualitative
Managers	100%	N=20	Focus Groups/Qualitative
Individual Contributors	17% (randomly selected)	n=40 (N=260)	Focus Groups/Qualitative
Directors	100%	N=8	Survey/Quantitative
Managers	100%	N=20	Survey/Quantitative

group (the *performance requirements*). The next step was to conduct focus groups that reflected all three levels of employees at DiversiCorp – directors, managers, individual contributors. Robert used the results of the director interviews to create focus group tools that included a prioritized list of competencies from DiversiCorp's leadership team. The director-level focus group was designed to capture directors' perspective regarding the challenges that both directors and managers faced on the job. Table 3 lists some of the results of their work. This list would be used to help determine potential needs for any instructional and non-instructional components to the project in the future.

Managers were organized into three focus groups, and further grouped into pairs or triads to brainstorm effective and ineffective examples of both director and manager behaviors in regards to specific ITIL competencies. For example, one pair of managers were tasked with listing specific examples of how a director would be

Table 3. Director feedback on biggest challenges

Level	Challenges
Director	• Honest open discussions. • Collaboration; making managers accountable to collaborate and solve problems. • Need to break down silos. • Directors are not strategic—all strategy is ROHS-driven. • Medical process is different than IT process. Justification between these two processes. Conflict between these two. Director has to justify these things. • Leadership: having the courage to take steps forward and inspiring team to take those steps. • Accountability/getting over victim mentality and going on offensive. • Moral leader/integrity. Doing what's best for organization and people. • Truly understanding how and why the technology we provide/support is used all the way through work processes. • Letting go of control over technical stuff and day to day details. • Keeping people engaged, excited, and feeling appreciated when they haven't gotten a raise in several years. • Organizational - stuck between ROHS and DiversiCorp. Real loyalty is to ROHS. • Pace makes planning difficult.
Manager	• DiversiCorp doesn't offer management training. • Different manager styles. • Technical mind-set of technical people. • Many have little management experience and if from outside we need to ensure that we hire with experience. • Used to have some management training from DiversiCorp, but now is not offered. • Managers need to form relationships with other managers. • Burning people out - working on weekends • Collaboration. • have moved technical people into manager roles. • We have some overlap in technology, so can be a power struggle. • ROHS decision making--ROHS can be slow to make decisions. • Don't always know what our budget is. • Lots of issues with network space--dire need of structure, process, discipline.

effective and not effective at "Listening and Collaborating." Similarly, they were tasked with listing specific examples of how a manager would be effective and not effective at "Encouraging Participation." Table 4 shows the results of these data. In this way, managers as a group provided feedback on all ITIL competencies for both director and manager behaviors.

Individual contributors were selected randomly from the DiversiCorp employee database by Margaret for their participation in one of six difference focus groups. At these focus group meetings, the individual contributors were grouped into pairs or triads to list effective and ineffective examples of both manager and individual contributor behaviors in regards to specific DiversiCorp competencies. As an ex-

Table 4. Manager focus group data on behavioral examples

Level	Data	
Director	**Competency – *"Listen and Collaborate Effectively"***	
	Example of "Effective Behaviors"	**Example of "Ineffective Behaviors"**
	Conducts regular meetings with teams and peers to keep abreast of issues or concerns on an organizational level.	Having a closed door policy where there is only one way communication.
	Being a mentor and coaching the chosen protégés.	Micromanaging the entire chain of authority thereby bypassing the right channel (implies lack of trust).
	Being readily available to subordinates to discuss any issues, concerns or new ideas.	Not showing up for important strategic planning meetings.
	Keeping the team focused and well informed of strategic directions of the organization.	Not building relationships with customers, partners, vendors, and employees.
	Delegating authority to managers to chose the correct path to lead their specific group.	Making unilateral decisions without listening to input from team, colleagues, other teams.
Manager	**Competency – *"Encouraging Participation"***	
	Example of "Effective" Behaviors	**Example of "Ineffective" Behaviors**
	Encouraging brainstorming sessions for new initiatives or problem solving- No bad ideas.	Not letting employees talk during meetings (monologue from manager).
	Enticing participation from reluctant employees by coaching them to actively participate.	Not conducting periodic staff dialogues.
	Creating actionable items based on teams input and brainstorming (effective decision making).	Discouraging ideas in a mixed forum meaning other teams, vendors, etc.
	Conducting timely one-on-one meetings with employees to discuss any issues, ideas.	Leverage and rotate resources for different functional areas within the group.
	Creating an environment where employees have ownership of key initiatives or projects. E.g. assigning a specific goal to the employee.	Not truly listening to ideas from the team (cutting them off in meeting or playing on phone, etc).

ample, one pair of individual contributors were asked to brainstorm both effective and ineffective examples of behaviors around the competencies of "Committed," "Meticulous," and "Innovative." In other cases, a pair of individual contributors created a list of single exemplars of each competency (see Table 5). These 10 competencies were developed by DiversiCorp prior to the project and provided to Robert, who confirmed their validity (though not necessarily their comprehensiveness) by drawing many examples of each from varied employees and focus groups.

In summary, through this data collection Robert identified key competencies at all three employee levels with full stakeholder involvement, indeed even stakeholder responsibility, because the stakeholders were the people who created the ranked lists and performance requirements. Importantly, these performance requirements demonstrated the competencies *specific to the needs of ITIL, ROHS, and DiversiCorp*, not simply generic ones. As a final part of needs assessment within the Design phase, Robert also reviewed existing hiring, promotion, and performance evaluation systems in order to identify where and how the competency-based system could help to improve them. Thus, the competency-based "operating system" provided a foundation for aligning multiple HR applications via the core set of competencies.

Table 5. Individual contributor focus group data on behavioral examples

Competency	Example of "Effective" Behavior	Example of "Ineffective" Behavior
Positive	In a meeting Manager calls out individuals that did good work.	In a meeting Manager calls out individuals that were performing poorly.
Accountable	Engineer taking ownership of a requested Change Control.	Failing to meet customers' expectations.
Communicator	Engineer mentoring individuals that want to learn a new technology.	Failing to communicate with customer or leadership.
Responsive	Engineer responding in a timely manner to IT requests.	On call engineer not answering pages or phone after hours.
Proud	Engineer taking ownership of a new cabling standard.	Not attending team building exercise.
Respectful	Engineer securing laptop while in the presence of patient.	Engineer leaving laptop unlocked in view of guests and patients.
Committed	Engineers assisted other team members proactively.	Engineer working on an island or in a bubble without outside assistance.
Meticulous	Reporting a spill to proper personnel to prevent injury.	Ignoring hazard and caution signs.
Innovative	Manager supplying new tools to engineers to help promote innovation.	Manager not considering or allowing new ideas to be heard or tested.
Diversity	Team members sharing ideas.	Team member not participating in discussions.

CURRENT CHALLENGES FACING THE ORGANIZATION

Robert collected, organized, and analyzed the data over the course of several weeks and then sat down with Thomas, Margaret, and Janet to review the findings. Many of the DiversiCorp team's initial perceived needs for IT managers were supported, especially those that had to do with improving the skills and knowledge of DiversiCorp employees who were promoted from within (e.g. such as hiring/interviewing skills). The breadth of data collected also pointed to other needs within the organization that address performance gaps at the individual, process, and organizational levels (Rummler, 2006). It should be noted that the purpose of this project was to focus on issues to improve performance, and despite the following summary of challenges there were a great deal of positive trends and successes that are not mentioned.

Individual Level

Directors were challenged to keep managers and individual contributors engaged, excited, and feeling appreciated. This was a demanding task, especially in a fast-paced environment that emphasizes business decisions over interpersonal ones. Though managers wanted to have honest and open discussions with directors, there was often a failure to communicate strategy and direction change. There were directors who had a "closed door policy" which reinforced one-way communication and unilateral decisions that excluded input from the team, colleagues, and other teams. Managers felt a need for a sharing of positive accomplishments with departments and teams coming from directors. Directors (and managers) needed to let go of control of technical work and day-to-day details, thus empowering individual contributors to do their jobs. There was a sense from managers of directors micromanaging the entire process chain thereby bypassing the right channels. Some directors had a lack of leadership experience as well as a lack of understanding of how and why the technology was used for ROHS all the way through work processes. Lastly, many managers felt that director decisions were often based on emotions rather than the skills of rational decision-making.

Managers are also faced with challenges. There was a feeling of insufficient sharing of information, wherein periodic staff dialogues allowed employees to be "in the know." But even when these dialogues did occur there was a tendency of managers to "monologue," and discourage ideas in a mixed forum meeting (with other departments or vendors), or not truly listening to ideas from the team (by cutting off the comments or being inattentive, such as being focused on a cell phone). This lack of openness was paralleled in some managers by being disengaged or disinterested in important business events. There seemed also to be an absence of responsibility taking, both in an unwillingness to accept responsibility for corrective actions from directors and also by buying time or delaying actions until issues resolved themselves or were escalated to directors. These issues contributed to the feeling that managers were unaware of the impact of their actions, and also unaware of how they were perceived by colleagues and individual contributors because of them.

Individual contributors have the task of making the hardware, software, and materials work. But, similar to both directors and managers, communication is a challenge. Often there was a lack of communication with the ROHS client or with DiversiCorp leadership. Email, which is the primary form of communication, was sometimes procrastinated and note responded to for several days. Similarly, voice mails went unresponded to for many days when the message came from another team. In meetings certain team members did not participate in the discussions, even though they were encouraged to do so. Accountability was an issue; teams had looked for a scapegoat instead of a solution during a root cause analysis of a technical problem. There was a feeling among some individual contributors that others were knowledge hoarders, and did not offer cross-training for self-preservation purposes. Finally, there were issues with attitudinal or motivational aspects, such as looking for the negative in a system instead of suggesting improvements, being non-enthusiastic, and having a "good enough" mentality.

Process Level

Directors were responsible for setting the standards for the organization, but often there existed unclear expectations and consequences, both in setting them and in communicating them to managers and individual contributors. This lack of clarity, especially in term of communicating client wants, worked to disengage the "IT do'ers." It also pushed the teams to have a lack of collaboration in which managers were not accountable to collaborate and solve problems. Instead of engaging in a pro-active continuous improvement process, improvement was often motivated by crisis. Even though DiversiCorp uses the ITIL framework as its service management process, the medical process is different than IT process. There was conflict between these processes and directors needed to do better at justifying the conflict between these two. Lastly, due to the pace and demands of the environment, directors tended to focus more on the beginning of initiatives than the rest of the process. This left a vacuum in a focus on follow through, initiative completion, and participation.

Managers often fell into the trap of letting their technical expertise trump their managerial responsibilities. This meant that they would often "roll up their sleeves" and jump in to a technical problem instead of letting individual contributors solve the problem. This undermined the teams feeling a sense of trust from managers as well as caused managers to lose focus on their managerial tasks. Also, there was a feeling that meetings were not standardized and were either effective or ineffective based on which manager was running it. In the cases of "bad meetings," managers had publicly called out individuals who were performing poorly, and had not considered or allowed new ideas to be heard.

Individual contributors had many process issues around change control. The first was team members who make undocumented changes; quietly fixing a problem, but not notifying team members of the problem. Another was not following the change testing protocol – applying changes to an IT system without first testing them in a controlled test environment. Also there were issues with following communication milestones; for example, when a change control was scheduled for a specific time window but required additional time due to complications. The team working on the change failed to contact the helpdesk to extend the change window, and as a result support tickets were generated, making more and unnecessary work for the team and other teams. There were also process issues around security. Individual contributors had used non-encrypted usb drives, putting patient data at risk (and exposing the organization to HIPAA violations). Similarly, individual contributors had left patient documents on the printer and left laptops unlocked in view of guests and patients.

Organizational Level

Directors were placed as heads of individual departments. Even though there was great deal of necessary cross-team functioning there existed silo-ing within DiversiCorp that diminished a sense of team and minimized effective communication. It was the directors' task to reduce this silo effect. There was also a strong feeling at all levels of the organization that it was a culture of "maintaining the status quo." Innovation is a core component of what DiversiCorp does - indeed it is a competency for team members - yet this culture was antithetical to innovation. Directors often felt the pressure of "being stuck in a middle position between DiversiCorp and their ROHS client." But as one director pointed out, "our real loyalty is to ROHS." There was a need at the most senior level of DiversiCorp to clarify this tension for directors, so that it could then be disseminated throughout the organization. Many directors felt that they were not strategic; rather all strategy came from ROHS and directors were simply heads of tactical units to implement that strategy. Finally, with the fast growth and requirements for new personnel most of the focus of HR had been on hiring. This had left existing employees, some of whom have not seen a pay raise in years, feel unappreciated and potentially leading to low motivation and turn-over.

Managers had the vital role of leading teams. There was a perception that managers needed to improve their leadership of having the courage to take steps forward and inspiring their teams to take those steps. Accountability was a recurring issue at DiversiCorp, and managers had been fearful for speaking up regarding accuracy to avoid accountability. Lastly, some individual contributors felt that there was reluctance on the part of managers to allow for healthy work-life balance, for example being able to use vacation time when needed.

Individual contributors were also affected by the "maintaining the status quo" culture. Many felt that things were done because "that's the way we've always done it." One employee noted that "we can't do that here statements are rooted in past failures, but overshadow the spirit of innovation." Additionally, the workforce at DiversiCorp, especially at the individual contributor level, was diverse. Yet there seemed to be instances where intolerance occurred. For example, opinions were discounted of those who were not of the same religious belief system, jokes were made that were ethnically insensitive in public areas, and managers did not learn how to correctly pronounce an employee's name. Though this intolerance manifests at the individual contributor level, a focus on diversity needs to be an organizational imperative.

SOLUTIONS AND RECOMMENDATIONS

Robert focused on solutions that created meaningful and measurable outcomes for DiversiCorp-ROHS. Ultimately, these outcomes were about supporting the ROHS vision of transforming lives and communities. To accomplish this, the team wanted to:

- Ensure they aligned leadership development efforts with the ROHS service culture competencies.
- Integrate ITIL, ROHS, and DiversiCorp competencies.
- Provide training, tools, support to directors, managers, and individual contributors to continually improve service.

Robert recommended a phased approach in which solutions could be rolled out over time while focusing on the most urgent needs immediately. This two-phase approach allowed core work to be done initially - defining the DiversiCorp "competency operating system" - and then designing and developing the interventions necessary to bridge DiversiCorp's performance gaps. The design of this phased roll-out was as follows:

Phase I

For Phase I of the solution Robert recommended:

- Development of the DiversiCorp "competency operating system."
- Behavioral interview training.
- Supporting tools.

The DiversiCorp "competency operating system" addressed all three levels of employee's: directors, managers, and individual contributors. In essence, it specifically identified clear behavioral examples of performance for each level by using a critical incident approach to determine "effective" and "ineffective" behaviors. Once this "competency operating system" was developed it could offer the benefits of clear descriptions of performance expectations to existing employees, improved hiring, strengthening the pool of potential managers and directors, and reducing turnover.

Because DiversiCorp was still experiencing fast growth and the need to hire new employees coupled with the fact that existing hiring managers did not have the skills and knowledge to conduct high quality legally-valid interviews, Robert next provided behavioral interview training.

These facilitated training sessions were for both managers and directors and contained content around hiring and the law, the DiversiCorp-ROHS IT Behavioral Competencies, how to developing behavioral questions, and also role-play practice interviewing using these new techniques. Table 6 displays an example of a behavioral/competency-based rating scale for managers. For this phase of the project the team created:

Table 6. Example of behavioral/competency-based rating scale for manager

Rating	Behavioral Example	Behavioral Example
5-- High Performance	Models the desired behaviors and develop the relationships to be regarded as a trusted leader	Makes immediate tactical decisions to deliver IT services knowing that the strategic plan could be re-aligned at a later date.
4		
3-- Expected	Resolves functional challenges and address opportunities by using appropriate functional tool and utilizing methods such as the Plan Do Check Act Model to examine evidence.	Validates and advocate the needs of end user. E.g., Creates value through the use of available technology.
2		
1--Low	Relies on inconsistent criteria to select candidates instead of objective evidence of qualifications (e.g. emotions, nepotism) they reward inconsistent delivery of service and incompetence while expecting the A player to stay engaged and appreciated.	Places blame for inadequate service delivery on others (colleagues, end users, customers)

- Behavioral/competency-based rating scales – Directors.
- Behavioral/ competency-based rating scales – Managers.
- Behavioral interview guide.
- Interview Job Aid – legal & illegal questions.
- Director training materials.
- Manager training materials.

Phase II

For Phase II of the solution Robert recommended:

- Integration of "competency operating system" with unique employee development needs.
- Alignment of "competency operating system" to performance evaluation, promotion, job descriptions, and training support.

Once the "competency operating system" had been developed and both directors and managers had been familiarized with it, all DiversiCorp staff could use it as a framework for understanding expectations, measuring performance, and identifying areas for improvement. Individual performance plans were developed and directors and managers could rely on on-going mentoring and support from Robert initially, and internal DiversiCorp employees on an on-going basis.

Directors and managers were facilitated through a 360 feedback tool built around the "competency operating system." For these two levels of staff this provided a key input towards the development of individualized development plans. Also, during this phase additional classroom training sessions were developed around topics such as business skills, communication skills, and other topics.

Key deliverables for Phase II included:

- 360 feedback tool.
- Individual development plans for leaders and managers.
- Prioritized group development needs (e.g. soft skills, communication, business skills, etc.).
- Promotion process and tools for leaders and managers.
- Enhanced performance evaluation tools.
- Leader and manager training based upon DiversiCorp priorities.

For example, the 5-point rating scales were used not only by interviewers to rank interviewees' answers to specific questions during a job interview, but they were also used for current employees' performance evaluations. Gaps between the desired levels of performances behaviors (e.g. a "Low" ranking in the Maturity scale) would be bridged through a custom coaching, mentoring, or training program.

The outcomes of these efforts included not only customized performance plans, but also updated job descriptions with key responsibilities and competencies. Director and manager skills sets were also enhanced. These leaders were able to hire better performers who had specific performance expectations which helped to drive accountability. Importantly, DiversiCorp also sent a message to ROHS about their commitment to on-going improved service performance.

REFERENCES

Arraj, A. 2013. *ITIL: The Basics. Best Management Practice*. Retrieved from http://www.best-management-practice.com/gempdf/ITIL_The_Basics.pdf

Gilbert, T. F. (1978). Human competence: Engineering worthy performance. *NSPI Journal, 17*(9), 19–27.

Guerra-Lopez, I. J. (2007). Evaluating impact: Evaluation and continual improvement for performance improvement practitioners (Vol. VI). Amherst, MA: HRD Press.

Rummler, G. A. (2006). The anatomy of performance: A frame-work for consultants. In J. Pershing (Ed.), *Handbook of human performance technology: Principles, practices, and potential* (3rd ed., pp. 986–1007). San Francisco, CA: Pfeiffer.

Solomonson, W. L. (2012). Trust and the client–consultant relationship. *Performance Improvement Quarterly, 25*(3), 53–80. doi:10.1002/piq.21123 doi:10.1002/piq.21123

ADDITIONAL READING

Applebaum, S. H., & Steed, A. J. (2005). The critical success factors in the client-consulting relationship. Journal of Management Development, 24(1), 68–93.

Bryson, L. (1951). Notes on a Theory of Advice. Political Science Quarterly, 66(3), 321–339.

Buchen, I. H. (2001). The trusted advisor revealed. Consulting to Management, 12(2), 35–37.

Cripe, E. J. (2012). Competency Development Guide. Fort Lauderdale, FL: Workitect, Inc.

Davies, I. K. (1975). Some Aspects of a Theory of Advice: The Management of an Instructional Developer-Client, Evaluator-Client, Relationship. *Instructional Science, 3,* 351–373.

Lucia, A. D., & Lepinger, R. (1999). *The art and science of competency models: Pinpointing critical success factors in organizations.* Hoboken, NJ: Pfeiffer.

Ganesan, S. (1994). Determinants of Long-Term orientation in Buyer-Seller Relationships. *Journal of Marketing, 58*(2), 1–19.

Gilbert, T. F. (2007). *Human competence: Engineering worthy performance.* John Wiley & Sons.

Karantinou, K. M., & Hogg, M. K. (2001). Exploring Relationship Management in Professional Services: A Study of Management Consultancy. *Journal of Marketing Management, 17,* 263–286.

Kessler, R. (2012). *Competency-based interviews,* (rev). Pompton Plains, NJ: Career Press.

Lusch, R. F., & Brown, J. R. (1996). Interdependency, contracting, and relational behavior in marketing channels. *Journal of Marketing, 60*(4), 19–38.

Rummler, G. A. (2007). *Serious Performance Consulting According to Rummler.* San Francisco: Pfeiffer.

Pershing, J. (Ed.), *Handbook of human performance technology: Principles, practices, and potential* (3rd ed.). San Francisco, CA: Pfeiffer.

Powers, T. L., & Reagan, W. R. (2007). Factors influencing successful buyer–seller relationships. *Journal of Business Research, 60,* 1234–1242.

Karantinou, K. M., & Hogg, M. K. (2001). Exploring Relationship Management in Professional Services: A Study of Management Consultancy. *Journal of Marketing Management, 17,* 263–286.

Robinson, D. G., & Robinson, J. C. (2008). *Performance Consulting: A Practical Guide for HR and Learning Professionals* (2nd ed.). San Francisco: Berrett-Koehler.

Sanghi, S. (2007). *The handbook of competency mapping: Understanding, designing, and implementing competency models in organizations.* Thousand Oaks, CA: Sage.

Solomonson, W. L. (2012). Trust and the client–consultant relationship. *Performance Improvement Quarterly, 25*(3), 53–80.

Smart, B. D. (2012). *Topgrading: The proven hiring and promoting method that turbocharges company performance* (3rd ed.). New York: Penguin Group.

KEY TERMS AND DEFINITIONS

Behavioral Interview: A structured hiring interview within which candidates are asked specific questions that elicit specific examples of previous performance in situations similar to those that they would encounter on the job, and based upon specific competencies known to be required for job performance.

Competencies: Knowledge, Skills, Abilities, and Other Characteristics translated into specific job- and organization-related behaviors.

Competency-Based System: A collection of competencies aligned with an organization's strategic direction (vis a vis, vision, mission, core values, etc.) that collectively align human resource applications such as recruiting, staffing, employee development, performance management, etc. with that strategic direction.

Critical Incident Technique: A method for acquiring examples by asking responders to provide exemplar situations that describe a particular object of study/interest. In this case, employees were asked to provide examples of "effective" and "ineffective" behaviors of specific competencies.

Maturity: The qualities and behavior expected of a reasonable adult; experience, discretion, responsibility, reliability, wisdom and emotional intelligence.

Needs Assessment: A systematic process to determine gaps in results, a prioritization of those gaps, and determine solutions to bridge them.

Performance: Meaningful actions resulting in measurable results.

Performance Consulting: Engaging with clients (internal or external) for the purposes of improving individual, process, and/or organizational performance.

Qualitative Data: Collected data which describes non-measurable factors.

Quantitative Data: Collected data which defines measurable factors.

Chapter 13
Branding Beyond Logo and Colors:
Case Study of FITC's Evidence Based Transformation

Lucy Surhyel Newman
FITC, Nigeria

EXECUTIVE SUMMARY

This case study presents FITC's evidence based application of ISPI's 10 Standards of Performance Improvement and theoretical insights from the author's doctoral dissertation to preposition a special purpose not for profit professional services organization in Africa. It describes the FITC mandate, FITC's trajectory and impact on identified stakeholders; reviews the various initiatives taken by FITC from May 2009 to May 2014, with a highlight of results attained. Thus, enabling the reader draw personal connections with interventions articulated in the organization. Consultants, Practitioners and Academics in the field of Performance Improvement, as well as those aspiring to these roles, would find this case study interesting.

ORGANIZATION BACKGROUND

The organization is Nigeria's FITC, otherwise known as the Financial Institutions Training Center, located within the Sub Saharan African region. The case study aligns with three critical organizational events. The first was the organization's maturity phase in view of the year 2009 being its 28th year of existence. The second was the

DOI: 10.4018/978-1-4666-8330-3.ch013

creation of a 2009-2014 strategy plan. The third was change in the organization's three permanent board roles by default and design – chairman, vice chairman, and the start of a five year contract employment of a new chief executive and managing director, the author of this chapter.

A close look at the updates to the mission and vision statements as well as core values as applicable to FITC as at close of 2008 and 2009 in Table 1 presents a high level perspectives.

FITC from Inception to 1990

FITC [also known as the Financial Institutions Training Center], was established in 1981 as a special purpose professional service organization. The decision to establish FITC was informed by a recommendation of the 1976 Okigbo Committee, a special committee established by the then Federal Government of Nigeria in 1976. The committee was to review the Nigerian Financial System, in search of a way to make the Nigerian Financial Services Sector emerge as a major driver of economic development for Nigeria. There was an acute shortage of managerial capability in the financial services sector at the time given dominance of the sector by foreign financial institutions, while citizens of Nigeria performed peripheral than core management and functional roles. The aspiration of the Federal Government, as indicated in the Pious Okigbo Committee's terms of reference, was that an institution be created to cater for the human capacity needs of the financial services sector in the short, medium and long term. As such, the committee's recommendation, as relevant to the

Table 1. Broad Corporate Direction Setting Variables

Corporate Variable	As at December 31, 2008	From December 31, 2009 - 2014
Mission Statement	"To be a provider of world class human capital development and advisory services to discerning clients, thereby adding value to their businesses"	"To provide best in class service quality and value to our stakeholders"
Vision Statement	"To be a Centre of excellence and the reference point in all matters relating to the acquisition, management and development of human capital needed to propel the Nigerian Financial System on a path to sustainable growth"	"To be the preferred provider of training, consulting and research services to the Financial Services Sector in West Africa by 2016"
Core values	• Professionalism • Transparency/Accountability • High ethical standard • Service quality • Teamwork	Acronym [**A-S-T--E-P**] • Accountability • Service • **Teamwork** • **Ethics** • **Professionalism**

creation of FITC, was that the Central Bank of Nigeria (CBN) should take initiative on this matter and accept responsibility to initiate and finance large scale training for the industry. The Federal Government accepted this recommendation and, via the Ministry of Finance, advised that the CBN take the initiative in consensus with all the licenced banks (under the auspices of the Nigerian Bankers' Committee), to set up the Financial Institutions Training Centre, known today as FITC. FITC came onto the Nigerian financial services scene as a special purpose organization and an aspired solution to a deep seated training and manpower development problem.

FITC was incorporated under the Company's Act of 1968 as a not-for-profit organization limited by guarantee, and it has been operational from September 1, 1981 to date. Its highest policy making body is the Board (formerly known as the Governing Council) which is chaired by the CBN's Deputy Governor, Financial System Stability, the Nigeria Deposit Insurance Corporation (NDIC) Managing Director/CEO serves as the Vice Chairman. Other members of the FITC Board are chosen from members of the Nigerian Bankers' Committee as well as one institutional representative from the cluster of Nigerian Universities and Management Development institutions on rotational basis of two years.

Originally, FITC was commissioned for training and manpower development in the financial services sector in general and the banking industry in particular. It is as such, a special purpose vehicle aimed at bringing dedicated focus to the acquisition, development, deployment, and management of the workforce in the financial services sector. It was also aimed at enhancing knowledge and skills required for effective practice of banking in Nigeria.

FITC's Turbulent Years and First Intervention in the Mid 1990s

With the exponential increase in the number of banks in the industry between 1986 and 1991, a large number of university degree and diploma holders were employed in banks, with many holding post-graduate qualifications in their areas of interest and expertise. The composition and profile of bankers changed drastically. They became highly educated and knowledgeable professionals, who were flashy, fashionable, and ambitious. The immediate challenge this posed to a human capacity development institution like FITC, was to grow its internal and external faculty to stay ahead of the new generation of bankers in service delivery. Besides, it was important for the existing bankers who were traditionally not graduates of banking related courses, but working in banks within grade categories from entry to board level, to acquire a wide range of knowledge and skills in areas including credit, banking operations, marketing, treasury and human resources management, amongst others, in order to help their institutions meet the increasing demands of modern banking and growing sophistication of customers.

For these reasons, FITC enhanced the content and delivery of its training pro-grammes to compare with off-shore courses in terms of quality and standards. It also engaged the services of consulting experts and employed many professionals in Banking, Accounting and Human Resources Management to grow its internal capacity. For instance, in 1991, nineteen staff were recruited to strengthen or comple-ment staff at various levels, and more office spaces were required. In 1992, twenty new staff were recruited bringing the total number of FITC staff to 105. Though this meant increased wages and overhead, it was without proportional increase in subscriptions or the internally generated revenue, as course fees were minimal and far below the market rate.

Meanwhile, by 1991, the Nigerian economy and the financial services sector were already passing through dire challenges. These included the increased pres-sures on the exchange rate with the parallel market premium rising to an all-time high of 60%, high fiscal deficits and inflation rate, aggressive monetary and credit expansion, and excess liquidity, all co-existing with increased incidence of distressed institutions and upward pressure on interest rates in the banking system.

A number of factors had led to this. Firstly, the deteriorating macroeconomic per-formance that persisted at that time was identified as a major factor that constrained the training budget of members and, consequently, impacted on the activities of FITC. By 1992, various economic indicators manifested in a downward economic trend, with GDP growth put at 3.6%. This further declined to 2.0% in 1993 and 1.3% in 1994. The low level of economic performance was aggravated by the political and social unrest that was generated by the June 12 imbroglio of 1993.

Between 1994 and 1995, the distress in the financial services sector had deep-ened, as many institutions became illiquid or technically insolvent or both. The CBN and NDIC resolved to revoke the licenses of some terminally distressed banks and some finance companies. Also, the failed Banks and Financial Malpractices Decree No. 18 of 1994 was promulgated to facilitate the recovery of debts owed to failed banks and penalise financial malpractices in banks. Due to this economic and industrial turbulence, many banks and non-bank financial institutions were faced with compressed operating margins. Their first line of action, as it seemed, was to rationalise training and cut back on the number of participants sponsored for various programmes, including those at FITC. The adverse effect of the systemic turbulence on FITC resulted in negative operating margins, accentuated by grossly inadequate receipts from members' subscriptions, some of whom were now distressed.

Other factors that contributed to the weak state of the institution in these turbulent years were a poor infrastructural base and unsuitable location (in the face of stiff competition); non-aggressive marketing of services; low staff morale, and weak and inefficient administrative structure and accounting systems. Given the fundamental nature of these internal problems and the reversal in the fortunes of the players in the financial services sector (the captive market of FITC), the need to revitalise and rejuvenate FITC became apparent. FITC also suffered an internal succession problem. The chief executive at that time was given a political appointment with the executive council of his state. He took a leave of absence, and a senior staff member was placed in an acting capacity at a very difficult time in the life of FITC. The person appointed was unprepared for the role, and had challenges dealing with the difficulties in FITC's operating environment.

Thus, the four-year period was dubbed the FITC's turbulent years. Turbulent not because of inability to execute its training calendar, as it ran a number of successful system-wide and in-plant programmes in the period. Rather it was because there was perennial economic turbulence that negatively impacted the sector, which demanded some fast strategic changes within FITC but somehow, business went on as usual. This was worsened by situational challenges in executive succession. FITC was literarily surviving on debts and needed be salvaged.

Concerned about how FITC might fulfil its mission in view of these challenges, the then Governing Council commissioned a firm of financial and management consultants to carry out a strategic study of FITC. This was to generate a scientific basis and direction for restructuring and repositioning FITC for sustainable delivery in human capacity development services in the industry. However, owing to the multiplier effect of the downturn in the nation's economy, and other internal challenges, FITC waded through some troubled waters in its operations from late 1992 to 1995.

By May 2009 when the author resumed as Chief Executive and Managing Director, FITC had matured into a viable professional services firm evident in its good reputation within the banking sector; policy advocacy role; institutionalized strategic management; successful collaborative international training programs with some international organizations; execution of major training and advisory services assignments for notable institutions and players in the financial services sector; and institutionalization of effective quality control process in its product design administration and delivery.

However, there were worrisome issues emerging in FITC's horizon prior to the author's resumption, which were concerns to the board, and the basis of discussions during the CEO interview processes. Obsolescence had started to creep into FITC's service delivery, infrastructure and approach to internal operations. Also, a corrosive corporate culture had crept in and staff turnover rates had been high, with abysmally low staff engagement as the corporate culture was getting increasingly autocratic. As such with the completion of this 13-year term, the foundation was laid for the next stage in the FITC journey. Taking FITC to the next level would put it on the same level and able to compete with the top training and consulting firms in the world. For FITC to take a place among the giants of the industry, more work still needed to be done. Several issues and challenges were impeding FITC from reaching its true potential because, since the banking industry consolidation of 2005/2006, the sector had gotten more sophisticated and FITC needed to remain value-added to its stakeholders and its primary constituency.

After three months of rigorous scrutiny of the situation from the author's resumption in May 2009 and issues described here-in, the author knew FITC had to immediately embark on another transformational agenda after the one initiated with the resumption of the author's predecessor in 1996, in order to move FITC to a higher level given developments in its sector, thus making it continually relevant to its stakeholders. As such, this case study is based on some findings derived from Newman's (2008) qualitative grounded theory doctoral dissertation, as well as application of the ISPI 10 Standards of Performance Improvement. The dissertation being a grounded theory study, exposed the author to the concept of open and axial coding in derivation of a grounded theory, as described in Creswell (2002). This is because as at the time the author took over as CEO, FITC was a mature organization in need of a transformation that can take it back to another round of the introductory phase of its corporate life cycle, thus deferring the natural process of decay and decline, post maturity. So based on the author's internalization of the 10 Standards of Performance Improvement and findings from the Newman (2008) study, FITC was led through a repositioning intervention, armed with all the required data, barely three months into my term as CEO. This case study is therefore a description of the transformation of FITC over a period of five years.

Diagnostics of FITC as of May/July 2009

Upon the author's resumption and in line with transformation plans promised the FITC Board during the executive selection process, the first six of the 10 ISPI standards of performance improvement were applied as follows:

Standard 1: Focus on results or outcomes.
Standard 2: Take a systemic view.
Standard 3: Add value.
Standard 4: Work in partnership with clients and stakeholders.
Standard 5: Determine need or opportunity.
Standard 6: Determine the cause and performance requirements.

Specific interventions as aligned to the first six standards are:

- An intermediary May – December 2009 work plan approved by the board [Standard 4].

- A detailed review of FITC's performance from inception to 2000 and then in a separate block, for the period 2000 to 2009 [Standard 1].
- A detailed review of the outgoing CEO's handover notes [Standard 3].
- A review of level of the key thrust of the inherited 2006 -2010 corporate strategy plan and level of attainment as at May 2009 [Standard 5].
- A review of the 1978 report of the Pious Okigbo Committee [Standard 2].
- Board minutes for the period dating back 10 years from 2000 to 2009 [Standard 6].
- The new CEO's personal review of individual staff confidential files [Standards 3 and 4].

Based on findings from these, it became expedient to run an anonymous employee engagement survey, to generate additional contextual scientific data, which was incidentally, the first employee survey ever done in the then 28 year old FITC. FITC introduced the annual staff engagement survey in 2009, to address the needs and interest of the institution's greatest asset, the staff, whose commitment and morale at the time were perceived to be at the lowest ebb. Since then, the survey has proved to be an effective instrument in eliciting staff inputs in many management decisions that have motivated staff, re-engineered the institution and redefined strategy, processes, culture, technology, communication, leadership and human resources management. The staff engagement survey aimed at requesting information and suggestions from staff, to assist management in evaluating and enhancing staff welfare and career in FITC, performance management, staff development, workplace suitability, leadership and motivation, as well as workplace culture.

The staff engagement survey parameters revealed the following situations:

1. **Performance Management:** Nearly 40% of staff did not know of any pre-agreed performance measures and 60% of respondents rated FITC performance appraisal system unfair or poor. It was even more disturbing when the data showed that 58 staff of FITC out of 61 could not agree on when the last appraisal was carried out, while 67.2% of staff felt it was between 6-12 months ago, 19% said it was in the last six months. Some said it was over a year ago. This confusion and obvious contradiction in the date of last appraisal suggest staff's high level of apathy to the exercise. The summary of staff's additional comments was that appraisal in FITC was not based on merit, as there was no level playing ground. This validated the need to review the performance management system. It was therefore, necessary to demonstrate key performance indicators across all levels so that they become understood, tangible, realistic and achievable – so that staff could truly relate with them.

2. **Staff Development:** Available data indicated that FITC was very poor in training its own staff. When staff were asked if they had been given adequate training for job performance, 69% of respondents either said "No, Somewhat, Can't say" or did not respond at all. On the level of contributions of available types of training to their (staff) development, only "On-the-Job training" and personal investment in self were seen to have contributed significantly. Others, like overseas training, were either not applicable to many staff or did not contribute much. About 70% of staff considered FITC training programme for staff as inadequate for achieving a high level of performance. This majority suggested an urgent need to match staff training with job requirements. Deliberate effort was therefore necessary to utilize various channels to identify the training needs for individuals and groups, and match these with learning options and FITC's training budget.

3. **Welfare and Career:** The rating given to FITC in 2009 on six factors relating to staff welfare and development, showed that FITC was very weak on its ability to retain high quality employees and on teamwork across departments. FITC was also rated low in caring about employees and average on appreciating diversity amongst staff. As regards to staff satisfaction with their jobs, the data showed nearly 30% of them were dissatisfied. This was high enough to checkmate FITC's progress in many ways. 43% of staff were not sure of staying in FITC in the next three years. Of those, most indicated that they would only be willing to stay there if the working environment improved. Surprisingly, 77.6% of respondents would recommend FITC as a great place to work. The question then was, "If close to 80% of staff believe in FITC and could proudly recommend it as a great place to work, why would they not want to stay there and work?

4. **Workplace Suitability:** Results indicated that staff were not satisfied with the following in FITC workplace: Catering Services at the Staff Canteen; Restrooms' Condition; Power Generation/Availability; Staff Bus Scheme; Health Insurance Scheme. Staff also believed that the provided channels of internal communication were not effective in FITC.

5. **Culture Assessment:** Culture assessment revealed the following;
   a. FITC leadership was perceived as not displaying behaviours and attitudes that depict FITC's core values.
   b. FITC leadership was perceived as weak in treating staff with respect, consideration and courtesy.

c.   Staff's level of trust for one another in the workplace was perceived to be low and there was a feeling that human resources management was not practiced in line with policy.

d.   FITC executives were perceived as not always consistent in what they said and did.

e.   FITC executives were perceived to lack sufficient skills comparable to the best obtainable in other organizations.

f.   Supervisors and executives were perceived as not committed to personally developing and improving themselves.

g.   Supervisors, executives and FITC's leadership were perceived not to demonstrate sufficient commitment to developing skill of supervised staff.

h.   Decision making in FITC was perceived not to be based on merit.

i.   It was perceived that supervisors did not always build "ownership' by involving others in determining how to achieve shared objectives and seldom encouraged individuals to take their own decisions with regard to their jobs.

Based on the engagement survey and other observations, FITC faced additional issues in 2009:

- **Unhealthy Staff Turnover Rate:** As at ending of 2007 and 2008, FITC had 30.9% and 18.6% staff turnover respectively.
- **Rigid Culture:** The staff came across as very stiff, not open and free in sharing their ideas and opinions, for fear of failure and being fired.
- **Bureaucracy:** There were a lot of unnecessary paper work and processes that delayed decision making, most of which did not add value.

The findings from the 2009 staff engagement survey, which was FITC's first ever staff survey in its 28 years of existence, laid the foundation to many of the internal capacity interventions that fed into the 2009-2014 strategy plan. FITC has so far deployed annual staff surveys and kept track of impact of policies introduced at each survey cycle and the transition of findings in the 2009, 2010, 2011 and 2013 are presented in Table 2 within this case study. For 2012, FITC participated in an external survey, the Great Place To Work [GPTW] survey and ranked 7th great place to work, out of 225 companies in Nigeria, FITC being the only not for profit organization in the top 20 organizations.

Table 2. FITC's Employee Demographics from 2009 to 2013 Staff Surveys

S/N	Concerns	2009 (%)	2010 (%)	2011 (%)	2013 (%)
1.	Male Population	60.3	63.2	63	60.7
2.	Female Population	39.7	36.8	37	39.3
3.	Between 26 & 40 years of Age	67.3	61.5	68.4	59.0
4.	Less than 50 years of Age (< 50)	96.6	94.7	91.3	85.3
5.	Above 50 years of Age	3.4	5.3	8.7	14.8
6.	5 - 10 years Post Qualification Experience (PQE)	20.7	22.8	30	42.6
7.	10 - 30 years Post Qualification Experience (PQE)	39.7	38.6	43.8	47.5
8.	Between 5 & 15 years' Service in FITC	24.1	29.8	43.8	72.1
9.	Professional Staff	62	67.6	66.6	52.5
10.	Junior Staff	38	32.4	33.4	31.2
11.	Degree Holders with PG Qualifications	48.2	54.4	60	55.7
12	Annual Staff Turnover [2007 - 30.9%, 2008 – 18.6%]	8.62	3.45	3.28	1.67
13.	**Total Permanent Staff**	**62**	**59**	**60**	**61**

SETTING THE STAGE

FITC Leadership from Inception to Date

Indications provided in the background section of this case study showed that FITC's existing status as an over 3 decades old institution in a sector and jurisdiction where corporate mortality rates are high comes with many advantages. First, FITC has lived through various seasons of the operating environment while making FITC's own internal adjustments and helping its stakeholders navigate their own paths. Second, FITC's continued improvement through multi-layered cycles of corporate transformation from inception to date has partly ensured that in spite of dynamisms in the environment, it has continued to fulfil its mandate.

Traditionally, board and executive level staff succession has based on lessons learned in the mid-1990s, become a critical factor for the owner institutions, and the FITC memorandum and articles of association made provisions for permanent membership of the board to reside within the roles of the chairman and vice chairman of the board, as well as the chief executive, with an additional 3 permanent members. The remainder of the board members serve two yearly terms on rotation amongst institutional members of FITC. As such, FITC has benefitted from successive terms of highly committed leaders at its board level, from inception to date, as detailed below. However, based on the survey findings, it appeared this strength of leadership did not drill down to the operational level. As such, this discovery informed the updates of the staff handbook to include whistle blowing, collaborative decision making by various committees including Management Committee and Procurement Committee at the Management Level.

CASE DESCRIPTION

Theoretical Frameworks and Concepts Applied

As earlier indicated, the theories applied to the FITC transformation process based on the Newman (2008) study include:

- Bertalanffy's (1972) General Systems Theory within the context of Khun's (1974) model.
- The Adult Learning Theory (1970) as extended by Speck (1996).
- Both theoretical contexts were taken within the focus of the Malcom Baldridge Model for Performamce Excellence 2007 and the ISPI 10 Standards of Performance Improvement to get FITC to its present status and ensure continued improvement in the years to come.

The 2007 Malcolm Baldrige Model for Performance Excellence was adapted for FITC's transition, in terms of aspired culture variables. Core values and concepts foundational to the seven Baldrige criteria include visionary leadership, customer-driven excellence, valuing employees and partners, management by fact, and a focus on results while creating value. Table 3 below presets a high level listing of the standards and criteria applied in a complimentary manner to provide some degree of iteration of interventions applies in the case study.

The Baldrige 2007 criteria for performance excellence were adopted as the 'essence' of the new FITC Culture deal with corporate and service culture issues identified in the surveys and these 7 criteria were validated by applying the ISPI standards 1-4 and 6-8 with integration into competency and mentoring based career progression in the performance cycle, while ISPI standards 9 & 10 were integrated into management and board processes at the management and board committee as well as board processes to track performance and make adjustments as deemed necessary during the financial year and at the end of each strategy plan cycle.

Table 3. Broad Corporate Direction Setting Variables

ISPI 10 Standards for Performance Improvement		Malcom Baldridge 2007 Criteria for Performance Excellence	
Standard 1	Focus on results or outcomes	Criteria 1	Leadership
Standard 2	Take a systemic view	Criteria 2	Strategic planning
Standard 3	Add value	Criteria 3	Customer and market focus
Standard 4	Work in partnership with clients and stakeholders	Criteria 4	Measurement, analysis and knowledge management
Standard 5	Determine the need or opportunity	Criteria 5	Workforce focus
Standard 6	Determine the cause and performance requirements	Criteria 6	Operation focus
Standard 7	Design the solution including evaluation	Criteria 7	Results
Standard 8	Develop the solution and test its feasibility		
Standard 9	Implement the solution		
Standard 10	Evaluate the results and impacts		

Therefore, the 10 ISPI standards of performance improvement that applied across the entire transformation process include;

- Focusing on results and helping clients focus on results at each intervention.
- Looking at situations systemically taking into consideration, the larger context including competing pressures, resource constraints, and anticipated change.
- Seeking to add value in how FITC executes projects and through the project itself.
- Working with client staff on each customised in plant training or a research project or consulting assignment.
- Using partnerships or collaborating with clients and other experts as required on a project by project basis.
- Always assessing the need or opportunity at first before determining intervention.
- Analysing the work and workplace to identify the cause or factors that limit performance and the requirements for aspired performance.
- Designing the solution by specifying the requirements of the solution early in the project.

- Developing some of the solutions and its elements, then performing formative evaluations of the solution and its elements as a pilot or test run pre implementation.
- Implementing the solution with the client staff.
- Evaluating the impact and the results together with the client.
- Stepping aside to watch the client run through unaided, but with FITC as an observer and coach.

This process has also been adopted for both FITC's internal projects and tasks, as well as all services to stakeholders and clients with great outcomes in terms of almost 50% of FITC projects being referral from existing clients, service quality awards based on client nominations, and spin-off engagements. In terms of grounded theory application, Creswell (2002) described the components of the *axial coding paradigm* as;

1. Causal conditions influence core category,
2. The strategies are specific actions that are outcomes of the core category,
3. Context implies specific conditions that influence strategy,
4. Intervening conditions are contextual conditions which influence the strategies, and
5. Consequences are the outcomes of implementing the strategies.

In view of the transformation project's aspiration to positively impact both service quality and operational efficiency aspects of the organization, FITC's three service departments as well as the two operational departments were taken as the five categories of the *open coding process* to enable a thorough subjection of each to the five stages of axial coding. FITC's five departments as referenced as categories, are FITC Training, FITC Consulting, and FITC Research which are external market or client facing and thus define our service offering, quality assurance and client feedback. The fourth department, FITC Central Services, embodies units that deal with FITC cost centers, thus requiring internal efficiencies. Lastly, the FITC Control Functions cluster, which require compliance to internal policies, corporate governance procedures, statutory requirements and service level agreements amongst internal departments and with 3rd parties. These formed the thrust of FITC's 2009-2014 Strategic Plan, one of the three critical events aligned to the case study.

FITC Evidence-Based Repositioning

After the survey, we developed the FITC 2009-2014 strategy and implementation model and then immediately commenced with the implementation. Certain intervention models were adopted. The two slogans coined to drive FITC's corporate repositioning initiatives were "Branding beyond logos and colours" and "Physician, heal thyself".

"Branding beyond logos and colours"- in 2007, FITC embarked on a corporate transformation project where its logo and colours were changed to reflect the new identity of a rebirthed FITC. This transformation had to go beyond the brand change to internalization of corporate transformation that would eventually lead to evidence-based results. We needed an injection of sprite and zest, in order to remain relevant to our stakeholders. This led to the development of the slogan "Branding beyond logos and colours."
"Physician heal thyself."- as a professional services firm we decided to conduct an internal diagnosis of problems with our human capacity. We believed that we had to first look inward before we act as advisors to our clients.

Under these two change projects, an eight intervention model was adopted to address the issues diagnosed. The Intervention model included; Strategy; Structure re-alignment; Infrastructure upgrade, Job design and performance tracking; Culture and workplace relationship, Internal Communication updates, Staff welfare and motivation, as well as Strategic alliances.

Intervention Process Outcomes

1. Strategy

We reviewed the entire mandate of FITC and dimensioned the entire financial system domestically and regionally to get a systemic view of the scope of the mandate. We then developed a collaborative description of what success will look like in terms of mission, vision, core values, structure, roles and suitability based performance plan that allowed for feedback and follow up coaching as well as mentoring. This process was useful in helping us dimension our various stakeholders and their expectations and in deriving the types and levels of partnerships required.

Strategic planning: The FITC's 2009 – 2014 strategy plan reviewed vision and mission as well as streamlined core values that align with the new FITC Brand. We knew we had to deepen our corporate and operational strategy definition as well as execution and monitoring capacities. The first step we took was to develop a five year strategy, so we drafted the 2009-2014 Corporate Strategy, which was a product of series of refinement and validation processes that included:

- Background research into the Pius Okigbo Report of 1976 that led to the establishement of FITC.
- Interface with predecessor and respective unit heads within FITC during my two week induction period.
- Review of the new brand essence and documents as submitted by the brand consultant, which was done in 2007.
- An audit of FITC's new Brand characteristics vis-a-vis the Centre's vision, mission, core values, etc.
- Results of a Staff Survey carried out in June 2009.
- Findings from the January – June 2009 Quality Assessment.
- Outcomes of a strategy summit involving all professional staff of the Centre-conducted on June 2009.
- Client feedback questionnaire.
- On the spot milestone surveys.

The 2009-2014 strategic plan launched our change process, because it gave us direction on how to and when to initiate changes that were needed to align us with our brand promise. We have so far deployed four series of annual internal surveys and participated in one internationally benchmarked survey – Great Place to Work survey. Feedback from these assessments form part of planning for each subsequent year, with initiatives tracked, discussed and improved upon. The results and improvements attained over these four cycles of such interventions have continued to provide ideas for sustained performance improvement.

In December 2013, we commenced drafting the 2014-2019 strategy, using the bottom-up approach. In the first strategy plan (2009-2014), a top-down approach was adopted, we conducted the surveys and background findings as listed above and then I used the generated data/information to draft the strategy and cascaded it downwards, because at the time I was a new CEO that needed to set the direction, based on aspired vision for the organization, and then sell the vision. The 2014-2019 strategy was developed collaboratively by each department to cascade upward in order to give them ownership of the strategy. Every member of each department was involved in designing their department's strategy. This is because the author is now in the second and final term, and needed to get the next set of leaders schooled in the art of realistic strategy planning and implementation, while owning the transformation process and institutionalizing change.

2. Structure Re-Alignment

In 2007, FITC changed its corporate identity and the designation of the chief executive from Director-General (DG) to Managing Director/Chief Executive Officer

(MD/CEO). The actions taken from 2009 to date are in a continuum of plans aimed at supporting FITC to be the best it possible could, during this period.

The key change here revolved around the evolvement of the strategy plan for 2009 – 2014 against the background of scoping the "roots" of FITC, examining its present and previewing its future. Thus, both the vision and mission statements of FITC as at December 2008 were updated by December 2009, to reflect FITC's three service areas and its expected best-in-class status. These updates to the mission and vision statements added to the streamlined core values, which were made to align with the new FITC brand as introduced in 2007, which seemed to have gained wide acceptability within the sector. Part of this alignment entailed the transformation of the highest policy level from Governing Council to Board, as well as updates to the FITC objectives. All these naturally culminated into an update of the FITC Articles and Memorandum of Understanding. The FITC Corporate Structure was further enhanced to enable creation of applicable Board Committees in line with the first FITC Corporate Governance Framework created late 2009. This further led to functional structure enhancements to the current structure with 5 departments and 16 units, using axial and open coding, as described.

Similarly, a brand alignment program was put in place to not only internalize the new FITC brand promise and features amongst staff, but also to enhance brand clarity amongst internal and external stakeholders. To a large extent, these dual objectives have been achieved. A lot has also been achieved in terms of internal structure re-alignment, especially in the areas of departmental restructuring, adoption of appropriate nomenclatures, job re-evaluation and analysis as well as redeployment of staff for improved alignment between personal behavior, qualifications, past working experience, job requirements and potential performance levels.

3. Infrastructure Upgrade

The infrastructure upgrade initiative had two components namely:

- Infrastructure upgrade in terms of a New FITC Building.
- Infrastructure upgrade in terms of Management Information Systems [MIS].

A very bold and obvious indication that a major change that has given expression to the new FITC, is the institution's movement after 30 years from its former rented office building that was rife with major facility issues to its own office building. The relocation took place in July, 2010. Upon resumption and after a review of applicable board minutes, the author discovered that the FITC Board had approved relocation from Apapa area of Lagos, as far back as 2008. However, that aspiration remained unrealized due to FITC's inability to find a suitable location. In view of this, FITC's aspirations for having its own office building in a suitable location became a major priority, to create the aspired work environment. Late 2009, FITC acquired a completed building and proceeded to remodel it to suit our purposes and features of the new brand, introduced in 2007. The new office is a three floor building, equipped with modern facilities, with an ambience that creates a suitable work environment. Since moving in July 2010, we have received over twenty institutions requesting a study tour of the facility and over five institutions including one from another West African jurisdiction, formally requesting directions for replicating such facility.

The movement and the new environment is a major shift in FITC work culture, professional service orientation and work tools and facilitates effective service delivery. This movement also demonstrates the "branding beyond logos and colors" concept and embodies all the transformation initiatives aimed at repositioning FITC in the short term and sets the tone for our future aspiration. The subsequent adjustment in staff attitude to work, team spirit and pride in their work was dramatic! To keep focus on FITC's medium term goal for the campus project on the land acquired in 2002, FITC obtained the Lagos State Government's Layout approval for its aspired long term 6.48 hectares campus project, which will be the permanent site for FITC, and a deliverable in the 2014-2019 Strategy Plan in progress.

The upgrade of FITC's MIS infrastructure over the last five years, has been sweeping. This is in addition to a number of information technology inclined innovations that include, but not limited to the following:

- Upgrade of the IT infrastructure, which ushered in a brand new Local Area Network (LAN) at the FITC's new ultra-modern building in Ebute-Metta, Lagos. The LAN comprises a standard data center with high capacity server machines to boost reliability. This included acquisition of SAGE Evolution Pastel as the new Enterprise Resource Portal [ERP]. Hitherto, FITC's ERP was the out dated SAGE100.
- Introduction of an online Performance Management solution, known as QPR being support by our South-African partners. This enables online real times performance measurement and tracking on a corporate, team and individual staff levels.
- Acquisition of new laptops to replace old desktop computers and enhance staff performance through upgrade of working tools, which has now facilitated a 1:1 computer-to-employee ratio and remote access for staff enabling mobility and work at home opportunities in instances of personal emergencies.
- Introduction of three e-products to expand FITC's service delivery reach to other jurisdictions and enable online payments. These products are:

   ◦   E-Recruitment Portal – an online recruitment solution which has formed a very useful tool in supporting FITC's numerous stakeholders in the area of human resources.

   ◦   Electronic learning (e-Learning) platform – an online solution targeted at delivering some of FITC's classic training services to stakeholders beyond the borders of the continent, on a 24/7 basis.

   ◦   Virtual Library – an online solution that enables library user remote registration, a review of catalogues, booking listed items ahead of visit and placing orders for FITC publications online.

- Virtual office (e.g. through virtual private network (VPN).

4. Job Design and Performance Tracking

Under this intervention process, we conducted several psychometric assessments to feed into employees' career plan and job role best fit. We scoped roles using diagnostic tools in 2009 to determine current and required technical and behavioral competence as well as capacity development programs, both local and international. The findings informed the training delivered from 2009 to 2011. The assessments have a shelve life of two years, as such it repeated 2011 and informs staff training for 2011 to 2013.

The psychometric assessments conducted on staff included;

- Personal Profile Analysis (PPA) from a self – assessment view, systemically generated report, for each staff and details staff behavioural profile and role compatibilities.
- M@GIC is an assessment for team cohesiveness and consistency (team maturity) – an indication of team development stage, of the management team.
- Management Action Profile(MAP) that provides a view of 8 key managerial success factors for staff of middle to senior management category.
- Sales Competency Assessment (SCA) which uses the 'Sales Cycle' to determine capability and performance from a 360 degree perspective, for all departmental and unit heads in both external and internal customer facing roles.

We also designed a new performance management system for staff and corporate performance tracking, individual staff coaching & development. The Employee Performance Management (EPM) Framework was redesigned to comprise of job description, Key Performance Indicators, job match & evaluation (Job Role), target worksheet (Quantitative using Balanced Score Cards), appraisal forms (Qualitative – in line with core value & culture), corporate budget & departmental objectives (Corporate Strategy). The variables generated from this, feed into the QPR in terms of performance metrics. The QPR integrates with the SAGE Evolution Pastel, the enterprise resource portal, thus enabling real time online performance tracking on the corporate, team and individual basis.

We also developed new incentives for career advancement and talent retention. This included methods of recognizing and rewarding excellence, creativity and innovation right through the grades. We also implemented internal capacity enhancement programs through strategic partnerships, training and certification of FITC professional staff to improve their competencies and acquire new business solution methodologies.

In the area of internal and external capacity building, within the five years, FITC has partnered with:

- Thomas International, a world renowned psychometric certification institution, to put the staff through the Thomas System Accreditation Programme. Now, not less than 23 professional staff are certified with strong competence to apply the Personal Profile Analysis and Job Profile in tandem, in respect of recruitment and selection of personnel anywhere in the world.
- Personal Global, Inc., an international management consultancy firm that specializes in providing robust, field-tested methodologies and metrics to organizational development (OD) practitioners. Of course, FITC staff are now kitted with relevant diagnostic tools in this area.
- Adams Gold Consulting and Sphere, Trusted Advisor training for FITC professional staff.
- The English School of Business and Social Etiquette, where 20e professional staff where trained on business and social etiquettes to give departmental and unit heads the necessary etiquettes for effectively representing the FITC brand at social and intellectual events.

As a result of all the transformation based learning initiatives aimed at enhancing staff skills, from May 2009 to April 2014, FITC has maintained a range of 46.5 – 80 training hours per staff per year, depending on the phase of the transformation process, with most of the trainings delivered between 2009 and 2012.

5. Culture and Workplace Relationships

Expectedly, many aspects of FITC's existing culture are changing rapidly while some traditional values were deepening, to make them a natural way of life. Nothing testifies of this more than insights from the two staff surveys deployed over the last five years – the first in June 2009 and the fourth one in August 2013. The staff engagement survey deployed in 2009 was the first for FITC and has now been adopted as an annual requirement. Table 4 shows a comparison of the culture element of the survey showed the following.

Also the culture of prudence in the use of resources generally, and paper products in particular, have been greatly enhanced as part of FITC's aspirations toward a paperless environment policy. For instance over the last five years, FITC's stationery consumption has been reduced by 30%, despite increased levels of stakeholder engagement. The process is a continuous one, for sustained performance improvement.

In the same vein, various internal policy and process manuals have been reviewed and updated to reflect global best practices. For institutionalization of these upgrades into an "FITC way" as aligned to best practice, in 2009 FITC evolved its own guidebook on corporate governance known as FITC's Code of Corporate Governance, this was the first of its type in the institution since it was established. FITC has developed other manuals, including the Management Information System Policy, while the Procurement Policy and Risk Assessment Policy is currently being drafted.

Our service providers and supplier contracts have also been reviewed to align with our new corporate governance framework requirements which include procurement processes, whistle blowing, disclosures, etc.

6. Internal Communication and Updates

Presently, there has been seamless communication between management and staff as well as with FITC's many stakeholders. All seemingly unused or underused communication media are now being fully employed to either exchange ideas or communicate developments with staff. Such media include internet, intra mail,

Table 4. Summary of culture change in FITC in 2009 and 2013

2009 Culture and Staff Orientation in FITC Revealed	2013 Culture and Staff Orientation in FITC Revealed
• Low level of trust amongst staff • Double standards in human resources management • Low staff morale • Low confidence in various leadership levels • High degrees of job dissatisfaction • Apathy to existing performance management system • Poor sense of ownership and accountability for work and actions among supervisors and executives • Unsatisfactory reward system.	• High level of trust amongst staff • Level playing approach to human resources management practices • FITC leadership consistent in what it says and does • Supervisors committed to developing and improving themselves • High sense of ownership and accountability for work and actions among supervisors and executives • Satisfactory reward system • Decision making driven by corporate vision and policies.

departmental meetings, management meetings, interactive "open house" meetings with staff, interface with Unit Heads and Heads of Departments etc. Expectedly, the efficacy of these media and the frequency of employing them to update staff on issues have significantly checkmated negative in office politicking and rumor mongering and psychological alienation in the system.

Essentially, there has been a redefinition of management style in FITC, in many ways. First the leadership runs an open and transparent system. Second, it gives opportunity to staff to bare their minds through constructive anonymous staff engagement surveys. Third, the leadership requests staff inputs to decision making on a regular basis. And fourth, the leadership involves staff in policy implementation, through the habit of making staff work in policy teams, committees and sub-committees. Today, the traditional "them and us" syndrome has almost disappeared, as staff own policies, programs and projects.

This is more so because in the last five years, committees have been set up to work on many assignments which include: Written Communication Standards, New Office Relocation, New Staff Handbook, New Payroll Allowances, Workplace Ethics, New Office Commissioning, Celebration of Leadership Excellence, FITC's Corporate Social Responsibility (CSR) program, Procurement Process, End-of-Year Programs, Disciplinary Matters, etc. Within the Service Units, there have also been further breakdown of departments into Sub-Units with each area's team leaders made responsible for efficiency and growth of leadership capabilities, enhancement of teamwork and productivity within the system. Indeed, FITC now places premium on teams as "our way of working".

7. Staff Welfare and Motivation

In the last five years, the welfare of staff has improved significantly (Table 5). Many factors have informed this. First, the FITC Board employed the services of a leading consulting firm to review the staff compensation. Secondly, the new performance management system (EPM) gives staff wide variety of options for career advancement and talent ventilation using corporate diagnostic tools, 360 degrees assessments, coaching and review by performance committee. More importantly, staff are being made to believe in themselves, while they are often recognized and commended for good performance, as well as receiving constructive discipline for errors and sub-optimal performance. Due process is more strictly followed when the need arises for disciplinary actions. Today, FITC not only has the capacity to attract talents, but has also demonstrated the capacity to retain them. The long troubling issue of high staff turnover, which was at an all-time high rate of 30.9% in 2007 has been effectively arrested. Now, staff rarely leave the system, except when requested to do so via termination. Voluntary turnover as of December 2012

Table 5. Summary of staff turnover at FITC 2004 to 2013

Year	No. of Staff	Staff Exit			% of Tunrnover
		Voluntary	**Termination**	**Total**	
2004	62	6	11	17	27.42
2005	59	10	2	12	20.34
2006	64	10	3	13	20.31
2007	55	15	2	17	30.91
2008	59	10	1	11	18.64
2009	58	4	1	5	8.62
2010	58	1	1	2	3.45
2011	61	2	0	2	3.28
2012	60	0	0	0	0.00
2013	60	0	1	1	1.67

and 2013 was 0% and many former staff of FITC who had left for other reasons other than discipline are returning either as full time employees or as associates on part-time project specific basis.

8. Strategic Alliances

FITC has over the years, continued to generate enough support and collaboration required to ensure that it remains relevant and value adding to its primary and secondary constituencies. One area the institution has explored for fresh collaboration in the recent times is an extension of the work done by the immediate past chief executive. It includes establishing additional strategic alliances and partnerships with reputable global firms and institutions to deploy services locally and internationally. Some of the strategic alliances that have impacted FITC's internal capacity include;

- Devex, a USA based network group of professionals, comprising of world leading organizations, firms and individuals. FITC's corporate membership of the group avails it the opportunity to network and become exposed to global opportunities.
- Featured in the British Chamber of Commerce publication on guide to African markets.
- Collaboration with the International Finance Corporation (IFC)'s Global Corporate Governance Forum on building capacity via indirect interven-

tion to develop FITC's capacity to deliver Board Leadership and Corporate Governance training for directors of Banks and Financial Institutions. This collaboration has potentials of a roll out across Sub Saharan Africa.

- Lafferty Group to introduce the International Academy of Retail Banking (LARB) in Nigeria. This collaboration with Dun & Bradstreet to introduce finance sector specific international programmes for both regulators and operators in the financial services sector. This collaboration has been terminated by mutual consent, upon expiry.
- FITC also has corporate memberships and affiliations with the following organizations:
  ○ Corporate membership of the Nigerian-American Chamber of Commerce.
  ○ Development Executive Group of Washington DC.
  ○ The Chartered Institute of Personnel Management of Nigeria (CIPMN).
  ○ Affiliate member of the newly established African Corporate Governance Network (ACGN).
  ○ The International Society for Performance Improvement (ISPI).

By and large, FITC's visibility has continued to increase significantly, not just because of its new alliances and partnerships, but also because of its increasing capacity to execute assignments with professional competence comparable to any of the leading professional firms in the world. Presently, it is competing with and winning assignments that would ordinarily have been won by the top four professional firms in the world, not based on pricing, but based on quality of delivery. We are currently executing two core projects on a consortium of consultants that include one of the global big four firms and executing a research project for another.

Where We Are Now: FITC as of May 2014

1. Improved Service Offerings

FITC had at inception, relied mainly on open courses to draw participants to its programs. Then during the banking industry consolidation periods of 2005 – 2006, the new bigger banks that emerged started to invest in staff development in customized form. As part of FITC's 2009 – 2014 strategy, there was a dramatic shift in focus that enabled FITC collaborate with respective organizations within the various industries in the financial services sector, especially banks, in designing and delivering customized institution-specific training programs. This shift in FITC's training paradigm has resulted in the bulk of the participants attending FITC's programs now being through FITC's customized in-plant training programs. The implication of this shift is that we now understand the needs of our stakeholders better, and have thus become their trusted advisor on issues relating to the delivery of training interventions in collaboration with the Human Resources and Training functions of the institutions.

Another positive development to the new impetus in FITC Training is the increasing number of participants attending FITC's courses and workshops from the Sub-Saharan African region. Lately FITC has been seeing increasing number of participants from Liberia, Sierra-Leone, Uganda and other African countries. This resonates clearly with FITC's vision to be the preferred provider of training, consulting and research services to the Financial Services Sector in West Africa by 2016 and potentially Sub-Saharan Africa in the medium term.

The strategic shift in the level and intensity of consulting services delivery as contained in the FITC 2009 – 2014 strategy plan enabled multi layered partnerships with some value adding international brands as well as franchised diagnostic tools which made FITC Consulting services evidence based interventions. As a result, FITC Consulting's core values to FITC stakeholders were updated to provide quality service in a reliable, efficient, cost effective manner. All projects of FITC Consulting are now undertaken on four cardinal points of quality cost effectiveness, efficiency and sustainability, particularly on organizational development projects, where FITC focuses fully on developing client stakeholders own capacity to sustain change in measurable terms over time for continued individual, team and corporate performance improvement. With a progressive strategic focus of getting at least 50% of its projects by referral, FITC has continued to evolve its solutions and processes in ways that have enabled 2 – 7 year retainerships with a number of key organizations in the financial services sector. While the main focus of activities has remained targeted at organizations in banking, insurance, capital market, development finance, pension and other ancillary industries of the financial services sector, FITC is increasingly being invited by special request, to support large-scale complex turn-around projects in other industries such as power and conglomerates, with demonstrated corporate transformation.

2. Brand Enhancement

We now have enhanced brand clarity amongst staff and external stakeholders. Our governance structure is now based on our new framework for corporate governance. Our vision, mission and core values are now aligned to the brand promise and have been used to influence our related due processes such as governance, procurement, whistle blowing, work tools, code of ethics, staff handbook, compensation, performance improvement and individual responsibilities. Our work environment, third party relationships, service quality and levels of self-actualization amongst staff are visible improvements. Our internal and external corporate communication is also completely overhauled.

FITC now has upgraded and re-energized staff profiles, new culture and orientations, new product packaging, new diagnostic tools that add value to institutional services, new capacity building initiatives, new job profiling and human job fits, new career management structures, new communication channels, new media outlook, new streams of goodwill, new corporate governance framework, new stakeholders' management approaches, new ground breaking service offerings, new approaches to business development and relationship management, new management-staff relationship, new team building spirit, new office complex and working environment, new ambience, new vista, new hope, new vitality, new zeal to work and to deliver, recognition and reward to those who demonstrate the aspires values at annual staff and family party, etc. The list seems endless.

3. Quantitative Performance

FITC is a nonprofit professional services organization that is limited by guarantee. As such its key performance indicators are:

- Net worth.
- Number and mix of training programmes delivered.
- Cumulative number of participants at the training programmes delivered.
- Number and mix of consulting assignments delivered.
- Number of books published.

In terms of net worth, as at December 31, 2008 FITC's net worth was N867.59m ($5.3m). However as at December 31, 2013, even with adjustments in assets valuation and provisions to fund staff gratuity fund as a fall out of FITC's conversion of its accounts from GAAP to IFRS, FITC's published annual accounts indicate a net worth of N1, 730,365,000($10.5m), more than a 100% increase in net worth, over the 5 year period ending 2013.

In terms of expansion in FITC operations, FITC delivered 86 courses in 2008, consisting of 57 open enrolment programs, 18 customized institution specific and 11 collaborative programs which included one delivered internationally. Total number of participants at all the eighty six courses was 2,002. On the other hand, FITC delivered 122 two courses in 2013, consisting of 61 one open enrolment programs, 54 customized institution specific and seven international programs. Total number of participants at all 122 courses was 4,822. To show impact over the five year time scale, it may be recalled that as at December 2008 FITC s cumulative number of participants from its inception in 1981 was 36, 523. However as at December 2013, FITC's cumulative number of participants from inception has risen to 54,061 participants, which indicates that 47.98% of FITC's incremental participants over its 32 years life span between 2009 and 2013. The impressive aspect of this outcome is that FITC's total staff number as indicated in Table 5, did not change. Thus, indicating outcomes of the initiatives aimed at enhancing its corporate efficiency by attaining much more, with basically same level of human resources.

4. Awards and Recognitions Received

The calendar years 2012 and 2013 can aptly be terms the season of awards and recognition to FITC, when taken in perspective of time, from its inception to date. The various awards received in 2012 and 2013 are:

1.   The Gold category award for Quality, received 2012 in New York, USA by Business Initiative Directions.
2.   The 2012 GPWT award - FITC emerged as 7th out of 225 workplaces in Nigeria. Thus, the only non-profit in the top 10 winners in the 2012 Great Place to Work awards in the maiden Nigerian edition and also obtained
3.   The West African Award for Training Excellence and Innovative Services, awarded by Aspire West Africa and received in Accra, Ghana
4.   The IFTDO [International Federation of Training and Development Organizations] 2013 award of excellence for FITC's outstanding contributions as Change Agent in Learning and Development in Africa
5.   2014 ADM [African Development Magazine] Award of Excellence as the Most Efficient Professional Services Firm for the Year.

5. Testimonial of Staff with over Ten Years of Service in FITC

In preparing this case study, given that FITC now has an easier culture that is open to giving and receiving feedback, the author requested for feedback in the form of FITC staff perceptions towards the recent five years of the transformation process, compared to previous experience in FITC. To ensure validity of data captured, the author requested the HR Officer, Mrs. Stella Ukadike to help the MD/CEO's special assistant, Ms. Glory Okang invite staff members who have spent a total of over ten years of continued employment in FITC. Response rate was 100% and almost all respondents exceeded to 120 words limit set by the survey administrators, as such the administrators had to edit each statement and return same of the respondents for confirmation. The interviews, for reasons of staff confidentiality as promised by the administrators, were not conducted by author and their confidence was assured. Thus, the author does not know the identity of the respondents, numbered 1-6 below.

Respondent 1

"Prior to the assumption of the current C.E.O the organizational climate was negative, morale was very low, attrition rate was high, leadership was dictatorial, organizational hierarchy was inflexible, and slow to respond to customers' needs, and creativity was not encouraged. The result: employee motivation was low especially for the experience staff. As result, the organization achieved sub-optimal performance. Today, the system encourages creativity and innovativeness, optimal leadership potentials, and growth within the system, core values and flexibility to adapt to changes occurring in the business world. The result: positive organizational climate, low attrition rate, highly motivated workforce, greater interaction between top management team and other employees, increased net worth, and FITC has become a great place to work."

Respondent 2

- Better Communication between management and staff.
- Increased automation and less use of paper.
- Removal of unnecessary protocol.
- Recognition and commendation of staff performance has increased tremendously.
- Low Staff Turnover - There has been a significant reduction in the number of staff turnover, which is largely due to the fact that staff morale is high and more committed to the work.
- Improved remuneration has increased staff motivation.
- Quick work turnaround time.
- Equal opportunity for all staff.
- Open door policy.
- More Publicity/Awareness initiated programmes.

Respondent 3

"The first five years of this management has witnessed a lot of notable achievements in many areas of the company's administration. The management took off with a transparent and open administrative style, relocation from Shippers' Property, Apapa to FITC House, Ebute Metta. There was also a successful hosting of FITC 30th anniversary and a documented history of FITC was published for the first time since its inception. The management also recognized suppliers and vendors as important stakeholders in FITC and increased interactions with them. A massive project on virtual learning was also concluded in the two core areas of banking, namely Bank Inspection and Internal Control and Credit Management and Analysis."

Respondent 4

"FITC has undergone profound changes in five years. The changes are manifest in FITC's strategic focus and alliances, staff welfare and development, processes, workplace suitability, culture, tools and infrastructure, performance management, brand positioning and, more importantly, leadership that is motivational and highly transparent. Compared to previous years, FITC has been drastically transformed, not just in physical asset building and aesthetics, but in human capital development, staff's zeal to make impact, team spirit within and across departments, and leadership styles. Staff members are now more stable emotionally, psychologically more proud of FITC and physically fitted for work and for their families. Staff attrition is now zero. These and more have combined to improve performance in FITC"

Respondent 5

"Staff Welfare/Morale - staff turnover rate is now at its barest minimum. FITC Staff are now very happy people, with a lot of laughter and positive energy in the working atmosphere and more cordial professional relationship. There are now enriched Staff Welfare Policies, a high level of well-deserved job security and work-life-balance is strongly encouraged in FITC. Leadership Style - The leadership of FITC now has a "human face". Work Environment - We are empowered with the right set of tools and resources we require to perform optimally, to grow professionally and intellectually. In summary, FITC now has a more conducive work environment that encourages team work, professional and intellectual growth; productivity, innovativeness, creativity and personal development and wellbeing."

Respondent 6

"Management style: the open, transparent and staff friendly approach seen has been countless, the style united the FITC to a degree that was not present prior to her coming. The corporate outfit of the organization is today an edifice of pride with the relocation of FITC office from Apapa to its own property on the mainland. Equitable sharing of yearly performance bonus – introduction of standardized sharing formula is highly commendable. The exposition of FITC to international collaboration is a demonstration of immense capacity in a leader whose vision of expanding our operational boundary is limitless. Indeed the performance of our beloved MD within the 1st tenure is excellent."

6. Insights from FITC External Stakeholders

In March 2014 as part of preparations for inputs to the proposed 2014-2019 strategy plan now I draft, a stakeholder survey was conducted for FITC strategic partners, training nominating officers and heads of human resource functions of stakeholder institutions, as well as external resource persons by a consulting firm based in the United States of America, to assess the services of FITC to its stakeholders and FITC service delivery to them. This is the first of this type of survey in the history of FITC. The results of the survey showed that 88% of respondents regarded FITC staff as helpful and friendly, 96% agreed that they will recommend FITC Training, Consulting and Research services to others and over 60% agreed that looking ahead, they were very positive of their relationship and dealings with FITC. The plan is to use feedback derived from this survey to feed some of the stakeholder expressed service needs in the short to medium term, into the draft 2014-2019 Strategy Plan. The decision going forward is that this survey will be repeated mid-term through the 2014-2019 strategy and the GPTW survey of 2012 will be repeated in 2016.

CHALLENGES FACING FITC

1. **Leadership Development:** Leaders across the system need to be developed and empowered to be leaders in true sense of the word, so they could be role models and mentors. In furtherance to this, all the heads of the five departments which served as categories from the axial coding process for grounded theory have taken turns to attend the Leadership Development Program of the Centre for Creative Leadership [CCL] in Brussels, Belgium in 2010, 2011, 2012 and 2014. The impact of this programme on their leadership styles are coaching issues directly involving the CEO, as coach for their leadership journey.

2. **Succession Planning:** Getting the right pool of possible candidates for the board to consider in succeeding the CEO after my second and final tenure which ends 2019, is a high priority agenda item for the FITC Board, traumatised by the bumpy leadership transition of the early 1990s which plummeted FITC into its dark days in the mid-1990s, thus leading to the recruitment of the author's predecessor as a turnaround CEO. The Leadership of FITC will require someone beyond leadership traits alone, but with a good blend of research, training and consulting skills as well as capacity to run FITC while delivering services to its stakeholders, with the required depth of experience and continually extending the boundaries for FITC.

3. **Addressing Issues Identified by ADKAR - ADKAR (Awareness, Desire, Knowledge, Ability, and Reinforcement):** Is an acronym for the five steps used in a methodology for assessing the level of awareness amongst employees regarding the changes they need to make to enhance their performance. The ADKAR process begins by creating awareness of the need for change, and desire amongst employees to want to succeed; next these employees must have the necessary knowledge of what is required for them to sustain the change. The next step in FITC's transformation post the 2009-2014 strategic plan period is to ensure that employees have the ability to execute what they are asked to do to change; while the final and most crucial step is the reinforcement through change management and sustainable planning as a culture than a corporate event.

In the 2013 FITC Staff Survey, given concerns for sustaining change, FITC staff members were evaluated using the ADKAR instrument. The result revealed that 97.56% of FITC staff were aware of the changes in FITC from 2009 to 2013 and had the ability to execute the change, 100% had the desire to change, 95.12% had the knowledge and 82.92% had the reinforcement to change. Comparatively on all measures, areas of improvement revealed that FITC staff members are relatively lower on Knowledge and Reinforcement compared to other variables. This implied that FITC will need to consistently improve and drive awareness on the changes implemented and will need to further design reinforcement measure to sustain these changes. Therefore, a component of the 2014-2019 strategy plan is a competency assessment by functional and grade category to address technical skills and professional certifications, as natural extension of the behavioural trainings generated from Staff PPA [Personal Profile Analysis] generated in 2011.

SOLUTIONS AND RECOMMENDATIONS

In view of FITC's experience of two in-depth transformation initiatives over its 33 years of experience and especially 2009 to 2013, the focus of this case study, lessons learned and recommendations for others faced with similar situations, recommendations from FITC' repositioning experience are:

*   Take a systematic view of the industry and organization nationally, regionally and globally.
*   Integrate strategy and roles with qualitative and quantitative performance indices.

- Incorporate a collective action that allows an iterative process for continued refinement.
- Ensure sufficient internal and external stakeholder engagement all through the process.
- Take a transformational leadership perspective by making the transformation enjoyable.
- Ensure applicable deployment of technology for real-time data collection.
- Derive effective and strategic, than just tactical, performance metrics.
- Ensure leadership transparency and leading by consensus for optimal buy-in.
- Always facilitate proactive feedback and collaboration for sufficient learning and knowledge management.

In summary, this case study has shown that there wasn't any *silver bullet* for a transformation as described. It was a mix of complimentary perspectives and methods, with underlying theoretical principles. It was a wholesome process that lasted five years and integrated various concepts from the 10 Standards for Performance Improvement to the Malcom Baldridge 2007 Criteria for Performance Excellence, to the process of axial coding using the grounded theory concept and application of a cocktail of organizational diagnostics and individual psychometric assessments. In view of this, it is a collective process from entry levels within the organizational hierarchy to the board level. One major factor, was the need for a very committed change champion that is able to constructively influence all stakeholders to stay the course with the required energy level and buy-in. The principles are universal, thus possibly easily replicated in other jurisdictions and regions.

REFERENCES

Baldrige, M. (2007). *2007 Business and nonprofit criteria: Baldrige model for performance excellence*. Retrieved August 7, 2007 from http://www.quality.nist. gov/PDF_files/2007_Business_Nonprofit_Criteria.pdf

Bertalanffy, L. V. (1972). The history and status of general systems theory. *Academy of Management Journal, 15*(4), 407–426. doi:10.2307/255139

Creswell, J. W. (2002). *Educational research: Planning, conducting, and evaluating quantitative and qualitative research*. Upper Saddle River, NJ: Pearson.

Creswell, J. W. (2007). *Qualitative enquiry & research design: Choosing among five approaches* (2nd ed.). London, United Kingdom: Sage Publications.

Fuller, J. (1997). *Managing Performance improvement Projects: preparing, planning, implementing*. San Francisco, CA: Pfeiffer.

Khun, A. (1974). *The Logic of Social Systems*. San Francisco, CA: Jossey-Bass.

Knowles, M. (1970). *Andragogy*. Retrieved April 13, 2005, from http://tip.psychology.org/Knowles.html

Newman, L. S. (2008). *Effects of Employee Performance Management Systems on Employee Learning and Development within Banks in Nigeria*. A qualitative method dissertation in partial fulfillment of conditions precedent to a Doctorate in Business Administration (DBA) submitted to the University of Phoenix, Arizona: USA. ProQuest UMI. ISBN 978-1-109-04887-2.

Okang, G. & Ukadike, S. (2014). *Perception of FITC staff with over 10 years continued work experience in FITC*. Being a special request qualitative survey for a case study on FITC.

Oladimeji, A. (2009). *Handover notes from Dr Oladimeji Alo out-going Managing Director/CEO, to Dr Lucy Surhyel Newman in coming Managing Director/CEO.*

Speck, M. (1996). Best practice in professional development for sustained educational change. *ERS Spectrum, 14*(2), 33–41.

ADDITIONAL READING

Addison, M. R. (2004). Performance architecture: A performance improvement model. *Performance Improvement, 43*(6), 14–16. doi:10.1002/pfi.4140430606

Alo, O. (1999). *Human resource management in Nigeria*. Lagos, Nigeria: Business & Institutional Support Services Limited.

Arveson, P. (1998). *What is balanced scorecard?* Retrieved April 21, 2005 from http://www.balancedscorecard.org/basics/bsc1.html

Aycan, Z. (2002). *Leadership and teamwork in developing countries: Challenges and opportunities*. Western Washington University. Bellingham: Washington. Retrieved May 3, 2005, from http://www.ac.wwu.edu/~culture/aycan.htm

Becker, B. E., Huselid, M. A., & Ulrich, D. (2001). The HR scorecard: linking people, strategy, and performance. *Working Knowledge: Harvard Business School*. Retrieved April 27, 2005 from http://hbswk.hbs.edu/tool.print_item.jhtml?id=2143&t=career_effectiveness

Benardin, H. J. (1989). Increasing the accuracy of performance measurement: A proposed solution to erroneous attributions. *Human Resource Planning*, *12*(3), 239–250.

Bowditch, J. L., & Buono, F. (2001). *A primer on organizational behavior*. Hoboken, NJ: John Wiley & Sons.

Boysen, C., Demery, A., & Shake, S. (1999). *Achieving organizational excellence through the performance measurement system: Consortium benchmarking study: Best practice report*. Houston, TX: American Productivity Center.

Chowdhurry, S. (Ed.). (2003). *Organization 21C: Someday all organizations will lead this way*. Upper Saddle River, NJ: Prentice Hall.

Chyung, S. Y. (2005). Human performance technology: From Taylor's scientific management to Gilbert's behavior engineering model. *Performance Improvement*, *44*(1), 23–28. doi:10.1002/pfi.4140440109

Galbraith, J. (1974). Organization design: An information processing view. *Interfaces*, *4*(3), 28–36. doi:10.1287/inte.4.3.28

Gibson, J. L., Ivancevich, J., & Donnelly, J. H. (1997). *Organizations: Behavior, structure, processes* (9th ed.). New York, NY: Irwin McGraw-Hill.

Gliddon, D. G. (2004). Effective performance management systems. *Performance Improvement*, *43*(9), 27–34. doi:10.1002/pfi.4140430908

Grosse, R. E. (2000). *Thunderbird on global business strategy*. New York, NY: John Wiley & Sons.

Gupta, A. K., & Govindarajan, V. (2004). *Global strategy and organization*. New York, NY: John Wiley & Sons.

Hamilton (n.d.). *Inspiring peak performance*. Retrieved April 1, 2005. From http://tma.bah.com/09/0901-b-.htm

Kirby, G. R., & Goodpaster, J. R. (2002). *Thinking* (3rd ed.). Upper Saddle River, NJ: Prentice Hall.

Latham, J., & Vinyard, J. (2004). *Baldrige user's guide: Organization diagnosis, design, and transformation*. Hoboken, NJ: Wiley.

Lussier, R., & Achua, C. (2001). *Leadership: Theory, application, skill development*. Cincinnati, OH: South-Western College Publishing.

McConnell, J. H. (2001). *Auditing your human resources department: A step-by-step guide*. New York, NY: American Management Association.

McFarland, D., & Sweeney, P. (2006). *International management: Strategic opportunities and cultural challenges* (3rd ed.). Boston, MA: Houghton Mifflin.

Murray, R. L. (2004). *A correlational study of leader's use of performance evaluation systems relating to manager – employee collaboration.* Dissertation retrieved from University of Phoenix Online Library, EBSCOhost database.

Newstrom, J. W., & Davis, K. (2002). *Organizational behavior.* New York, NY: McGraw-Hill Higher Education.

O'Connor, G., & Ayers, A. (2005). Building a radical innovation competency. *Research Technology Management, 48*(1), 23–31.

Pandit, N. R. (1996). The creation of a theory: A recent application of a grounded theory method. *Qualitative Report, 2*(4), 1–14. http://www.nova.edu/ssss/QR/QR2-4/pandit.html Retrieved July 29, 2008

Piskurich, G. M. (2006). The congruency between performance improvement and performance management. *Performance Improvement, 45*(8), 5–7. doi:10.1002/pfi.4930450802

Price, A. J. (2004). *Human resource management in a business context* (2nd ed.). London, UK: Thompson Learning.

Rainlall, S. (2004). A review of employee motivation theories and their implications for employee retention within organizations. *The Journal of American Academy of Business, 9*, 21–26.

Roberts, K., Kossek, E. E., & Ozeki, C. (1998). Managing a global workforce: Challenges, strategies & solutions. *The Academy of Management Executive, 12*(4), 93–106.

Romanoff, K. E. (1989). The ten commandments of performance management. *Personnel, 66*(1), 24–28.

Schermerhorn, J. R., Hunt, J. G., & Osbuorn, R. N. (2003). *Core concepts of organizational behavior.* Hoboken, NJ: John Wiley & Sons.

Scott, W. R. (2003). *Organizations: Rational, natural, and open systems* (5th ed.). Upper Saddle River, NJ: Prentice Hall.

Stewart, I., & Fenn, P. (2006). The motivation for innovation. *Construction Innovation, 6*(3), 173–185. doi:10.1108/14714170610710703

Stiffler, M. A. (2006). Moving from managing to driving performance. *Performance Improvement*, *45*(9), 17–19. doi:10.1002/pfi.4930450915

Swart, J., Price, A., Mann, C., & Brown, S. (2004). *Human resource development: strategy and tactics. Jordan Hill*. Oxford: Elsevier Butterworth-Heinemann.

Tidd, J., Bessant, J., & Pavitt, K. (2005). *Managing innovation: Integrating technological, market and organizational change* (3rd ed.). West Sussex, UK: Wiley.

Woolbridge, J. (2004). *Technology integration as a transforming teaching strategy*. Tech-LEARNING. Retrieved April 19, 2005, from http://www.techlearning.com/shared/printableArticle.jhtml?articleID=1770136

Wren, D. A. (1994). *The evolution of management thought* (4th ed.). New York, NY: John Wiley & Sons.

KEY TERMS AND DEFINITIONS

Branding Beyond Logo and Colors: Cliché adopted to extend FITC corporate identity change of 2007 into a more wholesome corporate rebranding including visible aesthetics enhancements, corporate culture change, underlying policies and work environment.

Evidence-Based Transformation: A corporate transformation approach that is based on findings from empirical data collection, analysis and reporting to show performance in collected data at the beginning and along milestone periods over the course of the transformation, which in this case study is 5 years.

FITC: Financial Institutions Training Center.

FITC Stakeholders: FITC stakeholders are those whose interests and expectations are affected by the decisions and actions of the FITC Board, Management and Staff. Their expectations from FITC include return on investment, product and service quality, FITC's sustainability and corporate social responsibility.

FPPN: FITC Professional Persons Network is a community of professional organizations and individuals bounded together by an appreciation of their role in FITC's success, their alignment to the FITC mandate and their interest in making contributions to FITC as may be required from time to time. Professional persons include those who have, at one point in time or the other, served as FITC Staff, Board member, Programme Director, Facilitator, Contracted Associate Consultant or been a participant at an FITC training programmes.

Nigerian Bankers' Committee: Is a National Committee, comprised of the Central Bank of Nigeria (CBN), Nigeria Deposit Insurance Corporation (NDIC), all deposit money banks and discount houses in Nigeria.

Physician Heal Thyself: Is a cliché adopted to make FITC take a critical review of itself as a corporate entity and then as a professional services firm in a way that challenged itself to first address its own corporate imperfections and by so doing, be in a better position to be a trusted professional services provider.

Theoretical Frameworks: Is the set of related concepts that were assembled to guide the broad scope of related ideas that guided the FITC evidence based transformation as described in the case study.

The Professor Pius Okigbo Committee: A Federal Government of Nigerian Committee that was created in 1976, under the instructions of the then Minister for Finance. The Committee was chaired by the late Prof Pius Okigbo and was called The Pius Okigbo Committee. The Committee's terms of reference were mainly to review the then Nigerian Financial Services Sector as constituted as at 1976 and recommend ways of enhancing the impact of the sector, on the national economy. The need for an institution like the FITC to serve the Nigerian Financial Services sector, was one of the Puis Okigbo Committee's recommendations.

Chapter 14
Blending Front– End Analysis

Beth McGoldrick
Fortune 500 Company, USA

EXECUTIVE SUMMARY

Performance problems come in all forms. The method presented in this chapter blends the models of three respected Performance improvement icons – Joe Harless, Thomas Gilbert, and Roger Chevalier. Their theoretical and practical approaches are applied to a case study. The three models – 13 Smart Questions (Front-end analysis), Behavior Engineering Model (BEM), and Updated BEM – when combined show ways practitioners can assess and improve performance. The practitioner will develop effective partnerships with clients, gain valuable perspectives on the issues, and their underlying causes. Finally the practitioner will be able to lead a department or an organization in fully analyzing problems and determining how best to solve them.

ORGANIZATION BACKGROUND

To onlookers, the award-winning team seemed to be running on all cylinders with work output at an all-time high. In reality, people were burning out and looking for jobs in other departments and companies. The annual employee satisfaction survey scores for the team had decreased by 10-30% in the 12 month period year-over-year. Why was this high-functioning team on the verge collapse?

DOI: 10.4018/978-1-4666-8330-3.ch014

This is an important question since many companies face situations like this that appear confusing, even hopeless and insurmountable. Some never know until it's too late. The choice many companies make is to continue as it is going and put band aids on the problems, cross their fingers, and hope it turns around when things slow down. This is especially true when the department is producing high quality work. But things usually don't slow down; to the contrary, things usually speed up.

As other departments and leaders see the success of the team, they ask for more. More is given and more is expected. This further exacerbates the problems creating a dangerous feedback loop. Employees are asked to do more and more until the morale decreases and productivity fails. Employees finally burnout and stay, leading to lower quality and quantity of work; or they take a job elsewhere, and the talent and knowledge is lost to the company forever. And those who remain have additional workload and expectations.

If a department really wanted to fix itself, how would they do it? Let's look at the department and company and then a real world example and see what solution they found. How would they make the correct diagnosis and take the proper steps to correct?

The company is a well-established and respected financial services company. They have been in operation for over 100 years. They operate in a highly-regulated industry selling a wide variety of financial products. The company supports and adheres to the regulations very strictly. This can lead to multiple layers of compliance and review of all communications and training produced by each product group to ensure the material is in compliance with not only the regulations, but also the company's high standards. The company prides itself on its reputation as an ethical and trustworthy organization.

The culture at the company is fairly hierarchical. There are additional marketing, communications and training in each different product-type departments across the company. Each product/function group within the company maintains their own communications and training teams, each working within a decentralized model in a heavily matrixed organizational structure. There is continuous work and desire throughout the company to remove barriers across product/function groups, and a lot of effort to encourage employees to work laterally as well as vertically.

The department is responsible for supporting financial product launches and sales strategies through communications and training for a medium wholesaling and a large advisor population. They do this through sales brochures and literature, sales strategy whitepapers, competitive updates, webpages, client seminars, instructor-led training, web-based eLearning, job aids, and additional print and digital collateral. There is an in-house design and project management department that supports the group.

The leaders of the marketing, communications and training department found themselves with the challenge to determine what was wrong; how to fix it; and how to keep the morale up. They wanted to do this while keeping the quality of the work as excellent as it had been. Everyone knew it was not an ideal situation for sustained growth and excellence. Something needed to be done, but what?

The leaders in this case could see that the employees were very good at what they did, but obviously there was something wrong. The employees were still performing at a high level and still winning awards for their work in both communications and training. They knew the satisfaction survey results were telling them something important. If asked, each employee had his or her own theory about what was wrong. Each leader had a theory about what was wrong. But no one really knew what was wrong.

The leaders decided to do something radical. They asked for volunteers from the employees in the department to be willing to look into the employee survey and find out what was wrong with the department. Since this was an employee satisfaction survey, they asked the employees to tell them what the problems were or at least, what was causing the problems. The employee volunteers would open up the employee survey results and tell the leaders what was really wrong. The leaders would then work with the group of employees to figure out what could be done.

When putting together the team to review the satisfaction survey, the leaders were seeking to find out what was wrong, why it was wrong, and how they could fix it. It was already determined that the department was important to the company and had to continue. The team had at that time eleven employees across the three functions, two managers, and one vice president. Six of the eleven employees volunteered to help determine what was wrong. The volunteer employees were dispersed across the three functions of the department and the leaders.

The volunteer employees and leaders met to kick off the program. In the meeting, the leaders provided copies of the full employee satisfaction survey for the department and asked the employee volunteers to keep it in confidence only among this sub-team. They could and would share results and recommendations to all of the employees in the department, but the survey itself was to be kept confidential at the request of the Human Resource department. The volunteer employee team was ready to go. The leaders asked for the team to provide them with a list of the problems prioritized within a few weeks. Then two weeks after that to provide a report that made recommendations on what could solve the problems. So the employee team set off with a goal to find out which problems were the most important, begin to discuss what caused them, and eventually make recommendations on how to fix them and the department.

SETTING THE STAGE

The performance improvement technologist will want to be very familiar with the Human Performance Technology (HPT) model. The model will guide them through the entire process of improving performance. When practitioners look at the Human Performance Technology map provided by the International Society for Performance Improvement (ISPI) (Figure 1), or any other performance improvement society's map, they see it starts with the Performance Analysis of Need or Opportunity, also known as front-end analysis (FEA) (Van Tiem, Moseley, & Dessinger, 2012). The front-end analysis is made up of the Organizational Analysis, Environmental Analysis, Gap Analysis, and Cause Analysis to determine what is wrong and why. The practitioner then moves to the Intervention Selection, Design, and Development and Intervention Implementation and Maintenance when the solutions are determined and put into practice. Then the practitioner progresses to the Evaluation phase to assess if the interventions are having the desired effect and improving performance.

Practitioners start to analyze the environment and organization then look at the actual and desired performance and any gaps; then they determine the causes of the problems before making recommendations of any interventions. As a word of caution, many clients and business partners try to jump to solutions before the process is complete and can miss the real underlying problem(s) causing the undesirable behavior and results. It is important for the practitioner to remind them that following the process is important to determine what problem(s) really need to get fixed in order to truly change and improve the desired performance.

Practitioners can improve their value to the business by listening carefully to the business partners and helping them by getting to the root causes. Unfortunately problems are often presented to the department in charge of fixing them as training problems. Performance Improvement Technologists often hear,

We need to train these people on _____. They seem to have forgotten everything and sales are down. If we train them again on _____, then sales will go back up.

Unfortunately, many training departments just go ahead and provide the training, counting the number of "butts in seats" and smiley satisfaction surveys, but not really delivering any results that matter or really improve performance in a meaningful way. In order to provide the end results that the business wants and needs – measurable improvement – the Performance Improvement Technologist needs to begin with a front-end analysis.

Front-end analysis (FEA) is the assessment completed at the beginning of a performance improvement program to identify if there is a problem. Front-end

Figure 1. The human performance improvement model (Used with permission)

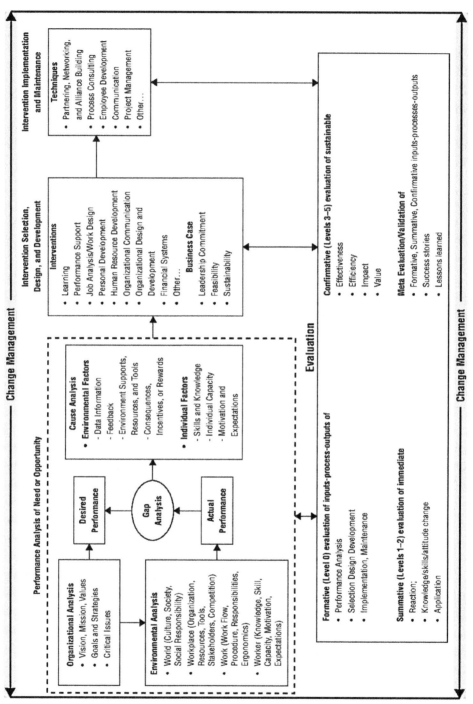

analysis models help determine up-front which actions need to be taken to solve the problems, and, sometimes more importantly, if the problem should be solved. The FEA will help the Performance Improvement Technologist and the leaders agree on what is really causing the decline in desired performance and help them determine together the correct solutions. This not only gets to the root causes of the problems, but builds the relationship between the training department and, in the above example, the sales department. The people in the training department will also be seen more as valued business partners, not just order takers. Sometimes training is the solution, but neither party – the training nor the sales department – should jump to that as the solution at the beginning without doing the analysis necessary to determine the real inhibitors to performance.

Fortunately, there are many models out there to guide the Performance Improvement Technologist through the analysis. The beauty of using a model is three-fold. First it's already been tested and proven useful. Many who have come before have used it and many will use the same model in the future because it has been effective in many other performance improvement situations both similar to and different from the current situation. Second, someone else already came up with the questions and steps the practitioner needs to follow to perform a front-end analysis to determine causes. Third, a model can be modified for each particular situation if it doesn't exactly fit, but the whole analysis doesn't need to be designed from scratch each time. Using performance improvement models that are time-tested and effective make efficient use of the Performance Improvement Technologist's time and show the business partners the value of consulting with a professional. Additionally, if the practitioner isn't fumbling around and designing tools as they go, they are more efficient, use less time, and make better recommendations. For all of these reasons, using Performance Improvement models raises the quality of work and the value of the consulting department in the eyes of the business partners.

The models used to help the volunteer employee team discover the solutions were existing well-known human performance improvement models; Joe Harless' 13 Smart Questions, Thomas Gilbert's Behavior Engineering Model or BEM, and Roger Chevalier's Updated Behavior Engineering Model. These three models were selected because they complement each other to help with the front-end analysis. The blended model shown in the case study follows this model and begins with the Gap Analysis

The three models were blended for the following reasons. The 13 Smart Questions are used as the framework and the driving force to move the process along. The questions simplify the process to make it not seem so overwhelming. The practitioner can take one step at a time and have productive conversations with the business partners as they work on the analysis together. The Behavior Engineering Model and the Updated Behavior Engineering Model provide the depth of analysis needed to get at the root causes in questions six through eight, and they even direct the practitioner to the interventions to apply in questions nine through eleven. The blended model provides a holistic, systemic, and systematic way of performing a Front-end analysis that wasn't possible before, when each model is used separately.

13 Smart Questions

Joe Harless and Thomas Gilbert were contemporaries. They were some of the early fathers of HPT and helped establish HPT as a profession. Harless coined the term front-end analysis. He often told people working with business partners who ask for training to give them what they need, but call it what they want. For example, if the business partner asked for training, but the practitioner determined after doing a front-end analysis that all they needed was a job aid, create the job aid and then train them on how to use the job aid.

The 13 Smart Questions in Table 1 provide the framework for the front-end analysis (Harless, 1973). The goal of the questions is to find out what is really causing the problem. Then the questions lead the practitioner to ask the business to consider if it is useful to the organization to fix it. The questions are grouped according to the phase of the FEA.

The first four questions identify the problem, what the problem means to the organization, and what it will mean to the organization if the problem is fixed. The gap in performance is identified and calculated in terms of value to the organization if the desired performance is achieved. Additionally the desired performance is defined and outlined.

Question five verifies that it is valuable to the organization to fix the problem and that resources will be allocated to fix the problem. If the business leaders determine it is worth the time and resources to fix the problem, then the practitioner

Table 1. 13 Smart Questions

1.	Do we have a problem?
2.	Do we have a (human) performance problem?
3.	How will we know when the problem is solved?
4.	Exactly what is the performance problem?
5.	Should we allocate resources to solve it?
6.	What are the possible causes of the problem?
7.	What evidence bears on each possibility?
8.	What is the probable cause?
9.	What general solution type is indicated?
10.	What are the alternate subclasses of solution?
11.	What are the costs, effects, and development times of each solution?
12.	What are the constraints?
13.	What are the overall goals?

will continue on the path of problem analysis. If the answer to question five is no, then the analysis stops and the organization moves on with very minimal time and effort spent on the issue. If the answer to question five is yes, then the organization commits time, resources, and effort to uncovering what is causing the problems.

A key point here is the first five questions do not get at solving or diagnosing the causes of the problem. The questions only determine what the problem is, how much of an impact the problem has on the organization, what it will look like if the problem is fixed, and whether it is worth it to try to fix the problem. This corresponds to the Gap Analysis from the HPT model. Questions six, seven, and eight seek to determine what is causing the problem. This corresponds to the Cause Analysis from the HPT model.

At questions nine and ten, the practitioner selects possible solutions. These help practitioners determine all of the possible solutions based on the cause of the problem. At this point it is important to identify the general interventions or solutions to use and the alternatives to those general solutions. Before the practitioner actually selects the interventions to implement, questions eleven, twelve, and thirteen help him/her identify the costs associated with each solution, the time and resources involved, and then identify the risks and the ultimate goals of solving the problem. These questions all correspond to the Intervention Selection, Design, and Development from the HPT model.

If the team is patient and takes the time to identify the root of the problem(s) and the benefit of solving them, and can help the business partners wait to determine solutions until they know what is really causing the problem, they will have a clearer path and be more effective. The 13 Smart Questions are useful because of the simplicity. They lead the practitioner through the process and conversation with the business partners. However, the 13 Smart Questions are a little light on how to dig deep into the cause analysis and that is why the Behavior Engineering Model from Gilbert helps supplement the 13 Smart Questions to provide a stronger blended model.

The Four Leisurely Theorems

Thomas Gilbert created what he called leisurely theorems. In his seminal 1978 book, "Human Competence, Engineering Worthy Performance," he introduced and described his leisurely theorems (Gilbert, 1978). His goal as a Performance Improvement Technologist was to improve performance, not behavior, and thus improve accomplishments. He drove practitioners towards changing and improving accomplishments, and not just any accomplishments, but worthy accomplishments or "worthy performance." He posited that if we could do this, then performance analysts would have a great impact on organizations and help improve human performance wherever they went.

Gilbert developed the four leisurely theorems to explain how to engineer worthy performance. Generally it is the third leisurely theorem people think of when they hear about Gilbert, but it's important to understand all four theorems to help with the implementation of the third leisurely theorem. The first and fourth leisurely theorems aren't applicable to the model, but will be explained briefly.

The first theorem aims to define worthy performance. Worthy performance is the goal of organizations. He explains that behavior is not what the organizations want. They want accomplishments. And they want worthy performance. The formula can be shown as worthy performance (W) equals accomplishments (A) divided by the costly behavior (B) or $W = A/B$. The value derived from the accomplishments needs to be greater than the behavior it costs to achieve the accomplishments in order to be considered worthy.

In the second leisurely theorem, Gilbert presented the formula for determining the organization's Potential for Improving Performance (PIP). The second theorem describes the difference between typical performance and exemplary performance. Gilbert discusses how to determine the quantifiable value to the organization to change the performance based on the difference between the typical and exemplary performance. He showed that worthy performance is derived from the ratio of exemplary performance (W_{EX}) over typical performance (W_T) or $PIP = W_{EX} / W_T$. The closer to 1 the formula is, generally, the more difficult it is to make big improvements in the performance between the exemplary performer and the average of all performers. For example, if the exemplary performer produces 100 widgets per hour and the average of all performers produces 95, the $PIP = 1.05$. However, if the exemplary performer produces 150 and the average produces 95, the $PIP = 1.57$. This is a much larger difference and improving the performance of the typical performers is more likely to produce the accomplishments desired by the company or organization.

The third theorem helps the practitioner diagnose what is causing the difference in accomplishment between the typical and the exemplary performer. Gilbert stated

[F]or any given accomplishment, a deficiency in performance always has as its immediate cause a deficiency in a behavior repertory (P), or in the environment that supports the repertory (E), or in both. But its ultimate cause will be found in a deficiency of the management system (M) (Gilbert, 1978, p.76).

Behavior is made up of two elements – the supporting environment and the person's repertory of behavior. When diagnosing performance problems, the causes will be found in these areas. Practitioners need to determine which of these will have a greater, more effective impact on behavior – altering the environmental supports or altering the person's repertory of behavior. This will determine the course of action. The first theorem stated that $W = A/B$. If we add in that $P + E = B$, then the formula can be restated as $W = A/(P+E)$ or we can determine if we have worthy performance when we have accomplishments divided by the sum of a person's repertory of behavior and their environmental supports.

The third theorem is generally called the Behavior Engineering Model or the "Management Theorem." Gilbert calls it the Management Theorem because he sees these areas as under the control of the manager or supervisor. So in order to improve performance, the manager can make improvements in one or all of the areas that need attention to improve performance.

The fourth theorem provides for a systematic way of evaluating the performance. It discerns between philosophical, cultural, policy, strategic, tactical, and logistic performance. The fourth theorem is a "system for sorting out the levels – the scope – of our viewpoints when we talk about value and accomplishment" (Gilbert, 1978, p. 112). Gilbert thought disagreements between people discussing accomplishments could be because they are each applying a different point of view. They weren't all looking at the accomplishments with the same understanding.

Gilbert's Behavior Engineering Model is shown in Table 2. The main categories are information, instrumentation, and motivation. There are six aspects of behavior that need to be in place to have worthy behavior. In the environmental supports three boxes, this is shown as data, instruments, and incentives – things that are outside of the individual person's behavior; what the work environment brings to the job. In the person's repertory of behavior three boxes, this is shown as knowledge, capacity, and motives; things that are within the individual's behavior; what the employees bring to the job.

Gilbert encourages performance analysts to determine which area(s) are impacting performance. In the Environment, does the employee have clear, frequent and

Table 2. Behavior Engineering Model

	Information	Instrumentation	Motivation
Environmental supports (E)	1. Data	2. Instruments	3. Incentives
Person's repertory of behavior (P)	4. Knowledge	5. Capacity	6. Motives

relevant feedback about their performance (Information). Do the employees have the materials, tools, and time to do the job (Resources). Are the employees motivated through financial and non-financial incentives to do the job (Incentives).

In the Person's behavior, do the employees have the necessary knowledge, experiences, and skills to do the desired performance (Knowledge). Do the employees have the capacity to learn and do what is needed to perform successfully (Capacity). And finally, are the motives of the employees aligned with the work and the work environment (Motives).

Gilbert taught practitioners to look at environment first and then move to the person's behavior second. He found that most problems with performance were somewhere in the Data, Instruments, Incentives, or Knowledge sections, sections 1-4. If employees have the clear and relevant feedback, have the tools, get the proper incentives, and either have or get the knowledge to do their job, then the majority of performance problems will be addressed.

He thought capacity and motives may change just by making a change in the other four. He called this Diffusion of Effect. Changes don't happen in a vacuum and practitioners can't, nor do they want to isolate the intervention to only the intended effect. Generally this is where Gilbert expected the personal motivation to change. If the data changes in the environmental supports and people now know how well they are performing against exemplary performance, the diffusion of effect would apply and there would be a positive effect on their motives without making any changes with regards to individual motives. For the volunteer team and the leaders, the diffusion of effect of making changes to the identified problems could have profound effects on the team that continue to build a stronger, more effective team and lift the entire organization.

Sometimes the Behavior Engineering Model needs to be supplemented to provide a more in-depth way to assess the causes of the problems and provide guidance to the practitioner on the order of implementing the interventions. This is where the Updated BEM helps further build out the blended front-end analysis model.

An Update to the Behavioral Engineering Model

Roger Chevalier first updated the performance gap, or PIP, valuation (Chevalier, 2003). Whereas Gilbert looked at the ratio of the exemplary performer to the typical performer, Chevalier simply asked, "what is the difference between the Present Level of Performance and the Desired Performance?" The answer gives the practitioner a Reasonable Goal. This is sometimes easier to understand than the PIP if the practitioner and the business partners are having difficulty putting measures on the performance gap.

The main difference between Gilbert's BEM and Chevalier's updated BEM is the order of the six factors. When Chevalier updated the BEM in 2003, he disputed Gilbert's order of knowledge before motives. Roger Chevalier looked at the BEM and determined that he would change the order in which the practitioner should apply the BEM. He thought the BEM should go across and wrap around rather than Gilbert's recommendation of across E then across I. He posits that a lot of time and money is expended in the Knowledge and Skills area in companies and produces only a small change. He also changed some of the names of the factors in the boxes. He changed "person's repertory of behavior" to "individual (I);" changed "data" to "information"; changed "instruments" to "resources" and added "skills" to "knowledge."

This case will retain Gilbert's original order and presume change in capacity and motives will occur as a diffusion of effect of changes in the other four areas. The questions added to the BEM by Chevalier will be added as they are valuable to guide the practitioner to diagnosing the underlying causes of performance problems. Table 3 provides an overview of the updates that were made to the Behavioral Engineering Model.

Table 3. Behavioral Engineering Updates

E	Information	Resources	Incentives
	• Roles and performance expectations are clearly defined; employees are given relevant feedback about the adequacy of performance • Clear and relevant guides are used to describe the work process. • The performance management system guides employee performance and development	• Materials, tools, and time needed to do the job are present. • Processes and procedures are clearly defined and enhance individual performance if followed. • Overall physical and psychological work environment contributes to improved performance; work conditions are safe, clean, organized, and conducive to performance	• Financial and non-financial incentives are present; measurement and reward systems reinforce positive performance. • Jobs are enriched to allow for fulfillment of employee needs. • Overall work environment is positive, where employees believe they have an opportunity to succeed; career development opportunities are present.
I	Knowledge/Skills	Capacity	Motives
	• Employees have the necessary knowledge, experience, and skills to do the desired behaviors. • Employees with the necessary knowledge, experience, and skills are properly placed to use and share what they know. • Employees are cross-trained to understand each other's roles.	• Employees have the capacity to learn and do what is needed to perform successfully. • Employees are recruited and selected to match the realities of the work situation. • Employees are free of emotional limitations that would interfere with their performance.	• Motives of employees are aligned with the work and the work environment. • Employees desire to perform the required jobs.

In addition to updating the BEM six boxes, Chevalier also introduces driving forces and restraining forces to help the practitioner determine which areas have the most negative or positive impact on the performance. Figure 2 can help the practitioner determine which general solution types would be most effective and efficient to implement based on how much force is helping them along or working against them. Let's go back to our volunteer employee team and the problem of poor satisfaction survey results. If the managers have provided the feedback the employees need, the figure would indicate that there are driving forces for the categories of providing employees clear and relevant feedback. But if the performance management system is complicated and difficult to use, then it would be a constraining force to the employees getting the relevant and clear feedback they need to know how to do their jobs and to know if they are doing them correctly.

Figure 2. Cause analysis worksheet (Adapted from Chevalier, 2003, p. 11)

Factors	Driving Forces					Restraining Forces			
	+4	+3	+2	+1	0	-1	-2	-3	-4
Information									
clear expectations	·	·	·	·		·	·	·	·
relevant feedback	·	·	·	·		·	·	·	·
relevant guides	·	·	·	·		·	·	·	·
performance mgmt system	·	·	·	·		·	·	·	·
Resources									
materials/tools	·	·	·	·		·	·	·	·
time	·	·	·	·		·	·	·	·
clear processes/procedures	·	·	·	·		·	·	·	·
safe/organized environment	·	·	·	·		·	·	·	·
Incentives									
financial	·	·	·	·		·	·	·	·
other incentives	·	·	·	·		·	·	·	·
enriched jobs	·	·	·	·		·	·	·	·
positive work environment	·	·	·	·		·	·	·	·
Motives									
motives aligned with work	·	·	·	·		·	·	·	·
employees desire to perform	·	·	·	·		·	·	·	·
expectations are realistic	·	·	·	·		·	·	·	·
recruit/select the right people	·	·	·	·		·	·	·	·
Capacity									
capacity to learn	·	·	·	·		·	·	·	·
capacity to do what is needed	·	·	·	·		·	·	·	·
recruit/select right people	·	·	·	·		·	·	·	·
emotional limitations	·	·	·	·		·	·	·	·
Knowledge/Skills									
necessary knowledge	·	·	·	·		·	·	·	·
necessary skills	·	·	·	·		·	·	·	·
proper placement	·	·	·	·		·	·	·	·
cross trained	·	·	·	·		·	·	·	·

Blending Front-End Analysis

The three models, when put together like this provide a systematic method for performing a front-end analysis (Table 4). The phase in the HPT model is added and identified in the left column of the table. The center column contains Harless' 13 Smart Questions along with Gilbert's PIP and Chevalier's Performance Gap,

Table 4. Blending Front-End Analysis

HPT Phase	FEA 'Smart Questions'	Your Analysis
Gap Analysis	**1. Do we have a problem?** What data supports that there is a problem? • Indicators & symptoms of problems • Description of tasks that may be deficient	
	2. Do we have a (human) performance problem? Do the indicators show that human performance or non-performance is the cause of the problem? • Observation of mastery performance • People aren't doing what they are expected to do • People are doing what they shouldn't be doing • A prediction of future should/shouldn't performance • Hypothesizing and testing of non-performance causes (e.g., technological inadequacies, Acts of God etc.)	
	3. How will we know when the problem is solved? What performance do we need/want? • Description of mastery performance at a level of task specificity • Description of problem-level goals	
	4. Exactly what is the performance problem? What is the performance gap? Desired Performance W_{ex} • Or PIP = ----- Present Level of Performance W_{i} --------------------------- Reasonable Goal	
	5. Should we allocate resources to solve it? What is the value or priority of allocating resources to resolving this performance gap relative to others? • Cost/benefit analysis	
STOP — If the answer to #5 is "no," stop; if the answer to #5 is "yes," continue.		
Cause Analysis	**6. What are the possible causes of the problem?** • What questions would you ask to investigate the causes of the performance gap? • How does the performance data you have collected relate to the possible causes you identified? Can you eliminate any? Do some seem more likely than others?	

continued on following page

Table 4. Continued

HPT Phase	FEA 'Smart Questions'			Your Analysis
	7. What evidence bears on each possibility? • Based on your analysis what is/are the most likely causes of the performance gap?			
		Information	**Instrumentation**	**Motivation**
	Environmental Supports (E)	**Data** • Roles and performance expectations are clearly defined; employees are given relevant feedback about the adequacy of performance • Clear and relevant guides are used to describe the work process. • The performance management system guides employee performance and development	**Instruments** • Materials, tools, and time needed to do the job are present. • Processes and procedures are clearly defined and enhance individual performance if followed. • Overall physical and psychological work environment contributes to improved performance; work conditions are safe, clean, organized, and conducive to performance	**Incentives** • Financial and non-financial incentives are present; measurement and reward systems reinforce positive performance. • Jobs are enriched to allow for fulfillment of employee needs. • Overall work environment is positive, where employees believe they have an opportunity to succeed; career development opportunities are present.	
	Person's Repertory of Behavior (P)	**Knowledge** • Employees have the necessary knowledge, experience, and skills to do the desired behaviors. • Employees with the necessary knowledge, experience, and skills are properly placed to use and share	**Capacity** • Employees have the capacity to learn and do what is needed to perform successfully. • Employees are recruited and selected to match the realities of the work situation. • Employees are free of emotional	**Motives** • Motives of employees are aligned with the work and the work environment. • Employees desire to perform the required jobs.	

continued on following page

Table 4. Continued

HPT Phase	FEA 'Smart Questions'	Your Analysis

Factors	Driving Forces				0	Restraining Forces			
	+4	+3	+2	+1		-1	-2	-3	-4
Information									
clear expectations	.	.	.	.		.	.	.	.
relevant feedback	.	.	.	.		.	.	.	.
relevant guides	.	.	.	.		.	.	.	.
performance mgmt system	.	.	.	.		.	.	.	.
Resources									
materials/tools	.	.	.	.		.	.	.	.
time	.	.	.	.		.	.	.	.
clear processes/procedures	.	.	.	.		.	.	.	.
safe/organized environment	.	.	.	.		.	.	.	.
Incentives									
financial	.	.	.	.		.	.	.	.
other incentives	.	.	.	.		.	.	.	.
enriched jobs	.	.	.	.		.	.	.	.
positive work environment	.	.	.	.		.	.	.	.
Motives									
motives aligned with work	.	.	.	.		.	.	.	.
employees desire to perform	.	.	.	.		.	.	.	.
expectations are realistic	.	.	.	.		.	.	.	.
recruit/select the right people	.	.	.	.		.	.	.	.
Capacity									
capacity to learn	.	.	.	.		.	.	.	.
capacity to do what is needed	.	.	.	.		.	.	.	.
recruit/select right people	.	.	.	.		.	.	.	.
emotional limitations	.	.	.	.		.	.	.	.
Knowledge/Skills									
necessary knowledge	.	.	.	.		.	.	.	.
necessary skills	.	.	.	.		.	.	.	.
proper placement	.	.	.	.		.	.	.	.
cross trained	.	.	.	.		.	.	.	.

HPT Phase	FEA 'Smart Questions'	Your Analysis
	8. What is the probable cause? • Based on your analysis what is/are the most likely causes of the performance gap?	
Intervention Selection, Design, and Development	**9. What general solution type is indicated?** Possible Solution Types include: 　d) Training, information and /or feedback. 　e) Re-engineering the performance environment. 　f) Incentives and behavior maintenance.	

continued on following page

Table 4. Continued

HPT Phase	FEA 'Smart Questions'	Your Analysis

	10. What are the alternate subclasses of solution?
	d) Training, information and/or feedback.
	    • Custom vs off-the shelf training
	    • Classroom vs E-learning
	    • Coaching
	    • Reporting
	    • Other
	e) Re-engineering the performance environment.
	    • Policies and procedures
	    • Systems, tools and equipment
	    • Other
	f) Incentives and behavior maintenance.
	    • Rewards and recognition
	    • Consequences
	    • Other	

	11. What are the costs, effects, and development times of each solution? Calculate the costs and likelihood of success of each option individually and in combination 	
	12. What are the constraints? Evaluate the limiting and enabling factors that may influence the success of the intervention	
	13. What are the overall goals? List the goals of the intervention.	

Gilbert's BEM, and Chevalier's Driving and Restraining Forces. The right column is for the practitioner to take notes. Supporting questions to aid in the analysis are included under the primary 13 Smart Questions.

To complete the Front-End Analysis, the practitioner needs to work with the business partners who own the problem and who will own the solution to gather all of the information and data needed to answer all of the questions. The combined model also provides Performance Improvement Technologists and the business partners with direction to determine the problems to performance. When neither party has access to the information or data to answer a question, they can determine from whom they can get the information and note it in the model. Then they can identify who will gather the data from the other department so they can analyze it and move to the next question.

CASE DESCRIPTION

Using the Employee Satisfaction Survey Team case as the example, the blended models shown in Table 4 can be used to determine what problems are affecting performance in the marketing, communications and training team, the cause, and the interventions that will improve the desired performance.

Application of the Blended Model: Gap Analysis Phase

First the practitioner begins with the "Performance Analysis of Need or Opportunity" section of the HPT Model and the gap analysis phase. The practitioner performs the Gap Analysis by using the first four questions of the 13 Smart Questions.

Final outcome: Yes, the solution to the problem is a very high priority and potentially worth over $100,000 per employee in cost savings. An increase in employee engagement is desired by the company and department and considered valuable.

Box 1.

FEA 'Smart Questions'

1. Do we have a problem?
What data supports that there is a problem?
    • Indicators & symptoms of problems
    • Description of tasks that may be deficient

    • The annual employee satisfaction survey results show the employees are very dissatisfied with their jobs and the department, especially over the previous year.

    • Scores went down significantly in eight out of nine categories from 2011 survey responses to 2012 survey responses.

    • Three out of the eight declining scores were -21, -19, and -14 over the year before.

Box 2. Final Outcome: Yes

FEA 'Smart Questions'

2. Do we have a (human) performance problem?
Do the indicators show that human performance or non-performance is the cause of the problem?
   • Observation of mastery performance
   • People aren't doing what they are expected to do
   • People are doing what they shouldn't be doing
   • A prediction of future should/shouldn't performance
   • Hypothesizing and testing of non-performance causes (e.g., technological inadequacies, Acts of God etc.)

   • The work is being completed on time by the employees, however many employees have stated that they've had to work many extra hours to redo work. Work that was approved by the group of approvers changes frequently when re-read and reconsidered. So then the approvals change and the employee is asked to rework the material again.

   • Additionally, in the survey 45% of this department's employees said they would be looking for a new employer within 1-2 years.

Box 3. Final outcome: Yes

FEA 'Smart Questions'
3. How will we know when the problem is solved? What performance do we need/want? • Description of mastery performance at a level of task specificity • Description of problem-level goals

   Desired performance would be satisfied and engaged employees.

   Proof of this would be

   • Employee satisfaction survey scores stop declining and start improving over 2012 scores.

   • Employee satisfaction with their jobs and desire to remain working in this department and staying with the company.

Box 4.

FEA 'Smart Questions'
4. Exactly what is the performance problem? What is the performance gap? Desired Performance W_{ex} • Or PIP = ----- Present level of Performance W_t --------------------------- Reasonable Goal =================

   The desired performance is retained employees. This is 1.5 times the salary of an employee* if they leave and need to be replaced, plus the cost of lost work while the new employee gets fully acclimated to and engaged in the job and culture. It is much less expensive to retain employees rather than hire new employees.

   *value obtained from the Human Resource department at this company

The answers to questions 1-4 indicate there is a human performance problem and there is value to the department and the company in finding solutions to improve the performance. Since the answer to question #5 is also yes, then the practitioner proceeds to Cause Analysis questions, numbers 6-8.

It is very important to get business leader support for all of the answers and data uncovered in questions 1-4 and to listen to the business leaders when it comes to question 5. This sets the stage for all of the possible cause analysis that will lead to intervention selection. If done well with support and buy-in from the business leaders, a very good case will be made by the business partners for the solutions and they will be looking at a holistic solution, not just what they think the cause and solution are. This will make the HPT practitioner a valued partner in solving future performance problems. Throughout the process, the practitioner will want to paraphrase the questions into the language used by the client or business. If the practitioner uses HPT jargon, they could distance themselves from their business partners and lessen their effectiveness and value to the business.

APPLICATION OF THE BLENDED MODEL: CAUSE ANALYSIS PHASE

The practitioner will continue the Performance Analysis of Need or Opportunity with the cause analysis phase. The practitioner performs the Cause Analysis with questions six through eight.

The volunteer employee team members met and reviewed the survey. They looked for any area on the survey where the "percent favorable" was less than 50% and the

Box 5.

FEA 'Smart Questions'
5. Should we allocate resources to solve it? What is the value or priority of allocating resources to resolving this performance gap relative to others? • Cost/benefit analysis

Box 6.

FEA 'Smart Questions'
6. What are the possible causes of the problem? • What questions would you ask to investigate the causes of the performance gap? • How does the performance data you have collected relate to the possible causes you identified? Can you eliminate any? Do some seem more likely than others?

"change from 2011" was more than -7. Key findings by the volunteer employee team from the Employee Satisfaction survey are: (numbers in parentheses are the % of employees who agreed with this statement – found it favorable)

- Policies/practices/procedures enable me to do my job the way it should be done (27%).
- Work processes are efficient and well organized in my department (27%).
- I am satisfied with the recognition I receive for doing a good job (36%).
- My leader gives me feedback that helps me improve my performance (45%).
- The company provides me with the opportunity for learning and development (36%).
- My department uses the feedback from this survey to make improvements (36%).
- The technology I have to do my job is comparable to the technology at other similar companies (36%).
- Communication in my department provides me with a clear understanding of why decisions are made (27%).
- I have the authority to make decisions that improve the quality of my work (27%).
- I am satisfied with my involvement in decisions that affect my work (27%).
- I understand the decision making and approval process as related to the work I do (45%).

There were other areas that warranted attention, but these were the most important and most critical to resolve by the department as identified by the volunteer employee team. The team decided that the remaining issues, if they persist, could be addressed after these critical issues were addressed.

To answer this question, the items the volunteer employee team identified can be applied to the Behavior Engineering Model.

In addition to the satisfaction survey, the volunteer employees were permitted to use any data source to help them. The employees interviewed other employees in the department, used past project documents including debrief meeting minutes to help in their search for the gap, cause and solutions to the department's problems.

Box 7.

FEA 'Smart questions'
7. What evidence bears on each possibility?   • Based on your analysis what is/are the most likely causes of the performance gap?

As they uncovered the reasons behind the poor scores in a variety of sources, they made a point of getting to the root of the causes with facts and documentation.

The team discussed all of the data they had and discussed the root causes of the problems. There were often heated debates about the causes of the problems in the volunteer team employee meetings. The practitioner, as the leader of the employee team, moderated through these. When items were being debated, the team looked for examples to prove their points. Generally stories were shared about incidents when a problem occurred and what had been done and how it had been handled by all of the parties involved. The group then discussed whether it was an isolated incident, or a pattern of behavior. Often more than one person in the group had a story to tell that supported the point and confirmed that it was a wide-spread problem. The group then documented the problems that were frequent and pain-points. They captured each of the issues and then ranked them by frequency or importance based on how difficult it was to work around the current situation to get the work done.

When all of the data gathering was said and done, the team each reviewed the data and highlighted on the BEM the items that they thought depicted the problems most accurately. The results of all of the completed forms showed the problems fell into categories 1-3, Data, Instruments, and Incentives.

Table 5 outlines the evidence that was obtained from the satisfaction survey.

Table 5. Evidence from the satisfaction survey

	Information	**Instrumentation**	**Motivation**
Environmental Supports (E)	**1) DATA** • My leader gives me feedback that helps me improve my performance. • My department uses the feedback from this survey to make improvements. • Communication in my department provides me with a clear understanding of why decisions are made. • I have the authority to make decisions that improve the quality of my work. • I am satisfied with my involvement in decisions that affect my work. • I understand the decision making and approval process as related to the work I do.	**2) INSTRUMENTS** • Policies/practices/procedures enable me to do my job the way it should be done. • Work processes are efficient and well organized in my department. • The technology I have to do my job is comparable to the technology at other similar companies.	**3) INCENTIVES** • I am satisfied with the recognition I receive for doing a good job. • The company provides me with the opportunities for learning and development.
Person's Repertory of Behavior (P)	**4) KNOWLEDGE**	**5) CAPACITY**	**6) MOTIVES**

The data from the survey and all other documentation used showed that the employees are motivated to work and in fact really enjoy working for this company and this department. They have the desire to improve the jobs and work so they can remain working in this department. Additionally, they have the skills, knowledge, and abilities to do the work, which is why such award-winning work is being accomplished even in the current system.

Table 6 demonstrates the alignment and how the leaders have done a good job of putting together a very good team.

Using Chevalier's driving and restraining forces table (Figure 3) gives the practitioner further details on which areas are helping the department succeed and which areas are impeding the success. The leaders verify that they have good employees with expert knowledge. The employees have the capacity to learn new tasks as needed and generally their motives are aligned with the work. The employees have a desire to perform for themselves and for the company. Additionally there is some benefit perceived from the jobs and positive work environment. These are all driv-

Table 6. Alignment between the models

E	Data	Instruments	Incentives
	• **Missing:** Roles and performance expectations are clearly defined; employees are given relevant feedback about the adequacy of performance. • **Missing:** Clear and relevant guides are used to describe the work process. • **Missing:** The performance management system guides employee performance and development.	• **Missing:** Materials, tools, and time needed to do the job are present. • **Missing:** Processes and procedures are clearly defined and enhance individual performance if followed. • **N/A:** Overall physical and psychological work environment contributes to improved performance; work conditions are safe, clean, organized, and conducive to performance.	• **Missing:** Financial and non-financial incentives are present; measurement and reward systems reinforce positive performance. • **Missing:** Jobs are enriched to allow for fulfillment of employee needs. • **Missing:** Overall work environment is positive, where employees believe they have an opportunity to succeed; career development opportunities are present.
P	Knowledge	Capacity	Motives
	• **In Place:** Employees have the necessary knowledge, experience, and skills to do the desired behaviors. • **In Place:** Employees with the necessary knowledge, experience, and skills are properly placed to use and share what they know. • **Missing:** Employees are cross-trained to understand each other's roles.	• **In Place:** Employees have the capacity to learn and do what is needed to perform successfully. • **In Place:** Employees are recruited and selected to match the realities of the work situation. • **N/A:** Employees are free of emotional limitations that would interfere with their performance.	• **In Place:** Motives of employees are aligned with the work and the work environment. • **In Place:** Employees desire to perform the required jobs.

Figure 3. Adapted from Chevalier's Driving and Retaining Forces (Used by permission)

Factors	Driving Forces				0	Restraining Forces			
	+4	+3	+2	+1		-1	-2	-3	-4
Information									
clear expectations	·	·	·	·		←———————			
relevant feedback	·	·	·	·		←———————			
relevant guides	·	·	·	·		←———————			
performance mgmt system	·	·	·	·		←———————			
Resources									
materials/tools	·	·	·	·		←——		·	·
time	·	·	·	·		←——		·	·
clear processes/procedures	·	·	·	·		←———————			
safe/organized environment	——————→					·	·	·	·
Incentives									
financial	·	·	·	·		←—————			·
other incentives	·	·	·	·		←———			·
enriched jobs	·	·	·	·		←—	·	·	·
positive work environment	·	———→				·	·	·	·
Motives									
motives aligned with work	——————→					·	·	·	·
employees desire to perform	——————→					·	·	·	·
expectations are realistic	——————→					·	·	·	·
recruit/select the right people	——————→					·	·	·	·
Capacity									
capacity to learn	——————→					·	·	·	·
capacity to do what is needed	——————→					·	·	·	·
recruit/select right people	——————→					·	·	·	·
emotional limitations	——————→					·	·	·	·
Knowledge/Skills									
necessary knowledge	——————→					·	·	·	·
necessary skills	——————→					·	·	·	·
proper placement	——————→					·	·	·	·
cross trained	·	·	·	·		←———————			·

ing forces, helping to make the workplace and performance better. Even though this is a very lean team with a lot of work, the employees are highly motivated and talented.

Based on the responses from the employee satisfaction survey, there are not very clear expectations, there isn't relevant feedback or guides, the right tools and materials aren't available, nor is there enough time or clear procedures and policies. Additionally there is less than desirable benefit perceived from the financial and other incentives. These are all restraining forces, helping to make the workplace and performance worse. There aren't clear expectations or direct tie-in to results of business by the results of the team. It was taxing to the leaders to maintain excellence with the newly expanded team and the higher than usual number of projects and product launches asked of the team. Everyone was striving to meet the needs being requested by the organization. The more the leaders can do to remove the restraining forces and enhance the driving forces, the better the work and the performance will be now and in the future.

Another challenge that can occur at this point for the practitioner is giving open and honest feedback to leaders. To sit and complain about leaders or any problem is not productive. To give honest, albeit difficult feedback is tricky. As in this case, the group discussed leader effectiveness and found some gaps; some ways leaders were not only ineffective, but were getting in the way and making the situation worse. The volunteer employee team stepped lightly, but purposely to deliver constructive feedback on ways the leaders were contributing to the team's problems and getting in the way of the process. The employee team discussed, heated at times, how this negatively affected projects and deadlines and then discussed potential solutions with the leaders.

As the volunteer employee team dug deeper into the employee satisfaction survey, they attempted to articulate the probable causes of the poor survey results. The key findings from the team were shared with leadership over a few meetings. The employees grouped the findings under two categories: Job itself and Leader effectiveness. Both of these categories contain further support of the possible causes and the evidence shown in the environmental supports sections of the BEM.

For the Job itself dimension from the satisfaction survey, the employees found the following relevant issues (items are not in order of importance):

Recognition/Work-Life Balance

- Acknowledge and recognize the team's accomplishments.
- Find fun ways to say "thank you."
- Celebrate our own results.
- Work from home options available.

Box 8.

FEA 'Smart questions'
8. What is the probable cause? Based on your analysis what is/are the most likely causes of the performance gap?

- More flexibility in work schedules.
- Create better link between yearly goals and how we are rewarded for our performance.
- Allow us to recognize other team members for accomplishments.

Respect

- Process interferes with good use of our time.
- Leverage expertise (strengths and talents) on projects while also providing opportunities for growth and development.
- Trust in the expertise on the team.
- Respect for the creative process.

Resources

- Training plans for new hires.
- Project coordinator to handle lower level work and act as back-up.
- Many people are extended beyond their roles.
- Many tools are cumbersome or not specialized enough for the team, making us inefficient and not able to communicate in manner we need.
- Color printer is antiquated and used by too many departments.
- Need social media access for greater impact.
- Mobile development software.
- Needs of a creative team are different than an accounting team, but the technology is the same.
- Culture doesn't inspire creativity, need colorful places where we can be inspired and celebrate past successes.
- Let the technology do some of the work for us rather than a manual process that's very cumbersome.

Development

- Need time to learn new trends and apply them.
- Flexibility to try new and innovative ideas and support through the learning curve.
- Encouragement to attend professional events, seminars, professional associations.
- Need departmental structure with career ladder and opportunities for specialization.

For the Leader effectiveness dimension from the satisfaction survey, the employees found the following relevant issues (items are not in order of importance):

Trust

- Rely on team members for expertise for which they were hired.
- Give decision-making authority to team members in addition to the accountability.
- Determine which items necessitate leader authority/input/feedback and turn over lower authority/input/feedback to the team member accountable for project.
- Address lack of trust of leaders for deadlines/importance/feedback.

Communication

- Team member success.
- Need to remove the hierarchy of sharing information.
- Communications/updates about projects should be proactively disseminated.
- Decision-making hierarchy hinders work and creates backlogs, wasted time, and overactive periods.
- Need clear method of getting decision-makers to understand urgency of issues and provide timely response.
- Better communicate leader expectations of what is meeting expectations and what is exceeding expectations.
- Kept in the loop about things that impact us like status of hiring vacant position and share info with us in-person before an e-mail to the entire company goes out – share with the team first.

Proactive

- Promote new trends in our field.
- Advocate for/promote employee achievements within the team and with outside leaders and business partners.

Process

- Improve processes to remove decision-making blocks.
- Have products developed before asking for implementation plans to improve output and remove confusion and duplication of work due to iterations.

- Remove cumbersome duplication of efforts by utilizing reporting functions currently available.

These probable causes align with the categories in the BEM boxes for environmental supports of Data, Instruments, and Incentives. The volunteer employees noted that these changes, if implemented, would bring about an overall cultural shift in the department based on the new trust and recognition. It would also necessitate more resources – process, people, and tools. Finally leader effectiveness would improve based on transparency and less gatekeeping.

The answers to questions 6-8 indicate there are basic themes of opportunities and challenges that fall within Gilbert's BEM. Primarily the Management Theorem shows the problems fall into the Environmental support area. It is time to determine Intervention Selection, Design, and Development.

An additional challenge for practitioners at this point can be resistance from the groups involved for ownership or fault. Generally there is partial responsibility for the problems from all sides. The practitioner needs to be diplomatic and use facts and pull back the emotion from the conversation, if it starts heading that way. The employees generally point at the leaders for the reason there are problems and the leaders generally point at the employees for the reason there are problems. One of the great things about this method is it looks for data and facts to support the gap and causes which takes the personal part out of the discussion, helping business partners to look at the situation systematically and systemically rather than problems with individual people.

Application of the Blended Model: Intervention Selection, Design, and Development Phase

Next the practitioner moves to the Intervention Selection, Design, and Development phase of the HPT Model. The practitioner performs this phase with questions nine through thirteen.

Box 9.

FEA 'Smart questions'

9. What general solution type is indicated?
Possible Solution Types include:
    a. Training, information and /or feedback.
    b. Re-engineering the performance environment.
    c. Incentives and behavior maintenance.

Looking at the items in the BEM identified as missing, give the practitioner the direction for recommending solutions and interventions. The general solution types indicated by the feedback from the employee satisfaction survey and the volunteer employee team research are located in the environmental support boxes – data, instruments, and incentives.

Recommendations for the Environmental support (E) area are (not in order of importance):

1. Descriptions of what is expected of performance.
2. Clearly defined roles and performance explanations.
3. Relevant and frequent feedback about performance.
4. Clear and relevant guides to describe the work process.
5. Materials, tools, and time to do the job.
6. Clearly defined processes and procedures.
7. Work conditions conducive to performance.
8. Career development opportunities.
9. Financial and non-financial incentives.

Recommendations for the Person's Repertory of Behavior (P) area are:

10. Cross-train employees to understand each other's roles and fill-in during a vacancy.
11. Provide flexible work schedules.
12. Provide additional staffing during peak capacity times.

Box 10.

FEA 'Smart questions'
10. What are the alternate subclasses of solution?
1. Training, information and/or feedback.
a. Custom vs off-the shelf training
b. Classroom vs E-learning
c. Coaching
d. Reporting
e. Other
2. Re-engineering the performance environment.
a. Policies and procedures
b. Systems, tools and equipment
c. Other
3. Incentives and behavior maintenance.
a. Rewards and recognition
b. Consequences
c. Other

Possible alternate subclasses of solutions could be:

- Better coaching of employees for performance, whether done by managers or by human resource professionals.
- Improved reporting including guides for reviewers and approvers.
- Clear policies and procedures.
- Upgraded systems and tools.
- Improved rewards and recognition.
- Positive consequences for exemplary performance

For the items in question 9, 1-4, 6-7, 10-11 the cost would be minimal. To put these into place, time would be the biggest resource needed.

1. Descriptions of what is expected of performance.
2. Clearly defined roles and performance explanations.
3. Relevant and frequent feedback about performance.

For these three, the Human Resource department could provide examples and potentially help put descriptions into place. They could provide assistance with clearly defining roles and what performance was expected by role. They could also show how to get the relevant feedback out of the existing performance support system and give the leaders help in coaching for feedback about performance. The development time would be moderate. The effects would be great as employees would know how they would be judged for performance and what they were expected to do.

4. Clear and relevant guides to describe the work process.

A Project Manager from the department who are already experts in developing process maps could help map out the work processes. The process maps could be developed to show not only what the current process is, but also highlight areas where the processes could be improved for better, more streamlined workflow. The development time on this would be minimal. The effects would be great as everyone in the department would know the work process and could support it.

Box 11.

FEA 'Smart questions'
11. What are the costs, effects, and development times of each solution? Calculate the costs and likelihood of success of each option individually and in combination

6. Clearly defined processes and procedures.
7. Work conditions conducive to performance.

After reviewing the process maps, the leaders could review with the team to determine what improvements to the process would need to be made and then the leaders could put the procedures in place. There would be on-going process improvement of the process maps and procedures until they were exactly what the department needed. The development time on this would be minimal. The effects would be very good as everyone knew what to expect and what they needed to do. This would contribute to a work environment that was favorable for the desired performance.

10. Cross-train employees to understand each other's roles and fill-in during a vacancy.

Leaders could identify parts of jobs that were critical once the roles were clearly defined. Then they could start cross-training similar roles to understand and be able to jump in to help for the critical processes when there was a vacancy or peak project time period. The cost would be minimal. The effects would be very good to alleviating stress during highly stressful peak times.

11. Provide flexible work schedules.

Leaders and staff could have more flexibility in their schedules of when they had to be in the office and when they could work from home. There would be no development time as the leaders could put this into effect immediately. The effects would be great as employees would have more control over their work-life balance.

The remaining items, 5, 8, 9, and 12 would take more cost to implement and require more resources. When leveraging the highest benefit for the lowest cost, these interventions may need more cost to implement so would not be good candidates for the initial wave of interventions. Additionally, many of these interventions require substantive discussions with other departments, e.g., Human Resources and Finance, to determine how to implement them. More analysis would be needed to determine how much benefit will be derived from implementing these and how best to implement them.

5. Materials, tools, and time to do the job.

Leaders would need to work with the list of tools the employees indicated would help them do their jobs better, assess each one and determine what were the most effective to purchase and implement. The Procurement department would need to be consulted to determine ordering and delivery time. The time to development could be significant. The effects would be moderate to significant. Leaders would need to do a deeper cost-benefit analysis on these before authorizing purchases to make sure they are selecting the best solutions for the biggest impact.

8.   Career development opportunities.

Leaders would need to work with the Human Resource department again to map out some career development opportunities for the team. Once the roles were clearly defined, the leaders and Human Resource could determine some stretch assignments and layout some possible career paths for the various roles within the department. The time for development would be significant and is contingent upon the work done to clearly define the roles and performance measures for the department. The effects would be very good as they would provide paths for employees to stay and grow within the company.

9.   Financial and non-financial incentives.

Leaders would need to work with the Human Resource department for guidelines on financial and non-financial incentives that fit within the overall corporate culture. The Human Resource department could also advise the leaders on a range of incentives from low-cost financial and non-financial incentives through high-cost financial and non-financial incentives. Once the incentives were determined, the Leaders could share the opportunities with the department and explain how the incentives could be achieved. The time for development would be moderate. The effects would be very good to retaining and rewarding the performance the department desired.

12.   Provide additional staffing during peak capacity times.

Leaders would need to work with upper management and with Human Resources to determine options for obtaining additional staffing during peak capacity times. Options could include job-sharing from other departments to hiring temporary staff for specific tasks during peak times. The time for development would be minimal. The effects would be significant for providing additional help to the already strapped and stressed team and would provide them with greater work-life balance on a continual basis.

A potential less expensive solution would be reprioritizing the work at peak capacity times. This would involve conversations with all the involved business partners, but could provide for full engagement of the existing staff on the key priorities and projects as deadlines approached. This could be accomplished for little to no cost.

Practitioners should also consult Chevalier's "Leveraging the Solution" graphic to help determine which interventions would have a higher impact for a lower cost (Figure 4).

The constraints to implementing the recommendations are:

- Time and capacity to create relevant feedback guides and to clearly define roles and performance explanations.
- Managers would need additional training in coaching.
- Project manager to help create work process maps.
- Cost for materials and tools to do the jobs.

Figure 4.

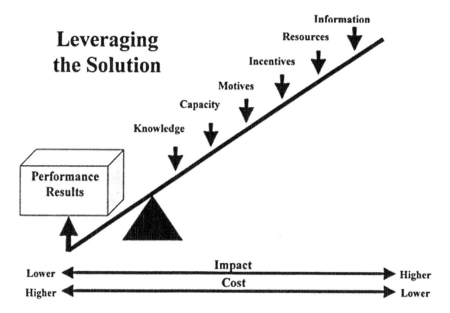

Box 12.

FEA 'Smart questions'
12. What are the constraints? Evaluate the limiting and enabling factors that may influence the success of the intervention

- Influencing business partners to build in the time to do the job.
- Career development opportunities.
- Costs and upper management approval for financial incentives.
- Costs and upper management approval for additional staffing during peak times.
- Restraining forces.
- Upper Management support of leader changes.

The outcome:

- Solve the process problems first.
- Improve communications about processes and procedures.
- Acknowledge team accomplishments.
- Implement non-financial incentives.
- Seek funds for further development and implementation of this project.

CURRENT CHALLENGES FACING THE ORGANIZATION

Hierarchical businesses often provide challenges to practitioners, employees, and leaders as the hierarchy must in some ways be followed. The employee team worked with leadership to combine reviews and steps in their processes whenever possible to minimize some of the hierarchy of reviews up and down. Work on this is ongoing. It takes effort on everyone's part to continually ask "Is the system working?" and work to improve it if the answer is no. Each person involved in the process needs to be accountable and responsible for helping to improve the process to make the business work better together to put out the best possible products.

The employees and leaders have committed to making the changes and improving the workplace. However, continuous work on the restraining forces is needed. To resolve this, the department has plans to continue working on the items and ideas discovered in the 2012 employee satisfaction survey and continue working to improve the policies, procedures and communication across the department and across the organization. Additionally they plan to keep a volunteer employee satisfaction

Box 13.

FEA 'Smart questions'
13. What are the overall goals? List the goals of the intervention.

team together to continue to assess the annual satisfaction surveys. The work of the department continues to receive awards and employees are more satisfied with their roles and performance.

The future outlook for the team is good. Team members are less stressed and communication about processes and procedures is greatly improved. Only the technology piece needs to be addressed to make this a complete success.

SOLUTIONS AND RECOMMENDATIONS

As a result of all of the work, the following solutions were determined to be the first to be implemented.

- Implement a new decision-making process for big projects.
- Improve communications and remove hierarchy.
- Reprioritize work load and projects during peak capacity times.
- Focus on team's accomplishments in staff meetings.
- Create a culture of fun through occasional happy hours, team meetings outdoors, more consistent recognition of work, and other developing ideas.
- Manage change and peak capacity times by quickly filling open roles and redesigning the team as needed as the projects and opportunities arise.

Everyone in the department eagerly awaited the results of the next annual employee survey. Would the hard work of everyone on the team payoff? The answers would be clear:

- Policies/practices/procedures enable me to do my job the way it should be done:
  - 2012 results = 27%; 2013 results = 50% - up 23%.
- Work processes are efficient and well organized in my department:
  - 2012 results = 27%; 2013 results = 64% - up 37%.
- I am satisfied with the recognition I receive or doing a good job:
  - 2012 results = 36%; 2013 results = 67% - up 31%.
- My leader gives me feedback that helps me improve my performance:
  - 2012 results = 45%; 2013 results 92% - up 47%.
- The company provides me with the opportunity for learning and development:
  - 2012 results = 36%; 2013 results = 75% - up 39%.
- My department uses the feedback from this survey to make improvements:
  - 2012 results = 36%; 2013 results = 100% - up 64%.

- The technology I have to do my job is comparable to the technology at other similar companies:
  - 2012 results = 36%; 2013 results 36% - no change.
- Communication in my department provides me with a clear understanding of why decisions are made:
  - 2012 results = 27%; 2013 results = 73% - up 46%.
- I have the authority to make decisions that improve the quality of my work:
  - 2012 results = 27%; 2013 results = 75% - up 48%.
- I am satisfied with my involvement in decisions that affect my work:
  - 2012 results = 27%; 2013 results = 67% - up 40%.
- I understand the decision making and approval process as related to the work I do:
  - 2012 results = 45%; 2013 results = this question was not included in the 2013 survey.

Except for one key area, all of the results were up 23-100% from 2012 to 2013. This was a huge success for the department, for the employees, and for the company. Additionally, the number of people who were looking to find a job at another company in the next 1-2 years dropped from 45% to 25%, with the majority of employees stating they planned to be at the company for 3 or more years.

Satisfaction with the company was the trigger that started this team on a search for solutions. If the situation continued as it was, the human performance was going to change (degrade) as the employees became even more dissatisfied. This would have resulted in lower quality of work or higher cost to the department as the employees left. The leaders correctly identified that there was a problem coming and they needed to solve it or lose.

Through the use of front-end analysis, the leaders and team were able to solve the majority of their problems with very little cost. Harless' 13 smart questions provided the overarching framework. Through his questions, the business was able to see there was a problem that would have a detrimental effect on the department and the business. Leaders and employees were able to agree on the problem, what it would look like if solved, and agree to solve it. Gilbert and Chevalier's BEM and Updated BEM helped answer the questions that Harless asked around cause analysis to provide details about what was causing the problems and showed how to prioritize the problems. Additionally, through the driving/restraining forces table, the department was able to see what was working and what driving forces would continue to help them be successful in the future when the restraining forces were removed. This allowed the department and leaders to prioritize the solutions to be most effective and efficient. When faced with a very difficult and challenging situation that could cause major upheaval in the company, the front-end analysis models helped bring to light what was really the problem.

REFERENCES

Chevalier, R. (2003). Updating the behavior engineering model. *Performance Improvement, 42*(5), 8–14. doi:10.1002/pfi.4930420504

Gilbert, T. F. (2007). *Human competence: Engineering worthy performance (Tribute Edition)*. San Francisco, CA: Pfeiffer.

Harless, J. (1973). An analysis of front-end analysis. *Improving Human Performance. Research Quarterly, 4*, 229–244.

Van Tiem, D. M., Moseley, J. L., & Dessinger, J. C. (2012). *Fundamentals of performance improvement: A guide to improving people, process, and performance* (3rd ed.). San Francisco, CA: Pfeiffer.

ADDITIONAL READING

Andia, L. (2008). Using the BEM for curriculum design: A case study. *Performance Improvement, 47*(6), 38–44. doi:10.1002/pfi.20008

Austin, J., & Garnier, L. (1998). The virtual office: A behavior engineering model (BEM) perspective. *Performance Improvement Quarterly, 11*(4), 7–21. doi:10.1111/j.1937-8327.1998.tb00104.x

Binder, C. (1998). The six boxes™: A descendent of Gilbert's behavior engineering model. *Performance Improvement, 37*(6), 48–52. doi:10.1002/pfi.4140370612

Bolin, A. (2006). Got tools?: Modified six-box model. *Performance Improvement, 45*(9), 20–21. doi:10.1002/pfi.4930450916

Brethower, D. M. (1997). Rapid analysis: Matching solutions to changing situations. *Performance Improvement, 36*(10), 16–21. doi:10.1002/pfi.4140361006

Chevalier, R. (1994). From a process to a system. *Performance And Instruction, 33*(10), 18–19. doi:10.1002/pfi.4160331008

Chevalier, R. (2014). Improving workplace performance. *Performance Improvement, 53*(5), 6–19. doi:10.1002/pfi.21410

Chyung, S. Y. (2005). Human performance technology: From Taylor's scientific management to Gilbert's behavior engineering model. *Performance Improvement, 44*(1), 23–28. doi:10.1002/pfi.4140440109

Crossman, D. (2010). Gilbert's behavior engineering model: Contemporary support for an established theory. *Performance Improvement Quarterly, 23*(1), 31–52. doi:10.1002/piq.20074

Dean, P. J. (1997). Thomas F. Gilbert, Ph. D: Engineering performance improvement with or without training. In P. J. Dean & D. E. Ripley (Series Eds.), Performance improvement Series: Vol. 1. Performance improvement pathfinders: Models for organizational learning systems (pp. 45-64). Silver Spring, MD: International Society for Performance Improvement.

Gilbert, T. (1988, July). Measuring the potential for performance improvement. *Training (New York, N.Y.), 25*(7), 49–52. PMID:10239570

Harless, J. (1970). *An Ounce of analysis is worth a pound of objectives.* Newnan, GA: Guild V Publications.

Harless, J. (1976). Speaking from experience. *Training and Development Journal, 30*(3), 10–11.

Kaufman, R. (1988). Preparing useful performance indicators. *Training and Development Journal, 42*(9), 80–83.

Lee, W. W., & Owens, D. (2001). Rapid analysis model: Reducing analysis time without sacrificing quality. *Performance Improvement, 40*(1), 13–18. doi:10.1002/pfi.4140400106

Marker, A. (2007). Synchronized analysis model: Linking Gilbert's behavior engineering model with environmental analysis models. *Performance Improvement, 46*(1), 26–32. doi:10.1002/pfi.036

Molenda, M., & Pershing, J. A. (2004). The Strategic Impact Model: An Integrative Approach to Performance Improvement and Instructional Systems Design. *TechTrends, 48*(2), 26–32. doi:10.1007/BF02762540

Rethaber, J. D. (2011). Bridging the performance gap with ergonomics: A case study. *Performance Improvement, 50*(7), 33–37.

Ripley, D. E. (1997). Joe Harless, Ed.D.: An ounce of analysis. In P. J. Dean, & D. E. Ripley (Eds.), Performance improvement pathfinders: Models for organizational learning (Chapter 6, pp. 92-107). Washington, DC: International Society for Performance Improvement.

Rossett, A. (1997). Have we overcome obstacles to needs assessment? *Performance Improvement, 36*(3), 30–35. doi:10.1002/pfi.4140360308

Rossett, A. (1998). *First things fast: A handbook for performance analysis.* San Francisco, CA: Jossey-Bass.

Rossett, A., & Volkl, C. (2000). First steps fast: Using technology to coach neophytes in analysis. *Performance Improvement, 39*(10), 25–30. doi:10.1002/pfi.4140391010

Rummler, G. A., & Brache, A. P. (1990). *Improving performance: How to manage the white space on the organization chart.* San Francisco, CA: Jossey-Bass Publishers.

Sostrin, J. (2011). A systemic cause analysis model for human performance technicians. *Performance Improvement, 50*(8), 17–23. doi:10.1002/pfi.20237

Stolovitch, H., & Keeps, E. (1999). What is human performance technology. In H. Stolovitch & E. Keeps (Eds.), *Handbook of human performance technology* (2nd ed., pp. 3–23). San Francisco, CA: Josey-Bass.

Taylor, R. (2005). Life in the pinball machine: Looking back with Bob Mager. *Performance Improvement, 44*(9), 5–8. doi:10.1002/pfi.4140440903

Wold, K. A. (2011). Blending theories for instructional design: Creating and implementing the structure, environment, experience, and people (SEEP) model. *Computer Assisted Language Learning, 24*(4), 371–382. doi:10.1080/09588221.2011.572900

KEY TERMS AND DEFINITIONS

Diffusion of Effect: Gaining benefits in a dimension when an intervention is applied in another dimension.

Environmental Supports: Data, instruments, incentives; things that are outside of the individual person's behavior; what the work environment brings to the job.

Front-End Analysis: A method to determine the gap and cause of performance problems in behavior before interventions are selected or implemented; a method to uncover the underlying causes of poor performance. Front-end analysis (FEA) is the evaluation completed at the beginning of a performance improvement initiative to identify if there is a problem. Front-end analysis models help determine up-front which actions needed to be taken to solve the problems, and, sometimes more importantly, if the problem should be solved.

Human Performance Technology: A systematic and systemic process, using a set of proven models, to improve the capability of people within an organization or department, generally including gap analysis, cause analysis, intervention selection and implementation, and evaluation.

Management Theorem: Also known as the Gilbert's Behavior Engineering Model or the Third Leisurely Theorem.

Person's Repertory of Behavior: Knowledge, capacity, and motives; things that are within the individual person's behavior; what the employees bring to the job.

Potential for Improving Performance (PIP): The difference between typical performance and exemplary performance, also shown as the ratio of exemplary performance (W_{EX}) over typical performance (W_T) or PIP = W_{EX} / W_T.

Worthy Performance: Worthy performance (W) equals accomplishments (A) divided by the costly behavior (B) or W = A/B.

Compilation of References

Adams, L. (2014, May). *Learning a new skill is easier said than done.* Retrieved May 31, 2014, from Gordon Training International: http://www.gordontraining.com/free-workplace-articles/learning-a-new-skill-is-easier-said-than-done/

America Institute of Medicine. (2013). *Best care at lower cost: the pat to continuously learning health care in America.* National Academy Press.

American Society for Safety Engineers (ASSE). (2009, January 1). *Criteria for accepted practices in safety, health, and environmental training* (ANSI/ASSE Z490.1-2009).

Ardichvili, A., Page, V., & Wentling, T. (2003). Motivation and barriers to participation in virtual knowledge-sharing communities of practice. *Journal of Knowledge Management, 7*(1), 64–77. doi:10.1108/13673270310463626

Arraj, A. 2013. *ITIL: The Basics. Best Management Practice.* Retrieved from http://www.best-management-practice.com/gempdf/ITIL_The_Basics.pdf

Bacdayan, P. (2008). Finding win-win forms of economic development outreach: Shared priorities of business faculty and community. *College Teaching, 56*(3), 143–148. doi:10.3200/CTCH.56.3.143-148

Baddeley, A. (1992). Working memory. *Science, 255*(5044), 556–559. doi:10.1126/science.1736359 PMID:1736359

Baldrige, M. (2007). *2007 Business and nonprofit criteria: Baldrige model for performance excellence.* Retrieved August 7, 2007 from http://www.quality.nist.gov/PDF_files/2007_Business_Nonprofit_Criteria.pdf

Banathy, B. H. (1968). *Instructional systems.* Palo Alto, California: Fearon Publishers.

Bannan-Ritland, B. (2001). Teaching instructional design: An action learning approach. *Performance Improvement Quarterly, 14*(2), 37–52. doi:10.1111/j.1937-8327.2001.tb00208.x

Barclay, R. O., & Murray, P. C. (2000, May 27). *What is knowledge management?* Retrieved from http://www.providersedge.com/docs/km_articles/what_is_knowledge_management.pdf

Bates, I., Taegtmeyer, M., Squire, S. B., Ansong, D., Nhlema-Simwaka, B., Baba, A., & Theobald, S. (2011). Indicators of sustainable capacity building for health research: Analysis of four African case studies. *Health Research Policy and Systems, 9*(1), 14. doi:10.1186/1478-4505-9-14 PMID:21443780

Compilation of References

Bath, P. A. (2008). Health informatics: Current issues and challenges. *Journal of Information Science*, *34*(4), 501–518. doi:10.1177/0165551508092267

Baytiyeh, H., & Pfaffman, J. (2010). Volunteers in Wikipedia : Why the community matters. *Journal of Educational Technology & Society*, *13*(2), 128–140.

Belson, K. (2010, July 23). *Soccer's growth in the U.S. seems steady*. The New York Times. Retrieved from http://www.nytimes.com/2010/07/24/sports/soccer/24soccer.html

Bennett, R. (2012, September 20). *Soccer's big takeover*. ESPNFC. Retrieved October 8, 2013, from http://espnfc.com/blog/_/name/relegationzone/id/262

Bertalanffy, L. V. (1972). The history and status of general systems theory. *Academy of Management Journal*, *15*(4), 407–426. doi:10.2307/255139

Binder, C. (1996). Behavioral fluency: Evolution of a new paradigm. The Behavior Analyst, 19, 163–197. PubMed PMID:22478257

Binder, C. (2012). *Get out of the training box! From training and development to performance improvement with The Six Boxes approach*. Bainbridge Island, WA: The Performance Thinking Network.

Bloom, B. (1956). *Taxonomy of education objectives*. Boston: Allyn and Bacon.

Blouin, D. D., & Perry, E. M. (2009). Whom does service learning really serve? Community-based organizations' perspectives on service learning. *Teaching Sociology*, *37*(2), 120–135. doi:10.1177/0092055X0903700201

Boshuizen, H. P. A., Wiel, M. W. J., & Schmidt, H. G. (2012). What and how advanced medical students learn from reasoning through multiple cases. *Instructional Science*, *40*(5), 755–768. doi:10.1007/s11251-012-9211-z

Botcheva, L., White, C., & Huffman, L. C. (2002). Learning culture and outcomes measurement practices in community agencies. *The American Journal of Evaluation*, *23*(4), 421–434. doi:10.1177/109821400202300404

Bourhis, A., & Dube, L. (2010). "Structuring spontaneity": Investigating the impact of management practices on the success of virtual communities of practice. *Journal of Information Science*, *36*(2), 175–193. doi:10.1177/0165551509357861

Brafman, O., & Beckstrom, R. A. (2006). *The starfish and the spider: The unstoppable power of leaderless organizations*. New York: Portfolio.

Brethower, K. S., & Rummler, G. A. (1976). Evaluating training. Improving Human Performance Quarterly, 5(3), 103–120.

Brethower, D. M. (2006). Systemic issues. In J. A. Pershing (Ed.), *Handbook of human performance technology* (3rd ed., pp. 111–137). San Francisco, CA: Pfeiffer.

Bringle, R. G., & Hatcher, J. A. (1996). Implementing service learning in higher education. *The Journal of Higher Education*, *67*(2), 221–239. doi:10.2307/2943981

Bringle, R. G., & Hatcher, J. A. (2002). Campus–community partnerships: The terms of engagement. *The Journal of Social Issues*, *58*(3), 503–516. doi:10.1111/1540-4560.00273

Broad, M. L., & Newstrom, J. W. (1992). Transfer of training: Action-packed strategies to ensure high payoff from training investments. Reading, MA: Perseus Books.

Brown, J. S., & Duguid, P. (2000). *The social life of information*. Boston, MA: Harvard Business School Press.

Butcher, N., Kanwar, A., & Uvalic-Trumbic, S. (2011). *A basic guide to open educational resources (OER)*. Commonwealth of Learning/UNESCO. Retrieved from http://dspace.col.org/handle/123456789/428

Carman, J. G. (2009). Nonprofits, funders, and evaluation: Accountability in action. *American Review of Public Administration*, *39*(4), 374–390. doi:10.1177/0275074008320190

Carr-Chellman, A. A. (2007). *User design*. Mahwah, New Jersey: Lawrence Erlbaum Associates.

Carver, R. L. (1997). Theoretical underpinnings of service learning. *Theory into Practice*, *36*(3), 143–149. doi:10.1080/00405849709543760

Celio, C. I., Durlak, J., & Dymnicki, A. (2011). A meta-analysis of the impact of service-learning on students. *Journal of Experiential Education*, *34*(2), 164–181. doi:10.5193/JEE34.2.164

Chevalier, R. (2003). Updating the behavior engineering model. *Performance Improvement*, *42*(5), 8–14. doi:10.1002/pfi.4930420504

Chyung, S. Y. (2008). *Foundations of instructional and performance technology*. Amherst, MA: HRD Press.

Chyung, S. Y., Wisniewski, A., Inderbitzen, B., & Campbell, D. (2013). An improvement- and accountability-oriented program evaluation: An evaluation of the Adventure Scouts Program. *Performance Improvement Quarterly*, *26*(3), 87–115. doi:10.1002/piq.21155

Clark, S., Collins, A., Kwan, J., & Sesnon, A. (2012). Tales from the field: Making service standards real for families in need. *Performance Xpress* (August 1). Retrieved from http://www.performancexpress.org/2012/08/tales-from-the-field-making-service-standards-real-for-families-in-need/

Clark, R. C., & Mayer, R. E. (2011). *E-learning and the science of instruction: Proven guidelines for consumers and designers of multimedia learning* (3rd ed.). San Francisco, CA: Pfeiffer. doi:10.1002/9781118255971

Cohen, H. H., & Jensen, R. C. (1984). Measuring the effectiveness of an industrial lift truck safety training program. Journal of Safety Research, 15(3), 125–135. doi:10.1016/0022-4375(84)90023-9 doi:10.1016/0022-4375(84)90023-9

Collins, J. (2005). *Good to great and the social sectors: A monograph to accompany good to great*. New York, NY: Harper Collins.

Commons, C. (n.d.). *Creative Commons Attribution 3.0 License*. Retrieved from http://creativecommons.org/licenses/by/3.0/

Conway, J. M., Amel, E. L., & Gerwien, D. P. (2009). Teaching and learning in the social context: A meta-analysis of service learning's effects on academic, personal, social, and citizenship outcomes. *Teaching of Psychology*, *36*(4), 233–245. doi:10.1080/00986280903172969

Cooke, M., Irby, D. M., & O'Brien, B. C. (2010). *Educating physicians: A call for reform of medical school and residency.* San Francisco, CA: Jossey-Bass.

Cooperrider, D. L., & Whitney, D. (1999). Appreciative inquiry: A positive revolution in change. In P. Holman & T. Devane (Eds.), *The change handbook* (pp. 245–261). San Francisco: Berrett-Koehler.

Correia, A.-P., Yusop, F. D., Wilson, J. R., & Schwier, R. A. (2010). *A comparative case study of approaches to authentic learning in instructional design at two universities.* Presented at the American Educational Research Association Annual Meeting, Denver, CO. Retrieved from http://files.eric.ed.gov/fulltext/ED509340.pdf

Creswell, J. W. (2002). *Educational research: Planning, conducting, and evaluating quantitative and qualitative research.* Upper Saddle River, NJ: Pearson.

Creswell, J. W. (2003). *Research design: Qualitative, quantitative, and mixed method approaches* (2nd ed.). Thousand Oaks, CA: Sage Publications, Inc.

Creswell, J. W. (2007). *Qualitative enquiry & research design: Choosing among five approaches* (2nd ed.). London, United Kingdom: Sage Publications.

Cross, R., Borgatti, S. P., & Parker, A. (2002). Making invisible work visible: Using social network analysis to support strategic collaboration. *California Management Review*, *44*(2), 25–47. doi:10.2307/41166121

Cross, R., Laseter, T., Parker, A., & Velasquez, G. (2006). Using social network analysis to improve communities of practice. *California Management Review*, *49*(1), 32–61. doi:10.2307/41166370

Curtis, R. V., & Nestor, D. (1990). Interpersonal skill-building for instructional developers. *Educational Technology Research and Development*, *38*(2), 51–59. doi:10.1007/BF02298269

Dailey-Hebert, A., Sallee, E. D., & DiPadova, L. N. (2008). *Service-eLearning: Educating for Citizenship.* IAP.

Davidson, E. J. (2005). *Evaluation methodology basics: The nuts and bolts of sound evaluation.* Thousand Oaks, CA: Sage.

De Laat, M., & Schreurs, B. (2013). Visualizing informal professional development networks: Building a case for learning analytics in the workplace. *The American Behavioral Scientist*, *57*(10), 1421–1438. doi:10.1177/0002764213479364

Dean, J., & Gilbert, T. (1997). Engineering performance with or without training. In J. Dean & E. Ripley (Eds.), *Performance Improvement Pathfinders: Models for Organizational Learning Systems.* Washington, DC: International Society for Performance Improvement.

Dean, P. (1997). Thomas F. Gilbert, Ph.D. Engineering performance improvement with or without training. In P. J. Dean & D. E. Ripley (Eds.), *Performance improvement pathfinders: Models for organizational learning systems* (pp. 45–64). Silver Spring, MD: ISPI.

Designers for Learning. (n.d.). Retrieved from http://designersforlearning.org

Dewey, J. (1938). *Education and experience.* New York: Macmillan.

Dornan, T. (2011). Developing learning resources. In T. Dornan, K. Mann, A. Scherpbier, & J. Spencer (Eds.), *Medical education: Theory and practice* (pp. 265–281). Edinburgh: Elsevier.

Driscoll, M. P. (2005). *Psychology of learning for instruction* (3rd ed.). Boston: Pearson Allyn and Bacon.

Egan, T. M., Yang, B., & Bartlett, K. R. (2004). The effects of organizational learning culture and job satisfaction on motivation to transfer learning and turnover intention. *Human Resource Development Quarterly*, *15*(3), 279–301. doi:10.1002/hrdq.1104

Eisinger, P. (2002). Organizational capacity and organizational effectiveness among street-level food assistance programs. *Nonprofit and Voluntary Sector Quarterly*, *31*(1), 115–130. doi:10.1177/0899764002311005

Expert OJT. (n.d.). *JobAid Writing System*. Retrieved 1 May 2014 from www.http://www.expertojt.com/

Fine, A. H., Thayer, C. E., & Coghlan, A. T. (2000). Program evaluation practice in the nonprofit sector. *Nonprofit Management & Leadership*, *10*(3), 331–339. doi:10.1002/nml.10309

Flanagan, J. C. (1954). The critical incident technique. *Psychological Bulletin*, *51*(4), 327–358. doi:10.1037/h0061470 PMID:13177800

Fontaine, M. A., & Millen, D. R. (2004). Understanding the benefits and impact of communities of practice. In P. Hildreth & C. Kimble (Eds.), *Knowledge networks: Innovation through communities of practice* (pp. 1–13). PA: Idea Group Publishing Hershey. doi:10.4018/978-1-59140-200-8.ch001

Fowler, S. A., Yaeger, L. H., Yu, F., Doerhoff, D., Schoening, P., & Kelly, B. (2014). Electronic health record: Integrating evidence-based information at the point of clinical decision making. *Journal of the Medical Library Association: JMLA*, *102*(1), 52–55. doi:10.3163/1536-5050.102.1.010 PMID:24415920

Fuller, J. (1997). *Managing Performance improvement Projects: preparing, planning, implementing*. San Francisco, CA: Pfeiffer.

Furco, A. (1996). Service-learning: A balanced approach to experiential education. *Expanding Boundaries: Serving and Learning*, *1*, 1–6.

Gegenfurtner, A., Veermans, K., & Vauras, M. (2013). Effects of computer support, collaboration, and time lag on performance self-efficacy and transfer of training: A longitudinal meta-analysis. *Educational Research Review*, *8*, 75–89. doi:10.1016/j.edurev.2012.04.001

Gilbert, T. F. (2007). Human competence: Engineering worthy performance (Tribute ed.). San Francisco, CA: Pfeiffer.

Gilbert, T. (1978). *Human competence: Engineering worthy performance*. Amherst, MA: HRD Press, Inc.

Gilbert, T. F. (1978). Human competence: Engineering worthy performance. *NSPI Journal*, *17*(9), 19–27.

Giles, D. E., & Eyler, J. (1994). The theoretical roots of service-learning in John Dewey: Toward a theory of service-learning. *Michigan Journal of Community Service Learning*, *1*(1), 77–85.

Gowdy, H., Hildebrand, A., La Piana, D., & Campos, M. (2009). Convergence: How five trends will reshape the social sector. Retrieved from http://www.lapiana.org/downloads/Convergence_Report_2009.pdf

Grace Centers of Hope. (n.d.). *Grace Centers of Hope Financial Information*. Retrieved from http://www.gracecentersofhope.org/Financial.aspx

Gray, B. (2004). Informal learning in an online community of practice. *Journal of Distance Education, 19*(1), 20–35.

Guerra-López, I. (2008). *Performance evaluation: Proven approaches for improving program and organizational performance* (1st ed.). San Francisco, CA: Jossey-Bass.

Guerra-Lopez, I. J. (2007). *Evaluating impact: Evaluation and continual improvement for performance improvement practitioners* (Vol. VI). Amherst, MA: HRD Press.

Guldberg, K., & Mackness, J. (2009). Foundations of communities of practice: Enablers and barriers to participation. *Journal of Computer Assisted Learning, 25*(6), 528–538. doi:10.1111/j.1365-2729.2009.00327.x

Handley, K., Sturdy, A., Fincham, R., & Clark, T. (2006). Within and beyond communities of practice: Making sense of learning through participation, identity and practice. *Journal of Management Studies, 43*(3), 641–653. doi:10.1111/j.1467-6486.2006.00605.x

Haney, D. (2006). Knowledge management, organizational performance, and human performance technology. In J. A. Pershing (Ed.), *Handbook of human performance technology: Principles, practices, and potential* (3rd ed., pp. 619–639). San Francisco, CA: Pfeiffer.

Hara, N., & Schwen, T. M. (2006). Communities of practice in workplaces : Learning as a naturally occurring event. *Performance Improvement Quarterly, 19*(2), 93–114. doi:10.1111/j.1937-8327.2006.tb00367.x

Harless, J. H. (1990). Diagnostic Front End Analysis. ABCD (Accomplishment-Based Curriculum Development) System. Newnan, GA: Job Aid.

Harless, J. (1973). An analysis of front-end analysis. *Improving Human Performance. Research Quarterly, 4*, 229–244.

Haythornthwaite, C. (2008). Learning relations and networks in web-based communities. *International Journal of Web Based Communities, 4*(2), 140. doi:10.1504/IJWBC.2008.017669

Hazlehurst, B., McMullen, C. K., & Gorman, P. N. (2007). Distributed cognition in the heart room: How situation awareness arises from coordinated communications during cardiac surgery. *Journal of Biomedical Informatics, 40*(5), 539–551. doi:10.1016/j.jbi.2007.02.001 PMID:17368112

Herrington, J., Reeves, T. C., & Oliver, R. (2014). Authentic learning environments. In J. M. Spector, M. D. Merrill, J. Elen, & M. J. Bishop (Eds.), *Handbook of Research on Educational Communications and Technology* (pp. 401–412). Springer New York. doi:10.1007/978-1-4614-3185-5_32

Herscovitch, L., & Meyer, J. (2002). Commitment to organizational change: Extension of a three-component model. *The Journal of Applied Psychology, 87*(3), 474–487. doi:10.1037/0021-9010.87.3.474 PMID:12090605

Hmelo-Silver, C. E. (2013). Creating a learning space in problem-based learning. *Interdisciplinary Journal of Problem-Based Learning*, 7(1), 143–156. doi:10.7771/1541-5015.1334

Hoffman, A. M., Wine, M. P., & McKinney, J. S. (2013). *A GED test for a Common Core world: Understanding the changes coming in 2014*. Presented at the Annual Meeting of the American Education Research Association, San Francisco, CA. Retrieved from http://www.gedtestingservice.com/uploads/files/6c97b538e2780491ee60d1d297d5d9f5.pdf

Holden, R. J. (2010). Physicians' beliefs about using EMR and CPOE: In pursuit of a contextualized understanding of health it use behavior. *International Journal of Medical Informatics*, 79(2), 71–80. doi:10.1016/j.ijmedinf.2009.12.003 PMID:20071219

Holland, B. A. (2001). A comprehensive model for assessing service-learning and community-university partnerships. *New Directions for Higher Education*, 2001(114), 51–60. doi:10.1002/he.13.abs

Hollender, N., Hofmann, C., Deneke, M., & Schmitz, B. (2010). Integrating cognitive load theory and concepts of human–computer interaction. *Computers in Human Behavior*, 26(6), 1278–1288. doi:10.1016/j.chb.2010.05.031

Hysong, S. J., Best, R. G., & Pugh, J. A. (2006). Audit and feedback and clinical practice guideline adherence: Making feedback actionable. *Implementation Science; IS*, 1(9), 9–18. doi:10.1186/1748-5908-1-9 PMID:16722539

Industrial Truck Standards Development Foundation (ITSDF). (2009). *Safety Standards for Low Lift and High Lift Trucks* (ANSI/ITSDF B56.1-2009).

International Society for Performance Improvement. (2013). What is HPT? Retrieved August 5, 2013, from http://www.ispi.org/content.aspx?id=54

International Society for Performance Improvement. (n.d.). *What is HPT?* Principles of Human Performance Technology. Retrieved from http://www.ispi.org/content.aspx?id=54

International Society for Performance Improvement. (n.d.). *What is HPT?* Retrieved from http://www.ispi.org/content.aspx?id=54

Jaskyte, K. (2004). Transformational leadership, organizational culture, and innovativeness in nonprofit organizations. *Nonprofit Management & Leadership*, 15(2), 153–168. doi:10.1002/nml.59

Jeon, S. H., Kim, Y. G., & Koh, J. (2011). Individual, social, and organizational contexts for active knowledge sharing in communities of practice. *Expert Systems with Applications*, 38(10), 12423–12431. doi:10.1016/j.eswa.2011.04.023

Jonassen, D. (1999). Designing constructivist learning environments. In C. Reigeluth (Ed.), *Instructional-design theories and models: A new paradigm of instructional theory* (Vol. 2, pp. 215–239). Mahwah, NJ: Lawrence Erlbaum Associates.

Jonassen, D. H., Tessmer, M., & Hannum, W. H. (1999). Procedural analysis. In *Task analysis methods for instructional design* (pp. 45–54). Mahwah, NJ: Lawrence Erlbaum Associates.

Kadushin, C. (2012). *Understanding social networks: Theories, concepts, and findings*. New York: Oxford University Press.

Compilation of References

Kaufman, R., & Guerra-Lopez, I. (2013). Needs assessment for organizational success. Alexandria, VA: American Society for Training & Development (ASTD).

Kenny, R. F., Zhang, Z., Schwier, R. A., & Campbell, K. (2005). A review of what instructional designers do: Questions answered and questions not asked. *Canadian Journal of Learning and Technology*, *31*(1), 9–16.

Kenworthy-U'Ren, A. L. (1999). Management students as consultants an alternative perspective on the service-learning "call to action.". *Journal of Management Inquiry*, *8*(4), 379–387. doi:10.1177/105649269984005

Khun, A. (1974). *The Logic of Social Systems*. San Francisco, CA: Jossey-Bass.

Kirkpatrick, D. L. (1996). *Evaluating training programs: The four levels*. San Francisco: Berrett-Koehler Publishers.

Kluger, A., & DeNisi, A. (1996). The effects of feedback interventions on performance: A historical review, a meta-analysis, and a preliminary feedback intervention theory. *Psychological Bulletin*, *119*(2), 254–284.

Knowles, M. (1970). *Andragogy*. Retrieved April 13, 2005, from http://tip.psychology.org/Knowles.html

Kolb, D. A. (1984). *Experiential learning: Experience as the source of learning and development*. Englewood Cliffs, NJ: Prentice-Hall.

Kraft, R. J. (1996). Service learning: An introduction to its theory, practice, and effects. *Education and Urban Society*, *28*(2), 131–159. doi:10.1177/0013124596028002001

Lakhani, K., & Wolf, R. (2005). Why hackers do what they do: Understanding motivation and effort in free/open source software projects. In J. Feller, B. Fitzgerald, S. Hissam, & K. R. Lakhani (Eds.), *Perspectives on free and open source software* (pp. 3–22). Boston, Mass: MIT Press.

Larson, E. L., Patel, S. J., Evans, D., & Saiman, L. (2013). Feedback as a strategy to change behavior: The devil is in the details. *Journal of Evaluation in Clinical Practice*, *19*(2), 230–234. doi:10.1111/j.1365-2753.2011.01801.x PMID:22128773

Larson, M. B. (2005). Instructional design career environments: Survey of the alignment of preparation and practice. *TechTrends*, *49*(6), 22–32. doi:10.1007/BF02763727

Larson, M. B., & Lockee, B. B. (2009). Preparing instructional designers for different career environments: A case study. *Educational Technology Research and Development*, *57*(1), 1–24. doi:10.1007/s11423-006-9031-4

Lassk, F. G., Ingram, T. N., Kraus, F., & Di Mascio, R. (2012). The future of sales training: Challenges and related research questions. *Journal of Personal Selling & Sales Management*, *32*(1), 141–154. doi:10.2753/PSS0885-3134320112

Leake, R., Green, S., Marquez, C., Vanderburg, J., Guillaume, S., & Gardner, V. A. (2007). Evaluating the capacity of faith-based programs in Colorado. *Research on Social Work Practice*, *17*(2), 216–228. doi:10.1177/1049731506296408

Lehman, C. M., & DuFrene, D. D. (2008). Achieving active learning through a service learning podcast project. *Journal of Business and Training Education*, 41.

Liaison Committee on Medical Education. (2013). *Functions and Structure of a Medical School: Standards for Accreditation of Medical Education Programs Leading to the M.D. Degree.* Retrieved from http://www.lcme.org/functions.pdf

Lin, A., Harris, M., & Zalis, M. (2010). Initial observations of electronic medical record usage during CT and MRI interpretation: Frequency of use and impact on workflow. *AJR. American Journal of Roentgenology,* *195*(1), 188–193. doi:10.2214/AJR.09.2946 PMID:20566815

Linnel, D. (2003). *Evaluation of capacity building: Lessons from the field.* Washington, D.C.: Alliance for Nonprofit Management. Retrieved from http://seerconsulting.com.au/wp-content/uploads/2009/09/Evaluation-of-Capacity-Building-Lessons-from-Field.pdf

Lohman, R. A. (2001). Editor's notes. *Nonprofit Management & Leadership,* *12*(1), 1–5. doi:10.1002/nml.12101

Madden, M., & Zickuhr, K. (2011). *65% of online adults use social networking sites. Report for the Pew Internet & American Life Project.*

Mann, J. A. (2012). *Creating collaboration among small nonprofit leaders using an appreciative inquiry approach* (Doctoral dissertation). Retrieved from ProQuest, UMI Dissertations Publishing. (1516533)

Marsick, V. J., & Watkins, K. E. (2001). Informal and incidental learning. *New Directions for Adult and Continuing Education,* *2001*(89), 25–34. doi:10.1002/ace.5

Mathison, S. (1988). Why triangulate? *Educational Researcher,* *17*(2), 13–17. doi:10.3102/0013189X017002013

McGregor, D. (1960). The human side of enterprise. New York, NY: McGrawHill.

Merrill, M. D. (2002). First principles of instruction. *Educational Technology Research and Development,* *50*(3), 43–59. doi:10.1007/BF02505024

Middleton, B., Bloomrosen, M., Dente, M. A., Hashmat, B., Koppel, R., Overhage, J. M., & Zhang, J. (2013). Enhancing patient safety and quality of care by improving the usability of electronic health record systems: Recommendations from AMIA. *Journal of the American Medical Informatics Association,* *20*(e1), e2–e8. doi:10.1136/amiajnl-2012-001458 PMID:23355463

Milen, A. (2001). *What do we know about capacity building: An overview of existing knowledge and good practice.* Department of Health Service Provision, World Health Organization, Geneva, June.

Mooney, L. A., & Edwards, B. (2001). Experiential learning in sociology: Service learning and other community-based learning initiatives. *Teaching Sociology,* *29*(2), 181–194. doi:10.2307/1318716

Moreno, R., & Valdez, A. (2005). Cognitive load and learning effects of having students organize pictures and words in multimedia environments: The role of student interactivity and feedback. *Educational Technology Research and Development,* *53*(3), 35–45. doi:10.1007/BF02504796

Musen, M. A., Middleton, B., & Greenes, R. A. (2014). Clinical decision-support systems. In E. H. Shortliffe & J. J. Cimino (Eds.), Biomedical Informatics (pp. 643–674). Springer London; Retrieved from http://link.springer.com/chapter/10.1007/978-1-4471-4474-8_22 doi:10.1007/978-1-4471-4474-8_22

Compilation of References

Natarajan, K., Stein, D., Jain, S., & Elhadad, N. (2010). An analysis of clinical queries in an EHR search utility. *International Journal of Medical Informatics*, (79): 515–522. doi:10.1016/j.ijmedinf.2010.03.004 PMID:20418155

National Center for Education Statistics. (2012). *Digest of Education Statistics, 2012.* U.S. Department of Education. Retrieved from http://nces.ed.gov/programs/digest/d12/

Navigator, C. (n.d.). Charity Navigator Rating: Grace Centers of Hope. Retrieved June 5, 2014, from http://www.charitynavigator.org/index.cfm?bay=search.summary&orgid=5309

Newman, L. S. (2008). *Effects of Employee Performance Management Systems on Employee Learning and Development within Banks in Nigeria.* A qualitative method dissertation in partial fulfillment of conditions precedent to a Doctorate in Business Administration (DBA) submitted to the University of Phoenix, Arizona: USA. ProQuest UMI. ISBN 978-1-109-04887-2.

Novak, J. M., Markey, V., & Allen, M. (2007). Evaluating cognitive outcomes of service learning in higher education: A meta-analysis. *Communication Research Reports*, *24*(2), 149–157. doi:10.1080/08824090701304881

Okang, G. & Ukadike, S. (2014). *Perception of FITC staff with over 10 years continued work experience in FITC.* Being a special request qualitative survey for a case study on FITC.

Oladimeji, A. (2009). *Handover notes from Dr Oladimeji Alo out-going Managing Director/ CEO, to Dr Lucy Surhyel Newman in coming Managing Director/CEO.*

Oshima Lee, E., & Emanuel, E. J. (2013). Shared decision making to improve care and reduce costs. *The New England Journal of Medicine*, *368*(1), 6–8. doi:10.1056/NEJMp1209500 PMID:23281971

Paas, F., van Gog, T., & Sweller, J. (2010). Cognitive Load Theory: New Conceptualizations, Specifications, and Integrated Research Perspectives. *Educational Psychology Review*, *22*(2), 115–121. doi:10.1007/s10648-010-9133-8

Park, P. (1993). What is participatory research? A theoretical and methodological perspective. In M. Brydon-Miller, B. Hall, T. Jackson, & P. Park (Eds.), *Voices of change: Participatory research in the United States and Canada* (pp. 1–19). Westport, CT: Bergin & Garvey.

Paul, L. (1999). Thinking together. *Inside Technology Training, 3*(8), 18-22.

Pershing, J. A. (2006). *Handbook of human performance technology* (J. A. Pershing, Ed.). 3rd ed.). San Francisco, CA: Pfeiffer.

Pimentel, S. (2013). College and career readiness standards for adult education. Washington, DC: U.S. Department of Education, Office of Vocational and Adult Education; Retrieved from http://lincs.ed.gov/publications/pdf/CCRStandardsAdultEd.pdf

Prell, C. (2012). *Social network analysis: History, theory and methodology.* London: Sage Publications Ltd.

Provan, K. G., & Kenis, P. (2008). Modes of network governance: Structure, management, and effectiveness. *Journal of Public Administration: Research and Theory, 18*(2), 229–252. doi:10.1093/jopart/mum015

Reichheld, F. F. (2006). *The ultimate question: For opening the door to good profits and true growth*. Boston, MA: Harvard Business School Press.

Renz, D. (2010). Reframing governance. *The Nonprofit Quarterly, Winter 2010*, 50-53.

Restler, S. G., & Woolis, D. D. (2007). Actors and factors: Virtual communities for social innovation. *Electronic Journal of Knowledge Management, 5*(1), 81–96.

Retna, K. S., & Ng, P. T. (2011). Communities of practice: Dynamics and success factors. *Leadership and Organization Development Journal, 32*(1), 41–59. doi:10.1108/01437731111099274

Retzer, S., & Yoong, P. (2009). Inter-organisational knowledge transfer and computer mediated social networking. In M. Purvis & B. T. R. Savarimuthu (Eds.), *Computer-mediated social networking* (pp. 76–85). Springer Berlin Heidelberg. doi:10.1007/978-3-642-02276-0_8

Richey, R. C., Klein, J. D., & Tracey, M. W. (2011). *The Instructional design knowledge base: Theory, research, and practice*. New York, NY: Routledge.

Richmond Strikers Soccer Club. (2014a). *Welcome to college advising*. Retrieved December 7, 2013, from http://www.richmondstrikers.com/Travel/College/393075.html

Richmond Strikers Soccer Club. (2014b). *Playing college soccer and the recruiting process*. Retrieved December 7, 2013, from http://www.richmondstrikers.com/Travel/College/404879.html

Rogers, E. M. (1995). *Diffusion of innovations* (4th ed.). New York: The Free Press.

Rosenberg, M. (1996). Human performance technology. In R. L. Craig (Ed.), *Training and development handbook* (4th ed., pp. 370–393). New York: McGraw-Hill.

Rosenberg, M. J. (2007). Knowledge management and learning: Perfect together. In R. A. Reiser & J. V. Dempsey (Eds.), *Trends and issues in instructional design and technology* (2nd ed., pp. 156–165). Upper Saddle River, N.J.: Pearson/Merrill Prentice Hall.

Rossett, A. (1999). Knowledge management meets analysis. *Training & Development, 53*(5), 62–68.

Rothwell, W. J., & Sullivan, R. L. (2005). Organization development. In W. J. Rothwell & R. Sullivan (Eds.), *Practicing organization development* (pp. 9–38). San Francisco: Pfeiffer.

Rummler, G. A. (2006). The anatomy of performance: A framework for consultants. In J. A. Pershing (Ed.), *Handbook of human performance technology* (3rd ed., pp. 986–1007). San Francisco, CA: Pfeiffer.

Rummler, G. A., & Brache, A. P. (2013). *Improving performance: How to manage the white space on the organization chart* (3rd ed.). San Francisco, CA: Jossey-Bass.

Saitwal, H., Feng, X., Walji, M., Patel, V. L., & Zhang, J. (2010). Assessing performance of an electronic health record (EHR) using cognitive task analysis. *International Journal of Medical Informatics, 79*(7), 501–506. doi:10.1016/j.ijmedinf.2010.04.001 PMID:20452274

Compilation of References

Satmetrix Systems. (2004). The power behind a single number: Growing your business with Net Promoter (White Paper). Retrieved from http://www.macu.ca/wp-content/uploads/2012/02/The-Power-Behind-A-Single-Number.pdf

Savolainen, R. (2007). Filtering and withdrawing: Strategies for coping with information overload in everyday contexts. *Journal of Information Science*, *33*(5), 611–621. doi:10.1177/0165551506077418

Schultz, M. (2013). 7 keys for sales training with maximum impact. *T+D Magazine*, *67*(3), 52.

Schwier, R. A., & Wilson, J. R. (2010). Unconventional roles and activities identified by instructional designers. *Contemporary Educational Technology*, *1*(2).

Scriven, M. (2007). *Key evaluation checklist.* Retrieved from http://www.wmich.edu/evalctr/archive_checklists/kec_feb07.pdf

Scriven, M. (1999). The fine line between evaluation and explanation. *Research on Social Work Practice*, *9*(4), 521–524. doi:10.1177/104973159900900407

Selden, S. C., Sowa, J. E., & Sandfort, J. (2006). The impact of nonprofit collaboration in early child care and education on management and program outcomes. *Public Administration Review*, *66*(3), 412–425. doi:10.1111/j.1540-6210.2006.00598.x

Shilbury, D., & Moore, K. A. (2006). A study of organizational effectiveness for national Olympic sporting organizations. *Nonprofit and Voluntary Sector Quarterly*, *35*(1), 5–38. doi:10.1177/0899764005279512

Smelcer, J. B., Miller-Jacobs, H., & Kantrovich, L. (2009). Usability of electronic medical records. *Journal of Usability Studies*, *4*(2), 70–84.

Snyder, W. M., & Wenger, E. (2010). Our world as a learning system: A communities-of-practice approach. In C. Blackmore (Ed.), *Social learning systems and communities of practice* (pp. 107–124). London: Springer London. doi:10.1007/978-1-84996-133-2_7

Solomonson, W. L. (2012). Trust and the client–consultant relationship. *Performance Improvement Quarterly*, *25*(3), 53–80. doi:10.1002/piq.21123

Speck, M. (1996). Best practice in professional development for sustained educational change. *ERS Spectrum*, *14*(2), 33–41.

Sports Scholarships. (2013). *Women's soccer scholarship.* Retrieved October 9, 2013, from http://sportsscholarship.com/womens-soccer-scholarships/

Stolovitch, H., & Keeps, E. (2004). *Training ain't performance.* Alexandria, VA: ASTD Press.

Templeton, G. F., Lewis, B. R., & Snyder, C. A. (2002). Development of a measure for the organizational learning construct. *Journal of Management Information Systems*, *19*, 175–218.

Trevor, C. (2001). Interactive effects among actual ease of movement determinants and job satisfaction in the prediction of voluntary turnover. *Academy of Management Journal*, *44*(4), 621–638. doi:10.2307/3069407

U. S. Census Bureau. (2012). *Educational attainment in the United States: 2012 detailed tables*. Retrieved from http://www.census.gov/hhes/socdemo/education/data/cps/2012/tables.html

U.S. Department of Commerce. (1995). *Special Publication (800 Series)*. National Institute of Standards and Technology Retrieved March 15, 2014, from http://csrc.nist.gov/publications/PubsSPs.html

Van Grove, J. (2010). *Social networking usage surges globally*. Retrieved from http://mashable.com/2010/03/19/global-social-media-usage/

Van Tiem, D. M., Moseley, J. L., & Dessinger, J. C. (2001). *Performance improvement intervention: Enhancing people, processes, and organizations through performance technology*. Silver Spring, MD: International Society for Performance Improvement.

Van Tiem, D. M., Moseley, J. L., & Dessinger, J. C. (2012). *Fundamentals of performance improvement: A guide to improving people, process, and performance* (3rd ed.). San Francisco, CA: Pfeiffer.

Van Tiem, D., Moseley, J. L., & Dessinger, J. C. (2012). *Fundamentals of performance improvement* (3rd ed.). San Francisco: Pfeiffer.

Venkatesh, V., Morris, M. G., Davis, G. B., & Davis, F. D. (2003). User acceptance of information technology: Toward a unified view. *Management Information Systems Quarterly*, *27*(3), 425–478.

W. K. Kellogg Foundation. (2004). *Logic model development guide*. Retrieved from http://www.wkkf.org/resource-directory/resource/2006/02/wk-kellogg-foundation-logic-model-development-guide

Waldner, L. S., Widener, M. C., & McGorry, S. Y. (2012). E-service learning: The evolution of service-learning to engage a growing online student population. *Journal of Higher Education Outreach & Engagement*, *16*(2), 123–150.

Warren, J. L. (2012). Does service-learning increase student learning?: A meta-analysis. *Michigan Journal of Community Service Learning*, *18*(2), 56–61.

Welch, S. (2012, November 29). Data opens doors: Grace Centers develops system to better track clients, outcomes. *Crain's Detroit Business*. Detroit, MI. Retrieved from http://www.crainsdetroit.com/article/20121125/SUB01/311259995/data-opens-doors

Wenger, E., & Wenger-Trayner, B. (2011a). *Slide: Levels of participation*. Retrieved September 03, 2013, from http://wenger-trayner.com/resources/slide-forms-of-participation/

Wenger, E., McDermott, R., & Snyder, W. (2002). *Cultivating communities of practice: a practical guide to managing knowledge*. Boston, Mass: Harvard Business School Press.

Wenger, E., Trayner, B., & De Laat, M. (2011). *Promoting and assessing value creation in communities and networks: a conceptual framework*. The Netherlands: Open University of the Netherlands.

Wenger, E., White, N., Smith, J. D., & Rowe, K. (2005). Technology for communities. In *Work, learning and networked: Guide to the implementation and leadership of intentional communities of practice* (pp. 1–15). Quebec: CEFRIO.

Wenger-Trayner, B., & Wenger, E. (2011b). *Communities versus networks*. Retrieved August 08, 2014 from http://wenger-trayner.com/resources/communities-versus-networks/

Wohlauer, M. (2012). Fragmented care in the era of limited work hours: A plea for an explicit handover curriculum. *BMJ Quality & Safety*, *21*(Suppl 1), i16–i18. doi:10.1136/bmjqs-2012-001218 PMID:23173183

Wohlauer, M., Arora, V. M., Horwitz, L. I., Bass, E. J., Mahar, S. E., & Philibert, I. (2012). The patient handoff. *Academic Medicine*, *87*(4), 411–418. doi:10.1097/ACM.0b013e318248e766 PMID:22361791

Wolcott, H. F. (2008). *Ethnography: A way of seeing*. Lanham, MD: AltaMira Press.

WordPress. (n.d.). Retrieved from https://wordpress.org/about/

Wulfeck, W. H., & Wetzel-Smith, S. K. (2010). Training incredibly complex tasks. In P. E. O'Connor & J. V. Cohn (Eds.), *Human performance enhancement in high-risk environments: Insights, development, and future directions from military research* (pp. 74–89). Santa Barbara, CA: ABC-CLIO.

Yorio, P. L., & Ye, F. (2012). A meta-analysis on the effects of service-learning on the social, personal, and cognitive outcomes of learning. *Academy of Management Learning & Education*, *11*(1), 9–27. doi:10.5465/amle.2010.0072

Zaheer, A., Gözübüyük, R., & Milanov, H. (2010). It's the connections: The network perspective in interorganizational research. *Academy of Management Perspectives*, (February), 62–77.

Zboralski, K. (2009). Antecedents of knowledge sharing in communities of practice. *Journal of Knowledge Management*, *13*(3), 90–101. doi:10.1108/13673270910962897

Zhang, X., & Venkatesh, V. (2013). Explaining employee job performance: The role of online and offline workplace communication networks. *Management Information Systems Quarterly*, *37*(3), 695–722.

About the Contributors

Jill E. Stefaniak is an Assistant Professor of Instructional Design and Technology at Old Dominion University. Prior to joining Old Dominion University, Jill was the Director of Education Training at the Oakland University William Beaumont School of Medicine. An experienced educator, Jill has trained medical students to become physician educators in community and hospital environments. She received her Ph.D. from Wayne State University in Instructional Technology, and holds a designation as a Certified Professional in Learning & Performance. Previously, she earned a Masters of Training and Development with a double concentration in Instructional Design & Technology and Organizational Development & Leadership from Oakland University in 2008 and a Bachelors of Commerce from the University of Windsor in 2006. Her research interests include learner-centered instruction, cognitive apprenticeships, informal learning environments, and medical simulation.

***

Paige Barrie is an experienced leader, strategist and collaborator with a passion for learning that leads to performance improvement. With more than 20 years of experience in the automotive learning space, she has significant experience leading the development of award-winning, evidence-based eLearning, classroom training and performance improvement solutions to drive measurable business results. A needs-based curriculum Paige's team created for a client was recognized in ASTD's Training and Development Magazine for its outstanding performance improvement results. Paige is currently the head of dealership and employee training and organizational development for VW Credit, Inc., the financial services division of Volkswagen Group of America. She has a B.B.A. from the University of Michigan.

Allison Bell is a Ph.D. student in Human Resource Development at University of Illinois at Urbana-Champaign and a Senior Analyst at Abt Associates. Throughout her career, Allison has served in a variety of workplace learning and development roles including instructional designer, performance consultant, and trainer. Her work has concentrated in the learning and change aspects of implementing information technology, as well as utilizing technology for learning. Her primary research interest is in the processes that support inter-organizational learning to improve organizational outcomes, particularly in organizations with a social mission. She is also interested in building stronger relationships between academic research and practice through research collaborations.

Bonnie Beresford, Ph.D., is an industry-recognized human capital strategist and performance consultant with over 20 years of experience in the field of human performance improvement. She has co-authored a book, *Developing Human Capital: Using Analytics to Plan and Optimize Your Learning and Development Investments*, which showcases how to link investments in people to measurable business outcomes. Bonnie's work with both Fortune 500 clients and non-profits has been recognized by Chief Learning Officer and T+D magazines including earning American Society for Training & Development's (ASTD) "Excellence in Practice Award" and three "Chief Learning Officer - Business Impact" awards on behalf of her clients. Bonnie's practitioner approach makes her a popular presenter at industry conferences including the Conference Board, ASTD, Chief Learning Officer Symposiums, International Society for Performance Improvement (ISPI), Corporate University Week, National Fund for Workforce Solutions, and Elliott Masie's Learning conferences. Bonnie holds a Ph.D. in human capital management from Bellevue University, an MBA from Wayne State University, and a BS with from Central Michigan University. She is an active member of ISPI, serving on both local and the international boards of directors.

Alison A. Carr-Chellman is head of Learning and Performance Systems, Penn State University's College of Education. She has focused her research and writing on User-Design, stakeholder participation, cybercharter schools, and re-engaging boys in education through gaming. She teaches courses on diffusion of innovations, instructional design, and interpretive research methods.

Seung Youn (Yonnie) Chyung is a professor in the Department of Organizational Performance and Workplace Learning in the College of Engineering at Boise State University. She teaches graduate-level courses on evaluation and quantitative research. She authored a book titled 'Foundations of Instructional and Performance Technology' (HRD Press), and has published research papers in various research journals including Performance Improvement Quarterly, International Journal of Training and Development, Journal of STEM Education, Advances in Engineering Education, Quarterly Review of Distance Education, American Journal of Distance Education, and The Journal of Experimental Education. She has presented papers at international conferences of professional associations such as American Evaluation Association and International Society for Performance Improvement. She can be reached at ychyung@boisestate.edu.

Stephanie Clark, MSc, is the Senior Editor and Lab Content Management Specialist for Learn on Demand. She earned her master's degree (2013) in Instructional and Performance Technology and the Workplace Instructional Design (WIDe) certificate (2012) from Boise State University. She has completed several instructional design projects both in her professional career and during her degree. She has eleven years of experience in the training industry and is a Certified MS Office Master Instructor and a Certified MS Office Specialist.

Ben Davis has over 12 years of performance improvement experience within the financial services industry, and is currently working as an instructional designer and program evaluation project manager at one of the leading banks in the country. He possesses a Master's Degree in Organizational Performance and Workplace Learning from Boise State University. His expertise includes needs assessment, instructional design, and program evaluation. Ben can be contacted at ben@battleborn.us.

Tom Giberson, Ph.D., is an Industrial/Organizational Psychologist and Associate Professor of Education in the Department of Organizational Leadership at Oakland University in Rochester, MI. His research interests include leadership and organizational culture and he has consulted with organizations of all sizes in multiple industries on issues of individual and organizational performance.

Annie Hernandez, Ph.D. serves as the Executive Director for the Los Angeles based Frieda C. Fox Family Foundation and leads their national initiative, Youth Philanthropy Connect. Previously, Annie led the Good Works Connect network of nonprofits in downstate Illinois for The Lumpkin Family Foundation. Her other experience includes service in a variety of roles in public and nonprofit organizations, including a management support organization, the State of Indiana's Rural Affairs, the J.W. Fanning Institute for Leadership at the University of Georgia where she was faculty with the Community Leadership Association, and Fiesta Indianapolis, Inc. where she was its first Executive Director. She received the inaugural Young and Emerging Capacity Builder Award from the Alliance for Nonprofit Management and earned her MS in Agricultural, Environmental Communication and Education at the University of Illinois, and her BS from Texas A&M University. She recently completed her Ph.D. in Leadership and Change from Antioch University with her dissertation focused on effective networked nonprofits. You can find out more at linkedin.com/in/anniehernandez1/.

Wenhao David Huang is an Associate Professor at Department of Education Policy, Organization and Leadership at University of Illinois at Urbana-Champaign. His research interests mainly focus on cognitive as well as motivational issues in technology-enhanced learning and performance settings across organizations. In particular he investigates the empirical relationship between cognitive and motivational processing afforded by highly interactive learning and performance environments enabled by technologies. His current projects focus on the design differences between genders (and other social variables) in the context of game-enabled learning. Dr. Huang also carries out research projects in the context of online teaching and learning on a regular basis, to promote learner- and instructor-friendly online instructional practices.

Robert Jordan is an instructional designer working in the federal government. His interests include informal learning and learning communities.

Karl Kochendorfer, MD, FAAFP is the Assistant Vice President for Health Affairs and Chief Health Information Officer at the University of Illinois Hospital & Health Sciences System (UI Health) and Associate Professor of Clinical Family Medicine at the University of Illinois at Chicago (UIC). Dr. Kochendorfer manages the deployment and evaluation of leading edge solutions to improve efficiency, quality reporting, and information retrieval at UI Health. Dr. Kochendorfer has helped nurture projects including: improvements to the PatientCentered Medical Home (PCMH) model of care, Population Health Management, and Mobile Computing.

Julie Kwan, MSc, is the Global Senior Specialist in Learning & Development at Hitachi Consulting, where she develops and manages content and delivery of learning programs for a global audience. She has over seven years of experience in the training industry. Julie completed her master's degree in Instructional & Performance Technology at Boise State University.

Jennifer Maddrell is the founder of Designers for Learning. As an instructional design consultant, her professional projects include work with Savant Learning Systems, the National Institute of Aerospace Associates, Baruch College, and the Metropolitan Transit Authority. Jennifer is appointed adjunct Assistant Professor in the Instructional Design and Technology program in the College of Education at Old Dominion University where she completed her PhD in 2011, and served as the Assistant Editor of the Journal of Computing in Higher Education. Recent courses taught include Principles and Practices of Human Performance Technology, Computer-based Multimedia Design, Cognition and Instructional Design, Instructional Strategies for Innovation, and Consulting Skills for Instructional Designers.

Jennifer worked for over 15 years within leading global insurance companies and progressed through various underwriting and management positions after completing a Bachelor of Business Administration degree in Finance at the University of Wisconsin -Madison and a Master of Business Administration degree in Strategic Management and Marketing at the University of Illinois – Chicago. In 2007, Jennifer completed the Master of Science in Education program at Indiana University where she received her degree in Instructional Systems Technology.

Beth McGoldrick is a Product Training Consultant for a Fortune 500 company, where she has won awards for training projects she designed and developed. She has over 18 years of experience in training & development in the insurance industry and academia, including skills in analyzing, designing, developing, and measuring training. She has a Master's of Science in Organizational Performance and Workplace Learning from Boise State University.

Misa Mi has over 28 years of experience working in higher education and different library settings. She is currently an associate professor in the Department of Biomedical Sciences of the Oakland University William Beaumont School of Medicine and a medical librarian at the medical library of the medical school. She is the recipient of a number of awards from the Medical Library Association and has won awards and grants from the National Institute of Health National Library of Medicine and the Arnold P. Gold Foundation Research Institute. She has authored numerous peer-reviewed journal articles and book chapters. She frequently presents and conducts workshops on topics related to instructional technology and informatics at local, regional, and national professional association meetings. She is a certified senior member of the Academy of Health Information Professionals of the Medical Library Association. Misa earned a doctorate from the College of Education at Wayne State University, a master's of library & information science from Wayne State University, and a master's in teaching from Oakland University. She completed her training in the Program for Educators in the Health Professions, a highly regarded professional development program, at the Harvard Macy Institute, Harvard University.

Joe Monaco is President and CEO of Monaco Group, Inc., a consulting firm specializing in the design and development of custom human performance systems that endure past the first change in management. Targeting forklift operator safety and speed, the LIFTOR Performance Management System is an enduring example of this. His LIFTOR.com site, a 20+ year labor of love, is a publicly available collection of evidence-based, systemic prescriptions and other useful information for preventing fatalities and serious injuries related to powered industrial trucks (forklifts).

He is a member of the ANSI/ITSDF B56.1 committee on the Safety Standard for Low Lift and High Lift Trucks. A life member of ISPI, he has chaired the Awards of Excellence committee, and has presented at many annual conferences. His B.A in Organization Behavior/Psychology is from Wilmington College/Ohio.

Lucy Surhyel Newman has 27 years of industry and consulting experience. She presents a hybrid of development finance, private sector commercial banking, performance improvement consulting and academic orientation, obtained from a public sector development finance institution, four commercial banks in Nigeria, and the business advisory performance improvement practice of the Nigerian firm of one of the global "big four" consulting firms. She has been the MD/CEO of FITC since May 2009 and has over the course of her career, gotten the reputation of being a results-focused person with proven success in aligning strategy, structure, people, policies and systems to optimize individual and organizational performance. Dr. Newman has a doctorate degree in Business Administration (Leadership and Performance) from the University of Phoenix, Arizona USA, an MBA [International Business] and a B.Sc. in Business Administration [Financial Management], from the Ahmadu Bello University, Nigeria. She is a Graduate of the Centre for Creative Leadership Colorado Springs USA's Leadership At the Peak Program [LAP], a Fellow of the Nigerian Institute of Management (NIM), a Fellow of the Institute of Credit Administration (ICA), a Certified Performance Technologist (CPT) of the International Society of Performance Improvement (ISPI) and the 2012/2014 International Director, on the Global Board of the International Society for Performance Improvement. Dr. Newman travels widely, has published three books, many articles and facilitated high profile sessions in Africa, Europe, the Middle East and the United States. She is a mother to three interesting male personalities aged between 26 and 12 years. She enjoys taking long walks, nature watch and traveling across cultures.

Stacey Olachea has worked in the financial, health, and government fields for the last 15 years applying her knowledge of human resource practices to enhance overall work environments and production. She is a recent graduate of the Organizational Performance and Workplace Learning program at Boise State University and may be reached at stacey.olachea@gmail.com.

Colleen Olson, Performance Improvement Specialist. Colleen has over 19 years of experience in the learning and performance field working in a variety of business sectors with employees across all organizational levels. She specializes in needs assessment, evaluation, and performance improvement solutions. She is a recent graduate of the Organizational Performance and Workplace Learning program at Boise State University and may be reached at coidesigns@msn.com.

Melanie Ross grew up in Ashburn, Virginia and attended Longwood University in Farmville, VA where she earned her bachelors degree in Liberal Studies with a teaching license in PreK-8. After teaching preschool for nearly two years in North Carolina's public school system, Melanie began pursuing her master's degree from Virginia Tech. Following her moving back to Virginia and transitioning to the private sector, Melanie earned her Master of Arts in Instructional Technology in May 2012. Shortly after, Melanie was accepted into Old Dominion University's Ph.D. Instructional Design and Technology program. She began pursuing her Ph.D. in January 2013 and is concurrently seeking an additional certification in Human Performance Technology (HPT). Her research interests focus on complex learning rooted in behavioral and cognitive psychology as well as the effects of instructional and non-instructional interventions on learner performance outcomes. Melanie anticipates graduating with her Ph.D. in December 2017.

Edward W. Schneider is the Proprietor of Peacham Pedagogics, a consulting firm that started out in 1984 specializing in research and development for interactive instruction, but has gradually broadened its scope to include other means of engineering human performance. A long-term member of ISPI, he has offered numerous presentations at ISPI conferences, and published in Performance Improvement Journal. He holds MS and PhD degrees in Experimental Psychology from Rutgers, the State University.

William L. Solomonson, PhD, is Assistant Professor of Education in the Department of Organizational Leadership at Oakland University in Rochester, MI. His research interests include topics in performance improvement and he has consulted with several Fortune 500 organizations. He is a Certified Performance Technologist (CPT).

Simone G. Symonette is a doctoral student in instructional systems technology at Indiana University with a minor focus in organizational behavior and human resource management. She earned her master's degree in public administration at the University of Central Florida and her undergraduate degree in international affairs from Bethune-Cookman College. She is also currently a performance consultant for a Fortune 500 Company. Previously, Symonette has served as a program research consultant for Indiana University RecSport and as an associate instructor in Indiana University's School of Education. Her research interests include human performance technology, specifically intervention set selection. She may be reached at simone.symonette@gmail.com.

Andrew A. Tawfik is an assistant professor of Educational Technology, Research, and Assessment at Northern Illinois University. He earned his PhD in Learning Technologies from the University of Missouri. Dr. Tawfik's research interests include problem based learning, case-based reasoning, case library instructional design, and computer supported collaborative learning.

Steven W. Villachica, PhD, is an Associate Professor of Organizational Performance and Workplace Learning at Boise State University. His current research interests focus on bringing academics and industry representatives together to decrease ramp-up time to competent performance in the workplace for newly hired graduates. A frequent author and conference presenter, Steve is a member of ISPI, ASEE, ASTD, and AECT. He completed his doctorate in educational technology at the University of Northern Colorado.

Index

CPSIA information can be obtained at www.ICGtesting.com
Printed in the USA
BVOW09*0324080515

399330BV00007B/145/P